This book explores the nature of, and conditions for, theoretical innovation in International Studies. Highlighting classic and new research problems, this collection of critically-minded, original essays pushes International Relations scholarship in uncharted directions. Bridging social theory and International Relations theory, it searches for sources of intellectual innovation in the everyday lives of ordinary people. The seventeen contributors are drawn from four continents and include such leading scholars as Richard Falk, James Rosenau, Yoshikazu Sakamoto and Susan Strange. Although a diverse group, they find the contemporary world order is in the throes of a structural transformation, which can be partly understood in terms of emancipation: the self-actualisation of human potential and community that looks beyond the current era in which neo-liberal globalisation is dominant, to a more democratic and just world order.

Innovation and transformation
in International Studies

Innovation and transformation in International Studies

edited by

Stephen Gill

York University, Toronto

and

James H. Mittelman

American University, Washington DC

PUBLISHED BY THE PRESS SYNDICATE OF THE UNIVERSITY OF CAMBRIDGE
The Pitt Building, Trumpington Street, Cambridge CB2 1RP, United Kingdom

CAMBRIDGE UNIVERSITY PRESS
The Edinburgh Building, Cambridge, CB2 2RU, United Kingdom
40 West 20th Street, New York, NY 10011-4211, USA
10 Stamford Road, Oakleigh, Melbourne 3166, Australia

First published 1997

Printed in the United Kingdom at the University Press, Cambridge

Typeset in 10/12 Monophoto Plantin by Servis Filmsetting Ltd, Manchester

A catalogue record for this book is available from the British Library

Library of Congress cataloguing in publication data

Innovation and transformation in international studies / edited by
   Stephen Gill and James H. Mittelman.
      p.   cm.
   Includes bibliographical references and index.
   ISBN 0 521 59105 8 (hardback). – ISBN 0 521 59903 2 (pbk)
      1. International relations.   2. International economic relations.
   3. World politics – 1945–   I. Gill, Stephen, 1950–   .
   II. Mittelman, James H.
   JX 1391. I555   1997
   327.1'01–dc20   96–47036   CIP

ISBN 0 521 59105 8 hardback
ISBN 0 521 59903 2 paperback

SE

Essays in honour of Robert W. and Jessie Cox
critical theorists
world order pioneers
esteemed colleagues and special friends

Contents

Contributors

ENRICO AUGELLI (1946–96) was an Italian diplomat and scholar whose published work covered a wide range from proposals for reform of the Italian foreign service, to discussions of North–South relations (especially in Africa), to more theoretical work applying Gramsci's and Weber's ideas to contemporary problems of world politics. His last publications included (with Craig N. Murphy), 'La nuova teorie delle pace delle Nazioni unite', in the Gramsci Institute journal, *Europa/Europe* (1995).

MITCHELL BERNARD is Assistant Professor of Political Science at York University, Toronto. He specialises in International and Eastern Asian Political Economy. He has recently published articles on the relation between region-formation, localism and globalisation with specific reference to Eastern Asia in *Third World Quarterly, New Political Economy* and *World Politics.*

FANTU CHERU is Associate Professor of African and Development Studies at the School of International Service, American University, Washington DC. His works include *The Silent Revolution in Africa: Debt, Development and Democracy* (1989) and *Dependence, Underdevelopment in Kenya* (1987); as co-author, *From Debt to Development: Alternatives to the International Debt Crisis* (1985); and as co-editor, *Ethiopia: Options for Rural Development* (1990).

RICHARD FALK is Albert G. Milbank Professor of International Law and Practice at Princeton University where he has been a member of faculty since 1961. His most recent books are *Explorations at the Edge of Time: Prospects for World Order* (1992) and *On Humane Governance: Toward a New Global Politics* (1995).

STEPHEN GILL is Professor of Political Science at York University, Toronto. He is the author of *The Global Political Economy: Perspectives, Problems and Policies* (1988, co-authored with David Law); *American*

Hegemony and the Trilateral Commission (1990); *Restructuring Global Politics* (in Japanese, translated by Seji Endo, 1996); and, as editor and contributor, *Atlantic Relations: Beyond the Reagan Era* (1989) and *Gramsci, Historical Materialism and International Relations* (1993).

JEFFREY HARROD is Research Professor at the Institute of Social Studies, The Hague, Netherlands. He is author of *Trade Union Foreign Policy* (1972), *Power, Production, and the Unprotected Worker* (1987), *Labour and Third World Debt* (1990) and co-editor with S. Frenkel of *Industrialisation and Labour Management Relations* (1995). He has taught at the Universities of Colorado, London, and the West Indies and at the Institute of Labour Studies, Geneva.

ERIC HELLEINER is Associate Professor of Political Science at York University, Toronto. He is author of *States and the Re-emergence of Global Finance: From Bretton Woods to the 1990s* (1994) and editor of *A World of Money: The Political Economy of International Capital Mobility*, a special issue of *Policy Sciences* (1994).

JAMES H. MITTELMAN is Professor of International Relations in the School of International Service at American University, Washington, DC. Previously, he served as Professor and Dean, Graduate School of International Studies, University of Denver, and as Professor and Dean of the Division of the Social Sciences, Queens College, City University of New York. His most recent books are, as editor and contributor, *Globalization: Critical Reflections* (1996), and with Mustapha Kamal Pasha, *Out from Underdevelopment Revisited: Changing Global Structures and the Remaking of the Third World* (1997).

CRAIG N. MURPHY is M. Margaret Ball Professor of International Relations at Wellesley College, Massachusetts. His recent publications include *International Organization and Industrial Change: Global Governance since 1850* (1994) and 'Seeing Women, Recognizing Gender, Recasting International Relations' (*International Organization*, 1996).

MUSTAPHA KAMAL PASHA is Assistant Professor of Comparative and Regional Studies in the School of International Service at American University, Washington DC, specialising in political economy, Islamic Studies and South Asia. He is the author of *Colonial Political Economy: Recruitment and Underdevelopment in the Punjab* (1997) and, with James H. Mittelman, *Out from Underdevelopment Revisited: Changing Global Structures and the Remaking of the Third World* (1997).

RANDOLPH B. PERSAUD is Sessional Assistant Professor of Political Science at York University, Toronto, and formerly Assistant Director of the York Centre for International and Security Studies. He specialises in International Relations theory, race and Third World foreign policy.

V. SPIKE PETERSON is Associate Professor of Political Science at the University of Arizona, Tuscon. She is the editor of *Gendered States: Feminist (Re)Visions of International Relations Theory* (1992) and, with Anne Sisson Runyan, co-author of *Global Gender Issues* (1993).

JAMES N. ROSENAU is University Professor of International Affairs at George Washington University, Washington DC. He is the author of *Turbulence in World Politics* (1990) and *The United Nations in a Turbulent World* (1992); co-author of *Thinking Theory Thoroughly* (1995); and co-editor of *Global Voices* (1993) and *Governance Without Government* (1992). His book, *Along the Domestic-Foreign Frontier: Governance in a Turbulent World*, is scheduled for publication in 1997.

MARK RUPERT is Associate Professor of Political Science at the Maxwell School of Citizenship and Public Affairs, Syracuse University. He is the author of *Producing Hegemony: The Politics of Mass Production and American Global Power* (1995).

YOSHIKAZU SAKAMOTO is Professor Emeritus of International Politics, Faculty of Law, University of Tokyo. He is the author of *International Politics in Global Perspective* (1990) and *The Political Analysis of Disarmament* (1988), both in Japanese, and is the editor of, and contributor to *Global Transformation: Challenges to the State System* (1994), *Asia: Militarization and Regional Conflict* (1988) and *Strategic Doctrines and their Alternatives* (1997).

SUSAN STRANGE is Professor Emeritus of International Relations at the London School of Economics. She is External Professor at the European University Institute, Florence and currently teaches and carries out research at the University of Warwick. She is the author of *The Retreat of the State* (1996), *States and Markets* (2nd edn. 1994), *Rival States, Rival Firms* (with John Stopford, 1991) and *Casino Capitalism* (1986). She was President of the International Studies Association in 1995–6.

KEES VAN DER PIJL is Reader in International Relations at the University of Amsterdam. He is the author of *The Making of an Atlantic Ruling Class* (1984) and *Vordenker der Weltpolitik* (1996).

Preface

Our book is an effort to conceptualise and analyse change in international relations and in International Studies. This is attempted in a collection of original essays that either review the work of major authors or that explore key theories or concepts in the light of two main themes: theoretical innovation and historical transformation. Although all the chapters in the collection are short (as a result of the editors' insistence), these essays show ways that new research problems and puzzles are appearing on a critical agenda for the study of global social relations in the emerging world order.

It needs to be stressed at the outset that this collection makes no claims to 'value-free' scientific inquiry along the lines of positivist and rational-choice approaches to international relations and political economy. Indeed, whilst there is no single epistemological position found in these pages, the authors adopt an approach that is 'critical', that is concerned to unmask and explain the underlying structures and social forces and discourses that constitute political and social life, whilst linking these to the idea of political emancipation – that people make history but not necessarily under conditions of their own choosing. Most of the contributions involve historicist, dialectical, hermeneutic or post-modern approaches. They seek to connect past, present and possible futures to an emancipatory political project.

Contributors were encouraged to consider the study of global problems and changes from an historical and social perspective in the spirit of Robert W. and Jessie Cox's contribution to the development of International Relations theory, and to their pioneering of an alternative conceptualisation of world order (see References, pp. 269–70). In this light, the work is intended to be an autonomous intellectual project that seeks to help shape an agenda for International and Global Studies, and, at the same time, a way to honour the Coxes' contributions.

Nevertheless, the reader might ask, what justifies yet another book on International Relations (a term that will be capitalised in this book when it refers to a field of study or a discipline, not actual practice)? In our

judgement, there are five reasons why this volume can contribute importantly to the field.

First, the collection widens the range or 'canon' of theorists considered
apposite to International or Global Studies. They include not only writers
customarily identified with International Relations *per se*, such as Hedley
Bull and E. H. Carr, but also others such as Adam Smith, Karl Marx,
Max Weber, Antonio Gramsci, Georges Sorel, Frantz Fanon, Fernand
Braudel and Karl Polanyi. What many of the theorists drawn together
here share is an integral and historical approach to social explanation
combined with emphasis on the need to apply this approach to contemporary problems and debates (for example, the nature of civilisation, economic and cultural globalisation, the role of transnational political forces
and political parties, or, more generally, the reconfiguration of global
political and civil society). These theorists then, can be regarded as both
critical and practical in their orientations and widening the scope of the
field of study.

A second reason is the centrality of the theme of transformation:
central because of a pervasive sense that we are in the throes of structural
change in world order. Thus the collection traverses various avenues for
considering the broad processes of structural change, whilst attempting
to root explanation in concrete situations and circumstances of people as
they organise their lives on a daily basis. Put differently, this volume seeks
to go beyond the idea that the end of the Cold War is somehow commensurate with the need for a paradigm shift in International Relations. We
argue, on the contrary, that signs of this shift were evident during the
Cold War era. Thus we adopt a long historical perspective to pose the
questions: what has fundamentally changed in world order and where are
developments taking us? How can these developments be channelled or
rechannelled by collective action? Thus the approach to transformation
involves consciousness and action in the making of history.

A third rationale is that for perhaps the first time in International
Relations, there is a work involving detailed and explicit consideration of
the question of, and the conditions for, theoretical innovation in the field.
Some contributors explicitly consider the way that particular authors
have produced innovations – in method, theory or perspective – and how
these innovations or insights have helped not only to shape a field of
study, but have had, or may have, a practical impact on how people think
and act. For example, the conditions under which innovations arise are
addressed in different ways by Stephen Gill, Enrico Augelli and Craig
Murphy, Richard Falk and Jeffrey Harrod. Gill stresses the interplay
between theoretical imagination, a sense of history and the construction of a critical social ontology as a way of interpreting and explaining

theoretical innovation. Whilst Augelli and Murphy use a genealogical method to closely identify cumulative historical moments of innovation, Falk examines the contemporaneous forces that give rise to innovation. Harrod stresses historical and present-day constraints set by the conditions of academic production, in particular by entrenched tendencies towards specialisation, positivism and empiricism. Innovation in historical method in studying social change is discussed by Eric Helleiner (in reviewing Braudel) and Mustapha Kamal Pasha (exploring Ibn Khaldun). Falk, too, mentions an historical method as setting apart the three innovative theorists he discusses (that is Carr, Bull and Cox). By contrast, Kees van der Pijl, Mark Rupert, Fantu Cheru and Yoshikazu Sakamoto discuss the way that theoretical-practical innovation occurs as a result of the political movement and consciousness of social forces. Their chapters suggest how socio-political innovation occurs, either from 'above' (for example, transnational ruling class formations) or from 'below' (right-wing populism, the democratic redefinition of civil society, the apparently spontaneous collective action of Third World peasants).

Fourthly, some authors in this collection link their work to the notion of emancipation – the creation of the possibility of a self-actualisation of human potential and community in the era of neo-liberal globalisation. Thus the issue of a creative moment or potentiality is examined, though never in the abstract – it is joined with concrete problems in the present age, such as those connected to political agency both locally and globally (for example, the prospects for a new internationalism). Also the moment of creative imagination is related to political and other problems in the emerging world order. Accordingly, some chapters probe prospects for the extension and development of an informal, fluid, open-ended and emancipatory political process, resembling in some respects a transnational political party or formation within and across political boundaries. Hence the role of critical theory in this sense is to help foster what van der Pijl in his chapter calls a new 'community of fate', concerned with the construction of novel forms of social solidarity sensitive to the interests of future generations and the ecological integrity of the planet.

Finally, the book shows how Coxian ideas are linked to broader perspectives and research agendas in critical theory, and how these agendas relate to the practical problems of our times. Indeed the breadth of perspective and concerns in this collection partly reflects an appreciation of the remarkable range of the Coxes' contributions and their healthy disrespect for the academic conventions that divide understanding of the world into 'disciplines'. (The Coxes' have made their mark not only in International Relations, but also in industrial relations, social and political thought, political economy, and, most recently, the study of civilisations.)

Both the transformative, innovative and emancipatory dimensions of theory are at the heart of the Coxes' work. Of course, Robert Cox's closest collaborator is Jessie Cox, who has participated in his research, sharpened his thinking, and helped make difficult concepts more accessible to the reader. Coxian historicism has been an inspiration to many scholars, especially a younger generation, and continues to influence research agendas in different parts of the world (Gill and Mittelman, 1996). We should note then, that in responding to the questions posed below most of the authors reflect an intellectual debt to the Coxes. Indeed, each contributor has been associated with Robert Cox throughout his two careers as, first, an international civil servant – Director of the International Institute for Labour Studies at the International Labour Organisation – and, second, as Professor at the Graduate Institute of International Studies in Geneva, Columbia University in New York, and York University in Toronto, where he is now emeritus. (This collection includes chapters by the first (Jeffrey Harrod, in Geneva) and the last (Randolph Persaud, at York) doctoral students supervised by Cox.)

In dealing with the themes of the book, the contributors were asked to consider matters of epistemology, ontology and method (theory and practice) in the study of history and society. The editors invited the authors to respond to some or all of the following questions:

1 What is the meaning and purpose of 'theory', critical or otherwise?
2 How is this definition related to an understanding and explanation of particular periods and historical transformations?
3 How far and in what ways can the writings of certain theorist(s) be termed 'innovatory', both in their times and with regard to the relevance of their contributions to the questions of world order today?
4 What are the key items for the agenda for study in contemporary international or global theory, in light of the purpose of theory in the present and the possible future?

As noted at the start of this preface, the contributions are varied and there is no single response to the complexities of theoretical innovation and transformation. Many contributors are motivated by a pervasive sense that the contemporary configuration of world order is in structural crisis. We seem to be undergoing a transition to something new, involving uncertain or even spectral and contingent conditions. What is common to the essays is a concern to respond critically to problems of our times. Some attempt this through reviewing former transformations and critical traditions so as to help us to innovate theoretically and perhaps influence politically the present global transformation.

One avenue for this is the development of a critical ontology of the emerging world order normatively linked to democratic and equitable values (Gill). Another is by exploring the 'crisis of masculinity' in the emerging world order (Spike Peterson). Pasha's contribution re-examines the relevancy of Ibn Khaldun for world order; that of Helleiner rethinks Braudel in the context of the need for a new historical approach to international – or as we would prefer it – global political economy. Others return to Sorel and Gramsci to elucidate the questions of myth and political agency (Augelli and Murphy), to Polanyi in search of a new global ecological politics (Mitchell Bernard), to Fanon to understand questions of colonisation, race and violence in the global order (Randolph Persaud); or to 'critical realism' to ask questions about the nature of world order (Falk). James Mittelman's essay warns against certain methodological pitfalls and calls for a return to Marx and Weber as a means of rethinking world order questions.

Some of the chapters involve attempts to synthesise components that may configure the emerging world order: for example, James Rosenau develops a 'fragmegrative ontology', a term that reflects a dialectic between social integration and disintegration, across a number of dimensions of lived reality. Others explore the transnationalisation of capital and structures of global authority (Susan Strange; van der Pijl); the need to synthesise the understandings of Industrial and International Relations (Harrod); the importance of the perspective of 'common sense' and how political mobilisation and contestation around concepts of nation takes place (Mark Rupert). Others consider resistance and the creation of self-protective and self-transformative mechanisms amongst rural and urban communities (Cheru); and finally forms of democratisation and contestation over and redefinition of 'civil society' in an emancipatory project (Sakamoto).

With this state of flux and theoretical complexity in mind, the organisation of the book is intended to be flexible and open-ended. There are four inter-related parts, each preceded by introductions that outline the aims and content of each. Part I contains essays that consider how a critical approach might contribute towards a renewal and a remaking of global political and social theory. Part II considers aspects of the reconfiguration and reconceptualisation of political economy and ecology in an age of globalisation. Part III explores social and political movements that represent, in varying respects, moments of transformation, innovation and in some cases, emancipation. A focus here is ways that political forces are shaped and constituted in the context of both global political and civil society. Finally, Part IV provides a series of reflections on aspects of the emerging world order. The concluding chapter identifies points of potential methodological confusion as well as some new directions in theory construction.

It is, of course, for the reader to judge whether the questions posed by the editors are sufficiently penetrating, and whether authors individually or collectively carried out their mission successfully in trying to answer them. We hope, however, that this book helps to push scholarship beyond International Relations theory as heretofore understood.

Stephen Gill
James H. Mittelman
Toronto and Washington DC, July 1996

Acknowledgements

The occasion for this book was our recognition that a work honouring Robert W. and Jessie Cox's many achievements was long overdue. Having shared important phases of Bob's and Jessie's career with them, both in New York and in Toronto as well as in some far-flung locales, we want to acknowledge their contribution to the personal and professional development of many students and established scholars. In addition, the Coxes' heart-felt collegiality and the depth of friendship they have offered on a truly transnational scale deserves tribute. Although we, the editors, confess to an abiding interest in big structures, Bob and Jessie evidence what agency can actually accomplish in challenging these structures, not only in terms of innovations in knowledge but also with important implications for an eventual transformation of world order.

In carrying out research and editorial tasks, we were assisted by two outstanding research assistants, Martin Hewson at York University and Ashwini Tambe at American University. Both worked tirelessly to help bring this project to a successful conclusion, especially Martin Hewson who, apart from his intellectual input, navigated the complexities of the internet in facilitating the development of drafts of the book across several continents. Ashwini Tambe contributed substantively in so many ways that all of her efforts cannot be recounted here. The team of Martin and Ashwini prepared the index – no easy task for a book of this scope – and for this, we are extremely grateful.

York University, through the Office of the Vice-President for Academic Affairs, the Office of the Dean of the Faculty of Arts and the Centre for International and Security Studies, graciously sponsored a dinner in Toronto in March 1997. This was a surprise for the Coxes. It gave us an opportunity to present the book to them. Members of the Cox family as well as representatives of York University joined most of the contributors at that happy testimonial. We are especially thankful to Astrid Eberhart for helping with communication and arranging the dinner with her impeccable taste. Linda Yarr, a long-time friend of the Cox family, also provided many excellent suggestions throughout the preparation of this volume.

All of the contributors to this book deserve praise for their co-operation – in some cases in terribly difficult moments – when being asked to honour short and inflexible time lines.

Finally we thank our editor, John Haslam, and copyeditor, Sheila Kane, for strengthening and polishing our work.

Rethinking and remaking the roots of global social and political theory

A central purpose of Part I is to begin to consider how to rethink and to reconstruct critical political theory. The four chapters in this part of the book seek to redefine some of the roots and to explore further the potential of critical theories in the making of world order. Authors approach the relationship between innovation and transformation in world order along three dimensions: historical, theoretical and practical.

Viewing innovation and transformation from a historical perspective, the contributors select important thinkers who grasped structural change in the past – so that we can learn to understand better the conditions of the present transformation. Theoretical innovation today does not mean consigning classical thinkers to the dusty confines of 'museum culture'. Rather it partly involves reactivating their key ideas and insights in the context of problems of the *emerging* world order. The next and most important dimension of Part I is theoretical. Authors take issue with, develop counterpoints to, and thus criticise a number of orthodoxies of left and right within the fields of social and international thought. They also highlight the importance of ontology, consciousness and normative aspects of theory.

Stephen Gill's chapter calls for attention to historically grounded and innovatory approaches that can help 'inform practical knowledge – about global politics, world order and the potential for the future that lies within the capacities for democratic collective action and political agency in contemporary civilisations'. He then argues that by focusing on ontology, a concept that relates to 'common sense' images of reality and the 'self-understandings' of an era, we can provide one pathway to theorise the dialectical relationships between historical transformations and intellectual and political innovation. To help clarify forces at work in the contemporary transformation the author sketches aspects of an 'ontological shift'. This involves changes in experiences of lived reality and social time, with contradictory implications for everyday life and expectations of the future. In calling for a reconstruction of theory to include a critical ontology, Gill seeks avenues to understand contradictory forms of consciousness in the present period of disorientation, anxiety and crisis in the emerging world order.

Enrico Augelli and Craig Murphy trace conceptual breakthroughs at the turn of the twentieth century that helped to underpin Gramsci's theoretical framework. Rational choice models, such as are central to present-day neo-classical economics, whilst sophisticated, still cannot grasp key aspects of consciousness. One such aspect is reflected in Sorel's concept of a motivating social myth. This concept draws on the emphasis by Bergson and Jung on intuition and feeling. Gramsci applied this seminal concept to problems of collective action, for example, to his concepts of the party and of hegemony, innovations that continue to have relevance, for example, in thinking of parties as transnational institutions comprising formal and informal, public and private entities and ideas.

By exploring innovations associated with three leading twentieth-century thinkers of 'critical realism', Richard Falk makes a generally applicable point. Often what is important for theoretical innovation is identifying prevailing orthodoxies against which theorists actively define their critique and their intellectual consciousness. Thus for E. H. Carr, it was Wilsonian idealism; for Hedley Bull, it was the pessimism of certain realists; and for Robert W. Cox, it involves contemporary orthodoxies – for example, associated with neo-realism and the rationalist-deductive geopolitical strategists. Falk suggests that Cox's version of critical realist theory is best able to explain current trends in world politics, for it embraces the interplay among states, markets and social forces. Part of its novelty lies in its prescient demystification of interstate power. Nevertheless, Falk reminds us of the importance of imagination, apart from rational intellect, in the process of innovation.

Mustapha Pasha argues for the need for theory to be self-conscious about its origins and history – a history that should include non-Western thinkers. For example, Ibn Khaldun's fourteenth-century thought provides a way to reconstruct our own intellectual and historical past. Indeed, appreciation of Islamic aspects of civilisation may free us from the cultural fetters associated with a range of orthodoxies in International Relations theorising. As Pasha puts it: 'Appreciation of various civilisational complexes and their notions of world order in *their* present manifestation and reality is needed to fully understand and to reflect upon real historical change.' Ibn Khaldun also provides an avenue for thinking about politics today by reference to his concept of '*asabiyya*: the spirit and social movement that informs the forces that give concrete potential to the development of a form of state (or political association).

Ibn Khaldun can also be read as a 'critical realist', attuned to state power (he was both a theorist and practitioner of statecraft). Like

Machiavelli and Gramsci, he was also a theorist of change who developed historically integrated concepts. Thus 'asabiyya can be compared to Machiavelli's concept of virtù. Virtù was a combination of active, prudent citizenship and coercive potential that created and sustained political community (or the state). Virtù was not a fixed quality: it was judged according to circumstances or fortuna. 'Asabiyya can also be compared to Gramsci's concept of the hegemonic historic bloc (blocco storico): the leading social forces in state and civil society that politically combine consent and coercion and give quality, movement, meaning and direction to a political community. Each of these three concepts – 'asabiyya, virtù and blocco storico – rejects the notion of the state as permanent and immutable, and emphasises its direction, movement and development.

Hence the final question posed by the contribution of Part I is how new forms of political community might be created in the emerging world order. Thus for Falk, our maps of reality – our ontology of the social world – necessarily include normative, prescriptive and imaginative aspects of thought. His main criticism of critical realism is that this element is down-graded, for example in explanations of global politics. Put differently, such an approach may err on the side of placing too much stress on what Gramsci called the 'pessimism of the intellect': it may not have enough 'optimism of the will'. Falk suggests that critical realism may be thus faulted in so far as it is insufficient in answering 'urgent claims based on conscience and action'. It seems 'agnostic on structural transformation'. Whether or not this is correct matters less than that it raises the question of the redefinition of political action and political agency as one of the most compelling issues of our times.

Part of the problem identified by Falk is to ask 'who are "we" and how are we to act?' As in Khaldun's era of decay and transformation – a period of intense ontological change – a central challenge in contemporary global politics involves the question of whether it is possible to generate a synthesis of social and political forces that might promote new political forms that have as their precursors concepts such as 'asabiyya and virtù. Put in Gramscian language, the problem is how to construct a counter-hegemonic blocco storico – analogous to a transnational political party – a 'we' that might comprise a new constellation of democratic and pro-gressive social forces. The 'how' needs to be both effective and open-ended, plural, inclusive and flexible, and it must be forged in terms of a realistic political optimism that is creative and forward-looking.

One key constraint on this potential is perhaps that our political imaginations may still be trapped in an ontology of world order that equates political action with territory and the state – although the con-straints and opportunities of a more economically globalised world order are increasingly palpable. We need then to rethink the questions of politics in both global and local frames of reference. Indeed, we need to do so by developing a role for the imaginative intellect in reconstructing the normative basis for collective action. Would this require a galvanising myth or a quite different form of political innovation? If so, how would this global 'imagined community' be created and by whom, and what might it consist of? Finally, 'we' need to ask ourselves the question posed by Augelli and Murphy: 'what is the best that can be achieved by collective action in the historical time in which we can imagine our actions making a difference?'

1 Transformation and innovation in the study of world order

Stephen Gill

> As the births of living creatures at first are ill-shapen, so are all innovations, which are the births of time. (Bacon, 1625)

This chapter explores the question of innovation as a prelude to reconstruction of theories of structural change and world order. A central goal is to integrate 'social' and 'international' theory, to transcend their limitations and to generate a theory that can help to illuminate and explain the present global transformation. This mandates 'critical innovation'. Such innovation involves exploration of sources as well as potential for theoretical development. With these aims in mind, the chapter makes the following arguments:

1 Critical innovation mandates ongoing questioning of and challenges to orthodoxy and the construction of an *alternative problématique*, one that is not only 'international' but also 'global'.
2 Critical innovation requires *a historical perspective*, drawing upon the imaginations of historians and critical theorists of the past. This can help to illuminate the dialectic between the long-lasting social and mental patterns of the *longue durée* and the forces of transformation. In this way, for example, Fernand Braudel's work helps to outline the limits of innovation and the weight of continuity in world orders.
3 Our ability to innovate can be improved by a *comparative historical method*. By making comparisons, for example, between the transformations in world order of the nineteenth and twentieth centuries, in the longer time frame of modernity, we can better assess the novelties of contemporary metamorphoses. We can then ask, 'what aspects of present-day change are contingent, and which are structural?'
4 Today, social and theoretical innovation requires us to *rethink ontology* and consider a possible 'ontological shift' or change in the 'common sense' of our era – understood not as something singular but as complex, contradictory and contested. In this context, a 'critical ontology' must rethink notions of space, time and social possibility, understandings of everyday life and expectations of the future.

5

5 Implicit in points 1–4 is a view concerning the *purpose of a theory* of world order. This is understood in a similar way to that in which Gramsci (1971), E. P. Thompson (1980) and E. H. Norman (1975) view the purpose of the study of history: as a necessarily incomplete perspective or guide that can inform practical knowledge about global politics, world order and the potential for the future that lies within the capacities for democratic collective action and political agency in contemporary civilisations.

Global transformation, ontology and innovation

A global transformation implies the emergence of a new epoch or configuration of global politics. Today, a sense of such a transformation has become pervasive. A 'transformation' here means change of a fundamental or structural quality.[1] A new age – or period – of flux and uncertainty relates to a sense that key institutional aspects of historical reality are in mutation: for example, forms of state, market and civil society; in the context of political economy: local, national, regional and global. It also relates therefore to changes in the way the world is perceived, understood and experienced – what is called here a shift in the ontology of world order. If there is a widespread sense that old political and theoretical models have exhausted their potential, students of world order have a responsibility to reconsider and to redevelop the roots of theoretical innovation.

For example, Eric Hobsbawm's (1994) study of the period 1914–91, *The Age of Extremes*, notes that following the 'golden years' of the 1950s and 1960s, we are now in the midst of a new age of uncertainty, decomposition and global economic, political and social crisis. This implies change in the self-understandings of the age. Hobsbawm's proposition has been reflected in a wide range of writings over the past two decades, for example, those that use the prefix 'post'. Indeed, the current global crisis has prompted a diverse range of innovations in critical thought in global studies – some of them represented in this book.

Theoretical innovation implies a moment when new methods, theories, perspectives or insights come to the forefront of social and political thought. A widespread sense of transformation may provide no more than the opportunity for theoretical innovation – and thus fall short of emancipatory potential – unless innovations-in-thought are related to and rooted in the real movement of social and political forces, institutionalised in civil and society in social movements, political parties, churches, universities, etc. This is how Gramsci conceived of theoretical innovation, that is, linked to the educative and political function of the party.

Ways to approach the problem of theoretical innovation are by no means self-evident. In this section we simply highlight key aspects of innovation. These include the sociological imagination, the ability to synthesise and to categorise, and a sense of social time that involves the question: 'how did we reach this point, and where are we going?' This question is an important prelude to innovations that may help to understand and channel structural change in a more humane, democratic and sustainable direction.

Theorising the 'international' in historical time

Put in more abstract terms, such considerations stem from a growing appreciation that we may be in the throes of an ontological change or shift: a redefinition of understandings and experiences that form basic components of lived reality. This includes mental frameworks – for example, the way that we think about social institutions and forms of political authority. Ontology more broadly involves shared understandings of the universe, the cosmic order and its origins; thus of time and space, and also of the interaction of social forces and nature. Ontology is connected to prevailing patterns of social reproduction, to the political economy of production and destruction, to culture and civilisational patterns. An ontology of the world includes our hopes, doubts, fears and expectations, our assessments of constraints and of human possibilities.

Hence one dimension of transformation is ontology – the theorisation of lived reality and the specification of its primary constituent units. Specifically, theoretical inquiry in the study of world orders rests upon particular ontological assumptions that provide basic units of analysis. It also gives definition to the significant forces or entities to be analysed and explained (and those less important and given secondary status in theoretical discourse).[2] Acceptance of a certain ontology has implications for the definition of a field of study or a discipline, as well as for the nature of research programmes, and indeed what is to be considered as useful and reliable knowledge (about global social and political relations). Thus the very term 'International Relations' may connote an ontology that may be inadequate to fully comprehend *global* structural change. For example, the 'international' as understood through the conceptual lens of neo-realism suggests that the most significant entities are states and the most important forms of interaction and movement are between or from national entities, in actions and foreign policies of governments or intergovernmental organisations. By contrast, when we speak of 'global politics' or 'global political economy' we have in mind an ontology that is more attuned to global social forces, structures and social relations. The term global political economy then, whilst still recognising the importance of politics, the state and territorialism, and the interstate system, recognises and reflects the existence of transnational forces (for example, in mass media, mass production and destruction) as well as global or biospheric forces. A global perspective may be more amenable to theoretical constructs that integrate social reproduction, production and ecology in the historical formation of world orders.

Indeed, although a number of contemporary discourses of International Relations have the prefix 'neo', with the implication of innovation (for example, neo-realism), what I find lacking in these approaches are conceptualisations that allow for the analysis of structural change. Often the impression of continuity is created in ways that may mask the transience of social forms and the complexities of social time. Examples are some forms of realism that stress the continuity of geopolitics and of sovereignty, the inevitable rise and decline of great powers and of the balance of power – propositions that sometimes assume that competitive states systems have existed in most civilisations. Another example involves those forms of feminism that stress a basic continuity of public–private distinctions and the patriarchal form of political power. Foucault's analysis of power relations and the pervasiveness of 'capillary' power may also be considered a conceptualisation that emphasises deep continuities in power relations and forms of subordination over time – that is after what he calls the 'epistemological break' of the Enlightenment and the onset of scientific rationality (1972: 176–7). Indeed Weber (1946) seemed to outline the continuity of the process of rationalisation stretching back even further – perhaps to the emergence of the world religions. The problem this poses for a theorisation of change is how far to recognise continuity within the context of structural transformations? At risk of oversimplification, a common difficulty in each of the above examples is that they tend to lead to sociological abstractions ('the anarchic interstate system', 'the patriarchal state', 'governmentality', 'the iron cage of modernity') as opposed to historicised concepts that are specific to time and place. I would suggest that the construction of concepts needs to be more dialectical and historical, so that a sense of the movement and the making of history is integrated conceptually into the lexicon of social and political theory. Put differently, the epistemological process needs to be understood as one of thought-in-movement in ways that are relevant to the practical problems of our times.

The social and historical imagination

In this sense, ontology and theoretical innovation are closely inter-related. An innovation in social thought may be defined initially as an original or ingenious conceptualisation of lived reality, rendered clearly comprehensible. But it is more than this. An innovation introduces something new – a new method, a new theory, a new perspective – in ways that have some practical effect on the way that we may think about and potentially act in the world. Often this simply involves the act of writing, synthesising, codifying or clarifying ideas current for over half a century, such as the central ideas in Marx's *Capital* concerning exploitation; or else rearticulating existing Republican arguments in different political contexts, for example, Tom Paine's *Rights of Man* in Britain in the early 1790s against the backdrop of the American and French Revolutions (for details of each, respectively, see Thompson, 1980: 217–22, 84–130).

Theoretical innovations may not be immediate in their effects and relevancy for human action which in any event cannot be predicted or fully anticipated from a theoretical postulate. Marx's ideas were of course bastardised and instrumentalised under the aegis of Marxism–Leninism and the social forces associated with Paine's individualism and egalitarianism were harshly repressed in England in the 1790s.

One way to approach the dialectic of continuity and transformation is by comparing Marx, Weber, Braudel, Smith and Polanyi. For Weber the process of theoretical innovation – or what C. Wright Mills called that of the 'sociological imagination' – came in a moment of Platonic frenzy as the theoretician created the conceptual categories that would shape the mental frameworks of the age. Weber was thus self-conscious of some of the political implications of his generic constructions, for example, that of 'Scientific Man' (*sic*) and also that of the Calvinist capitalist hero as one of his key agents of history. The latter concept was counterpoised to Marx's idea of the proletariat. And of course Weber emphasised the individual as the basic unit of analysis and this was central to the construction of his social ontology – whereas for Marx social ontology was based upon the processes of objectification (the self-creation and transformation of individuals in relation to each other and in relation to nature, that is in social relations in a particular historical situation) in an emancipatory project. By contrast Weber's notion of rationalisation implied a form of historical closure – an 'end' to history in a situation of disenchantment. Each perspective thus had radically different implications for political action and for emancipation – and each implies a quite different approach to and conceptualisation of, social ontology. Weber's appears to be an ontology that emphasises historical continuity, whereas that of Marx emphasises potential and transformation.

Going back further, one of the key innovations in the theory of political economy was Adam Smith's 'imaginary machine', the Providential process that would be unleashed if individuals were to be able to pursue their own self-regarding interests under conditions of competitive capitalism: the 'unseen hand' that would provide for the wealth of nations. The system – or machine – of Smithian political economy was built from ideas drawn from Newtonian mechanics, and it was imaginary because it was invented in a mercantilist, heavily regulated economic world, configured by powerful notions of moral economy (for example, a 'just price' for bread, which, when transgressed inevitably led to food riots in the eighteenth and nineteenth centuries). This mercantilist system, with its tendency towards centralisation and absolutist power in the hands of the forces of the state was the object of Smith's critique. His system, however, was and still is imaginary because it has never materialised in any known society (Smith, 1967 (1776)). However, Smithian political economy has helped to shape modernity in so far as it has served as a central basis for both classical and neo-classical political economy, as well as a justification for the power of the incipient bourgeoisie – or the power of capital – a power Smith warned against, especially the tendency for manufacturers to combine to oppress labour and to defeat competition.

For each of the three great thinkers just noted, their ability to innovate was rooted in a profound study of history as well as of contemporary conditions: each studied political economy from ancient times and integrated this knowledge into his work. This is, of course, quintessentially true of that doyen of modern historians, Fernand Braudel. Several years after Braudel was released from a Nazi war prison he embarked on detailed research for an economic and social history of post-medieval Europe.[3] Braudel notes that he became aware of the fact that the evidence 'did not seem to fit, or even flatly contradicted the classical and traditional theories of what was supposed to happen' (1979a: 23). Braudel realised that to attempt to explain what are conventionally called 'economic transformations', he would need to use and assemble 'a number of parahistoric languages – demography, food, costume, lodging, technology, money, towns – which are usually kept separate from each other and develop in the margin of traditional history' (1979a: 27). In this spirit, a theme of this collection concerns how the organisation and form of the disciplines is constitutive of particular forms of knowledge and understandings of the world.

The limits of the possible and the dialectic of duration

On the basis of very detailed empirical research over a period of roughly twenty years, Braudel found a methodological means to elaborate the idea of the 'limits of the possible' and thus the scope of actual and potential transformations. This method encompassed space and time, production and power, and biological and ecological dimensions of social life. Braudel thus developed an elaborate, detailed and differentiated social ontology, constructed for different regions of the world between the fifteenth and eighteenth centuries. Although using a quite different method, like Gramsci and Marx he established a way of approaching the question of the nature of and limits to historical transformation and the potential for collective action in the making of history. This approach allowed for elements of continuity within a broader discussion of social change, always grounded in concrete and specific social contexts.

Braudel used this apparatus to sketch a three-dimensional model of society, economy and civilisation. Linked to this was a theory of time similar to that developed – albeit often more implicitly – by Gramsci in the *Prison Notebooks*.[4] What Braudel calls the 'dialectic of duration' is the way in which historical situations and transformations are the product of the interplay between 'events-time' (François Simiand's notion of *l'histoire événementielle*) and deeper socio-historical structures, the latter being sets of ideas, patterns of interaction and institutional forms that may persist 'for an infinitude of generations'. Important in this latter respect as a way of understanding the continuities of history is the idea of the *longue durée*: the long passage of history associated with the embedding of fundamental social structures, that may take on an almost geological, quasi-permanent character. The *longue durée* is a multidimensional concept that includes the patterning of habits and expectations in everyday life. It also includes philosophical systems which may last for very long periods, as well as associated conceptions of space and social hierarchy. The *longue durée* therefore includes the mentalities that prevail in a given era, and the way that these are manifested in different historical conjunctures.

An example of the latter is the permanence of a certain conception of geometric pictorial space – or perspective – that was invented in the Florentine Renaissance and which lasted until the Cubists and other forms of twentieth-century pictorial representation. Prior to the Renaissance metaphysical and social dimensions of representation had tended to predominate in the pictorial arts. With regard to conceptions of the universe, 'The Aristotelian conception of the universe persisted unchallenged, or virtually unchallenged, right up to the time of Galileo,

Descartes and Newton's system of thought; then it disappeared before the advent of a geometrised universe which in turn collapsed, though much later, in the face of the Einsteinian revolution' (Braudel, 1980: 33). Braudel points out that it is paradoxically more difficult to discern the *longue durée* in matters economic, since the cycles, inter-cycles and structural crises tend to mask the longer-term regularities (33). Nevertheless, here we could cite the increasing monetisation and commodification of socio-economic relations as aspects of the economic *longue durée* of modern capitalism – a process that began to accelerate in the nineteenth century. This point can be illustrated with reference to innovation in the work of Karl Polanyi (1957).

The emergence of a new social ontology

Polanyi's thesis – one that is largely commensurate with Braudel's – is that the late eighteenth and early nineteenth century constituted a moment of historical discontinuity, or of rapid structural change that encompassed an historical and epistemological rupture. This change was coincident with the emergence of modern industrial capitalism, and the deepening of capitalist social relations in England (the onset of intensive change) with their extension globally (the creation of a world market order). Central to this was not technological innovation as such but, more importantly, a process of theoretical and political innovation that was partly inspired by the ideas of Adam Smith (and others like Ricardo), and also by the ideas of Bentham and the utilitarians. Of course some of Bentham's ideas or inventions never became practical innovations, that is, never applied directly (for example, his plans for the perfect prison/manufactory/poor house, the Panopticon) whereas others did (for example, his ideas about public administration premised upon the central concept of 'inspectability').

In other words, the creation of the market society – an entirely new form of society – drew on a strong and reorganised liberal state that could roll-back mercantilist regulations and practices in a process that today would be called 'systemic transformation' (for example, the role of the International Monetary Fund and World Bank in the former communist-ruled countries of Eastern Europe). Nature, people and the means of exchange were redefined through political action so that they became part of a new social ontology (which Polanyi called the 'fictitious commodities' of land, labour and capital). These fictions became real in so far as they were treated and thought of *as if* they were factors of production, a process that was extended geographically and socially as the new global market order was constructed. For Polanyi, this change is central to the explanation of modernity, and to the crisis of world order in the 1930s, that is after an attempt was made to reconstitute an unfettered world market order premised upon liberal political economy. Indeed Polanyi suggests that the revolt against the discipline and deflation of world market forces – and especially of mobile financial capital – produced Nazism and fascism and was the key to the explanation of the outbreak of the Second World War. The origins – and the contradictions – of our times are largely to be found in the great transformation that emerged in Britain about 200 years ago. In sum, this change involved the emergence of a new social ontology.

From a Marxian viewpoint an ontological shift would involve changes in consciousness and processes of objectification: forms of self-creation of people and their interactions with nature. Thus in the more specific and restricted sense of political economy, the appraisal of an ontological shift would imply a need to reconceptualise the dialectic between what Marx called the relations of production (ideas, ideologies and theories, shared understandings of the world, class and other social relations such as race and gender, political institutions including the state) and the forces of production (power potentials for production and destruction) in a partic-ular world order. Above all, however, such an appraisal would need to recognise that the process being theorised is historical and it involves the 'common sense' of a given period. As E. P. Thompson put it, the English working class was present at its own making. In arguing against the econ-omistic orthodoxy of modernisation theory and a certain 'Marxist ortho-doxy' that 'supposed that the working class was the more-or-less spontaneous generation of new productive forces and relations', Thompson notes 'we cannot understand class unless we see it as a social and cultural formation, arising from processes which can only be studied as they work themselves out over a considerable historical period' (1980: 14, 11). Powerful social and cultural forces that helped shape working-class formation included Wesleyism and Methodism more generally (with contradictory implications for English Radicalism) as well as English Dissent and Jacobinism. Of course, there were many other cross-cutting political, religious and social currents at work during the indus-trial revolution.

Indeed, a longer historical perspective indicates that contemporary forms of social relations are often the product of long and sometimes violent historical struggles. For example, agitation for political reform by middle-class Dissenters and working-class forces in the 1790s in Britain was interpreted by parliament and crown in terms of the threat of the French Revolution. This produced 'among the higher orders . . . a horror of every kind of innovation' (Thompson, 1980: 61, citing Sir Samuel Romilly). 'Innovation' was shorthand for attempts to widen the franchise and to root out parliamentary corruption. Burke referred to such agitation as the threat of the 'swinish multitude' (26) and it was met with systematic repression. More broadly, 'The commercial expansion, the enclosure movement, the early years of the Industrial Revolution – all took place within the shadow of the gallows' (66).

A critical ontology thus helps us to identify the mental frameworks for understanding and action that prevail in a given epoch and some of the potential for change. It helps to explain how, in a given historical situation, dominant forces – for example, the rising power of the industrial bourgeoisie in the creation of nineteenth-century self-regulating market society under a strong state – premise their supremacy not simply on coercive capacities but also on the hegemony of a particular perspective and the political framework that this entails: for example, a utilitarian and neo-classical form of political economy in contrast to a moral economy form, or a political economy of utopian or Marxian socialism. More broadly this involves a struggle over the politics of knowledge production and the institutionalisation of a certain pattern of possibility and potential within universities and other social entities. In other words, the historical process may prioritise certain modes of understanding or perspectives on the world, involving conceptions of society and representation that have significant – although uneven – implications for social change.

In sum, since the eighteenth century there has been an acceleration in the scope and intensity of change within given social frameworks (for example, the integral nation-state, the spread of capital, the processes of industrialisation and rationalisation) as well as a shift in the very categories and intersubjectivities associated with this process. However, what seem unprecedented in scale are the rapid growth in population and degradation of the environment – again the turning point seems to have coincided with the emergence of industrial capitalism at the end of the eighteenth century (Kates *et al.*, 1990). The scale and scope of these process have accelerated since 1950, such that virtually all human-induced ecological change in history has occurred since then, and the rate of this change is quickening, although with uneven effects in different regions of the planet. Hobsbawm also notes that this has involved, at least in the OECD, the virtual elimination of the peasantry as a class – perhaps the most profound social change in the last millennium.

Towards a critical ontology of world order

How then can we proceed towards an innovatory social ontology that may have a transformative and emancipatory dimension? In my view this involves clarification of criteria to outline the components of ontology, and the application of these criteria to assess propensities towards transformation in the emerging world order as both an aspect of and a prelude to further theoretical innovation.

Thus this section first briefly sketches elements of previous world orders in order to elucidate different historical configurations, and certain conceptions of social time. This is a means to highlight the distinctiveness of contemporary conceptions of time (and, by implication, of social organisation) and to identify some of the potentials for change.

Historical configurations of world order: a schematic

A world order configuration involves a persistent pattern of international relations – or global social relations – over time. It is a term that helps to define and to outline the conditions of war and peace in a given era. Hence 'world order' does not necessarily imply stability or a desirable set of international arrangements – it is an analytical phrase that principally seeks to represent the actual configuration of social forces in a given era. When used in the context of a critical perspective, it is also a term that implies an attempt to theorise the tensions, contradictions and limits that may give rise to historical transmutation, and an effort to consider the possibilities for new forms of world order to emerge.

Thus the term 'world order' can be used to analyse very violent and chaotic periods, such as the Thirty Years War that preceded the Peace of Westphalia in 1648; or the 1914–45 period, when there were two world wars, a collapse of the world economy and a general increase in violence. Both periods can be characterised as ones of 'systemic chaos': a situation of disintegration and breakdown in the normative and material structures that constrain violence (Arrighi, 1993, 1994). 'World order' can also be used to describe periods when interstate conflict may be at a much lower level, such the 'Hundred Years Peace' after the defeat of Napoleon in 1815. According to Polanyi, in this period there was no 'world' war, or one in which a significant number of the great powers were involved (despite internal repression and violence to suppress revolts, revolution, regional conflicts and wars, as well as imperial expansion and colonialism). The same can be said for the post-1945 order. Here there has been no major violent conflict between the great powers (although over 200 'local', 'regional' or 'civil' wars).

As was the case in the early nineteenth century, towards the end of the Thirty Years War, demands for 'order' and for a reduction in interstate violence increased. Thus in the seventeenth century a new form of world order was made possible in part because of the superior 'power resources' of the United Provinces (this involved military power due to war-fighting techniques and technologies pioneered by Prince Maurice of Nassau; the economic centrality of Amsterdam in commerce and finance), and perhaps most crucially, because of the shared interests of rulers in the emerging nation-states in sustaining their own survival and power within their own territories. The Westphalia settlement ratified emerging conceptions of sovereignty, and outlined norms and rules for interstate competition and for resolving the religious conflicts that were central causes of the Thirty Years War. State powers and capacities were reconstructed and created; put differently, sovereignty, authority and legitimacy were rearticulated both within and between the emerging nation-states. At the same time, the political basis of rule was very narrow (about 90 per cent of the population lived in conditions of what Braudel called 'material civilisation' and were excluded from both the fruits of market society and world capitalism and from representation or participation in rule). The role of Amsterdam and merchant capital might also be emphasised as a core of class forces seeking to establish a transnational dominance of merchant capital.

Whilst realists might stress the power and primacy of Britain in the nineteenth century, especially naval power and commercial superiority based on the leading role in industrialisation, Gramscians would also emphasise the growth of the capitalist class and the way that a new form of international politics went with the construction of a world market, so that in Smith's terminology, the 'wealth of nations' could develop. The construction of hegemony here – to follow Giovanni Arrighi (1993) and a certain extent Robert W. Cox (1987) – involved emulating the path of economic development laid down by British industrialisation and agreeing to new rules of international commerce and finance with Britain and the City of London in a co-ordinating role. It was an order that did not rest upon preponderant power as such. Rather it reflected a new balance of interstate and class forces (a balance of internal and external power), as well as the ratification of a global racial hierarchy. This hierarchy changed over time: for example, in the great powers it was reflected in a shift from predominantly reactionary to more liberal-constitutional forms of rule, linked to the dominance of *haute finance* in the world market. It entailed the spread of what Weber called rationalisation and Marx called capitalist social relations of production. Britain sustained centrality and primacy through exploitation of the empire, especially of India. Nevertheless, industrialisation tended to create an urban working class and demands for wider political representation, many of which were ruthlessly suppressed, for example in Britain in the 1790s in defence of the political settlement of the Glorious Revolution of 1688 (and against Jacobinism). Indeed, struggles for representation were the primary form of political action by subordinate classes for several centuries prior to the age of imperialism in the late nineteenth century – struggles that at this point in history had not included women in the extension of the franchise.

The nineteenth-century order lost its coherence, and the propensity to interstate violence began to increase. This was partly because of the rise of the newly industrialising and militarising nations of Germany and Japan, the United States and to a lesser extent Russia. Attempts to consolidate and extend the power of these nation-states led to an age of imperial rivalry, economic concentration, protectionism and a renewal of violent forms of colonisation. In this period political rule widened gradually to include the 'labour aristocracy' or skilled workers. Thus between roughly 1876 and 1914, new social forces and conditions emerged: the late nineteenth and early twentieth century was a period of the second industrial revolution. Mass production, mass communications, mass political parties and universal ideologies emerged, generating the capacity for total mobilisation and war. The Great War of 1914–18, along with the Russian Revolution, meant the eclipse of the Eurocentric world order configuration despite unsuccessful attempts to reinstate its institutional form with the League of Nations in the 1920s. Revolution was not confined to Europe – other key examples were in Mexico and China.

In each of these world order configurations, following Cox (1987) there were different sets of social forces at work – that is different configurations of ideas, institutions and material capabilities, as well as different forms of production, state and world order.

Elements of contemporary ontological change

Our schematic of world orders can now be related to contemporary ontological change. What follows summarises six elements of ontology as I understand them. They are partly a distillation of earlier discussion in this chapter. Here, I have drawn on and elaborated Esteve Morera's (1990) outline of Gramsci's approach to ontology:

1 Social relations and social structures are the basic elements to be established, because they constitute the source of and limits to the possibility of social transformation in any given epoch.
2 These social structures and social relations are conditioned by the transience of social forms.
3 The historical situation, understood as the interplay between different rhythms of social time and structural forces, constitutes the main object of analysis, and it is within this situation – or configuration of world order – that the significance of events is to be interpreted and explained.

4 Historical events are the product of a range of social forces, rather than of a single set of forces. These forces are of varying nature, form, scope, intensity and duration.

5 World orders are a product of the interplay between social forces and forms of state in the context of the 'dialectic of duration': the pattern of world order entails both events-time and socio-historical time (conjuncture and *longue durée*). This process involves agency and structure. It may be identified within as well as across different societies and civilisations.

6 Although society, economy and the state, understood as distinct and separate entities cannot exist unless they are reproduced through the actions and thoughts (intersubjectivities and particular ideologies) of individuals, the nature of these social institutions is such that they cannot be reduced to individual action: Gramsci called this the dialectic of the transformation of quantity into quality (Morera, 1990: 187).

Changing conceptions of social time

Like the sketch of world orders above, my outline of ontology is preliminary and tentative; it needs to be elaborated and extended, and made more sophisticated in each of its moments, and then related systematically to different configurations of world order. For example, in each configuration there may be varied conceptions of time that inform the frameworks of thought and self-understandings of an age. Martin Hewson has compiled a number of these instances.[5] One is 'scholastic time', that is the natural and metaphysical notion of time based upon the idea of the immutable laws of God and nature that was to be found in the church-dominated universities of early modern Europe. This conception began to be challenged in some ways in the fifteenth and more widely in the sixteenth century with the early emergence of individualism and the doctrine that Morse (1976) called that of 'masterless man' (*sic*), linked to a Promethean sense of social possibility. Another example is 'civic Republican time': the temporality of cycles in which republics are founded, rise to greatness and fall to corruption – a view that has prevailed in some contemporary theories of hegemonic cycles among world systems and realist theories of world order, as well as the writings of modern thinkers from Spengler to Paul Kennedy (1987). This conception seems to have been associated with the humanist intellectuals in commercialised cities and states of early modern Italy, England, France and America.

Indeed, the sense of time – both in science and in history – changed dramatically during the Enlightenment. Scientific speculation circulated concerning the history of the earth and the deep origins of the universe was linked to the idea that the world was in a continual state of change. These new ideas were counter-poised to those that stressed the fundamental continuity of life on earth in the Providential order. Prevailing scientific ideas concerning the fixity of the species had been connected to medieval concepts of the Great Chain of Being. The new dialectic of thought confused some philosophers: 'Leibnitz made the best of both worlds by relegating the time when change was possible to a region that was certainly dim and presumably distant' (Hampson, 1968: 225). Voltaire remained wedded to a Providential explanation of a (fixed) Newtonian universe. Nevertheless the significance of this ontological shift was the way society was gradually emancipated from 'an Old Testament chronology that made human and natural prehistory unintelligible. With this went the partial rejection of a static conception of the universe' (1968: 231). For historians this change allowed a new freedom to decide on which were the key forces of historical change and how they might operate.

Some historical thinking – mainly of aristocrats or disinterested scholars – therefore broke away from the cyclical pessimism of the fifteenth to the early eighteenth centuries. Some began to think of recent history in terms of (technological) progress and the 'reason' of history. Others, such as Vico, whose *New Science* of 1725 was largely ignored by contemporaries, argued that scientific knowledge deals with the appearance of things, whereas historical knowledge, since it is linked to the motives that underlie human action, can explain both how and why. Human nature was a social creation, in continuous evolution. Thus the values of a society were only explicable in terms of that particular society. For Vico, 'abstractions such as a social contract between primitive men were absurdities' (Hampson, 1968: 235). Vico argued that any period was as significant as any other, and was configured by its particular forms of socially constructed understanding. Vico implicitly repudiated myths of progress and the 'reason' of history as a guiding force, in ways that anticipate twentieth-century thinkers.[6]

Aspects of the emerging world order: consciousness and time

This section outlines selected aspects of the current configuration of world order that might be taken into consideration in moving towards a critical ontology – space restrictions preclude a more developed exploration. Of course, often cited in contemporary discussions of the changing ontology of world order is the collapse of communist-ruled states and the globalisation of capital, the redefinition of conceptions and practices of sovereignty, with the links between authority and territory becoming apparently less clear-cut. Yet it still needs to be established how far and in what ways, for example, the events of 1989–91 can be explained – especially given that orthodox theories failed to predict it. The Soviet collapse requires us to ask questions about the relationship between 'events-time' and the *longue durée* and the post-Soviet limits of the possible.

Stepping back from the moment of the collapse of the USSR, another way to understand the dialectic of duration in terms of a wider ontological shift is that, in many parts of the world, we may notice a fragmented, immediate and ahistorical outlook that seems to be linked to an extension of possessive individualism. Simultaneously, there is a pervasive sense of structural crisis, a widespread sentiment of uncertainty and anxiety, of exhaustion of political alternatives, and in some manifestations, a yearning for 'order': a new order or an attempt to reconstitute the old order. This is akin to the condition of disorientation and flux that Arrighi (1993) associated with periods of 'systemic chaos' such as the 1640s and the 1790s. The perception of immediacy and, simultaneously, of structural change, helps to form the contradictory set of mentalities that seems characteristic of our age.

Thus some have noted a disturbing dimension of this process: a tendency for the collective historical memory to be supplanted by a consciousness preoccupied by the instantaneous and the evanescent. In some parts of the world it is associated with a revival in millennial thinking (for example, some of the Christian right in the United States; some strands of Islamic fundamentalism). As Hobsbawm (1994:3) puts it: 'The destruction of the past, or rather of the social mechanisms that link one's contemporary experience to that of earlier generations is one of the most characteristic and eerie phenomena of the late twentieth century.'

The form of consciousness Hobsbawm refers to is partly based upon the internalisation of a uniform, rationalised and absolute form of time (associated with the mechanics of Isaac Newton). This mode of thinking is economistic in so far as it shapes hopes and expectations and sense of possibility in narrowly material ways. It entails a myth of progress premised upon the realisation of self through linear accumulation and consumption – often with scant regard for ecological consequences or responsibility for the welfare of future generations. Whilst acceptance of this mental framework is central to the supremacy of neo-liberalism, its social myopia, its limits and contradictions, lie in the anxiety and insecurity, economic instability, social polarisation, growing inequality and structural violence it engenders – it reflects a preoccupation with the immediacy of events-time, an economism of morality, as well as other social pathologies (Gill, 1995b).

One specific hypothesis about the contemporary situation is that there is a mutation of forms of political economy, involving a greater commod-ification of the basic principles of operation of government, which is itself reshaped by economistic modes of thinking just noted (points 1 and 2, above). That this dimension of the ontological shift is real and is of direct practical relevance to the everyday lives of people is revealed by exploring the links between the globalisation of finance, the rise in the structural power of (mobile) capital and the fiscal crisis of the state (Gill and Law, 1989). In brief, financial pressures have provoked redefinition of desir-able and necessary action by governments. A shift is occurring away from socialisation of risk provision (health care, pensions, unemployment insurance and so on), towards a privatised system of self-help. In this situation the individual is made to fight in the marketplace for survival and to protect him or herself against sickness and the vulnerability of old age. What is materialising is an internal and external transformation in forms of state (a shift from the welfare-nationalist form towards the neo-liberal 'workfare' and 'competition state') and in prevailing under-standings of the purpose of politics. Indeed, the latter conception of the instrumental state presiding over a liberal economy that supplants an older moral economy can be traced back to the ideas of Smith, Ricardo and Bentham and Polanyi's account of the *Great Transformation*.

Much public and private neo-liberal discourse about political economy and social possibility suggests that there can be 'no alternative' to the present world order configuration. In concrete terms this project depends to a large extent upon how far national and transnational fractions of capital and labour, and their counterparts in government, see their inter-ests as tied to the mast of a neo-liberal market-based system of global eco-nomic governance. Many workers are not only consumers but also increasingly becoming investors – as pension provision is privatised and their savings are placed by institutional investors in mutual funds, government bonds, etc. It is institutional investors and bond-traders, along with private credit-rating agencies, that influence, and in some cases directly pressure governments to adopt neo-liberal policies associ-ated with the reconfiguration of welfare and risk provision noted above (Useem, 1996). However, even privileged workers are experiencing alien-ation and a rising rate of exploitation (longer work hours, harder and more knowledge-intensive work, sleepless nights), as the workplace becomes part of a wider social Darwinist struggle in more polarised soci-eties. Attempts to protect this type of order through 'enclavisation' (for example, the construction of guarded production/finance facilities, as in export-processing-zones or 'offshore' financial centres, or walled, pri-vately policed residential developments such as in Los Angeles, Buenos Aires or London) mean, necessarily, that it has a divisive, incomplete and unrealisable quality (Hirsch, 1976; Gill, 1995b).[7] The alternatives to this order may, of course, not necessarily be progressive ones, especially given the resurgence of the reactionary right and different forms of authoritarianism in the last twenty years.

Conclusion

This chapter has highlighted selected issues of transformation, innovation and ontological change in the study of world orders. A preoccupation with ontological change is also evident in the reflections of authors in other fields: what is occurring is an intense reordering of prevailing conceptions of space and time. This is seen as part of a process whereby social and cultural relations are being restructured in an era of 'postmodernity' relative to the reconstruction of political economies. As David Harvey (1989) notes this is partially reflected in post-modern visual and written art as the collision and superimposition of different ontological worlds (for example as in collage/montage), as well as in its emphasis on indeterminacy and immanence and the perpetual interweaving of texts.[8] This is a factor in the transience of social forms (point 2, above) and indicative of a shift in intersubjectivities (point 6, above).

It has been suggested that new ontologies emerge as part of an ongoing dialectic of social being and becoming, perhaps represented as negations of accepted or prevailing ontologies. This occurs most acutely under conditions of structural crisis, such that new ontologies emerge from the historical experience and actions of people creating their destinies but not necessarily their destinations – a journey in which the 'is' and the 'ought' may undergo a transformation.

Indeed, as people confront the limits and the contradictions associated with a particular set of forces that come to dominate socio-economic life, that is as they undergo both intensified exploitation and growing insecurity and experience associated ecological, psychological and health problems, prospects for ontological transformation may emerge. As Robert Cox observes: 'where there appears to be a disjuncture between problems and hitherto accepted mental constructs, we may detect the opening of a crisis of structural transformation' (1992c: 138). Reformulation of ontology and forms of popular political innovation are taking place not only in the context of cultural movements – but also in conjunction with new conceptions of civil society and a process of 'reflexive democratisation' or 'innovation from below' (see the chapters by Yoshikazu Sakamoto and Fantu Cheru). Thus although increased exploitation in the workplace (partly because of the decline of the countervailing power of unions) tends to squeeze time available for workers for reflection and political association, the capacity for reflexive democratisation should therefore not be underestimated.

Implicit in my discussion is a critique of the form of political economy that prevails in much of the present English-speaking world: it is represented as if it is subject to quasi-natural laws, so that there can be no alternative to neo-liberal forms of globalisation. This is an acute issue in a period when socialist and communist alternatives seem to have been marginalised or destroyed in public discourse. Yet one thing that the study of history teaches us is that it never 'ends'. Indeed, control over and use of time, for reflection, for thought, for organisation, for pedagogy, as well as for the development of material resources and networks, are centrally important for theoretical development and as an object of struggle – or action – in the attempt to create an open-ended, non-totalising and innovative form of global politics. Indeed, reflexive moments, as well as moments of resistance in the mental and material prisons of our everyday lives, are part of the same processes of self-creation, and of innovation, emancipation and historical transformation.

NOTES

I am indebted to Martin Hewson for insightful comments and suggestions.

1 Historical structures are 'abstract' representations of persistent patterns of thought and action, incentives and constraints. However, structures are 'real' and concrete in that they are produced by human action as people respond to actual or imagined circumstances they face. Thus structure and agency are dialectically interrelated through theory and practice in a historical process – as Karl Marx argued, people make history though not under conditions of their own choosing. A historical transformation implies forms of structural change that range from the details of everyday life (intensive change) to the scope of social or world order practices (extensive change).

2 Several chapters deal with dimensions often ignored in neo-realist and liberal institutionalist discourse. See the chapters by Spike Peterson (gender) Randolph Persaud (race) and Kees van der Pijl (class).

3 This explains why theoretical innovation is possible under conditions where it may appear to be impossible. Braudel and Gramsci wrote much of their best work whilst in prison (Gramsci was incarcerated by the Italian fascists).

4 Cf. St Augustine, writing in the fifth century, who developed an early theory of time. Augustine postulated that there are three 'times': 'a present of things past, a present of things present, and a present of things future' (*Confessions*, Book XI, Chapter xx, cited in Russell, 1946: 374).

5 M. Hewson, 'Some Forms of Time-Culture'. Research Note. December 1995.

6 Recent conceptions and experiences of temporality – associated with modern industrial capitalism and productive innovation include: labour time: a principal medium of capital's power over labour (control over and length of the working day; time management; labour redefined as an abstract quantity of

commodified time), and 'discipline time': the ethic of not wasting time and avoiding idleness; this has a long and complex lineage from Protestant churches to Taylorist and Fordist methods of 'scientific management'. These forms of temporality help to shape not only our consciousness and social experience. In addition there are two other forms of time that can be noted. The first is 'life-time', the natural cycle of birth, youth, ageing and death. The second is 'bio-spheric time', – the life spans of particular species.

7 Mrs Thatcher coined the phrase 'there is no alternative'. When she was replaced as prime minister, she and her husband were offered an enclave property, replete with walls, surveillance cameras, patrolling security personnel, etc., at a premium price by the property developer. However local residents protested that their security would be threatened if the Thatchers were to live there. The Thatchers were therefore forced to look for an alternative.

8 (Harvey, 1989: 39–65, esp. plate 1.6, p. 51). Harvey cites Foucault's concept of heterotopia: the coexistence of 'incommensurable spaces that are juxtaposed and superimposed upon each other'. Harvey defines the emergence of 'the postmodern condition' in terms of the compression of space and time. However, the commercial and finance capitalists of seventeenth-century Amsterdam experienced an early form of 'time-space' compression of global reach.

2   Consciousness, myth and collective action: Gramsci, Sorel and the ethical state

Enrico Augelli and Craig N. Murphy

Many students of International Relations would consider Robert W. Cox's greatest contribution to be his opportune introduction of Antonio Gramsci's work to a field that seemed bent on forgetting its own traditions of rich, historicist theorising about fundamental social change. Gramsci offered a non-economistic way to understand fundamental questions about collective action at a time when the dominant liberal and 'realist' traditions began to embrace neat (and often simplistic) models of individual rational choice – and when at least one important group of *critical* scholars (scholars orienting their work towards the transformation of the social worlds that the dominant traditions treat as given) adopted a 'rational-choice Marxism' that passed over many of the same issues ignored by 'structural realists' and neo-liberal 'new' institutionalists.

Yet, as we argue here, much of the specific power of Gramsci's non-economistic and critical analysis that first attracted many students of International Relations to his work comes not from his own innovations in theory, but from the core conceptual breakthrough in the politically much more ambiguous theory of Georges Sorel. It is Sorel's concept of the motivating social 'myth', and his modern exemplar, the proletarian general strike, that provide Gramsci with a fundamentally different answer to the collective action 'problems' posed by liberal rationalist social theorists. The field of International Relations, as yet, may not have fully absorbed the distinctively 'Gramscian' contribution of identifying the fundamental progressive social myth of the industrial age not as that of Sorel's general strike, but as that of the party oriented towards the creation of an ethical state where the distinction between ruler and ruled is no longer essential. We suggest some ways in which Gramsci's broader analysis of the party might motivate further fruitful International Relations research and then return to the contrast between the model of consciousness adopted by Gramsci's followers and the liberal model that is otherwise relatively ubiquitous in International Relations research.

Sorel's 'Myth'

In the last decade of the nineteenth century and the first decade of the twentieth century, Georges Sorel, a retired French civil servant, used the leisure provided by his pension to study and write about what he perceived as the decadence of the society of which he was a part. He became a public intellectual, an advocate of socialism on ethical grounds, an extreme critic of modern bureaucratic organisation along with the consolidation of power that regularly comes with privilege, and a leading proponent of voluntarism and syndicalism – an advocate of the transformation of bourgeois society by the spontaneous collective action of working men and women whose centrality to industrial production assured that, in theory, they always had it within their hands to make a moral, egalitarian society.

In Sorel's analytical work on the history of what he understood as moments of moral regeneration of society, and on the reasons that men and women rebelled, Sorel focused on motivating myths, stories that created unity among the group bent on social transformation by describing the process by which the group could triumph and by promising ultimate victory. He often presented the early Christian story of redemption as his ultimate model. That myth, 'produced many heroic acts, engendered a courageous propaganda, and was the cause of considerable moral progress' (Sorel, 1961: 35). Sorel was convinced a new myth, that of the general strike – the moment when working people would rise together, expose their collective power within industrial society, and, in doing so, transform it – would have the same historical function.

Sorel's idea of a motivating social myth rested upon a fundamentally different understanding of human psychology than that underlying both today's rational-choice theories of human behaviour and their precursors in the works of Sorel's contemporaries such as Vilfredo Pareto. Pareto, like his rational-choice followers today, found it perfectly reasonable to reduce the font of human action to individualistic, rationalistic judgement of the relative desirability of things apprehended by the immediate senses. Rational-choice man (*sic*) is a thinker and a calculator who knows what is and what is likely to happen on the basis of mundane experience alone. Sorel, in contrast, adopted the psychology of Henri Bergson, who saw men and women drawn to decision by an inner, rarely conscious model of a complete, true self that becomes manifest not merely through the faculty of rationalist judgement of things as presented to the senses, but also via profound emotional attachment and leaps of intuition about things as they might be (see Bergson, 1955). For Bergson, collective decision and collective action arose out of a unified affirmation of a course of action by all the faculties of perception and judgement (Sorel, 1961: 47–8). Thus, Sorel, in contrast to Pareto and to the bourgeois economists of his day, could distinguish between courses of action that someone might affirm via her rationalist judgement of her immediately apparent self-interest, and courses of action more powerfully motivated by all aspects of her being – courses of action revealed by transformative social myths.

It is perhaps not too much of a distortion to argue that the psychology of economic man, the psychology of rational-choice analysis, assumes the existence of only two of the four dimensions of human cognition identified by another of Sorel's contemporaries who was also influenced by Bergson, C. G. Jung (1933).[1] Economic man understands the world via what Jung calls 'sensation' and judges the world via what Jung calls 'thought'. Bergsonian (and, hence, Sorelian) man also apprehends the world via Jung's 'intuition' and judges the world via Jung's 'feeling'. To use an older analogy: in terms of Aristotle's logic and rhetoric, economic man decides on the bases of *logos* and knowledge of immediate causes, while Sorel's is Aristotle's more complete man who is also moved by *pathos* and knowledge of ultimate causes. Thus, the core of Sorel's insight is that the most powerfully motivated decisions are those equally affirmed by everything and every way that human beings can understand and judge including all the passion and the eschatology that disappears from narrowly rationalistic versions of social science.

One consequence of Sorel's adoption of Bergsonian psychology was Sorel's suspicion of simple, ahistorical accounts of collective behaviour in which, for example, well-tried rationalist recipes for effective collective action could be used again and again (extending the 'shadow of future', providing side-payments for compliance, creating 'false consciousness', and so forth). In Sorel's psychology, moments of real decision – moments at which the self is grasped (and, in being grasped, is transformed) – create people anew. They give time an arrow, changing the way judgements will be made from that point forward – even the petty, incomplete rationalist judgements we make when acting as an 'economic man'. In that way, effective social myths, those that become the basis for collective action, make history. Therefore, they require us to understand human action *historically* and not as the consequence of recurrent, essentially similar, ahistorical individual rational choices.

Myth and International Relations

Students of International Relations influenced by Gramsci have used Sorel's insight, even if sometimes less than fully self-consciously. In the face of a contemporary scholarly culture that seems to affirm the contrary, we have acted as if myths and history are integrally connected and as if both deeply matter. We have argued, either directly or indirectly, that one cannot explain effective collective action without taking into account the emotional power of the narratives aimed at binding people together. We have contended that those powers can and should be compared, that is, that the study of motivating myths and ideologies is central to social science and effective praxis. We have demonstrated that collectivities bound together historically by particular myths – and the individuals within them – are, themselves, transformed, that their 'interests' change, and that, as a result, collective actions that would have been predicted before the advent of the new collective identity often become less and less likely.

Myth matters in Cox's (1979) account of the conflicting elite ideologies and programmes for reconstructing 'world order' in the wake of the first phase of the current global crisis, and one particular myth mattered in the (at least temporary) triumph of the neo-liberal-Trilateralist programme whose rise was so carefully documented by Stephen Gill (1990). In North–South relations the weakness of the peculiar international analogue to the myth of the general strike proved central to an explanation of the failure of the 'global Keynesian' solutions to the crisis of the early 1970s, even though that programme remained in the rational, relatively short-term, self-interest of most of the powerful states who could have made the global Keynesian vision a reality (Augelli and Murphy, 1988: 149–51). Later, as William Robinson's (1996) work has demonstrated, popular democratic movements in all parts of the world – from Poland to the Philippines, to Haiti, to South Africa – motivated by something more than a mere analogy to the general strike have created a second, more political stage in the current world order crisis.

Recent International Relations scholarship has not only demonstrated the usefulness of the Sorelian concept as part of any understanding of the genesis of historically significant collective social action, but has, arguably, even clarified the way it fits into Gramsci's overall political theory (Murphy, 1994: 17–18). In almost every case in which Gramsci uses the concept (and in the most important modern cases in which Sorel uses it) the motivating social myths have the peculiar characteristic of being somewhat self-fulfilling. Thus, although we, as modern rationalists, would hardly expect the Second Coming to occur tomorrow even if all Christians suddenly began to act as if they believed that to be true, we would expect a general strike to be more or less effective depending on the degree to which workers believe in its efficacy. Similarly, most myths of nationality – myths that a certain 'we' are, in fact, a 'nation' – are even more self-fulfilling;

which is why, as Mark Rupert (1995a) has shown, contestation over the elaboration of the national myth of a dominant society can become central to the structure of a particular historical world order, as it did in the American-dominated 'free world' after the Second World War.

In almost every case, International Relations scholars influenced by Gramsci have used Sorel's concept in the course of discussing the ways in which intellectual leaders of one or more political movements have attempted to motivate collective political action that would maintain or transform a significant aspect of world order. We have analysed 'myths' in the course of examining the way in which social movements that could be considered 'political parties' have gone about a central part of their business. This is in keeping with Gramsci's own use of the concept. Gramsci sees 'myth' as central to *part* of the business of political parties, an initial and fundamental phase of the formation of collective will, of making 'I', 'we'.

Gramsci uses Sorel's idea to provide what a liberal rationalist might call an 'initial answer' to the 'problem of collective action', and it is in that sense, that students of International Relations have, for the most part, done the same. For Gramsci, of course, the 'problem' of collective action is not really a problem; it is only a problem for those who have assumed the ontological priority of separate, narrowly rational, egoistic individuals. Not surprisingly, then, Gramsci's use of Sorel's concept is not really at the centre of his political analysis. It is only one very small part of a more elaborate theory of the role of parties, and, in particular, the transformative party, a theory that has not, as yet, been fully absorbed into International Relations.

Gramsci's party

Gramsci relies on Sorel's concept of 'myth' in two ways. On the one hand, Gramsci considers social myths to be at the centre of the persuasive apparatus of any party, no matter what the social forces to which it is organically linked. A social myth is a 'concrete phantasy' which allows a group to 'organise its collective will' (Gramsci, 1971: 126). Myths give parties something akin to the 'state spirit' promoted by nationalism. This 'spirit' links party members backwards and forwards in time, both emotionally and rationally, connecting them to powerful 'forces which are materially "unknown" [not completely predictable] but which nevertheless feel themselves to be active and operational' (Gramsci, 1971: 146; cf. Anderson, 1983: 17–25). Some such myths that are central to contemporary international relations include the liberal-fundamentalist notion of the inevitable triumph of the marketplace, the more recent bourgeois internationalist assertion of 'the end of history', and all the tropes that define the various 'missions' of crusading nations like the United States or revolutionary Iran (cf. Augelli and Murphy, 1988: 58–70).

Yet, on the other hand, Gramsci critiques the particular myth that Sorel offered as a means of organising the collective will of the working class, and Gramsci proposes his own 'concrete phantasy' of the revolutionary party, in its place. Gramsci (1971: 127–8) argues that Sorel's 'general strike' was merely one moment in the strategic transformation of capitalist societies by a self-conscious working class. In contrast, it was the working-class party, the party directed towards the abolition of class society itself, that could be conceived of as the historical actor linking past and future and providing both a rational as well as an emotive ground for collective action.

Although Gramsci's critique of Sorel's myth is carried on entirely in rationalist terms (that is, as a matter of logic and fact), the party that Gramsci proposes as the more complete and effective instrument of transformation retains some of the emotive, eschatological and even the 'fantastic' characteristics of Sorel's general strike. Gramsci's party is not necessarily to be equated with any real, existing party, even though, of course, Gramsci understood his own work in building Italian communism as an effort to create the kind of party he imagined. Nonetheless, Gramsci argued that the ideal party's concrete reality as the expression of working-class aspirations may appear only at moments of crisis as leadership blocs break up and recoalesce. Even then, unless appropriate numbers of leaders, intermediate cadres, and active mass members have been mobilised, the party will be ineffective (Gramsci, 1971: 147–57).

Gramsci relies upon the party-ideal to catalyse recurrent working-class collective action aimed at the 'realistic' utopia of a state in which the distinction between ruler and ruled is abolished; 'realistic' because that classless state, as Marx argued, would be in the collective interest of the working class. This ultimate ideal also provided Gramsci with one of his means for judging the actions of existing parties and states. Gramsci recognised the ways in which his endpoint mirrored the Hegelian ideal of an 'ethical' state in which ruler and ruled have become indistinguishable, or, even more narrowly, the left-Hegelian identification of the more ethical state (or party) as the one which acts to create the conditions for the abolition of class distinction, and, therefore, the abolition of the conditions which necessitated the institution in the first place.

Thus, real-world parties that make appeals to the working class can be judged not only by the degree to which their strategies to abolish class-riven societies are effective, but also by the degree to which their strategies move towards the abolition of such distinctions within the party itself.

The leaders of the emergent ideal party would not only be effective, they would, themselves, never lead party cadres and members by either force or fraud, but, rather, lead as teachers and educators, creating the conditions under which the need for a separate party leadership stratum would disappear (cf. Augelli and Murphy, 1988: 124–5).

Gramsci's analysis of parties and International Relations

Even in the last decade of Gramsci's short life, when he decided to try to write something *'für ewig'* in the fascist prisons where he remained incarcerated for his leadership of the Italian Communist Party, Gramsci remained, fundamentally, a man of action, which is why his analysis of the transformative political party looms so large within his political writing. The detail and nuance of that theorising can provide a richer mine for those students of International Relations who, thus far, have taken advantage only of Gramsci's understanding of some of the sources of collective action. Gramsci's theory provides at least three other sources of insight for International Relations. They have to do with, in turn: (i) the organic relationship between party leaders and fundamental social forces; (ii) the organisational attributes of a party, especially as discussed in Gramsci's reflections on 'The Theorem of Fixed Proportions'; and (iii) the degree to which party programmes, and parties themselves, provide effective answers to questions about the meaning of individual and collective life within history, that is, the degree to which they effectively link party members to the past and to the future.

It is important to consider at the outset one major objection to seeking insights into international relations in Gramsci's theory of political parties: today's key problems of international relations, the objection might go, are just not the stuff of political parties. Those problems are ones of economic globalisation and 'global governance', problems of the forms of multilateral and transnational regulation of economic processes that are no longer reasonably bound within any nation-state; in the realm of 'global governance' (even in the relatively well-organised realms of multilateral governance such as the North American Free Trade Agreement) political parties encompassing the whole realm hardly exist, or, if they do, as in the case of (say) the European Parliament, they are relatively powerless and ineffective.

However, this objection is based on a misunderstanding of Gramsci's notion of a 'party'. For Gramsci, a party is an institutional structure that binds together intellectual and political leaders with a mass base that can be a fundamental economic class. 'Parties may present themselves under the most diverse names, even calling themselves anti-party or the "negation of the parties"', and, under certain circumstances 'a newspaper too (or a group of newspapers), or a review (or group of reviews), is a "party" or a "fraction of a party" or a "function of a particular party"' (Gramsci, 1971: 146, 148). In today's multilateral and transnational settings, Gramsci's sort of 'parties' include, in fact, the conflicting ideological tendencies, social movements and transnational 'voluntary' associations that have been the focus of so much of the critical theorising within International Relations.

Parties as the expression of concrete social groups

Nonetheless, International Relations theorists who explore such movements do not always ask what is, for Gramsci, the most fundamental question about any party. Which social group does it represent? In part this may be because, as Mark Rupert (1993) argues, so many International Relations Gramscians have dropped the Marxist political economy – and the class analysis – on which Gramsci's own theory was based. However, we think there is also something else going on: the identification of the concrete social groups that are connected most organically to a particular party is, as Gramsci himself recognised, extremely difficult and likely to be highly contentious.

Yet great rewards could come from taking the resulting risk of mis-identification. At the very least, raising and answering the question: 'which fundamental social forces are represented by which transnational collectivities?', would allow many scholars to be more explicit about the transformative potential of different groups that they highlight and discuss.[2] For example, scholars who (like ourselves) have often done research that may appear to champion the solutions to current world-order problems offered by the 'globalist Keynesians', should probably make clear to readers and to ourselves that these intellectual leaders are, ultimately, working for the preservation and extension of capitalist industrial economies, and, therefore, for the classes that benefit most from the current order.

On the other hand, if students of International Relations were to ask the question: 'which institutions act the most like the political-party expression of the working-class?', over some specified globalising economic space, we might arrive at fruitful, and often quite provocative answers. Specific political parties of the left within some states? Small, fractional institutions within specific 'international' trade union movements? Perhaps even institutions whose immediate foci of organisation are not 'working-class' issues, but issues of gender or the environment?

The theorem of fixed proportions

Central to Gramsci's theorising about political parties are not only questions about for whom parties act, but also questions of who does the acting: the members, organisers or leaders of the party? Throughout his *Prison Notebooks* Gramsci regularly returns to the problem of maintaining the optimum proportion of each party stratum, 'the mass element', 'the principal cohesive element' (the leadership), and the 'intermediate element which articulates the first element with the second and maintains contact between them, not only physically but also morally and intellectually. In reality, for every party there exist "fixed proportions" between these elements, and the greatest effectiveness is achieved when these "fixed proportions" are realised' (Gramsci, 1971: 153).

This last insight, a rather standard one in Organisational Studies, has yet to be reflected on widely within International Relations. The hypothesis that the proportions of different organisational elements within competing transnational 'parties' may help explain their relative success is certainly worth investigating. The apparent triumph of neo-liberalism in the 1980s may, in fact, have something to do with the ready availability of a vast middle cadre, made up of academically trained neo-classical economists, at the very moment that a powerful leadership element formed in reaction to the economic crises of the 1970s. On the other hand, it is possible that the size of this middle element may be disproportionately large compared to the 'mass' element of the transnational neo-liberal 'party', and that a broader public reaction to the 'arrogance, impudence and short-sightedness' of economists – who *do not* reflect the interests of most of those they try to 'educate' and 'improve' – may turn out to be one of the weaknesses of transnational neo-liberalism.

Similarly, attention to Gramsci's conclusions about the organisational dilemmas of political parties may make critical International Relations scholars a bit more sceptical about one of the more hopeful conclusions found in Robert W. Cox's recent work. Cox (1992b) has argued that what Gramsci might have identified as intellectual leadership of today's transformative 'party' (which must be, of necessity, transnationally oriented) may arise 'within the shadow' of the work of the multilateral organisations that are required to keep the current, inegalitarian world order in place:

The responsibility of this second sector of international institutions is to become the point of contact, the interlocutor, for the new social forces. The debate about alternative forms of economic organisation, about alternative development strategies, will also be a debate within the UN system. Different segments of the system develop policy approaches that respond to the interests and needs of different social groups. I have in mind particularly the needs of the relatively disadvantaged and the imperative of ecological sustainability. (Cox, 1992b: par. 39)

Cox (1992b: par. 32) makes a persuasive case that the history of the UN system should lead us to predict the regular development of such centres of intellectual leadership, 'the ECE during the early Cold War Years under the directorship of Gunnar Myrdal, or the ECLA under Raul Prebisch, and one could add to the list' (including, of course, the International Institute for Labour Studies under Cox). Unfortunately, Cox is not able to make the same case that the 'intermediate element' – the cadres that organise the mass base – in this transnational party can be expected to appear. He asserts that, 'The segments of multilateralism that take on the task of envisaging a world order in this perspective will also foster linkage among supportive social forces in different countries and thereby help to build a political base for a globally coherent alternative set of policies' (Cox, 1992b: par. 40), but the task of identifying or creating the concrete groups that will make those linkages remains. Certainly no ready-made cadre – like neo-liberalism's neo-classical economists – is readily apparent.

Meaningfully linking parties to the past and future

Gramsci's ideas about the organisational characteristics of an effective party, link insights about *who* needs to act with *what* they need to do. At the centre of Gramsci's theory are ideas about a party's intellectual leadership and its role in developing a strategy and conception of the world. When writing about that role in his notes on the ideal party (collected as 'The Modern Prince') Gramsci reiterates Sorelian and Bergsonian themes, critiquing Bergson's confusing discussion of the metaphysical, intuitive linkage of the self to past and future that creates meaning through a sense of *durée*. Gramsci (1971: 147) argues that such an awareness is, indeed, fundamental to assuring that people act *politically*, that is, with an eye towards collective and long-term goals, rather than with 'brutish' short-term individualism (which Gramsci calls that 'picturesque' and 'bizarre' attitude, 'like the behaviour of the inmates of a zoological garden'). Nonetheless:

It is obvious that such awareness of 'duration' must be concrete and not abstract . . . we feel ourselves linked to men who are now extremely old, and who represent for us the *past* which still lives among us, which we need to know and to settle our accounts with, which is one of the elements of the present and one of the premises for the future. We also feel ourselves linked to our children, to the generations which are being born and growing up, and for which we are responsible. (Gramsci, 1971: 146–7)

Thus, effective political parties must provide an understanding of the world and a political programme that binds us towards collective goals in the concrete historical time that we know and can understand.

Arguably, in this light, one of John Maynard Keynes's greatest *political* insights was his recognition that in this modern 'post-Christian', rationalist age people tend to believe that 'in the long run, we are all dead'. Today, political myths commanding collective action that will lead us towards some sort of final redemption in what may be an unknowably distant future do not 'work'. But the capitalism-preserving middle-run promise of the wealth that would accrue to the working class from the Keynesian class compromise *could* bind together an effective collectivity (cf. Przeworksi, 1985).

As yet students of International Relations have rarely investigated the relative effectiveness of the different projections of past to future offered by different international 'parties'. International Relations analysts have not considered the degree to which those analyses are convincing to the women and men whose collective action is needed to make the vision offered by different parties a reality. Certainly, though, the recent inability of Marxist intellectuals to offer a convincing vision of the transformation of global capitalism within the lives of our children and our children's children helps explain the waning significance of fundamentally egalitarian international political movements, especially when, at the same time, *convincing*, coherent Keynesian, social-democratic visions of desirable, middle-run class compromises with our globalising economy are also in short supply (cf. Strange, 1981).

The question for critical International Relations scholars is whether a radical vision of the transformation of global capitalism within 'politically-real' time is at all possible, given what we now know about the world economy (much of which, of course, people of Gramsci's generation did not know). World-systems theorists (some of the few historical materialists who still have a relatively strong teleology in their models) tend to put the transformation of global capitalism to socialism some century or two into the future (Chase-Dunn, 1989: 86–7). That is well into Keynes's 'long run'. The question for those who would desire such a transformation is: what is the best that can be achieved by collective action in the historical time in which we can imagine our actions making a difference?

Complex understanding of consciousness versus the liberal model within International Relations

Of course, the central questions for critical International Relations are not really about creating helpful myths for parties concerned with the transformation of global capitalism. Cox (1992b: par. 9) is correct in his conclusion that the essence of critical theorising is to 'stand back from the existing order of things to ask how that order came into being, how it may be changing, and how that change may be influenced or channelled'. Cox writes of the way in which interstices of the UN system have provided political space for the making of critical International Relations theory, but there is another realm (which Cox has also inhabited) that performs the same function: the realm of academic International Relations.

Within the UN system, and within other realms of government sponsored research, the existence of space for critical theorising depends on the capacity of the same institutions to generate the kind of intellectual work that solves the problems immediately faced by their sponsors, what Cox calls 'problem-solving theory'. In the academic world, the space for critical theory is generated somewhat differently. Those who attempt to do critical work must create the space for it through their capacity to carry out scholarship that is judged as a contribution within the broader disciplinary norms of the field. As Gramsci argues, despite what may be the 'ultimate' links between any formation of intellectuals and the practical problems faced by some particular social group, the disciplinary norms of every stratum of 'traditional intellectuals' have a real and material influence. Disciplinary norms of 'intellectual progress' make a difference.

Currently, in many parts of the world, some shifts in those norms may be working to reduce the space that can be occupied by those critical International Relations scholars who rely on many of the concepts and theories discussed in this chapter, especially the relatively complex model of human consciousness that provided Sorel with an answer to the collective action problem, and that Gramsci adopted in order to develop a historical understanding that affirmed human autonomy and responsibility. Room for articulating that model may be closing simply due to the relative success of its 'mainstream' alternative, the model of individualistic, egoistic, narrowly rational, economic man taken from liberal economics.

International Relations scholars influenced by Gramsci would do well to understand that, today, the importation of rational-choice theorising from neo-classical economics does not necessarily leave the field without means for understanding fundamentally 'social' action. Quite the contrary, the game-theoretic research programme that is shared by neo-liberal institutionalists, many neo-realists and by rational-choice Marxists provides a language in which most of the common problems of collective action and truly social behaviour can be discussed.[3] Nor is it the case that rational-choice theorising need eliminate time's arrow, in the way that the simple, ahistorical models of an older liberal economics invariably did.

Neo-classical economic historians now develop rigorous, diachronic ('path-dependent') accounts of historical processes.

As a result, it now appears that the fundamental difference between rational-choice theorising in International Relations and the accounts given by scholars influenced by Gramsci has to do with the relative simplicity of the former's model of human consciousness, and the relative complexity of the latter's model.[4] Rational-choice theorists point out that we can go very far in understanding the social world by beginning with the assumption that humans are guided by a very simple psychology of the rational pursuit of individual interests, however 'brutish' and 'bizarre' that may make our subjects seem to be. Gramscians, in contrast, see men and women as fundamentally motivated by *both* relatively short-term and individual interests, and relatively long-term, collective aspirations that are determined by their social class. Moreover, for Gramscians, neither of those fundamental motivations is expected to be immediately operative in any specific case. Rather, people come into consciousness of their individual interests (as well as their collective aspirations) via interaction with others, via learning. Gramsci's complex human beings are rarely merely narrowly 'rational'. Not only do they have the capacities of intuition and non-rational (however consistent) moral judgement that would be attributed to them by Sorel or Bergson, but under 'normal' conditions human thoughts are complexly *irrational*, the consequence of a 'contradictory consciousness' made up of overlay upon overlay of folklore, rules of thumb and the historical residue of generation after generation of philosophy. Humanity's contradictory consciousness assures that a central role of progressive political leaders is educative; it is to help people erase the irrationalities of their contradictory consciousness and to see their collective interests.

Within International Relations, there are psychologists who regularly defend the case that complex models of human consciousness are needed to understand nationalism, identity formation, group loyalty, and, through those factors, the dynamics of most of the internationally significant violent conflicts that are now commonplace (Druckman, 1994). They have also demonstrated the practical validity of their related conclusion that the transformation of such identity-based protracted social conflicts must, of necessity, involve a complex educative process not dissimilar from the one that Gramsci described as central to the work of his ideal party (Kelman, 1979, 1992).

In some of the Gramscians' own 'problem-solving' intellectual work – for example, in our attempt to derive lessons for more effective UN action in such protracted social conflicts such as those in Somalia and Rwanda (Augelli and Murphy, 1995) – there are clear parallels to the lessons found in the social psychology literature. It would probably be worth-while to make such parallels more explicit.

There is also a second, more difficult task, but one that should prove to be more significant both intellectually and 'politically', in terms of its contribution to the preservation of space for historicist critical work in International Relations. We need to elaborate and further explicate the model of consciousness implicit in Gramsci's work and identify the range of its similarities and differences with the complex social psychological models in use in other parts of the academic discipline. This critical task will, in part, involve further investigation into the common roots of both models in the turn-of-the-century metaphysics/psychology that was the common currency for both Gramsci and Sorel. We hope this brief essay may suggest a place to begin.

NOTES

1 This is one set of Jung's concepts that have become standard in mainstream Cognitive Psychology and the fields that it most influences such as Organisational Behaviour. See Hirsh (1985).
2 Kees van der Pijl (1993) provides a good example of how this might be done in the regular course of an analysis of the competing forces trying to restructure one part of the regulatory network of the globalised industrial economy.
3 Nelson (1991) does an excellent job of explaining the broad limits within which the game-theoretic research programme can serve as an effective means of uni-fying different approaches to social action.
4 See Augelli and Murphy (1988: 16–25) for citations and a broader discussion of Gramsci's model of consciousness. Much of his theorising can be made explicit only by pulling it out of his discussions of intellectuals and of ideology, although at other points, for example, when critiquing Bergson or liberal theo-rists, he is more direct.

3 The critical realist tradition and the demystification of interstate power: E. H. Carr, Hedley Bull and Robert W. Cox

Richard Falk

American-centred efforts in International Relations theorising during the last several decades have struggled hard to discipline academic inquiry and understanding by a reductive, totalising focus on the power relations among sovereign states. In a certain sense, this neo-realist orthodoxy can be treated as nothing more or less than a geopolitical snapshot of the Cold War period. Even this restricted image of the subject matter of International Relations invites a serious misinterpretation of recent world history, making the present preoccupation with the dynamics of the world economy seem overly discontinuous from the past, and providing little, if any, insight into the various stages in the complex interplay between state and market that are so characteristic of this emergent era of globalisation.

Within the broad domain of realist thinking, that is, analysis grounded on an assessment of the realities of power in all forms of international life, there exists a counter-tradition that is more historically and philosophically oriented. This tradition accords priority to the dynamic diversity of political arrangements, spatially and temporally, offering overall lines of interpretation of a given world order rather than positivistic hypotheses about statist behaviour that are analytic and scientifically rigorous, constructs, purportedly true or false independent of time and place. Critical realism, by its stress on context, thus contrasts with neo-realism even taking full account of the range of orientations encompassed by the latter (Gilpin, 1986). Critical realism highlights future possibilities with respect to the character of world order, but projects these alternatives to the present with a sensitive acknowledgement of the limits of knowledge giving rise to a posture of radical uncertainty about the future of international relations. At the same time, the critical side of the approach is suspicious of indulging fanciful interpretations of the future, and is committed to the rootedness about world order. A sharp distinction is drawn by critical realists between their sense of future possibilities and those interpreters whose work is characterised as 'visionary' or 'utopian'. In this regard, critical realists seem as eager to exhibit their anti-utopian, anti-visionary convictions as do their mainstream neo-realist counterparts.

There is an initial difficulty of classification, especially with respect to E. H. Carr and Hedley Bull. Should their work be treated as early embodiments of critical realism or as variants of what has been called 'traditional' or even 'classical' realism? (George, 1994: 91ff., 191–200). If critical realism is to be understood essentially as a reaction against the dominating position of neo-realism, then clearly Carr and Bull are best regarded as traditional or classical realists. But if their insistence on an historical, interpretative orientation towards knowledge about international relations is viewed as fundamental to their approach, then despite their own obliviousness about 'critical theory', it still seems more appropriate to regard them as critical realists of the early, non-self-conscious variety. This uncertainty as to disciplinary orientation contrasts with the clarity of Robert Cox's intellectual affinities. He is both an explicit respondent to neo-realism (see formative essay, Cox, 1981, reprinted with special note in Keohane, 1986a) and an avowed critical realist with his own research agenda.

An emphasis on the work of E. H. Carr, Hedley Bull and Robert Cox serves the dual purpose of selecting intellectually distinguished figures who are representative yet diverse enough to insinuate the range of thought suggested by the label 'critical realism'. What such fundamentally different world views share is an insistence on grounding their analysis on an existent system of political actors, especially sovereign states, whose dynamics are predominantly shaped by the actualities of power relations among them, but whose character is a matter of historical evolution arising from the play of social, economic and ideological forces, as well as from the impact of defining political moments, especially war and economic trauma. These thinkers about International Relations are all, in some manner, committed to theorising in interpretative modes about interstate relations as a whole, premising their expectations about the future on an understanding of how current international society is evolving and what sorts of changes are likely to be both feasible and beneficial. Although the work of these thinkers is to some extent sequential in relation to the stage of international history and with respect to successive readings of each other, their overlapping, yet distinct, concerns and assessments can be more organically, less mechanically, considered by discussing their particular contributions topically, rather than biographically. A difference in their stance towards interstate relations is suggested by the unquestioning reliance by Carr on an interstate framework of inquiry and by Bull on an historically contingent, yet currently dominant statism. In some contrast, Cox deliberately, after reflection, adopts, although with what he signals to be an idiosyncratic meaning, the terminology of 'world order' to the more fluid and indeterminate structure of power that he associates with the current phase of global politics. Cox's move is clearly motivated by his empirical sense that the study of politics of global scope can no longer be understood merely, or even primarily, as the interaction of states, and that this expansion of agency relations must be recognised as formative and cumulative rather than treated as incidental and static. Whether Carr and Bull living in the 1980s and 1990s would have reached a comparable conclusion cannot be known, although both were especially sensitive to alterations in the historical conditions bearing upon analysis and interpretation.

My overall purpose is to depict the terrain of critical realism in a generally appreciative spirit, but at the same time to problematise the orientation by reference both to its underlying theoretical claims and with respect to its approach to the domain of human possibility as it bears on the potentialities for global reform.

The distinctness of International Relations

Critical realists consider that the nature of international life should be studied as a distinct whole, a disciplinary undertaking that can contribute to our knowledge and improve diplomatic practice. Unlike neo-realism there is no supposition that the existing reality is comprehensible by reduction to the structure of interaction among the dominant units or that the character of human and political behaviour can be properly studied by analogy to rational behaviour in the marketplace, conceptualised as a matter of ordering and allocating preferences (see Keohane, 1986a: 1–16).

E. H. Carr is mainly responding to the instabilities of diplomacy in the interwar period between 1919 and 1939, and to a climate of ideas that he felt exaggerated the role of moral factors and neglected the importance of power and geopolitical ambition (Carr, 1939, 1945). In a typically insightful overstatement, Martin Wight contends that Carr's achievement 'is essentially a brilliant restatement of Hobbesian themes' (Wight, 1966: 121). Carr's concerns were definitely historically conditioned by the challenge of fascism, and more generally of totalitarianism, his assessments being then directed at the elites in the liberal democracies, particularly Great Britain. Carr's didactic intention was to shift attention from utopian expectations of the sort that were associated with the promotion of and reliance on the League of Nations or schemes of world government, to the more relevant tasks of preparing for war against aggressive adversaries and managing power relations among states in a stabilising manner. Carr believed that nationalism as a motivating and mobilising force was the fundamental explanation for why conflict among states was so prevalent and virulent. For Carr, then, interstate relations, as such, need not produce endless warfare of a more and more destructive character. It was contemporary linkage between statist forms and intense nationalism that was responsible for generating destructive political passions that supported massive assaults upon and defences of the established international order.

Hedley Bull maturing a generation later was influenced in his thinking by the pedagogy and cynical strictures of the early realists, particularly by Carr, but notably also by Hans Morgenthau, Reinhold Niebuhr, and George Kennan, distinguished intellectuals who were primarily out to slay the (American) dragons of legalism and moralism in foreign affairs so that the new epoch after the Second World War would not reproduce the diplomatic failures and idealistic illusions that allegedly held sway in the period between 1918 and 1939.

Bull from his earliest writings onwards sought to elevate realist sights above the contingencies of the emergent Cold War and offer a more durable and constructivist reading of International Relations than was being provided by the essential realist insistence that modern world history is the story of the state system told with geopolitical sophistication, and a strong belief that human societies were inherently conflictual. Although conservative by disposition, Bull was less interested than other prominent realists of his day, possibly because of his Commonwealth ties, in sermonising to the Americans, possibly believing that the message of learning from the mistakes of the 1930s had got through, indeed too well. Bull's view, clearly bearing the imprint of two influential figures on the British academic scene, Martin Wight and C. A. W. Manning, was that the Hobbesian contrast of the international and domestic domain, while structurally correct, had been misleadingly construed as an inherently anti-social milieu. Bull argued persuasively that despite anarchy, states had succeeded in forming and sustaining an 'international society' that made life more tolerable, by far, than would result from an uncritical acceptance of the idea that where there is no government there is no law, no security and no reliable ordering instruments available.

Bull looked upon the balance of power, including even wars fought to maintain the balance, and great power diplomacy, as providing a type of international security that had compiled a respectable historical record and was generally beneficial for the whole of humanity, and was preferable to feasible alternatives, although admittedly deficient in serious respects (Bull, 1977). In this sense, Bull was a supreme realist, in the living room sense of keenly appreciating the strengths and weaknesses of the object of inquiry, perceiving more extant order and security on the international level than prior realists and yet remaining on guard against those whose vision of international society was, in his terms, unduly 'solidarist', thereby minimising the independence and selfishness of states, and more seriously, eroding the genuine ordering capacities of the prevailing states system. Bull argued eloquently that a more evolved international society that embodied more community solidarity was not an impossibility, but that it did not yet exist, and that by acting as if it did, the genuine ordering capacities of international society as presently constituted would be undervalued, even repudiated (Bull, 1966a). For Bull, then, the state system could be made to work by building upon its distinctive capacities for limited types of co-operation, so as to maintain a balance among dominant states, and in certain circumstances allowing for order in a form that later realists would identify as 'hegemonic stability'.

Robert Cox came last in time, and did his influential theorising about the character of world order during the penultimate and terminal phases of the Cold War, and he has continued to do valuable work since 1989. While making use of the insights and interpretations of Carr and Bull, Cox was drawn by temperament and ideology, as well as by his academic training as an historian, to a less Anglo-American, more Continental tradition of philosophical and historical inquiry. Cox distanced his work from the style and preoccupations of the reigning American orthodoxies, especially the various expressions of neo-realism and its endorsement of an hegemonic geopolitics. Instead of neo-realists, Cox chose as his intellectual forebears Machiavelli, Vico, Marx and Gramsci. The intention was to explore and depict the material and ideological underpinnings of state power, to condition these interpretations on a non-linear view of historical process, and to examine the role of social, cultural and economic forces in constituting and reconstituting the established order and in generating those specific oppositional tendencies that arise among the ranks of the oppressed. A vital part of Cox's originality and significance as a 'realist' is to conceive of power in Machiavellian/Gramscian terms that stress the influence of ideas and cultural primacy rather than to conceive of 'reality' by exclusive reference to the equations and hierarchies of brute force. Such an intellectual framework of analysis shifts the emphasis from stability and continuity to change and discontinuity.

Unlike Carr and Bull, Cox is reluctant to conceptualise even the current global domain as one of primarily interstate power relations. He regards the state as pulled in one set of directions by market forces and in another by societal pressures, giving rise to an historically original and unresolved encounter between states that are 'internationalised' (that is, responsive to regional and global market forces despite adverse territorial impacts) and those that remain 'territorialised' (that is, giving priority to the economic and social well-being of the territorial citizenry) (Cox, 1993a, 1994a; also the programme on Multilateralism and the UN System). Well before the end of the Cold War, Cox adopted a political economy orientation to world order in contrast to both realist and neo-realist preoccupations with war/peace issues and international security (Cox, 1981). In his most recent writings Cox has complemented the emphasis on global political economy with a new concern about the char-acter of inter-civilisational relations. In a genuine sense, Cox's Gramscian approach to political economy anticipated the relevance of cultural factors to the quality of world order (Cox, 1983).

It is also illuminating to inquire as to the identity of the 'other', the active alternative that shapes consciousness by its otherness. Note that the identity of the other is not to be confused with that of the enemy. The latter is the obvious opponent, challenge, even menace: the former is con-cerned about the choice of an intellectual strategy of interpretation and response. The identification of the other seems particularly complex, and somewhat elusive, for critical realists. For Carr the other was clearly the Wilsonian idealists, and especially their European analogues, an identification facilitated by the potent challenge to humane politics being posed by totalitarian ideologies, which for Carr included nationalism. For Bull, the credibility of visionary geopolitics had been considerably eroded, and the other was primarily the pessimistic strain of realist thought that failed to perceive the humane achievements and potential-ities as actualised by that form of anarchy embodied in international society. For Cox, the other was partly the neo-realists with their strident claims of objectivity and their unabashed stress on celebrating continuity and the existing order, partly the statists who minimised the significance of market tendencies, production styles and social/cultural factors, and partly those who covered the face of American geopolitics with the mask of rationalist, deductive theorising. Of Waltz, for instance, Cox observed: 'There is an unmistakably Panglossian quality to a theory published in the late 1970s which concludes that a bipolar world is the best of all possi-ble worlds' (Cox, 1986).

In my terms, Cox is mistaken to conclude that Marxism was 'the great "other"' for 'American social science' in the period of the Cold War because it was 'the ideology supportive of the rival superpower' (Cox, 1986). It is mistaken because these American practitioners were, by and large, ignorant about Marxism, and the intellectual environment in the United States suppressed or, at least, marginalised any serious presenta-tion of Marxist alternative standpoints on the great issues of the day. In this regard, American academic life, as compared to that in Europe and the Third World, was provincial and ideologised; Marxism was the other only in the most primitive polemical sense. The true other for neo-realism was specified epistemologically, rather than politically or ideologically. Its identity had to do with traditional, interpretative social science. The neo-realists brought positivistic and behavioural orientations to bear, hoping to exert influence by becoming 'scientific', more or less infatuated with the academic success and societal stature of economics, which provided them with the proper model for inquiry. Because of this methodological turn, which in its more extreme tendencies relied upon game theory and rational choice models, with maximal recourse to formal theorising and even mathematicising, there was a simplifying and professionalising bias evident that insisted on reducing world politics to what it had been in the time of Carr and Bull, a matter of interstate power relations, but formulating their assessment in esoteric social scientific jargon. Only after the Cold War became history did neo-realists strongly respond to the world as an existential reality by shifting their concerns to the subject-matter of political economy, although Robert Gilpin's work is a distinguished exception (Gilpin, 1981).

In another sense the other for Cox was the world system orientation of Immanuel Wallerstein. Wallerstein's work was critical, historical, holistic and centred upon issues of political economy, but it also shared with neo-realism a primary concern with explaining the present system. Cox consciously rejects the world system approach because of its more static sense of history, resulting in a disappointing conception of change and discontinuity (Cox, 1981).

Envisioning the future of interstate relations

One of the features of critical realism is to identify possibilities for positive adaptation, conceiving of positive largely by reference to the changing agenda of primary concerns about historically salient issues in international life. As generic forms of inquiry, critical realists, along with neo-realists, are concerned with the quality of the whole system, while classical realists have focused on participation by actors in the system. Closely related is the shared realist insistence that such adaptation is not a matter of normative preference, but of the evolutionary potentials associated with the exercise of power. The critical realist, with historical consciousness, is aware that the state and the state system have emerged, evolved, are resilient, are being superseded, and will continue to evolve in response to contradictory pressures.

Carr, Bull and Cox envision this evolutionary potential in quite different ways, reflecting their distinct political and ideological orientations and their varying relationships to and perceptions of a changing global setting as interpreted by an unfolding historical consciousness. Such a view of the possibilities for change and reform is at odds with values-driven or idealist orientations that believe in the potentially animating influence of ideas and ideals, provided the conditions for their realisation, including mass receptivity and innovative leadership, exist. It is evident that the political space available for idealistic innovation has been associated, especially in this century, with the aftermath of trauma, which in international life has usually meant the periods following upon wars disruptive of the social fabric of leading countries (Kolko, 1994). The First and Second World Wars gave rise to a series of such idealist innovations, most notably the League of Nations and the United Nations, but also initiatives associated with procedures for the peaceful settlement of international disputes, war crimes trials, and frameworks for the protection of human rights and the promotion of international justice. The Cold War, in contrast, provoked no social trauma and its settlement produced no idealist openings, although the Gulf Crisis of 1991 allowed George Bush to claim the start of 'a new world order' as a kind of geopolitical *trompe-l'œil*.

Neither Carr nor Bull would have been prepared to regard their role as one of demystifying interstate relations. Both believed that the state, while not a permanent fixture, will remain the decisive unit constitutive of international political life for the foreseeable future, and given their hostility to universalist solutions to the problems of international order, were not particularly discouraged by this prospect. For Carr the quality of international order could be improved by a combination of sensible balance of power geopolitics and the spread of citizen-oriented states, as well as by trends that he believed pointed to the decline in the mass mobilising capacity of appeals to nationalism. For Bull reliance was placed on the intelligent and moderate use of the external instruments of diplomacy, including great power willingness to confront by warfare any serious challenge mounted against the proper functioning of the balance of power. Of our three critical realist thinkers, it is only Cox, with his political economy orientation and an historical vantage point that is shaped by the accelerating dynamics of globalisation, who envisions a future world order structured by the interplay of states, material conditions and social forces, including civil initiatives and social movements. Even Cox views the main constructivist energy with respect to the future of world order to involve the creative tensions arising from the encounter between 'internationalised' and 'territorial' states that are not likely to be resolved until well into the next century (Cox, 1993a). In this regard, it is within this current, more methodologically self-conscious phase of critical realist thinking that the comprehensive demystification of interstate power is beginning to occur, at least to the extent of bringing actors and agencies other than the state into the consideration of how future restructurings are most likely to occur.

Carr's critical fame rightly rests on his insistence that the study of International Relations must be grounded upon a non-sentimental account of the role of power and the consequent rivalry that occurs among states that are objectively and subjectively unequal. In this regard, Carr provided a realist account of international history between the two wars that was prescriptive in its implications, especially the repudiation of universalist solutions and ahistorical musings on grand designs for a peaceful world.

Carr's conception of normative potential is tied closely to the evolution of the state in relation to its international behaviour, attributing great significance to the transition from the absolute, royal state of early modern Europe to the national-state as it was prefigured in Rousseau's writing, entering history by way of the French Revolution and the Napoleonic Wars. It was Carr's view that this pre-modern state had a limited capacity to mobilise resources, that its leaders were joined together by ties of family, their membership in a noble class, and their shared adherence to Christianity. Such a state system tended towards moderation and limited warfare, with a common culture supporting adherence to common standards of morality and law. In contrast, the modern state was subject to the nationalist passions of its peoples that could be manipulated by ambitious, expansionist leaders. These tendencies associated with nationalism were further accentuated by the labour movement, the influence of socialist ideas, and by the emergence and spread of support for the principle of national self-determination that naturally led to frequent wars of secession, as well as intervention on behalf of national minorities (Carr, 1945).

Carr saw a turn for the better in international life arising from an ethos he discerned after World War II as 'beyond nationalism', the title he gave to a spirited series of lectures. His relative optimism was associated with this decline of nationalism that he seemed to regard as a spent force in international life, so much so that he could not imagine a future international order that was as fragmented as the present order, reflecting essentially non-viable states fashioned out of nationalist sentiments rather than functionalist considerations. Of the smaller states of Europe, Carr wrote: 'They can survive only as an anomaly and anachronism in a world which has moved on to other forms of organisation', and then cryptically, 'But it remains to consider what these forms may be, and whether there is any hope of making them more tolerable to mankind than the forms of the recent past' (Carr, 1945: 35ff.). Carr never makes clear whether these new forms will be multinational entities of a statist character or some entirely different associative entity.

But surprisingly, given his realist profile, Carr seems to anticipate the extension of human rights within states, quoting with approval Hersh Lauterpacht's view that '[t]he driving force behind any future international order must be a belief, however expressed, in the value of individual human beings, irrespective of national affinities or allegiance and in a common and mutual obligation to protect their well-being' (Carr, 1945: 45). There is a terrible irony contained in Carr's critique of universalist pretension and his view that the inclusion of the Monroe Doctrine in the League Covenant was a good thing as it 'bears witness to the persistence of attempts to escape from the theoretical and unworkable universalism into a practical and workable regionalism' (46). Unlike what Carr somehow imagined, American diplomacy in the Caribbean and Central America, the region delimited by the Monroe Doctrine, operated brutally as the most consistent force against the extension of a life of decency to ordinary citizens (Smith, 1993).

Carr was similarly wrongly optimistic about statist evolution, believing that 'the socialised nation . . . cannot be spirited out of existence', and that 'the service state' of the welfare era had permanently replaced what he called 'the night-watchman state' (Carr, 1945: 48, 63). This sense of providing fulfilling lives for women and men was thought by Carr likely to create human satisfaction of a sort that would naturally lead to the drastic erosion of the nationalist ethos, so much so that the pressure of 'nations' to possess their own states would virtually disappear. So strongly did Carr entertain this vision of the future that he forecast a sharp decline in the number of states: 'We shall not again see a Europe of twenty, and a world of more than sixty, independent sovereign states' (1945: 53; preface). For the future peace of the world Carr placed his hopes on a mixture of a 'balance of power between great powers' and the 'success of common policies directed toward the realisation of equality of opportunity, of freedom from want, and of full employment', that is, his programme for the realisation of economic and social rights (1945: 71). Carr's misapprehension of the future is an unexpected, and largely unnoticed, complement to his acute critical perception of international history between the two world wars, expressive of the gap in his thinking between critical reflection on the past and the normative potential of the future.

Bull's sense of the future is essentially an extension in time of his interpretation of the past and present, but further sophisticated by a sceptical view of human capacity to discern future possibilities. He concludes *The*

Anarchical Society with a strong respect for any enquiry, whether realist or not:

The search for conclusions that can be presented as 'solutions' or 'practical advice' is a corrupting element in the contemporary study of world politics, which properly understood is an intellectual activity and not a practical one . . . The fact is that while there is a great desire to know what the future of world politics will bring, and also to know how we should behave in it, we have to grope about in the dark with respect to the one as much as to the other. It is better to recognise that we are in darkness than to pretend that we can see the light. (Bull, 1977: 319–20)

Of course, such epistemological caution saves Bull from the kind of inaccurate anticipations that afflict Carr in *Nationalism and After*. But Bull sees plenty of light in the darkness of the present that provides guidelines for approaching the future, thereby identifying the zone of normative potential.

Bull's main contention is a negative one: that the reality of international society is neither a Hobbesian domain of perpetual conflict nor a Kantian teleological preserve of emergent universalism. For Bull these alternative readings of international relations are out of touch both with the past and present, which have been shaped by social forces that have endeavoured, generally successfully, to keep conflict limited. Bull conceives of international relations as essentially carried on by states through the mechanisms of international law, diplomacy, balance of power adjustments and Great Power collaboration in enforcement roles (Bull, 1966a: 48). His realism centres on an unsentimental, yet conceptually coherent, view of the ambiguous place of force and war in international life. Given his major premise of sustaining tolerable relations by keeping conflict limited, Bull takes the view that order depends on maintaining the security and autonomy of the states, which may from time to time require a benevolent recourse to war by the great powers. For Bull, accordingly, war has 'a permanent and perhaps even a necessary place' in international society, whereas ideological and normative correctness is inappropriate and unnecessary (49). Bull generally was opposed to interventionary diplomacy, regarding as one of the positive features confirmed by history that 'order is best founded on agreements to tolerate ideological difference' (1977: 248). In this regard, Bull was sceptical about the capacity of the superpower diplomacy of his day, especially given its intolerance towards ideological difference, whether it was a matter of preserving the Soviet sphere of influence in East Europe or the American paranoia about the emergence of any left-oriented government in the Third World. Such intolerance violated Bull's central pluralist convictions about the character of international society.

It follows for Bull that trying deliberately to impose a legal framework on the behaviour of states in the domain of security policy is not only misguided in the sense of being ineffectual, but positively damaging as it shifts the focus from the decentralised behaviour of states to an artificially posited centralisation of authority. In Bull's influential essay attacking what he calls the Grotian conception of actual and latent international solidarity, the undertakings that he singled out for criticism are the Nuremberg and Tokyo war crimes trials, the effort by the League of Nations to impose economic sanctions on Italy in response to its aggression against Ethiopia, and the recourse to collective security by the United Nations in response to the North Korean attack on South Korea (Bull, 1966a: 71). Bull's critical contention here is a subtle one, namely, that rules for restraint in international society cannot be meaningfully converted usefully into 'rules of law' without diverging from and inflicting damage upon the pluralist and statist conception of international society that Bull believes can alone help keep conflict limited and international political life tolerable. In essence, Bull argues that a pluralist world order cannot act as such for the sake of a just international society, and that the premature attempt to do so invites perceptions of hypocrisy and unwarranted pessimism.

What Bull counsels is the need to subordinate international law and the activities of international institutions to the more significant role played by balance of power geopolitics. In his words, 'one of the weaknesses of the Grotian and neo-Grotian doctrines' is their failure 'to take account of the theory of the balance of power' and to 'face up' to 'the relationship between the prescriptions emanating from this theory and prescriptions of international law' (Bull, 1966b: 72). It is not that threats to the balance and the plural character of international society are not challenges requiring responses, but that these responses need to be fashioned at the level of the state, really by the great powers, both to retain their true character and role, but also to discourage more ambitious objectives associated with seeking justice as well as order, a pursuit that Bull regards as weakening the effort to limit conflict. Bull's final word on this issue is to admit uncertainty about the future, but clarity about the recent past, saying that 'although the solidarity exhibited by international society may increase in the future, just as it may decrease, it can still be argued that in the twentieth century the Grotian conception has proved premature' (73). Similarly, on the basis of international experience, Bull critically analyses and discounts influential perspectives on global reform, including a new great power concert, global centralism, regionalisation and Marxist revolution, before concluding that 'the states system can remain viable only if the element in it of international society is preserved and strengthened' (1977: 315). This latter presupposes great power co-operation on minimum conditions of order, but also a responsiveness to the altered global setting arising from decolonisation. Bull impressively counselled the need to 'take account [of] the demands of Asian, African and Latin American countries that are weak and poor . . . who represent a majority of states and of the world's population', if the old Eurocentric order expects to endure (315). In retrospect, Bull probably overestimated the solidarity and leverage of the Third World, as well as neglected to appreciate the rise of global market forces.

Bull's critical realism focuses exclusively on the security dimensions of international relations, thereby treating political economy concerns as essentially irrelevant to his view of international society. His claim that the interaction among states is best regarded as 'a society' rather than 'a system' is coupled with the contention that international society is a very special sort of society built around maintaining tolerable limits of conflict. This 'social construction' of reality works against the build-up of international institutions concerned with peace and security, disarmament and individual accountability for those leaders of states that embark on warfare or commit atrocities as a matter of state policy. Such a preferred international reality deliberately inverts the optimistic Wilsonian expectation of evolutionary progress based on institutionalising at a global level the regulation of force in international relations, thereby abandoning the balance of power and replacing it by collective security under the auspices of international institutions guided by the Rule of Law.

The views of Robert Cox are more elaborate, yet not necessarily discontinuous with those of Carr and Bull. Cox shares with Carr the belief that power relationships dominate international life, and that the form of organisation in the world economy helps to disclose the historical dynamics that will shape the future. What is distinctive about Cox is his acceptance of a dialectical view of history, in the manner of Gramsci, that shifts attention to the likely discontinuity between past and present likely to result from a present clash of opposite social forces. In explaining the choice of Ibn Khaldun's fourteenth-century thought as a basis for understanding the present phase of global history, Cox explains that Khaldun also confronted a prospect of fundamental change and 'was aware of living and acting in a period of historical change, a period of decline and disintegration of the social and political structures that had been the underpinnings of past glory and stability; and he wanted to understand the reasons that lay beneath the brute facts of historical events, reasons that, when understood, could become guidelines for action' (Cox, 1992c: 136). Cox makes clear that this special sense of political flux extends beyond the historical narrative to include our most basic ontological and epistemic ideas about reality. The clash that lies at the centre of Cox's interpretation of world order is primarily brought about by the globalisation of capital, with its tendency towards according priority to claims external to the state arising from pressures mounted by market forces. As a consequence, those persons not integrated into the global market tend to be less protected, both because of the drive towards competitiveness and the diminishing willingness of states to discharge welfare responsibilities towards their own citizenry. By way of Cox's dialectical understanding of history and politics, he considers the most plausible scenario of change to arise from a countervailing set of pressures that are likely to be mounted by the territorial victims of globalisation, who have started to organise themselves on a transnational basis with the objectives of restoring the human service functions of the state and to uphold territorial, economic, and in some instances, cultural interests. Perhaps the most impressive feature of Cox's critical realist interpretation of the global setting is the degree to which his sense of the global future, already in 1981, was not dominated by a Cold War outlook or the accompanying delusion of bipolarity, so central to the credibility claims being made then on behalf of neo-realism (Cox, 1981).

In thinking about 'Future World Order Prospects' Cox then believed that the three most likely futures for the state system were a new type of hegemony associated with 'the internationalising of production' and sustained by a coalition of states that benefit most from globalisation, a non-hegemonic order dominated by several rival core states that were implementing a neo-mercantilist approach to policy, and, finally, by the 'more remotely possible outcome' based on a counter-hegemony associated with 'a Third-World coalition' that enabled 'autonomous development of peripheral countries and the termination of the core–periphery relationship' (Cox, 1986: 237–9).

From the perspective of the late 1990s Cox's interpretation of the global setting seems much more fruitful than those of Carr, Bull and the neo-realists. First of all, it anticipates geoeconomic preoccupations, and correctly identifies the trends and tensions most likely to assert themselves, and through its dialectical sensitivity highlights the most plausible prospect for change. Implicit in this Coxian vision is the Carr view that nationalism is no longer shaping the behaviour of core states, but with a different construction of the sequel to nationalism, as well as the sense that the leading states, Bull's great powers, are no longer capable of shaping world order by reference to classical balance of power mechanisms. True, core states may make war to uphold globalisation, that is, a variation on the role of great powers in preserving international society, if necessary by recourse to war.

Cox's interpretation of the Gulf War insightfully links the role of military power to the dynamics of globalisation, rather than associates it with either a legalist response to Iraqi aggression or a Bullian instance of great power co-operation. As Cox notes, 'US military power in defence of world-economy interests has become a *quid pro quo* for foreign support of the US economy' (Cox, 1993a: 151). Surprisingly for a theorist with as little interest in polemics as Cox, he ends his discussion of the interstate diplomacy that was mobilised to fight and pay for the Gulf War, especially the uneasy military/financial collaboration between the United States and Japan, with the arresting comment that 'The asymmetry in the relationship of the two powers . . . brings to the back of the mind the spectre of Japan as America's Kuwait' (154). Cox does not pose the next question, namely, whether in such an encounter China would become Japan's America!

Cox's reconceptualising of an interstate system as essentially subordinated to the complex dynamics of a globalised world economy was fashioned while the Cold War dominated both the public mind and disciplinary activity. It is also notable that Cox's variant of critical realism was sensitive to the emergence of transnational social forces, an aspect of his Gramscian sense of people and cultural ideas as primary agents of historical change. By the 1990s Cox came increasingly to appreciate the agency role that was being played by transnational social forces connected with such goals as human rights, the status of women, and environmental enhancement, and to depict the emergent global order as one constituted by interpenetrative levels of interaction in which states were only one among several categories of relevant actors (Cox, 1994a). He also acknowledged that on the plane of action it was important to specify to the extent possible the shape of 'a more desirable world order', which he now associated with a more regulated world economy, a more democratic structure of multilateral institutions, especially with the United Nations, and a greater understanding of those intercivilisational features that called for respect for difference and those that transcended difference. In other words, critical realism in a period of historical transition has become for Cox not only a tool for understanding and interpretation, but also a source of guidance for action, not in an immediate or concrete sense, but as an orientation that could achieve specificity in concrete settings of struggle between social forces aligned to the global market and those connected with more limited human communities of local, national and regional scope.

A concluding assessment of critical realism

The critical realist perspective coheres mainly around its critical attitude towards the orthodoxies of political thought about global issues. Further, it is self-consciously conditioned by historical circumstance, relying on an interpretative presentation of reality rather than claiming to be scientific in a positivistic sense, although Carr's epistemological stance is somewhat ambiguous as he was clearly in some sense trying to put the case for treating International Relations as a science. The critical realist position also differentiates itself from transcendental projects to redesign the world according to the dictates of a normative agenda. At the same time, critical realists are interested in doing more than solve current policy problems facing leaders of states. Their interest is in the whole flow of global politics from past to present to future, with the hope of distinguishing between prospects for 'improvement' by reference to criteria of plausibility.

With respect to the interstate system, critical realists because of their historical conditioning are not biased towards either continuity or discontinuity, and thus, unlike neo-realists have no intellectual investment in the permanence of world order in the form of a states system, nor do they, as is the case with advocates of world government, hold the conviction that the only path to a desirable future for humanity is to dismantle the states system. The critical realist outlook tends to be agnostic on structural matters, appreciating the positive and negative aspects of the state as the basis for political participation in global politics, as well as acknowledging the role of other actors, including transnational corporations, banks, regional organisations, functional regimes and social movements.

The shortcomings of critical realism as an orientation towards the construction of reality in international life need to be distinguished from disagreements on an interpretative level with a specific scholar about how to 'read' the historical present. I find the interpretative orientation congenial, but I am less convinced about the anti-visionary, anti-utopian aspects of the position for two broad sets of reasons: I don't believe that our interpretative capacities are sufficient to provide contours for the domain of the desirable. Looking back just a decade confirms the eruption into history of a series of 'surprises' (including the end of the Cold War, the collapse of the Soviet Union, the collapse of apartheid and the electoral appeal of religiously based political parties). And secondly, I think the tendencies towards abstraction that seem characteristic of efforts to encompass the whole of world order push into the background the urgency of certain concrete claims based on conscience and action (such as, continuing French nuclear testing, eruptions of genocidal politics in Rwanda, Burundi and Bosnia, the suffering of the poor of civilian populations subject to long-term sanctions).

In concluding, it might be relevant to compare critical realism in these respects with the outlook of the World Order Models Project (WOMP), which is informed, admittedly, by a far less convincing account of existing international reality than that offered by the three critical realists whose work has been examined in this essay. But WOMP has the virtue of putting suffering, urgency, alternative arrangements and the fluidity of the future at the centre of its analytic and prescriptive efforts. Is this 'utopian' in the adverse sense of historical irrelevance? My response is that only future generations will be able to know enough to tell us. Since we can't know what is possible, it seems justifiable to focus on what is desirable, necessary, and feasible. Such a path of normative conjecture does not imply an indifference to constraint or tactics, and in this sense the outlook is one of 'rooted utopianism', a posture towards thought and action that seeks to combine what we do know with what we need and aspire to achieve, but reliant on the imagination as much as on the rational intellect (Falk, 1995).

4   Ibn Khaldun and world order

Mustapha Kamal Pasha

> The world of the things that come into being as the result of action,
> materialises through thinking. (Ibn Khaldun, 1958, II: 413)

The promise and challenge of globalisation, with radical shifts in global economic activity, rearticulations in political space, and the emergence of new forms of cultural identity portend both opportunities and perils for International Relations theory. Although existential dislocations may yield theoretical innovation, established patterns of thought – or what can be termed here the dominant orthodoxies of neo-realism and liberal institutionalism in International Relations theorising – continue to discipline the imagination of those with power and privilege.

Against this dialectic of transformation in the world order and dominant thinking in International Relations lies the promise of an alternative approach. To realise this promise, it is important to identify fresh avenues for both innovation and emancipation. Appreciation of various civilisational complexes and their notions of world order in *their* present manifestation and reality is needed to fully understand and to reflect upon real historical change. Such complexes should not be understood as entities that are outside of the driving forces of historical transformation or assigned the disparaging status of 'pre-history' – they are part of the movement of history. Also, to fully appreciate, for example, the complexities and contradictions of Islamic aspects of civilisation may help free our imagination from the cultural fetters associated with prevailing orthodoxies. This would then enable us to move towards a more universal conversation on international relations.

This essay focuses on the writing and life of Ibn Khaldun as a modest step towards broadening International Relations theory to account more fully for those alternative conceptions that actually constitute the emerging world order. Ibn Khaldun's thought is apposite today in as much as it enables a reconstruction of our own intellectual and historical past. His philosophy of history, ideas on politics and society and thoughts on culture and civilisation provide signposts to understanding both the problems of constituting an alternative world order, and more specifically, the dilemmas of social transformation in the Islamic sphere of a globalising world order.

Ibn Khaldun confronted a shifting ontological terrain similar to our own, when his fourteenth-century world was being overturned. In our own times, a globalising market-based order appears to unleash new forces with far-reaching implications for imagining and building collective or individual life (Gill, 1995a). Resistance to such forces, as conceived by Ibn Khaldun, is recognisable less as an embodiment of tradition, irrationality or particularism and more a rejection of the market's *social* form. More generally, Ibn Khaldun's ideas also reclaim the humanistic tradition in International Studies, a tradition salvaged from a Europeanised discourse of the Enlightenment. Ibn Khaldun thus reinforces non-positivist emphases on holistic thinking arising from an awareness of historical embeddedness.

History and the philosophy of history

Writing in a period which saw the basic structure of medieval Islamic civilisation unravel, Ibn Khaldun experienced first-hand the shifting fortunes of Muslim political authority and material conditions. Yet, Ibn Khaldun's significance is not solely *as an Islamic thinker*, whose vision is bounded by the relativity of his circumstances, but a thinker *from* the Islamic world whose thought embodies the highest expression of human civilisation.

Wali ad-Din 'Abd-ar-Rahman Ibn Khaldun was born in 1332 in Tunis, when North African civilisation was in decline and the Reconquista reduced Muslim Spain in size and influence. His eminent family background, combined with renown as a scholar-politician, gave Ibn Khaldun relative facility in negotiating power, wealth and status in various North African and Andalusian courts. But realising the futility of politics in effecting renewal, he sought – especially in his Universal History (*Kitab al-ibar*), and its Prolegomena (*The Muqaddima*) – an understanding of the meaning of history.

An astute observer of an age of Islamic–Arab decline, Ibn Khaldun is concerned with knowing the *actual conditions* in the life of a (political) community. Ibn Khaldun's reflections on world history emanate from the ontological spirit of his times. Yet, his general conception of social organisation and development renders him a pioneer among the philosophers of history. Ibn Khaldun's 'science of culture' (*'ilm al-umran*)[1] offers a synthesis of *falsafa* and the Divine Law as well as an attempt to provide general principles to understand particular circumstances, the actual unfolding of 'information about human social organisation' (Ibn

Khaldun, 1958: 71). Imbued in the Islamic philosophical tradition, Ibn Khaldun's primary object of study is to grasp the real meaning behind historical events.

Ibn Khaldun is above all a theoretical synthesiser whose ideas violate established boundaries of modern social science. Practitioners in today's rival disciplines may claim Ibn Khaldun as one of their own – a sociologist, historian, philosopher, anthropologist or political theorist – but he escapes these disciplinary walls. His 'science of culture' (*'ilm al-umran*) deals with the totality of actual human existence. He is ultimately a theorist of *necessity*, where necessity is both a natural compulsion and natural condition. Ibn Khaldun paints a picture of a world with real constraints and possibilities, not a utopian or imaginary social order. An inner necessity, not tied to any idealised telos, pulls human society in specific directions.

Following the distinction in Islamic mysticism between things that are visible (exoteric) and those that are unseen (esoteric), Ibn Khaldun's reflections on history challenge knowledge claims that remain mired in recording appearances. Beneath external (*zahir*) events-history, there is an internal (*batin*) logic. Multiplicity follows unity, an important Islamic belief (Leaman, 1985). Whereas the method of collating historical information may take external data as a starting point in analysis (a favourite staple of contemporary positivist methodology), real knowledge flows from the rational structure that orders data. The *zahir* and *batin* aspects of history are intertwined: information yields the raw material to ascertain the causes; a knowledge of causes makes data intelligible. Philosophy and history, while based on different principles are, therefore, unified in Ibn Khaldun's 'new science of culture'.

Combining philosophical concerns with theology, Islamic theorists had long recognised both divine revelation and natural reason as two modalities of knowledge. Contra dialectical theology in which tradition supersedes philosophy, Ibn Khaldun takes reason as the basis for approaching both theoretical and practical sciences. In his time, Islamic philosophy was preoccupied with the task of reconciling reason with religion. Prophecy and polity pulled the Muslim community in opposing directions. Identifying a rational element in both, Ibn Khaldun's work falls squarely within this Islamic philosophic tradition. Rejecting neo-Platonism, with its proclivity towards theoretical reasoning divorced from real history, Ibn Khaldun tackles real history, but he chooses 'not only to write history but also to write about history' (Mahdi, 1957: 113).[2]

For Ibn Khaldun, a universal pattern is discernible in social evolution. Acknowledging unity in human diversity, Ibn Khaldun held that history is a universal science which tries to grasp the essence of human organisation. The 'science of culture' follows the logic of deductive reasoning to establish general principles before addressing specific instances, but experience also furnishes the basis for reworking categories. However, there is no definite telos or grand design in history leading up towards perfection. Ibn Khaldun also breaks with the annalistic method and would reject Vico's (1970) notion of a repetitive cycle of an ideal history against which human history must necessarily correspond. Essentially a theorist of transformation, Ibn Khaldun attempts to explain the cyclical pattern of history. Ultimately, the rise and fall of civilisations is not an iron law of history, but a principle that affirms the *changeability* of societal phenomena within a bounded structure. The necessary causes of change are distinguished from the contingent; the general from the particular. Only a longer view of historical evolution reveals a recognisable pattern. The seeds of development and destruction lie within the same social order.

By sensitising readers to the susceptibility of *all* civilisations to enerva- tion (attendant on the depletion of creative and consolidating capacities) Ibn Khaldun draws attention to an *historical* consciousness. To the extent that civilisations are historical (and thereby human) constructions, we are left with none of the promise of transcendental orders.

Ibn Khaldun situates his science within Islamic metaphysics which stresses the transitory character of human existence. Islamic cosmology places men and women in an intermediate position – God on one side, nature (and the animal world) on the other (Khalidi, 1985). In developing this idea, Ibn Khaldun proposes a symbiotic relationship between the various parts of a human being (body and soul) and the elements of the universe, establishing an organic link between humans and the environ- ment. Islamic epistemology, in Ibn Khaldun's terms (following Aristotle), distinguished the theoretical, practical and productive sciences, each with a distinct object. Ibn Khaldun accepts this distinction, but seeks to under- stand real history as an autonomous object of study. His break lies in treating history not as a chronicle of events, but as a science geared towards understanding the different forms of culture. Taking the distinc- tion among the essential, the accidental, and the implausible causes, Ibn Khaldun's project is to penetrate the inner workings of culture. Throughout, he underscores the need for *historical*, not formal under- standing. Implicit here is a critique of pure exegetical reasoning that fails to address the real conditions of humanity, and of formal dialectics in favour of historical dialectics. In Ibn Khaldun, both genetic and analytical methods are blended. The former yields an understanding of culture through its various phases of development; the latter helps comprehend the particular aspects of culture.

Politics and society

Ibn Khaldun posits the rationality of historical processes. Extending Islamic metaphysics, he sees reason as the distinguishing mark of human beings. Human intentionality – the capacity for purposeful activity – lies at the root of any social order and its cultural manifestations. Intentionality covers human capacity to order acts in both social relations and in relations with nature. The basis of intentionality, however, is not self-interest and a prefabricated human nature, but action. Unlike social contractarians, Ibn Khaldun rejects the idea of a state of nature. Co-operation *in* society is the human condition. Material existence is the common problem facing different human collectivities. Anarchy may follow given competition and social strife, resulting in new forms of social control, but it is not (as in neo-realism) the defining metaphor of society. Indeed, Ibn Khaldun has a complex, multifaceted conception of human nature which combines animal and human attributes. Proposing a hierarchy of desires, linked to human capacity, habit and learning, Ibn Khaldun sees perfectibility and its realisation as intrinsic to the human condition.

A central concern for Ibn Khaldun is the tripartite relationship between the rise of civilisation, economic prosperity and social disintegration. For him, human society is the collective product of three basic elements: reason, social reproduction *and* social cohesion. Both nature and nurture must coalesce to ensure the existence and development of society.

Anticipating Adam Smith, Ibn Khaldun links the division of labour to wealth creation: in the shape of a division of labour, human co-operation satisfies greater needs. What begins as an initial step towards survival advances social wealth. Co-operation, and the need to keep society cohesive, leads to the rise of the state. Hence, the state is the natural outcome of co-operation, not anarchy. Society must take a state form to subsist. Society and state are, therefore, natural, not in a primordial sense alone, but in a rational sense of having a primary cause. Wealth creation and cultural identity, in turn, interact at multiple levels.

The focal point of Ibn Khaldun's analysis is the state (*dawla*), which is quintessentially the form civilised culture must take. The rise and decline of states, his primary concern, is neither the consequence of great personages in history nor dependent upon individual human action. All states experience five phases in their evolutionary path: establishment, consolidation, prosperity, complacency and decline. A similar, though not the same, trajectory is followed by the city, economic life, and the relation between sedentary and primitive forms of culture.

Unlike his Greek predecessors, Ibn Khaldun does not seek an ideal state (*madina fadila*), but an analysis of *historical* states distinguished by the ends regimes pursue. Broadly conceived, forms of governance are tied to the animating spirit of the regimes. Hence, regimes of law are characterised by an inner justification sanctioned by Divine Law. By contrast, rational regimes either pursue the public good or the good of the ruler. Actual states are gradations of different hues, combining elements from these modular forms. Hence, Ibn Khaldun's criterion for classifying states emanates from an internal principle, not imposed from an *a priori* typological scheme as in recent discourses on Third World democracies.

Culture and civilisation

In an hierarchically arranged order of principles, Ibn Khaldun places human beings in a two-fold relation to nature and the spiritual world. Within this scheme, he sees culture as a product of human existence and endeavour; he seeks to lay out the foundations of the rise of primitive culture and its transition to civilised culture, the development of culture through different modalities (economic activity, for instance) and its formal aspect – the state. In turn, culture develops in distinct phases, each phase characterised by a distinct ethos. Culture is the outcome of material necessity, desire and reason. To the extent that culture embodies reason, it can be rationally apprehended. Whether in institutions or the arts, individual or collective habits, or economic life, culture is ultimately a reflection of the application of human capacity to think.

Ibn Khaldun repudiates the notion of culture as a primordial substance. Culture, for him, is never static. Distinctive in the manner in which he construes the evolution of culture in different historical contexts, Ibn Khaldun would not share the orientalist predilection to view culture as a monadic set. In terms of quality, quantity and space, mutation is the natural state of culture. Hence, the forms of *'asabiyya*[3] (social solidarity that underpins each political order) change when religion reinforces mechanical solidarities; as does culture in primitive or civilised contexts; or the character of material production. Islamic intersubjectivity affords only one important synthesis of materialist and spiritual components of (human) social association. Demographic change, the rise and decline of urban culture, also heralds transformations. The rearticulation of territorial boundaries, in turn, alters the ethos of human society.

In this elaborate theoretical structure, *'asabiyya* and its formal organisation in the state are the motor-force of historical change. As forms of social solidarity change, so does culture. Ibn Khaldun sees a dialectical link between *'asabiyya* and human capacity: without *'asabiyya*, the possibility for a culture to last for very long is negligible. All civilisations must experience growth, limits and decline; civilisations obey laws of change, so do elements that compose them. Yet, aware of their dynamic nature, Ibn Khaldun accords relative autonomy to these elements. In the concept of *'asabiyya* lies the potential for tracing the genealogy of civilisations, but also (in a contemporary sense), the source of inner weakness in Muslim society as it negotiates a market-based order in the closing decade of the twentieth century.

Ibn Khaldun and world order

What guidance can the ideas of a fourteenth-century thinker provide for rethinking an emerging world order on the eve of the new millennium? Ibn Khaldun is a bridge between the past and the present, but in more poignant terms, a link between a more inclusive historical consciousness and a hegemonic (and therefore, exclusivist) stance in mainstream International Relations.

To begin with, Ibn Khaldun represents an embedded consciousness of the Islamic world. Recognising alternative intersubjectivities means to acknowledge the *internality* of social development in other contexts, processes integral to the realisation of universal history. From this vantage point, Ibn Khaldun affords the opportunity to recover Islam's internal dialectic, both as it predates European hegemony and as it was radically reconstituted with the rise of the West. In examining the particularity of distinct civilisations within the common framework of universal history, Ibn Khaldun provides insight into the Muslim world, understood in the context of world history. In this sense, Ibn Khaldun allows an appreciation of the deeper reasons for the ferment in the Islamic world. At the same time, Ibn Khaldun is a philosopher of world history, a universal thinker, one whose thought engages a much wider object: human society in the aggregate. He provides a *synthesis* of human civilisation at a particular moment in time.

Next, Ibn Khaldun's 'pre-scientific' thought anticipates the post-positivist humanist current of historicism. Social orders are neither eternal nor natural, but historical. In Ibn Khaldun's world view, material forces, states and civilisations are subject to dialectical change. Therefore, the present world order is ultimately a congealed form of social relations on a global scale, imbued with human intentionality. In comparison, positivism often creates the fiction of permanence or order. One implication of stasis – the world of neo-realists – pertains to understandings of cultural encounters: a temporal separation is maintained between epochs organised under alternative civilisational principles. The past survives, but as undertheorised history, with neither movement nor consequence. Hence, Columbus's voyage, the rise of Western capitalism, or Westphalia become familiar signposts to modernity, lacking in conceptual under-pinnings for what drives these momentous occurrences. Another implica-tion is to mistake alternatives to an existing order as chaos or anarchy, or to fail to pose the possibilities for transformation.

Additionally, on Ibn Khaldun's reading, an acceptance of other civilisa-tional principles, especially those that combine reason and faith, may temper economic development with spiritual concerns. Ibn Khaldun saw no contradiction between his 'science of culture' and the Divine scheme. In the context of profound ecological challenges, largely the consequence of a basic disregard for nature in extant 'models' of development, a moderated notion of technological progress may be entirely legitimate.

Finally, from Ibn Khaldun's perspective, social solidarity or ʿasabiyya is not determined *a priori*, but is historically embedded. Ibn Khaldun's realism (not mainstream realism in International Relations theory) makes ethics contingent upon social forces and their resolution in particular forms of social and political community. Hence, he would dismiss recent claims on ethics in discussions of a global civil society, cosmopolitanism or global democracy as utopias, failing to recognise the importance of his-torical causes. For Ibn Khaldun, all *a priori* claims about idealised and preferred worlds disown the societal context of their inception. The basis of a universal civilisation lies in *the world as it is*, but also a world that has been made with human intentionality that congeals Divine purpose. On Ibn Khaldun's reading, an understanding of history is a basic precondi-tion for speculation about better worlds, and on that basis, one may add, an awareness of the consciousness that undergirds social orders.

The Islamic world

The significance of Ibn Khaldun's thoughts on universal history becomes pronounced against the background of rethinking the relation of the Islamic world to the emerging world order. Following Ibn Khaldun, the reassertion of Islamic consciousness is placed within a framework that avoids either essentialism or relativism, the former treating Islam in fixed, unchanging terms, and the latter viewing Islam as particularistic and standing outside universal history. Ibn Khaldun would recognise that the Islamic world on the eve of the twenty-first century, as in his times, is enmeshed in a crisis. A source of the crisis in the nineteenth and twentieth centuries was the assault of the West on Islamic society, producing new tensions and conflicts. However, Ibn Khaldun would also acknowledge that the roots of this crisis are primarily *internal* to Islamic civilisation, only reinforced by outside forces. Western impact on Muslim society appears in the form of economic subordination, but significantly it is provoking a shift in the terms of political and social discourse. Externally driven norms of conduct have captured the imagination of Muslim dominant classes, while the vast majority seek meaning and succour in non-colonised sensibilities. Replacing an internal dialectic with a potential for resolution, rival notions of politics, ethics or civility abound. In their encounter with the West, Muslims began to see themselves not in their own civilisational terms, with an appreciation of *their own history*, but as a subordinate community of believers. Even the forms of Islamic reform and renewal became mere reactions to the West, not responses to internally driven historical forces.

The crisis of Muslim society encompasses a number of factors, including the loss of *'asabiyya*; economic degeneration; political corruption, schisms and state decline; and the enervation of a culture that is unable to renew itself. There are no guarantees that the impetus of change would correspond to piety, but to a combination of *'asabiyya* and Divine Law. But on Ibn Khaldun's reading there are no remedies; history can be understood, not escaped. Ibn Khaldun's Islamic civilisation in the Maghreb could not transcend its historical constraints. The last great Almohad Empire in the Maghreb had ceased to exist even before Ibn Khaldun's birth in 1332. Until his death in 1406, he personally observed the passing of an era, in which he had played an important role as a prime minister, advisor, political counsel to several monarchs. His deep historical consciousness led him to see political reform in the Islamic community constrained by the materiality of the times.[4] Neither good intentions nor shifting political fortunes could surmount these conditions.

In the time separating Ibn Khaldun's world from our own, the Muslims have not only lost their former glory, but the crisis that once inflicted the Arab–Islamic Maghreb is now *globalised* to affect the Islamic civilisation as a whole. Once a thriving culture and trading civilisation, straddling three continents, Islam had lost its momentum due to the internal fragmentation. Similarly, despite individual achievements, the Islamic civilisation today also seems unable to establish a material basis for realising an alternative vision. The quest for a perfect Islamic state appears remote.

Following Ibn Khaldun into the present implies a repudiation of an *external* reading of Islamic history in favour of an investigation of the *internal* debate and conjuncture within Islam: between various strands of philosophy and Revealed Law; between Islamic *shari'ah* and *kanun*; between faith and reason (Fakhry, 1970; Corbin, 1993). An *internally* structured dialectic is sustained or diminished by *international* relations. Though a commitment to Islam appears non-negotiable, the quotidian practices of Muslim society reveal heterogeneous expression. In this internal debate, reform is neither new to Islam nor singularly propelled by external determinants, notably Westernisation. Efforts to reconcile a living faith with the imperatives of reason or philosophy are intrinsic to Islamic history, an essential backdrop to Ibn Khaldun's 'new science of culture'. Closure in the debate within the Islamic community, on the other hand, reflects the perceived threat by some Muslims of an imminent harm to the *ummah*, to the vital sources of Islamic belief and practice. Reform treats Islam as a dynamic faith, whose true realisation is historical, underlining the unfinished nature of history; closure freezes the dialectic. In the name of recapturing the 'golden past', it privileges an uncompromising faith in the texts and implementation of the *shari'ah* in virtually all walks of Muslim social life (Pasha and Samatar, 1996).

Beyond Islamic reform or closure, Muslim anxieties are real: how to reverse an historical tide that has pitted modernity against their civilisation. Generally, in times of acute crisis, Muslims have been willing to trade in their local traditions in favour of more abstract and universal interpretations of the *Quran, Sunnah* and *Hadith* (Gellner, 1981). The presumption that local traditions are usually the product of a compromise in the original teachings of the faith, could only yield closure in debate, but provide a simpler explanation of societal ills. Appreciating the character of heated debates over different modalities of reason and faith *within* the totality of Muslim sensibilities averts external interpretations of Muslim society. This also prevents orientalist constructions of Islamic politics and its apparently unrecognisable patterns.

How can Muslims constitute *'asabiyya* so that it recognises the challenges and constraints of globalisation? This may be the central question facing the Islamic world in our times. As Ibn Khaldun recognised, religion does not exhaust the compass of social cohesion. In the context of a global political economy, Muslims cannot expect the *Shari'ah* alone to help overcome centuries of subordination, misrule, neglect and economic marginalisation. To realise the Law would depend upon rational principles of administering both economy and state. Muslim culture, like any sedentary culture, for Ibn Khaldun, was a complex structure of its productive capacity and urban institutions; forms of state that had arisen throughout Islamic history; *'asabiyya*, which made it possible to coalesce; and the notion of the common good.

Yet, in times of crisis, those who are at the margins of world order may be better situated to propose alternatives. Removed from a closer ideological commitment to that order's survival, their intersubjectivity may capture opposing elements. And as in Ibn Khaldun's times, when 'the material foundations of Islamic hegemony were much weakened', while its 'cultural pre-eminence' remained (Cox, 1992: 147), Islamic resurgence today appears more conspicuous in the cultural arena than in the materiality of its political economy. This unequal dialectic between accumulation and Islamic culture unveils new global dynamics, misconceived either as a 'clash of civilisations' (Huntington, 1993) or a 'return of Islam' (Lewis, 1976).

In the context of global political economy, the Islamic civilisation must rediscover the sources of vitality, not only in faith, but in new constellations of politics that afford the rise of a new *'asabiyya*. Extrapolating from Ibn Khaldun's basic distinction between nomadic and sedentary groups, with *'asabiyya* being stronger in the former but corrupted by the development of civilisation and luxury, a key feature of Islamic societies in our own times appears to be the perverse relation between wealth and culture. The sources of renewal tend to coalesce around sectors of the population who find themselves marginalised; the affluent seem removed from the wellsprings of Islamic culture, preferring the materialist and often shallow accoutrements of West-centred modernity.

Ibn Khaldun's distinction between theoretical and lived Islam also finds a parallel in extant Islamic states, those with a token commitment to Islam and the larger Muslim society that takes Islam's ethos as its motor. The rupture between those who seek comfort and those with the capacity to establish *'asabiyya* may have grown with the advent of market civilisation. The compression of space and time, a crucial element of globalisation (Mittelman, 1996b), adds yet another dimension to the dialectic between the need to preserve and renew the faith and establish a self-sustaining material civilisation. In several Islamic cultural areas, there is a lively conversation on these issues without a definite resolution.

A new synthesis of faith and *'asabiyya* alone, recognising material constraints and the resources of culture, can yield pathways towards a reconstitution of an unequal world order. And yet, the primary impetus for innovation and transformation must arise from *within* the Islamic cultural areas with a rethinking of the state, patterns of justice, economic organisation and cultural development. However, the burdens placed on those who are least prepared to withstand them, an integral feature of a market order, must be redistributed in the reverse direction. Injustice and decline of a civilisation are inextricably related, in that the former creates the conditions of division and dissension, undermining *'asabiyya*. Without addressing the issue of justice within the *ummah*, calls for redressing history may be irrelevant.

Conclusion

In the face of the market's homogenising, if socially disintegrative, force, the task of harmonising the demands of accumulation with the yearning for cultural autonomy appears more tenuous. Although riddled with irreconcilable contradictions, often concealed in proclamations of the 'end of history' (Fukuyama, 1992) or calls for a new world order, global neo-liberalism presents itself as the new heavy artillery in our own era to batter down all cultural walls. Offering little solace to those who resist its path, the thrust towards homogenisation leaves room for a shallow vision for mutual cultural recognition. Without a durable social base, the global reach of market civilisation is unable to realise its imaginary future, giving the struggles for cultural heterogeneity and autonomy both purpose and salience. On this reading, political assertiveness in the Islamic cultural areas becomes recognisable as an aspect of globalisation itself, rather than simply a reaction to globalisation.

Ibn Khaldun's analysis of a declining Islamic civilisation yields a closer scrutiny of the historical context and logic of Muslim sensibilities. It also gives the quest for a supra-intersubjectivity a rational and real foundation. By appreciating the internal dialectic of other civilisations, the nominalism of recognising difference can give way to a genuine acknowledgement of their agency, and development. Islam's temporal-historical structures have rarely entered the study of world politics, emptied out in the problematic of anarchy that homogenises space and time, or appended to West-centred global capitalism, *merely* following the latter's drum-beat. Instead, denying the received temporal sequence of history is to recognise its partiality, not particularity.

Many extant readings of Islam often fail to recognise the integrity of Muslim civilisation. Ibn Khaldun allows us to understand the wholeness of Islam's internal dialectic, an alternative to partial readings that arbitrarily connect different aspects of phenomena without capturing their embeddedness. The real causes of the Muslim predicament may not be so readily apparent; they require careful theoretical scrutiny, as in Ibn Khaldun's 'science of culture', not solely for immediate practical purposes. The *longue durée* of Islamic history furnishes an understanding of the mutual interaction and development of different, but interconnected, elements.

Recently, culture has appeared as an alternative to *both* 'anarchy' and 'political economy' as the grand metaphor for explaining a post-Cold War world order. In place of an appreciation of intercivilisational dialogue, established on an acknowledgement of the diversity of *internal* principles embodied in *particular* historical-structural contexts, liberal triumphalism (Fukuyama, 1992), or an imminent 'clash of civilisations' (Huntington, 1993) show up as successors to the received paradigms – the new organising principles. In these constructions, however, the stasis of Western hegemony has been recycled. Alternatively, recognition of 'difference' has assumed a ceremonial status in numerous post-structuralist and post-colonial writings – the recognition of particularism as the defining motif of conceptualisation. Contra Ibn Khaldun, the universal character of human civilisations is overlooked in these formulations.

Avoiding particularism, critical forms of theoretical innovation are embedded in a recognition of the universal nature of human association *and* its spatio-temporal realisation. On Ibn Khaldun's historicist terms, this would involve a repudiation of mere exegetical reasoning and an appreciation of actual historical conditions as a starting point for conceptualisation. The main purpose of Ibn Khaldun's 'science of culture' is to furnish an awareness of the real reasons behind events-history. But this seemingly elementary task can also become the source of critical reflection. Every epoch is imbued with a distinctive logic, yet the common problem of human association gives history a universal configuration. Assuming the rationality of historical phenomena, an understanding of the spirit of the times provides the basis for transcending the immediate world of sensory data. Historical consciousness affords reflexivity. Taking this initial premise, Ibn Khaldun's historicist thinking laid the path for subsequent theoretical innovations prominent in Vico, Machiavelli and Gramsci.[5]

Following Aristotle and anticipating future generations of philosopher-historians, Ibn Khaldun locates the meaning of any epoch only in the completion of its historical cycle. Once an historical process has exhausted its possibilities, understandings of its latent structure become plausible. Ordinarily, with 'a general change of conditions', as Ibn Khaldun notes, a world may be 'brought into existence anew'. Reflexivity is often the main harvest of structural transformations.

Ibn Khaldun's 'science of culture' appears to originate necessarily with the decline of Muslim civilisation in North Africa. Yet, on a careful reading of Ibn Khaldun, theoretical innovations are not linked to crises in a linear relationship. Indeed, as any mindful study of civilisations would show, social dislocations have even suppressed reflexivity or dislocated embryonic transformation. Great transformations in social and political association or imagination rarely follow the same trajectory. Innovation does not hinge only upon an awareness of the actual conditions of our own world, but is contingent on propitious social forces. The meaning of history lies precisely in rejecting the notion that there are direct pathways from here to there. Thus, Ibn Khaldun's 'science of culture' is not only a product of a crisis of North Africa, but it draws heavily from heterodox intellectual achievements of Islamic civilisation *in its totality*. Perhaps the brilliance of Ibn Khaldun lies in his ability to simultaneously respond to a crisis of a specific historical epoch and to synthesise Muslim thought in its advanced permutations.

In our times, a globalising economy appears to produce a unified material world. An awareness of its basic contradictory impulses offers an *initial* step towards innovation. A recognition of different inter subjectivities and *their* constitutive principles, distributed across space and time, may create the intellectual spaces to identify the diverse cultural expressions of globalisation. Paradoxically, globalisation also occasions a recognition of the particularistic nature of extant IR theory. In this context, theoretical innovation may require a synthesis of different civilisational perspectives. Specific investigations of multiple modes of thought from a variety of perspectives may help overcome the constrictions of the basic categories of (Western) social thought, reveal the cultural foundations of both 'normative' and 'positive' social science, and challenge the hegemony of normalised epistemologies. Nevertheless, the process of theoretical innovation must be discerned as open-ended: as an integral aspect of the social process itself.

With a dislocation in the nature of the world comes the hope of new imaginings. But the new need not originate with the present. A rediscovery of the past and the recognition of its repressed consciousness may yield openings to rethink how we envision and remake our world. With such a rediscovery, epochs, artificially sealed off from one another, may be reunited, and the possibility of transcending the constrictions of the present arises.

NOTES

I am indebted to Stephen Gill, James Mittelman and Ritu Vij for their comments on earlier drafts of this chapter. All errors are my own.

1 By culture Ibn Khaldun meant 'the totality of conventionalized social habits, institutions, and arts' (Mahdi, 1957: 289). The 'science of culture' included a study of all the available religious and rational sciences, whose main object was to understand history. Ibn Khaldun was particularly interested in the effect of the environment on society and social organization and the relation between productive forces and social forms. Therefore, *'umran* covered a very wide range, from geography and demographics or the *oikoumene* (the populated world) to social relations. In this sense, *'umran* covers the totality of human phenomena. For analytical purposes, Ibn Khaldun distinguished between *'umran badawi* and *'umran hadari*. In Mahdi's opinion, the relationship between the two was a dialectical one. For Mahdi, *'umran badawi* refers to 'primitive culture' and *'umran hadari* to 'civilization' (Mahdi, 1957).

2 This section draws from several interpretations of Ibn Khaldun's thought, notably Mahdi (1957), Lacoste (1984) and Schmidt (1967).

3 The concept of *'asabiyya*, like most other concepts in Ibn Khaldun's philosophy of history, is a highly contested term. Two broad lines of interpretation are recognisable in the literature. In the first sense, *'asabiyya* refers to social solidarity of a group. Durkheim's concept of *mechanical solidarity* comes closest to this

sense (Gellner, 1981). Other scholars treat *'asabiyya* as a more flexible concept which refers to the animating spirit of any social or political order, for example, Machiavelli's notion of *virtù*. In this essay, *'asabiyya* is understood as a dialectical term which develops in the logical sequence, from generality to particularity. Hence, depending upon the specific context, *'asabiyya* evolves: different elements combine to constitute the spirit or solidarity that undergirds a community, state or civilization.

4 Ibn Khaldun writes in *The Muqaddima*: 'When there is a general change in conditions, it is as though the whole world has been altered . . . Therefore there is need at this time that someone should systematically set down the situation of the world among all regions and races' (1958, I:65).

5 I am grateful for Stephen Gill's important advice on this section, especially on the link between ontology and theoretical innovation.

Political economy: the social and ecological anatomy of transformation

The purpose of Part II is to widen the focus of approaches to International Studies so as to provide for a more integrated and global form of analysis. In so doing, contributors consider the productive, ecological and social anatomy of the political economy. They stress that transformations called 'globalisation' require historical analysis. Indeed, each contributor develops a critique of orthodoxies, for example orthodox Marxist methodological postulates such as 'the primacy of the economic', 'base' and 'superstructure' or 'determination in the last instance'. They also criticise the liberal separation of the 'political' and the 'economic', the 'domestic' and the 'international'. Finally, each chapter considers theoretical and practical innovations, for example those associated with 'imagined communities' in a process of 'global transformation'.

Indeed, the first chapter in Part II by Mitchell Bernard reminds us that Polanyi's approach was an innovative 'substantive' form of political economy, going beyond 'formal economics' that abstracted states and markets from a real social context. Polanyi analyses how particular societies are actually constituted and reproduced, allowing for a theorisation of political economy as an anthropology and ecology of human reproduction. Polanyi's account of the emergence of nineteenth-century liberal capitalism is prescient for those concerned with contemporary forms of globalisation. Polanyi's analysis of the destructive aspects of 'market mentality' underlines its subordination of human life and nature to the imperative of competitiveness. A Polanyian perspective thus involves ethical and ecological dimensions of explanation.

Further, Eric Helleiner discusses how the historian Fernand Braudel's work can provide a perspective on the significance of 'economic' globalisation. Braudel provides an innovative alternative to the conventional 'states and markets' ontology, since he located developments in terms of the different dimensions of 'economic life' within a much broader context. Braudelian observation points of space, time, social order and hierarchy help to indicate that integrating tendencies (precursors of globalisation) both predated the modern nation-state and also help to understand how such tendencies today may contribute to its decline. Braudelian theory implies that innovation lies not simply in the content of theory, but in the wide range of interpretative possibilities it can offer.

Braudel's framework is similar in some respects to Harrod's attempt to reach a theoretical synthesis, though his thesis is that production, broadly defined, is a methodological universal that can provide a 'social anthropology' of present-day globalisation. Harrod's argument also stands in the tradition of Polanyi who combined anthropology, economic history and political economy in his analysis of the 'Great Transformation'. As regards theoretical innovation, Harrod explains how the fragmented organisation of disciplines within the university shapes knowledge. Indeed, as other authors note, specialisation is in some respects an important constraint to theoretical innovation. This is explored in the context of the difficulties of synthesising 'Industrial' and 'International' relations as fields of study, particularly because of the dominance of functionalism and empiricism found in each. Harrod calls for linking studies of the workplace (for example, the rural commune, the household, the factory, the office, etc.) to the study of world orders. This is a subversive move in the current academic context especially since there has been a regressive trend in recent innovations in theory: a shift in International Political Economy from power and production to 'states' and 'markets'; in the study of the workplace from 'industrial relations' to 'human resource management'.

By analysing the *longue durée* of transnational class formation since the Glorious Revolution in England in 1688, Kees van der Pijl is able to develop a method analogous to that of Marx and Polanyi. Van der Pijl speaks of the dialectic between alienation/commodification/exploitation and socialisation. There are contradictory tendencies in world capitalism that promote global economic integration and social disintegration: the development and extension of capitalist social relations of production disrupt prior traditions, real communities and existing forms of political association. However, the reproduction of accumulation depends on the prior existence of community. In this context, Pijl analyses processes of transnational class formation and reproduction of state forms: a contradictory dialectic that is open-ended and generates a continuous transformative process. Today's global neo-liberalism can be interpreted as an effort to extend globally what he calls, following Benedict Anderson, a particular type of 'imagined community'. This Lockian complex of state and civil society is the social dimension of a cosmopolitan form of capitalist expansion. It has particular national origins but it is potentially global in scope and thus clashes with other political communities that are more locally or nationally configured.

Reflecting points made in Part I, van der Pijl calls for the formation of 'a new community of fate', perhaps understood as a Sorelian or Gramscian myth (see the chapter by Augelli and Murphy). This idea concerns the possibility of a world-wide political association or imagined community of the progressive counter-movements. Polanyi's concept of the 'double movement' is useful here in thinking about this globally, since, as in the 1930s, some of today's counter-movements involve attempts to reassert democratisation whereas others are highly reactionary: the neo-liberal globalisation tendency is being challenged politically in complex ways. However, for van der Pijl, such an alternative community would seek to restrict the scope of commodification in the definition of social forms and institutions. Indeed the investigation of this potentiality in social movements anticipates discussion in Part III and opens up the question of what will be the key problems for the critical study of political economy and ecology in the foreseeable future – part of the attempt to set an agenda for study which is a central purpose of this book.

Perhaps the most general of these big issues in the study of political economy are transformations associated with the restructuring of production and consumption patterns, and their link to deepening exploitation, commodification and alienation in social relations, and the reshaping of the hierarchy and nature of state forms. What do these changes mean for the constitution of social life in lived communities? Put differently, what are the socio-ecological limits to existing patterns of power, production and consumption? In this regard, there is a need to consider whether there has been a depletion of the ethical dimension of political and economic life, partly as a result of the economism of prevailing perspectives and forces in the global political economy – in accord with social Darwinist tendencies. For most of the contributors in this collection, these tendencies are associated with growing social polarisation and widening inequality both within and across state forms, in an era when financial power and the values of Mammon seem to predominate in defining economic alternatives and systems of political accountability and representation (for a somewhat different interpretation see the chapter by Susan Strange in Part IV).

The second big issue concerns the sustainability of present world order structures. Given the associated social, political and military processes of enclavisation (see the chapters by Gill and Persaud) which imply that key nodes of globalisation are, in Polanyian terms, largely 'disembedded' as well as guarded from the local society and political economy, the question is how far and in what ways is this situation sustainable? Can the major beneficiaries of economic globalisation continue to live under conditions where their capacities for continued accumulation and personal modes of existence increasingly dictate that they be protected by public and private militias? A third 'big question', that has unprecedented implications, concerns the interface between new technological and scientific innovations and patterns of accumulation and legitimation – a point that is touched upon in the chapter by Harrod, and later in this volume (for example, by Susan Strange, with reference to scientists and bankers).

The potentials and constraints of social movements, trends and ideas are discussed in more detail in Part III of this collection.

5 Ecology, political economy and the counter-movement: Karl Polanyi and the second great transformation

Mitchell Bernard

This chapter examines the contribution of Karl Polanyi to a critical theory of ecological political economy. It is argued that whilst Polanyi's work contains significant ambiguities over questions of political agency – for example, his arguments sometimes seem to invoke a form of technological determinism – other aspects of his writing contain theoretical innovations that enable a richer and deeper understanding of the limits and contradictions of political economy and ecology in the so-called age of globalisation.

My objective here is to examine the possibilities of integrating these two interrelated aspects of global transformation through the perspective of Karl Polanyi. Polanyi's work has been of interest to a number of international political economists who see parallels between globalisation and his analysis of nineteenth-century capitalism. Polanyi's framework has also inspired political ecologists who have seized upon his critique of how industrial society began to understand nature in economic categories and subordinated the surface of the planet to the needs of accumulation (Rogers, 1994; Worster, 1993; Eckersley, 1992; Henderson, 1991).

The remainder of this chapter will seek to make explicit the method and purpose to which Polanyian ideas could contribute. It will focus on three particular concepts in Polanyi's analysis that may serve to link global political economy and ecology; those of 'embeddedness' and 'disembedding', 'fictitious commodities' and the 'counter-movement'. It will discuss them in the context of some of Polanyi's larger themes, as well as identify the strengths and limitations of these ideas for the study of world order. The conclusion will critically assess the way Polanyian thought has been used in International Political Economy (IPE) and consider how his work can shed light on those areas where resistance and change are possible. In this regard, some of Polanyi's ideas – for example, his notion of the 'double movement' – are useful in theorising the question of global transformation at the end of the twentieth century.

Transformation and globalisation

The structural transformation in world order associated with globalisation, the restructuring of state–society relations, tensions between territorial and non-territorial forms of power, and potentially dramatic technological change have become a central theoretical focus in the study of global politics. This transformation, in conjunction with the end of the Cold War, has precipitated debates in International Political Economy concerning the appropriateness of conventional theorisations of world order.

There is another aspect to the current transformation that receives less attention from so-called International Political Economy scholars: the ecological crisis. Current rates of resource harvesting and waste generation, for example, are depleting nature faster than it can regenerate. In 1986, Stanford biologist Peter Vitousek calculated that human activities were by then already 'appropriating' directly, or indirectly, 40 per cent of nature's land based biological production, and recent work suggests that exploitation of continental shelves is approaching similar levels (Wackernagel and Rees, 1996). This ecological dimension of structural transformation has precipitated a debate among political ecologists and ecological economists that has paralleled but, for the most part, not penetrated the core concerns of International Political Economy. Both aspects of the current historical conjuncture are transpiring in a context where the wealthiest 20 per cent of the world's population take home more than sixty times more than the poorest 20 per cent, a disparity that has doubled over the past three decades (UNDP, 1992).

Sitting on the cusp of dramatic changes in world order at the height of the Second World War, economic historian Karl Polanyi reflected back on the causes of the war in his magnum opus, *The Great Transformation* (Polanyi, 1957). Polanyi argued that nineteenth-century attempts to subordinate society to the 'self-regulating' market resulted in the subjugation of individuals and the natural world by turning both into 'commodities' to which monetary value was ascribed through markets for labour and real property. Societies rose up to protect themselves in what he likened to a dialectical 'counter-movement' that precipitated a range of political configurations from Nazism to 'New Deal' America.

It is therefore worth exploring how Polanyian thought might contribute to an international political economy that incorporates a systematic treatment of the contemporary ecological crisis into its analysis of global transformation. In so doing, this inquiry will critically assess the strengths and limitations within Polanyi's work for conceptualising the relationship between political economy and ecology for the purpose of arriving at a historical materialist political economy that might better discern what constitutes the 'limits of the possible' for change towards more sustainable forms of social life. The argument put forward here is that Polanyi identified a method and ontology central to his study of the transformation of nineteenth-century European society that provides a basis for opening up International Political Economy and the study of world order to incorporate the ecological dimensions of structural change. Nevertheless, aspects of Polanyi's history, at the same time, potentially undermine this contribution.

Method and purpose in political economy

Questions of theory and method are inseparable from purpose. Robert Cox, in an often quoted passage, has referred to two kinds of theory, critical and problem solving theory (Cox, 1986: 208–9). Practitioners of each embody a different purpose: critical theorists seek to transcend the milieu they are located in by uncovering its historically contingent origins, and the ideas and power relationships that sustain it, and inquiring as to how it may be changed. Problem solving theorists, on the other hand, see problems as isolated from complex wholes. The particular context is taken as given. The purpose of theory then becomes to solve the particular problem to restore the *status quo ante.*

This chapter attempts to contribute to a critical theory perspective, to contribute to what C. Wright Mills has termed the 'fragile power' that a critical theory of world order might possess (Mills, 1959: 185). I will focus on six components of a critical theory approach to political economy. Most of these are central to Polanyi's own work. The first is a historicism that sees the world as historically constituted and eschews theorising that strives to measure or predict social process or human action on the basis of trans-historical essences. Second, critical theory should involve a synthetic approach that demonstrates the structural relationship among all parts of a social whole without ascribing an ontological primacy to any one. Third, Polanyi's work points to the importance of theorising change. Both methodological holism and historicism require this to be done dialectically. It is out of the contradictions in any historical context that resistance, potential struggle and ultimately transformation result. Fourth, a diachronic political economy requires the theorising of agents in relation to structures rather than fixating on the decisions of disembodied actors or ascribing change to natural forces beyond anybody's control. A recognition of the importance of agency within a given historical context compels us to locate specific agents, their purpose and the power relations in a given context. It allows us to ask in whose interest is a given process, action or idea. It also allows us to see the possibilities for action in any historical context. Fifth, critical theory has to examine the connection between material circumstances and intersubjective understanding, acknowledging that ideas shape material conditions but not as disembodied 'discourse'. Ideas themselves emerge out of particular material conditions and are the products of human agency. Finally, and consistent with Polanyi's purpose, critical theory must highlight the possibilities and obstacles in any given context with regard to realising a more just and sustainable future, even if it means lighting a candle in the dark.

Innovatory concepts in Polanyi's 'great transformation'

There are three aspects of Polanyian thought that will be considered for their potential to contribute to innovation in the study of world order by providing concepts that suggest the way to a more ecologically oriented critical International Political Economy: the concepts of embedding and disembedding; fictitious commodities of land and labour; and the counter-movement. These ideas need to be understood in relation to Polanyi's methodology and ontology. Central to this is his distinction between a formal and substantive understanding of economic practice. This distinction forms the basis for a critical approach that historicises the theory and practice of contemporary social life while allowing us to imagine alternatives to it.

To Polanyi, a 'formal' understanding of political economy focuses on the rational choices actors make to economise scarce means, to make the most efficient use of what is available for particular ends (Polanyi, 1968: 140). Polanyi contended that this choice-theoretic approach leads inexorably to seeing economic life as essentially the same in all societies. To Polanyi this was no more than an ideologically driven ahistorical assumption that what is dominant in a market society has been 'natural' throughout history. He refers to this as 'the economistic fallacy'. In contrast, he understood the substantive economy to constitute a historically contingent, instituted process of interaction between humans and their environment (1968: 145). Thus:

The substantive meaning implies neither choice nor insufficiency of means; man's [sic] livelihood may or may not involve the necessity of choice and if choice there be, it need not be induced by the limiting effect of scarcity of the means; indeed some of the most important physical and social conditions of livelihood such as availability of air and water or a loving mother's devotion to her infant are not, as a rule, so limiting. (1968: 140)

Out of this distinction comes the basis for a historically grounded dialectical understanding of the relationship between social relations, institutionalised economic practice and ecology. Polanyi operationalises this understanding of substantive economy in his depiction of the transition to capitalism, which he terms 'the great transformation'. Classical liberal political economy has portrayed the transition to capitalism as a liberation of the 'market' from political and cultural constraints (Wood: 1994). Capitalism, in this conception, is simply the expansion and unfettering of acts of exchange that are inherent to human nature and have taken place since the dawn of history.

Polanyi, on the other hand, makes the crucial distinction between the earlier existence of 'markets' and the advent of a 'market society'. He understands the emergence of capitalism in terms of the agency that brought it about. Rather than seeing it as something natural or inevitable, to Polanyi it was a discontinuity brought about by the exercise of state power. As he put it: 'There was nothing natural about laissez-faire; free markets could never have come into being merely by allowing things to take their course' (1957: 139). Prior to the transformation, economic life was embedded in society. It was determined by kinship, communal, religious or political relations (Polanyi, 1977: 47–62). He depicted exchange relations in various precapitalist social contexts as being organised around principles alien to capitalism, such as tribute, reciprocity or redistribution. It is only with the emergence of capitalism that economic life becomes disembedded from society and it becomes possible to speak of the 'market' as the organising institution to which society must adjust. Only now could the economic motivations ascribed to people by liberalism prevail because they existed amidst institutional mechanisms that made human survival dependent on economic drives (Block and Somers, 1984: 63).

A central aspect of this 'disembedding' of economic life from society was the incorporation of labour and land into a market economy as 'factors' of production. To Polanyi, as labour and land are no other than human beings and the natural surroundings in which they exist, to subordinate them to the market mechanism means, in essence, to subordinate the substance of society itself (Polanyi, 1957: 71). He termed these 'fictitious commodities' because, whilst they were incorporated into a sphere of scarcity and assigned value that is determined by a market, they are not produced by markets. As fictitious commodities became incorporated into the hegemonic discourse of liberalism, the basis was created for human identity to be conceived of in terms of the requirements and imperatives of production and consumption, with nature seen as existing only to provide the resources to serve that mechanism.

It is precisely in dialectical reaction to this disembedding that what Polanyi referred to as the counter-movement took root. Polanyi believed that the subordination of these fictitious commodities was not sustainable for any period of time and would precipitate society rising up to protect itself in response to the utopian liberal project. Here Polanyi's analysis turns orthodox historiography on its head. Whereas conventional accounts view the crises of the 1890s and 1930s as caused by political interference with free markets, Polanyi argues that they emanated from attempts to remove all constraints on markets and the power of capital (1957: 231). The counter-movement entailed several locally specific attempts to re-establish some semblance of social control over increasingly unfettered markets.

These concepts were central in crafting a critical political economy of the transition to market society in the nineteenth and early twentieth centuries. The next section assesses what Polanyi's depiction of 'The Great Transformation' might contribute towards innovation in theorising the second great transformation, the globalisation of capitalism and the crisis of the global commons.

Polanyian contributions to an ecological political economy

Polanyi's insight that markets do not arise naturally but are constituted only as the result of the exercise of state power has provided a basis for understanding historical change in terms of the agency that brings it about. It has proved invaluable in the work of a number of critical scholars who have attempted to retheorise the second great transformation, that of late-twentieth-century neo-liberal globalisation, in political terms. Critical global political economy, by examining the historical processes precipitating globalisation, has been able to highlight the agency of powerful social forces within and across states, as well as the role of ideology and multilateral institutions in promoting the transnationalisation of production, finance and ideas (Gill, 1995b; Helleiner, 1994; Bernard, 1994; Panitch and Miliband, 1992; Cox, 1987). This stands in contrast to mainstream scholars who have depicted globalisation as a product of impersonal market forces with the promise for unprecedented prosperity for all who embrace the tenets of global competitiveness.

Polanyi's conception of agency fits well with a historically informed critical approach to the construction of markets. While his argument that markets are historically contingent creations of agents contains important insights, closer scrutiny needs to be paid to how Polanyi understands this agency. Indeed, one of the problems of Polanyi's contribution to a critical theory of global transformation is the very ambiguous way in which he deals with the question of political agency. To him, fictitious commodities were derivative of the pressures of technological change (Polanyi, 1957: 74–6). According to Polanyi, as long as the machine was an inexpensive and unspecific tool, industrial production, in the form of the 'putting out' system, could remain 'a mere accessory to commerce' (1957: 74). The advent of the elaborate and capital-intensive machinery of the industrial revolution, however, transformed the merchant into capitalist and ushered in the factory system. The long-term investment and risk inherent in purchasing the new machinery necessitated greater control over production including the need to purchase labour. It is here that the state established a labour market by removing the social institutions that inhibited the commodification of labour. The creation of fictitious commodities was thus the 'inevitable consequence of the factory system in a commercial society' (1957: 75).

As will be taken up below, three aspects of this understanding of agency sit in tension with his more general framework for a critical methodology. First, in some parts of his writing there is a technological determinism that, ironically, Polanyi shares with more conventional theorising. His portrayal of the emergence of industrial capitalism, like other technologically deterministic ones, attempts to explain social change as a consequence of changes in production technology. This is perhaps because he viewed the transition as one from 'putting out' to the industrialised factory. Recent historical research, however, has illustrated that artisanal shops and centralised manufactories co-existed with the 'putting out' system, and the latter in particular was the organisational forerunner of the factory Polanyi described (Bruland, 1990: 157–8). Rather than the centralised factory emerging in response to the cost structure of new technology, it was changing social relations of production in these workplaces that chronologically and causally preceded industrialisation (165–9). Whilst other readings of Polanyi stress the way he emphasised the role of political agency and social scientific innovation as crucial in generating the transition to a self-regulating market society (see chapter 1 by Stephen Gill) it is worth remembering that the notion of an autonomous development of technology is a depoliticising one, that is abstracted from historical processes. It resonates today when we are constantly subjected to the idea that it is telecommunications and information technology themselves that are propelling globalisation and the restructuring of social life, when, in fact, it is a change that involves shifts in the social relations of production, or social structure of accumulation.

This leads to a second concern, that it is precisely because agency is ascribed to an autonomously evolving technology that change cannot be understood in terms of the social forces deploying technological innovations and the power relations, institutions and ideologies that shape the context in which they emerge. Nor can the state, the power of which was necessary for the institutionalisation of markets for the fictitious commodities of land and labour, be understood in terms of its relationship to society or location in the world. Ambiguities in Polanyi's work do not help to clarify these issues – issues that involve the power relations, as well as political power and the state (Cox, 1987). Finally, Polanyi depicts the great transformation as a general European phenomenon, but one that reaches its culmination in England. Yet the specific processes whereby market societies emerge in the multitude of contexts of nineteenth-century Europe are never explored in his *magnum opus*. This again raises questions about the relationship between agency and local specificity that are equally germane to an understanding of globalisation and the tensions between those who see globalisation as a homogenising process and those who argue that it can only be understood as manifesting itself in terms of local conditions. The problem of agency in Polanyi's history thus serves to highlight a tension between the historicist inclinations and appreciation of the agency inherent in social change in his method and the lack of historical specificity and social depth in his actual history.

Whilst the problem of agency illustrates the antinomies in Polanyi's work, his idea that liberal political economy resulted in a disembedding of society, in the form of the commodification of labour and land, provides a significant point of departure for incorporating ecology into a critical theorisation of world order. This would serve to both deepen critical political economy approaches and provide an alternative to recent problem solving attempts in International Political Economy, and in International Relations more generally, to understand ecological crisis. Realist approaches, for example, have incorporated 'the environment' into an analysis of the interstate system as a new area of potential interstate conflict (Buzan, 1992). Similarly, neo-liberal institutionalist writings have been concerned with the way strategic interaction between states may lead to interstate co-operation producing norms, rules and institutions for the management of transnational environmental problems (Young, 1989). These views seek to graft environmental problems on to their state-centric ontology by portraying ecology as an exogenous, passive sphere to be acted upon and controlled. Not only do they implicitly accept the idea that human action is decoupled from the natural world, but ecological problems are understood in isolation from the particular configurations of power, the organisation of production and finance, or the ideological context (which includes a particular theory of the environment) that produced them. The result is what Wolfgang Sachs describes as reducing 'ecology to a set of strategies aimed at resource efficiency and risk management. It treats as a technical problem what in fact amounts to a civilizational impasse' (Sachs, 1992: 35–6).

Polanyi's notions of embedding and disembedding open up the possibility for a profound ontological shift rather than the cataloguing of environmental problems as merely another 'new issue area' in world politics. Polanyi suggested that there is an interdependent relationship between social organisation and the natural world. Prior to the disembedding brought about by liberalism, nature, he argued, was bound up with labour and the institutions of social regulation in an articulate whole (Polanyi, 1957: 178). While he did not systematically delineate a method for theorising this relationship, it bears remembering that Polanyi was writing at a time when his concern with the ecological consequences of industrial society could be seen as almost visionary. His focus on the discontinuity marked by the advent of market society centred on his idea that people's livelihood and nature had been disembedded from the new society. This should not be taken to mean that somehow prior to the rise of liberalism there was an essential harmony between human organisation and the ecological structures to which they were connected. Countless societies have refashioned, depleted or degraded their ecological base to the point where they became unsustainable. For example, it would be impossible to understand the 'political' contradictions in eighteenth and early-nineteenth-century Tokugawa Japan without examining how social organisation undermined the society's ecological base, which in turn led to political turmoil (Totman, 1993). What distinguishes a market society is that, for the first time, not only is nature refashioned, but it is capitalised, i.e., turned into a commodity the worth of which is determined by its exchange value.

Critical political economy has concentrated on the commodification of labour and the disembedding of economic practice from an anthropocentric conception of society. Polanyi's concern with disembedding from nature provides the opportunity to extend this to the biosphere as well. Recasting the relationship between political economy and ecology in a way that sees ecological structures as integral to politico-economic processes, shaping and being shaped by social organisation at the local and global levels, requires an ontological reformulation of the field. This would allow for a retheorisation of key aspects of political economy, such as the notion of hegemony, to include their ecological dimensions. The political economy of imperialism provides an example of a process that has been understood in terms of its socio-economic, political and, more recently, its cultural dimensions. Polanyi, however, also took account of how the commodification of land came to encompass one key aspect of imperialism (Polanyi, 1957: 182–3). While Polanyi's conception of the problem of 'land' may be excessively narrow, it provides the opening for a more nuanced and systematic ecological reading of different historical manifestations of world order by breaking down disciplinary boundaries that inhibit students and researchers of International Political Economy from engaging and incorporating the work of scholars in other disciplines such as ecological history.

A concern with the ecological dimension of political economy, by extension, allows for greater awareness of spatiality in our understanding of world order. Critical geographers have argued that the rich tradition of historicity that has characterised critical theory needs to be matched by a better understanding of the relationship between time and space (Soja, 1989). Critical political economy has had little to say about how the organisation of social life affects space. This is curious for a field so concerned with the processes of globalisation. Spatiality is one way to link the biosphere to human organisation. As Altvater notes, structures of production and consumption 'manifest themselves spatially as cultural landscapes, buildings, cities, streets . . . deserts, garbage dumps and so on' (Altvater, 1994: 79). But spaces also need to be understood dialectically as constituting a basis for social organisation and particular sets of social relations. In addition, we can consider the spatial forms associated with an array of structures and practices from hegemony to macro-regionalisation.

Polanyi's juxtaposition of the 'double movement' as a response to the disastrous consequences of the 'great transformation' of the nineteenth century has also provided an exceedingly important conceptual basis for theorising the potential limits of globalisation. A number of scholars have portrayed globalisation in the same dialectical terms set out by Polanyi, highlighting the contradictory nature and the socio-political limits of the discourse and practice of globalisation and exploring the sources out of which might emerge a second counter-movement to re-embed the market (Hettne, 1995; Mendell and Salée, 1991). It is here that the Polanyian concepts of embedded economy and fictitious commodities, as they pertain to the biosphere, can extend this analysis from the social realm by highlighting the ecological limits of globalisation.

Ecological limits could be understood in terms of the incompatibility of the scale of economic activity or the disruptions caused by their waste outputs or their undermining of minimal levels of biodiversity with important ecological cycles (J. O'Connor, 1994: 137). Ecological limits of globalisation may also be reached as transnational pharmaceutical and biotechnology companies, aided by the US state and multilateral institutions, apply patents and property rights that are deepening commodification of the biosphere by sanctioning corporate ownership over the very forms and processes of life (Shiva, 1993a: 120–1). Ecological limits to a deepening of this process of capitalising ecology also lies in the resistance engendered by local groups being dispossessed of their local ecological assets or the transformation of their ecological space. Theorising of local resistance in turn requires approaching counter-movements with Polanyi's sensitivity to the relationship between the incorporation of the biosphere into markets and the tragedy of the commons whilst avoiding his lack of attention to local specificity. This militates against assuming that ecological problems will be theorised in one way across space and time.

There is one last aspect to Polanyi's political economy that enriches an ecological International Political Economy in the critical spirit referred to above. To Polanyi, the disembedding of the land from society and the commodification of the biosphere had both a material and an ideational dimension. The subordination of land to a capitalist political economy had a material component as manifested in the way changes in social relations associated with capitalism forced peasants off the land into towns and labourers' settlements with a concomitant conversion of the land into sites that met the unlimited demands of the new society for food and raw materials. But it also involved a reconceptualisation of the natural world in the image of the new society, with the living, the biosphere, now subordinated to the dead, defined as commodities that could be valued in monetary terms and utilised in industrial processes. Polanyi's conclusions about the retheorising of nature require us not merely to examine the physical limits of the extension of market society, but to remember and transcend the 'fictitiousness' inherent in attempts to deal with the ecological crisis in ways that unquestioningly accept the 'naturalness' of a disembedded ecology.

The second great transformation?

This chapter has so far attempted to suggest how the work of Karl Polanyi might contribute to a theory and method of studying world order while at the same time being cognisant of the limitations of Polanyi's actual historical narrative. The section that follows attempts to look more closely at the applicability of Polanyian political economy to the post-Second World War international political economy by considering some of the ways Polanyian concepts have been applied by others. Then, by way of conclusion, the possible contribution Polanyi's ideas can make toward highlighting the 'limits of the possible' for change towards more ecologically sustainable forms of social life will be taken up.

Polanyi understood disembedding in terms of the creation of fictitious commodities and the reorganisation of society around the institution of a self-regulating market. It was the unsustainability of this project that precipitated the counter-movement. Some of Polanyi's followers see the culmination of this counter-movement in the post-war Fordist settlements in the advanced capitalist countries. There was no generic Fordism but rather a series of locally specific social bargains that included significant state involvement in economic management, an elaborate social welfare system, institutionalised bargaining between labour and capital resulting in high wages for unionised blue-collar workers and controls on financial capital. These social arrangements were in turn underpinned by American hegemony. John Ruggie (1982) has termed these social arrangements 'the compromise of embedded liberalism'. By this he meant that liberalism was constrained *within* advanced capitalist countries by the social arrangements produced by the counter-movement, but was enshrined in the principles of the General Agreement on Tariffs and Trade (GATT) and other organisations of world order that helped institutionalise economic relations *between* countries.

It is here that the ambiguity in Polanyi's 'critical purpose' becomes salient. Polanyi appreciated that the counter-movement took place in societies that were already capitalist. While the counter-movement produced various mechanisms for social protection he explicitly points out that there was no possibility of removing capitalism. The market may have come to be constrained in a manner consistent with the orientation of reformists such as Keynes, but it remained the dominant institution of social life and, as Ralph Miliband argued, the power of capital within these societies was undiminished (Miliband, 1968). The counter-movement that Polanyi described was thus incapable of re-embedding economic life as Polanyi originally understood embedding, but it is not entirely clear from Polanyi's writings if he understood this as a contradiction-laden compromise or some sort of actual re-embedding.

With the use of 'embedded liberalism', 'embedding' has come to be used in a way that unequivocally accepts market society as a given. It has come to mean a regulated capitalism that was embedded within the nation-state. It also opens the possibility for the argument that in a world where capitalism is a given, this actually constitutes social protection. Eric Helleiner (1995: 151–2) for instance, refers to Bretton Woods as ushering in an 'embedded international financial order'. This is a long way from Polanyi's original idea that re-embedding meant removing the market as the dominant institution of society, rather than merely modifying its worst excesses but in a context that fully accepts liberal rationality. Nor is it possible to argue that this view of embedding takes into account the ecological dimensions of disembedding that Polanyi saw as so central to structural change in the nineteenth century. In fact, it is precisely in the world order characterised by 'embedded liberalism' in the advanced capitalist world that ecological disembedding increased exponentially in intensity and came to subsume literally all corners of the planet.

To the extent that embedding is theorised in terms of the capacity of states to act as gate-keepers to the world to regulate finance and trade to maintain the integrity of domestic political compromises, then the 'second great transformation', globalisation, can also be seen as a kind of disembedding. But to the extent that globalisation involves the reconfiguration of domestic structures, this kind of 'liberal re-embedding' can no longer come about through renationalisation. This may lead to the conclusion that a re-embedding is possible if only states possess the necessary will to affect 'proper' co-ordination of policy formation among state elites. Re-embedding could thus come about by achieving an environmentally sustainable political economy within the framework of corporate control and market rationality, as was promoted at the 1992 'Rio Summit' (Hildyard, 1993).

But if we locate power by examining the configuration of social forces that have promoted and sustained globalisation at both the local and world order levels, then disembedding ceases to be an issue of policy co-ordination and becomes one of struggle and resistance. The case could be made that a re-embedding that comes closer to Polanyi's original inclinations would require some form of re-nationalisation, but this would have to entail more than simply re-regulating finance and trade, returning to Fordist regulation or imposing more stringent environmental regulations. It would require a reorganisation of work, a democratisation of state structures, and the socialisation of decision making about technology and the relationship between economic activity and local, regional and national ecological carrying capacities. But none of this is possible without a shift in power relations and ideologies at local and global levels. It is here that Polanyian thought can contribute to a more sustainable second counter-movement.

Polanyi and the limits of the possible

Just as Polanyi's work has the potential for contributing to the method and ontology of a critical theory of global transformation, so too does it contain possibilities to advance the praxis of critical theory. As suggested above, one of Polanyi's unsurpassed contributions lies in his juxtaposition of a world prior to and subsequent to disembedding. His insights into the historically contingent ideology associated with liberalism and the developmentalist view of ecology suggest the crucial task of identifying and resisting what Martin O'Connor (1994: 143–4) calls the 'semiotic domination' of those social forces which seek to insert all debate about ecological crisis into a framework that *a priori* accepts capitalism as the legitimate social form within which theorising must take place. Polanyi provides a framework for looking back to and drawing upon precapitalist intersubjectivities as well as to exploring those practices that exist around the globe that are not yet completely subordinated to market society, including the traditional notions of political economy of various aboriginal peoples.

The difficulty of this task should not, however, be underestimated. We are a good deal further removed from premarket societies than was Polanyi. Our sociological imagination has also been constrained by a perception of an absence of alternatives to the market, our attenuated sense of history and a fixation on the potential for the ever greater material affluence that neo-liberalism holds out. Post-colonial societies are temporally closer to premarket societies and in an absence of liberal hegemony, often contain social practices and institutions that compete with capitalism. But we need to be aware of how the capacity for resistance, as in the way Asian philosophical or religious belief systems might have tempered the liberal obsession with material mastery, has been eroded by the diffusion of the discourse of development. Post-colonial state elites have appropriated traditional practices and incorporated them into the project of nation-state formation and the establishment of capitalism. Indigenous practices and ideas appear in elite discourse not as being at odds with market society, but as giving it a distinctly 'non-Western' flavour. Resistance to the processes that Polanyi saw as dislodging the economy from its social moorings does continue to exist, but it does not reside with the elite stratum of poor and 'newly industrialising' societies, but with those who are marginalised within these societies. They are not merely recipients of repression but are actively engaged in what James Scott (1985) refers to as 'everyday resistance' against the agents and structures of social and political power, even though they have neither the means nor necessarily the intention of successfully challenging that power (see also the chapter by Fantu Cheru).

Polanyi's concern with 're-embedding' economic life has been used to inspire grass-roots movements to organise non-market relationships on the bases of either local currency systems or co-operative production and consumption arrangements in the advanced capitalist world. These types of movements are gaining in popularity and often rely on the strand in Polanyi's historical narrative that views capitalism as epiphenomenal and industrialisation as the real source of unsustainability (Polanyi, 1974: 213; Uchihashi, 1995; Eckersley, 1992: 142). We can understand their emergence in Polanyian terms as acts of social protection. But these movements, as acts of resistance that try to create non-market islands within a capitalist world, invariably raise questions about whether meaningful change can be precipitated by simply circumventing the power of the state and that of capital. It is here that we would do well to return to what I take to be the core of Polanyi's original critique in *The Great Transformation*: that 'disembedding' was precipitated by the creation of a 'market society'. It is only through challenging the power relations and institutional frameworks that continue to sustain market society that Polanyi's goal is ultimately attainable. At a time when the hegemony of neo-liberalism appears so robust, it is the insight that there is nothing natural about liberalism, and the sociological imagination to envision the alternatives to it, that are most needed. Polanyi's framework offers us both.

6 Braudelian reflections on economic globalisation: the historian as pioneer

Eric Helleiner

In the 1990s, the focus of the field of International Political Economy (IPE) has come to be centred on the phenomenon of 'economic globalisation'. It is a phenomenon that seems to both describe and explain many of the momentous changes in the global political economy of the late twentieth century. Although economic globalisation is now at the centre of the field's concerns, its precise meaning and significance remain hotly contested among International Political Economy scholars. This is hardly surprising. In this latest phase of its development, International Political Economy has begun to attract scholars from a wider diversity of disciplinary backgrounds than ever before. No longer is the field restricted to a dialogue between political scientists and economists. Geographers, sociologists, anthropologists and historians have also come to assume a central place within the field's debates. The task of arriving at a common intellectual approach to the study of economic globalisation for scholars from such a broad range of disciplinary backgrounds is obviously a daunting one.

As the definitional and conceptual debates surrounding the phrase 'economic globalisation' have heated up, one response has been to advocate the abandonment of the phrase altogether on the grounds that it is contributing more to confusion than to understanding. Although understandable, this response is likely to be a futile one; 'economic globalisation' is a phrase that will not quickly disappear from academic and policy debates. For this reason, another strategy is needed, one that outlines a way of thinking about economic globalisation that both clarifies the debates and can be embraced by as broad a group of International Political Economy scholars as possible.

In this chapter, I suggest that the work of French historian Fernand Braudel may be useful to this task. The relevance of Braudel's thought to contemporary International Political Economy stems from the fact that he was engaged in a lifelong project to foster a more sustained dialogue between the various social sciences as well as between the social sciences and history. As I have explained elsewhere (Helleiner, 1990), this project led him to develop a set of analytical tools that were designed to encourage scholars to adopt a more interdisciplinary approach to their subject material. Specifically, Braudel suggested that any social phenomenon must be analysed from the perspective of various observation points along four distinct axes which represent space, time, 'social orders' and hierarchy. As I aim to demonstrate, this approach proves particularly valuable in investigating both the meaning and significance of economic globalisation. I suggest in the conclusion that it may also have broader relevance for the field of International Political Economy as a whole at this moment in its development.

Economic globalisation and space

An overarching theme in Braudel's work is the importance of locating social life in a spatial context. Indeed, one of the most significant contributions of the *Annales* school of historians, of which Braudel was a leading member, was the incorporation of spatial and geographical analyses into the study of history. In perhaps his most famous work, *The Mediterranean and the Mediterranean World in the Age of Philip II*, Braudel (1978 [1949]) demonstrated the power and usefulness of this approach particularly effectively, devoting the first third of the book to a fascinating discussion of the importance of the geographical setting within which human history took place in that region during the sixteenth century.

Braudel's insistence on the need to locate social phenomena in space is particularly relevant to an analysis of economic globalisation. It is perhaps most important to the task of describing the phenomenon. Economic globalisation is, after all, partly a spatial phenomenon. As Anthony Giddens (1990: 64) notes, globalisation is perhaps best seen as an 'intensification of world-wide social relations which link distant localities in such a way that local happenings are shaped by events occurring many miles away and vice-versa'. As this description suggests, globalisation can be viewed as a kind of process of 'spatial compression' in which the significance of distance is increasingly reduced.

Giddens' quotation also highlights a second important point about the definition of economic globalisation. This is a process much broader than economic 'internationalisation', a word with which it is often confused. While the latter describes growing economic linkages across the borders of nation-states, the former is concerned with the broader process of spatial compression involving individuals and local communities on a world wide scale and without regard to state boundaries. As discussed below, this is a process that originated before the creation of the nation-state and may also be contributing to the nation-state's demise in the current era.

In addition to being central to a *definition* of economic globalisation, space is also important for any analysis of the *significance* of economic globalisation. Some might question this claim, arguing that globalisation is eradicating space as an important variable in human affairs because of its role in reducing the importance of distance. But this view incorrectly associates economic globalisation with an 'end to geography' (O'Brien, 1992). Although globalisation may compress space, it does not in any way eliminate its significance. There are several ways in which we can see the continuing centrality of space for examinations of the meaning of economic globalisation.

To begin with, if one were to view economic globalisation from different spatial locations around the globe, its importance would clearly vary considerably. Some regions of the world are swept up in the process to a considerable degree, while others are much less so. The 'uneven' nature of economic globalisation often manifests itself very dramatically between countries in the contemporary period (e.g., North Korea vs. Singapore) (Holm and Sorensen, 1995). Important differences can also exist within countries. 'World cities' such as London or New York, for example, experience economic globalisation in much more intense form than many rural regions which are not as 'wired' to the world. Indeed, this parallels the experience of the first wave of 'economic globalisation' in the early modern period when wealthy merchants living thousands of miles apart in the great sea-ports of the world were linked more closely to each other than they were to the peasant population that lived in the surrounding inland regions. Economic globalisation is, thus, not at all a homogeneous phenomenon in a spatial sense. Rather, it must be located in specific spatial contexts in order to understand its significance.

Far from eradicating space, economic globalisation should also be seen to be reconfiguring it in novel and interesting ways. For example, it can easily be forgotten that today's globalised markets still take place in specific geographical contexts, contexts which have often been considerably restructured to accommodate their needs. The most globalised of contemporary markets, financial markets, demonstrate this well. The globalisation of finance has in fact encouraged a concentration of financial market activity in London, New York and Tokyo, cities whose emergence as major financial centres in recent years has produced important internal transformations in their urban space. Financial globalisation has also encouraged a proliferation of new geographical centres of finance in unusual locations such as the micro-states of the Caribbean (Corbridge, Martin and Thrift, 1994).

Also accompanying the economic globalisation trend since the 1960s have been a number of reconfigurations of space that challenge the territoriality of the nation-state. One of these is the rise of 'offshore' economic spaces in which business is transacted according to special rules that do not apply to the rest of the national economy in which they are located. Another is the rise of macro-regional blocs, such as the European Union, which seem to challenge the territorial nation-state from above. Economic globalisation also appears to have encouraged a proliferation of interest in micro-regional spaces in political and cultural affairs. Instead of bringing an 'end to geography', then, economic globalisation in fact appears to be raising the profile of spatial issues by challenging conventional conceptions of space and territoriality (Ruggie, 1993; Agnew, 1994).

There is a final reason to focus on geography in analysing the significance of economic globalisation. One of the key contributions of Braudel's work was to highlight the importance of the ecological space within which all human activity takes place. In Braudel's conception, this is not an inert and unchanging space, but rather an active and living one which sets 'the limits of the possible' for human activity (Braudel, 1985a). A Braudelian perspective on economic globalisation would thus locate the phenomenon also within the ecological space of the global biosphere. Particularly important would seem to be an analysis of the extent to which economic globalisation is testing the ecological 'limits of the possible' of the global biosphere. Alfred Crosby (1986) shows how early phases of economic globalisation in history often brought distinct ecological zones into contact with each other with devastating environmental and human consequences. In the contemporary period, economic globalisation also appears to be undermining ecological sustainability by encouraging the global spread of industrial production processes as well as by challenging traditional patterns of human life that had often developed in long-standing and viable relationships with local ecosystems (Shiva, 1993a).

Economic globalisation and time

In addition to being a spatial phenomenon, economic globalisation is also clearly an historical process; that is, a process of change over time. But what kind of historical change is it in a temporal sense? Braudel offers a way of thinking about time that is useful in answering this question. He argues that history can be viewed from the perspective of three different speeds of time. One is the *'l'histoire événementielle'* or 'the short-time span, proportionate to individuals, to daily life, to our illusions, to our hasty awareness – above all the time of the chronicle and the journalist' (1980: 28). A second is the medium-term or 'conjunctural' perspective where historical change takes place according to cycles, movements and 'slow but perceptible rhythms' that may span a decade or more (1978: 21). Braudel also insists that history must be viewed from a very long-term perspective – the *'longue durée'* – where change takes place at 'a slower tempo which sometimes almost borders on motionless' (1980: 33) and where one is studying deeply embedded structures of social life that last over centuries.

To define economic globalisation in a comprehensive way, it should be viewed simultaneously from each of these temporal observation points. From the perspective of the *longue durée*, for example, economic globalisation clearly represents a long secular trend originating in the fifteenth century. During that era, various human communities across the world – particularly those close to the major seaports, as mentioned already – first began to experience a collective economic destiny on a global scale or what Braudel calls a common 'world time' (Braudel, 1985c: 17). Perhaps not surprisingly, as Waters (1995: 2) points out, the first use of the word 'global' dates back to this period.

Economic globalisation is also a conjunctural phenomenon which has accelerated rapidly in certain moments of history. One such acceleration phase took place in the 1850–1914 period in response to technological innovations, a new stage of capitalist development and the European economic and imperial expansion of that era. Since the 1960s we have clearly been living through another, although its causes are more hotly disputed. Some highlight the role of the accelerating pace of technological change, which has both reduced transportation and communication costs as well as forced firms to sell to global markets as a way of recouping their increasing development and production costs (Cerny, 1995). Others point also to the significance of political changes that have encouraged states to foster the globalisation of trade, production and finance in this period (Helleiner, 1994). Whatever the causes of this latest conjunctural phase of economic globalisation, its importance is recognised by all. Once again, some linguistic history is also interesting: the word 'globalisation' was first used around 1960 near the start of the evolution of this latest conjunctural trend (Waters, 1995: 2).

Finally, the sudden popularity of the phrase 'economic globalisation' in the last decade suggests that it also usefully describes a more immediate and short-term intensification of both the secular and conjunctural trends taking place at the moment. Robert Cox's (1992a) use of the phrase 'global perestroika' as a synonym for economic globalisation sums up well one meaning of the phrase from this short-term perspective. It is linked closely in many people's minds to the intensified global integration that has accompanied the end of the Cold War and the embrace of neo-liberal ideas across the world. Contemporary debates about the need to either embrace or resist 'economic globalisation' also usually use the word with this kind of meaning assigned to it.

There is one further way in which Braudel's temporal axis is useful in thinking about how to describe the economic globalisation process. In addition to being a process compressing space, economic globalisation can also be seen to represent a compression of time. As the influence of distant current events and trends within local settings is increased and the significance of enduring local historical structures is diminished, economic globalisation can be viewed as embodying an acceleration of the speed of historical change. Decontextualised synchronic dimensions of economic life emerge ascendant, while diachronic dimensions that are deeply embedded in local settings and tradition are increasingly marginalised. In this way, economic globalisation might well be described as a process that is altering the relative significance of Braudel's three speeds of time in favour of '*l'histoire événementielle*' (Cox, 1995b).

Braudel's three temporal perspectives are useful not just in describing economic globalisation but also in interpreting its significance. From the perspective of the *longue durée*, globalisation appears as a deeply embedded structure of the global political economy. While contemporary observers highlight the seeming novelty of globalised economic activity, continuities with the past seem more striking from this temporal vantage point. The global reach of today's financial markets in New York, for example, is not dissimilar to that of London markets in the nineteenth century or even Amsterdam markets in the eighteenth century. To the extent that there is change from this perspective, economic globalisation appears as a slowly expanding spatial envelope within which social life has been forced to exist since the fifteenth century. From this vantage point, the very gradual and durable nature of the trend also makes it seem an almost irreversible one.

By contrast, economic globalisation from a conjunctural perspective appears more significant as a transformative force which is challenging existing structures. The economic globalisation trend since the 1960s, for example, is seen to be a central force eroding the foundations of the post-1945 world political-economic order and perhaps also at a deeper level the territorial nation-state. From this vantage point, economic globalisation is not a deeply embedded structure but rather a phenomenon promoting discontinuity from the recent past. The emergence of globally organised production processes and the instantaneous nature of money transfers, for example, signal something profoundly new. As a conjunctural phenomenon, economic globalisation is also clearly a reversible process (as was the globalisation trend in 1850–1914) and scholars debate the extent to which it will be influenced by other conjunctural historical processes such as the trajectory of US hegemony and the changing balance of various social forces.

At the level of '*l'histoire événementielle*', the significance of economic globalisation as an agent of change is even more pronounced. From this temporal perspective, it often appears as a political weapon used and promoted by certain groups to bring local conditions more in line with global norms and dynamics. This is a project in which the local is increasingly 'globalised' – to use Shiva's (1993b) phrase – in an active and deliberate way. In this globalised context, short-term temporal perspectives and synchronic cosmologies become prioritised over conceptions of social life that derive from a sense of time that is more long term. The almost infinite time horizons of the premodern world give way to what Benedict Anderson (1991: 22–4) calls more 'empty' forms of time that are experienced in a 'homogeneous' manner across space. As Cox (1995b: 22) points out, it is for this reason – rather than that suggested by Fukuyama (1992) – that the era of 'global perestroika' can be seen to represent a kind of 'end of history'. It is this aspect of globalisation that generates such concern among environmentalists who favour a more deeply embedded sense of 'ecological' time which would value the future as equally significant as the present.

Economic globalisation and social orders

According to Braudel's way of thinking, any social phenomena must be viewed not only from various spatial and temporal perspectives but also from the standpoint of four distinct 'social orders'. By this, he means standpoints that correspond to the lens we adopt when we view a development from an 'economic', 'political', 'social' and 'cultural' perspective. These four perspectives are not meant to imply that economic, political, social and cultural realms should be seen as separate 'systems'. As he puts it, each 'is in real life inextricably mingled with the others . . . One could formulate the following equations in any order: the economy equals politics, culture and society; culture equals the economy, politics and society etc.' (Braudel, 1985c: 45). Each social order simply corresponds to a distinct vantage point from which to view the social whole.

This approach can be usefully applied to an effort to define economic globalisation. The phenomenon is obviously defined most straightforwardly from an economic perspective. From this observation point, it is seen as a phenomenon in which goods and services as well as various factors of production are increasingly exchanged on a world-wide scale. From a *longue durée* perspective, it began in the fifteenth to eighteenth-century era with the first globally integrated long-distance trading of luxury goods and precious metals by European merchants. It then accelerated in the conjunctural globalisation phase of the 1850–1914 period with the rapid growth of world-wide financial transactions and trade in more bulky goods as well as a more extensive movement of people on a global scale. Since the 1960s, economic globalisation has once again resumed and intensified in the financial and trade spheres and it has also been characterised by the emergence of a new kind of highly integrated world-wide production structure.

But economic globalisation has not just been an 'economic' process. From a 'political' vantage point, it has also been a phenomenon characterised by the emergence of increasingly dense and extensive governance structures with global reach. These have taken different institutional forms in each phase of the economic globalisation trend. Between the fifteenth and eighteenth centuries, they were very limited, perhaps only visible in the weak and often unsuccessful efforts by European states to build integrated empires on a world-wide scale. These efforts, of course, became more substantial in the 1850–1914 period and during that era economic globalisation also was accompanied by the global extension of the governance norms and practices associated with the European sovereign state system (Krasner and Thomson, 1989). The contemporary conjunctural and short-term economic globalisation phase has also witnessed the proliferation of global regimes and institutions, as well as the increasing 'internationalisation' of the state in regions across the world (Cox, 1987).

Economic globalisation is also clearly a social phenomenon. As Philip Curtin (1984) highlights, economic globalisation in the early modern period was characterised by the growth and global spread of 'trade diasporas' or merchant communities who were linked across wide geographical spaces by complex social networks. The conjunctural trend of the 1850–1914 period also saw the emergence of a 'cosmopolitan bourgeoisie' and '*haute* finance' class with global vision and world-wide presence (Jones, 1987; Polanyi, 1944). Similarly, a central feature of the acceleration of economic globalisation since the 1960s has been the consolidation of what Cox (1987) calls a 'transnational managerial class', a class that includes not only global business elites but also officials of those international organisations and elements of state bureaucracies which are most responsive to the needs of the emerging world economy. Some analysts also argue that economic globalisation in the current age has been accompanied by the growth of transnational social movements which increasingly act as if they were participating in a broader kind of 'global civil society' (Lipschutz, 1992).

A cultural vantage point provides one further perspective on the economic globalisation trend. In a *longue durée* context, Giddens (1990) sees economic globalisation as a process that has been characterised by the spread of the values of modernity. From a more conjunctural standpoint, the economic globalisation trend since the 1960s has also been associated closely with the diffusion and penetration of American values, ideas and pop culture on a global scale. From the perspective of the short-term time span, economic globalisation is often synonymous with the global triumph of neo-liberal ideas and the spread of what Susan Strange (1990) terms the emerging world-wide 'business civilisation'.

Economic globalisation is thus not just an economic phenomenon. Only by viewing it also from a political, social and cultural vantage point is it possible to arrive at a more comprehensive depiction of the phenomenon. Similarly, the significance of economic globalisation should not be viewed only from the isolation of one of the 'social orders'. For example, the post-1950s economic globalisation trend can be analysed from a strictly economic perspective; that is, in terms of its impact on efficient production and distribution of goods and services. But this is only one way in which the significance of the trend can be analysed.

From a political observation point, for example, economic globalisation appears more significant in terms of its impact on the power and legitimacy of the state and state system. Some analysts, for example, view economic globalisation as a process that is dramatically undermining the power and coherence of the state in ways that are challenging conventional notions of citizenship and the spatial boundaries of political communities (Archibugi and Held, 1995; Cerny, 1995). Others reject this analysis, suggesting that economic globalisation is in fact strengthening the state and its coercive powers (Panitch, 1994).

The current conjunctural economic globalisation trend can also be viewed from a social perspective in terms of its diverse impacts on social groups. From the standpoint of class divisions, for example, the trend appears to be granting a new kind of structural power to capital over labour in countries around the world (Gill and Law, 1988). The globalisation of economic life also appears to influence other social divisions such as those associated with gender, as recent feminist studies of worldwide economic restructuring have demonstrated (Bakker, 1994).

From a cultural perspective, the post-1950s economic globalisation trend is significant in additional ways. According to David Harvey (1989) (and in some contrast to Giddens' broader point noted above), this 'time-space' compression has given strength to the post-modern cultural movement of the last two decades. Economic globalisation may also be prompting reconceptualisations of identity, partly in the form of new transnational and supranational affiliations and partly in the form of a resurgence of localist and micro-regional identifications. More broadly, economic globalisation in the contemporary era is also intensifying inter-civilisation encounters that began on a global scale with the first wave of globalisation after the fifteenth century (Cox, 1995b).

Economic globalisation and hierarchy

From Braudel's point of view, a comprehensive perspective on any social phenomenon is not complete until it is also viewed from distinct hierarchical observation points. All societies, according to Braudel, are characterised by various layers of hierarchy which manifest themselves within each of the various 'social orders'. As he puts it, the 'power apparatus' in society 'is the sum of the political, social, economic, and cultural hierarchies' (Braudel, 1985b: 555). Given the pervasiveness of hierarchy, Braudel argues that it is important to locate all social phenomena within a hierarchical perspective.

This argument has important relevance for any effort to describe the meaning of economic globalisation. If economic globalisation represents an 'intensification of world-wide economic relations', this is a phenomenon which is clearly hierarchical in addition to being spatial, temporal and manifest across different 'social orders'. It involves an intensification of relations between the various layers of social hierarchy. The description of economic globalisation as 'time-space compression', thus, appears too limited. It can also be seen as a process of 'hierarchical compression'.

This has been a particularly notable feature of economic globalisation in the conjunctural trend of the 1850–1914 period and since the 1960s. Braudel provides a particularly useful way to think about this hierarchical compression in the economic realm. He suggests that the economy is best pictured as divided into three layers. The top layer – labelled 'capitalism' somewhat controversially by Braudel – is dominated by powerful corporations and privileged elites operating in large-scale oligopolistic and speculative markets for high stakes and 'exceptional profits' (1985b: 428). At the next level down, we find the 'market economy' of smaller scale markets characterised by greater 'transparency and regularity, in which everyone could be sure in advance, with the benefit of common experience, how the processes of exchange would operate' (1985b: 455). Finally, the bottom level is comprised of 'material life' which represents 'a sort of bargain basement . . . made up of all the activities outside the market and state controls – fraud, barter of goods and services, moon-lighting, housework' (1985c: 630).

Before the nineteenth century, Braudel's 'world time' was experienced in most regions of the world primarily only at the top level of 'capitalist' activity. The world-wide movements of bills of exchange and precious metals, for example, had little influence on the world of material life and the 'market economy' in which the majority of population participated. During the 1850–1914 period, however, economic globalisation increasingly brought the world of 'capitalism' into closer contact with the other two levels of economic life. World commodity prices and the movements of high finance became what Polanyi (1944: 18) calls a 'central reality' in the everyday life of millions of peasants across the globe in this period. The relationship also went the other way: as their production became linked more closely to global markets, the experiences of those same peasants increasingly affected the 'capitalist' world inhabited by the Rothschilds and Morgans.

This kind of hierarchical compression has also characterised the economic globalisation trend since the 1960s and in a more intense way. The influence of giant transnational corporations and high-level foreign exchange trading has increasingly penetrated downwards into the realm of the local shopkeeper and material life in this period. Few aspects of Mexican economic life, for example, were insulated from the effects of the late 1994 frenzied speculation against the peso in the office towers of the world's leading financial centres. At the same time, the impact of developments at the lower levels of economic life is increasingly felt at the top. Which of the world's financial speculators could afford to ignore the local activities and concerns of Chiapas peasants at the time of the peso crisis?

A focus on the hierarchical dimension of social life is also important to adopt if the significance of economic globalisation is to be fully understood. To begin with, a key consequence of economic globalisation has been the reconfiguration of hierarchical structures and relationships. In a *longue durée* context, for example, economic globalisation fostered the emergence of relatively durable global core–periphery economic relationships across the regions of the world that persist into the contemporary period. As Herman Schwartz (1994: 43) points out, inequality also assumed a new spatial dimension as a consequence of this long-term economic globalisation trend: '[w]hat was novel about inequality consequent to the expansion of the north-western European maritime economy was its *spatial* aspect: inequality existed and persisted not just inside countries but also among regions and nations'.

The contemporary conjunctural and short-term economic globalisation phenomena also appear to be intensifying certain forms of geographical economic inequality. Most dramatically, sub-Saharan Africa appears to be increasingly marginalised in the new globalised economy of the late twentieth century. According to some accounts, this marginalisation reflects the fact that countries in this region are not incorporated within the economic globalisation trend (Camdessus, 1996: 21). This view is hard to accept. While sub-Saharan African countries may receive very little inward investment, they experience enormous outflows of capital flight to financial centres in the OECD region. Similarly, their goods may find few external export markets, but their internal markets are increasingly flooded with foreign food and manufactured products, including such items as the toxic waste by-products of Northern countries (Clapp, 1994). Sub-Saharan Africa is, thus, integrated in the economic globalisation phenomenon, although in a particular fashion that appears to be intensifying its dependent and peripheral status.

The contemporary economic globalisation trend also appears to be intensifying hierarchical structures within countries. Cox (1992a) suggests that within the new globalised economy 'periphery' and 'core' are no longer just geographical concepts but also useful ways of describing emerging social relations at the domestic level. In many countries across the world, a 'core' group of workers – Robert Reich (1991) labels them 'symbolic analysts' – is emerging whose services are in high demand by global markets and who are experiencing rising wages and secure employment conditions. At the same time, other workers are increasingly being pushed into employment situations that are increasingly precarious and without high wages or stable benefits. As Reich suggests, the growing gap in the experiences of these two groups of workers may be emerging as one of the key sources of social friction and political conflict in this age of economic globalisation.

The growing hierarchical divisions within and between countries also highlight the need to view economic globalisation from a variety of hierarchical observation points. From the standpoint of someone near the top of the world's social hierarchy, the phenomenon appears to be one that widens intellectual horizons and enhances individual freedom and choice. It is experienced through the pages of The Economist magazine, travels through the leading airports of the world, and everyday life in a world city. From the perspective of someone closer to the lower hierarchical levels, economic globalisation appears more threatening. It might be experienced through greater job insecurity or forced geographical mobility or the destruction of a long-standing pattern of local everyday life. Thus, only by gaining the perspective from the 'top' and 'bottom' can more comprehensive interpretation of the meaning and significance of the various dimensions of economic globalisation be gained.

Conclusion

Does Braudel provide a way of thinking about 'economic globalisation' that might help to address some of the confusion which surrounds the meaning and significance of the phrase? Does he provide a set of analytical tools that may be able to be embraced by scholars from very diverse disciplinary backgrounds? In this chapter, I have suggested that the answer to these questions is yes. In terms of the meaning of economic globalisation, Braudel's four axes can be used to build on Giddens's definition in a helpful way. From a Braudelian perspective, economic globalisation is an 'intensification of world-wide economic relations' that can be seen as an economic, political, social and cultural process taking place at several different historical speeds and involving a compression of space, time and hierarchy. This definition is more nuanced and elaborate than many of the simpler definitions often used and it could help to clarify the complex and uneven nature of the phenomenon being described. At the same time, because it highlights the multifaceted nature of economic globalisation, it may also be wide enough to embrace the various developments that different International Political Economy scholars are discussing when they use the phrase.

As I have suggested, Braudel's analytical tools may also be helpful for those seeking to analyse the significance of globalisation. Not only do they remind us that the phenomenon has important implications for the organisation of social life along each of his four axes corresponding to space, time, 'social orders' and hierarchy. They also call attention to the fact that the full significance of economic globalisation will not become clear until it is viewed from diverse observation points in space, time, 'social orders' and hierarchy. These analytical tools thus provide a rich research agenda for those interested in the significance of economic globalisation. This agenda is also quite an inclusive one that encompasses and actively encourages the kind of multidisciplinary research that is now being done within the field.

In addition to their potential practical use for the study of economic globalisation, Braudel's analytical tools may also prove helpful at a more theoretical level in encouraging International Political Economy scholars to shed some of the more problematic assumptions that have characterised their thinking in earlier years. To begin with, as geographers now entering the field point out, International Political Economy scholars in the past have shown little sensitivity to the spatial and ecological context within which political and economic life exists. Because of the prenineteenth century era on which he focused, Braudel's work may provide a particularly important model for those seeking to understand how these weaknesses might be addressed. Not only was this preindustrial era one in which the ecological setting exerted an enormous influence on the course of human history, as Braudel so effectively demonstrates. It was also an era before the territorial nation-state was consolidated, ensuring that

Braudel did not fall into the 'territorial trap' (Agnew, 1994) of ignoring the diverse spatial contexts in which social life can take place.

Braudel's discussion of historical time may also be helpful for those International Political Economy scholars beginning to think through the relationship between agency and structure in a more systematic way. In Braudel's conception, this relationship is seen not as an abstract theoretical problem but rather as one involving the relative importance of different speeds of historical time in a concrete context. His three-fold categorisation of time also highlights a more nuanced way of thinking about this issue than the rather stark contrast between agency and structure that is usually presented. For between the world of agency and that of the almost unchanging structures of *longue durée*, Braudel places the structures of conjunctural time span, structures which are more flexible and more easily influenced by agency and '*l'histoire événementielle*'. These conjunctural structures are the kind that Cox (1987) points to in his discussion of the importance of 'historical structures' for the study of International Political Economy.

Finally, Braudel's methodology also pushes International Political Economy scholars to think of political economy as embracing more than just the study of states and markets. Like many of the sociologists and anthropologists now entering the field of IPE, Braudel argued that political economy could not and should not be divorced from broader sociological, cultural and civilisational issues. A focus on states and markets also presents a limited view of the economy from Braudel's point of view. As his three-level hierarchical model suggests, a large part of economy exists outside the realm of the state and market in the level of material life, a point that feminist and green analysts in International Political Economy have also begun to emphasise (Waring, 1988; Helleiner, 1996). Similarly, Braudel is keen to encourage political economists to recognise the distinction between the high level of 'capitalism' and that of 'market economy'. Indeed, from his perspective, a central task of political economy was to understand the changing relationship between each of these three levels of economic life – what in today's language might be called the study of the relationship between the global and the local.

An acceptance of the Braudelian approach to studying globalisation, thus, implicitly involves an embrace of a wider vision of the task of International Political Economy. No longer would the field be restricted to the study of the 'politics of international economic relations' or the study of 'states and markets'. Instead, it would focus on the study of the relationship between politics and economy in a global context, where politics is understood broadly as the study of social decision making and economics is equally broadly defined as the study of the production and distribution of goods and services. Those who have seen International Political Economy from its origins as a subfield of International Relations will resist this move. But it should be welcomed by those who have always seen International Political Economy as one of the few 'open ranges' within the social sciences, a field whose innovative nature stems from the fact that it is 'still unfenced, still open to all comers' (Strange, 1984: ix). For those with this wider view of International Political Economy, Braudel should be viewed as an important pioneer within the field.

NOTE

For their comments on an earlier draft of this article, I am grateful to Stephen Gill, James Mittelman and Randolph Germain.

7 Social forces and international political economy: joining the two IRs

Jeffrey Harrod

The editors of this volume announced in one of their earlier communications an ambitious purpose: 'to conceptualise and analyse change in international relations and International Relations theory'. From the standpoint of a holist, generalist, eclectic, or student of the condition of humankind, such a purpose, is however, already constrained. Constrained, that is, by the distinguishing of a separate, specialised, compartmentalised and professionalised segment of human activity, labelling it 'International Relations' and then endowing that segment with theory of its own.

This compartmentalising process is, of course, part of the structure of knowledge production of the twentieth century. It is the century of fragmentation, specialisation and the denial of intellect as a potentially all-encompassing capability for comprehending the human condition. This process may make it more difficult to achieve the stated greater purpose of this volume – to examine the 'prospects for the transformation of the present world order in a more just, democratic and sustainable direction'. Such a project would, in my view, be difficult within the existing professionalised academic area of International Relations. It would require a firmer base in philosophy, history and social theory and other such fields which have an original and fundamental intent to examine universal orders of humankind to which dissidents can, in the last resort, appeal when pushed towards greater specialisation, 'scientism' and empiricism.[1]

This chapter argues for a more integrated approach towards social knowledge in seeking an understanding of and the creation and transformation of world orders. But to demonstrate the current difficulty of such a project it uses as an example the attempt to incorporate within International Relations the concept and knowledge relating to 'social forces'. Hence the 'two IRs' in the title: International Relations dealing with world orders and Industrial Relations dealing with social forces created from the sociological, psychological and political effects of the power relations surrounding the universal occupation of work and production and the universal preoccupation with its distribution and allocation.

To this end, in this chapter I will cite developments in the field of Industrial Relations, which up until the mid-seventies were an important source of information on 'social forces', and which Robert Cox in *Production, Power and World Order: Social Forces in the Making of History* (1987), and myself in the connected volume *Power, Production and the Unprotected Worker* (1987a), tried to make an essential component to be studied for an understanding of the construction of world orders.[2] The incorporation of social forces into the current analysis was proposed as the main component of a new International Relations or rather the development of an eclectic International Political Economy.

Specialisation and the corporate age

Specialisation as a barrier to theoretical transformation or development has concerned thinkers long before the twentieth-century founding of the social sciences. Kant had the idea of an 'anthropology' as the basic discipline to consider humanity in the cosmos. The use of that subject for colonial purposes, however, relegated it largely to the study of rituals and kinship practices 'out there' (Apthorpe, 1980). Perhaps even more important were the ideas of Wilhelm Dilthey who was a thinker, at the beginning of the century, involved in the foundation of hermeneutics as a discipline with the objective of understanding all forms of human expression. For Dilthey the relativity of human expression was comprehended from a basic unity of human nature and it was the purpose of those in the human sciences to explore and define such unity through the medium of history. As Van Harvey notes in relation to Dilthey: 'Ultimately, history is the variety of ways in which human life has expressed itself over time. Indeed we can grasp our own possibilities only through historical reconstruction and understanding. Through understanding (*Verstehen*) of life-expressions (*Lebensausserungen* and *Erlebnisausdrucke*) of past persons, we come to understand the humanity of which we are a part' (Van Harvey, 1987: 203) and therefore the world order we create or wish to create. Dilthey's attempt was born precisely at the moment when the organisational foundations of specialisation were being put in place at the beginning of the century. In the current circumstance it would not be sufficient to simply seek a unifying intellectual basis without using or distinguishing the 'data' produced by the empiricism and positivism of the past seventy years. Thus to achieve the ultimate purposes of this collection it is necessary either to intensify the specialisation of International Relations and hence convert a large part of its personnel to empiricist testing and, at the same time, found another department charged with a holist approach; or to convert the whole of International Relations into such a department or field to holistic purposes. Given that such a new field would have to synthesise the positivistic production into a comprehension of the total meaning, such a field could be called, for example, crasisology. *Crasis*, the Greek word for synthesis or mixture, might be used as the name for the study of and activity of synthesising all information and theories derived from the past segmentation of human knowledge. Such an activity would not only have as its function to produce grand works of synthesis but also to promote the lost teleology that is currently denying humanity to itself.

Such an activity is not being undertaken currently (except perhaps for this volume) because for the majority of practitioners specialisation becomes the crutch for intellectual cripples (Harrod, 1986) and the professional status quo is easier and less stressful than joining or creating a coalition to overthrow the hegemony of specialisation. If such a challenge to specialisation is to be made it can begin with the analysis of the origins of the current nature of knowledge production and, in particular, the rapidity with which, in the past quarter century, many fields and branches have so willingly been denuded of their contemplative framework. In this respect I have noted elsewhere:

Any approach should be welcome which can integrate or accommodate into policy and strategies the different dynamics, power groups, and consciousness emerging from different patterns of power relations. In general, as noted in the opening chapter, in policy planning, in devising strategies for political and social change, and in investigating the nature of human societies any social scientist or general observer of the human condition who ignores, or fails to analyse rigorously, the variety of patterns of power relations in production is likely to produce at best uneven or at worst self-defeating results. (Harrod, 1987a: 325)

Part of the hegemonic structure of world orders is the dominant institution which, in turn is a dominant organisation within a dominant form of power relations in production. It could be argued that the dominant structures in Western Europe (and which have been given to the world via colonialisation) have been based successively on the predominance of four organisations/institutions – the manor, the church, the state and, now, the corporation. Both the church, with its production of morals, and the state, with its production of the norms of justice, were holistic in ambition, and the ideologies promoted by them reflected that ambition of establishing something concerning the condition of humanity and its desirable future. The current development of industrial feudalism under the aegis of the corporation is thus, like the medieval feudalism before it, functionalist, fragmentary and specialised in intent.[3] It could be then that intellect has been arrested in its movement from the one philosophically holistic order of the Church to another holistic order centred on the state. Instead it has been forced back to the functionalist fragmentation needed for organisations which have the unmitigated and unique purpose of production of material goods and services.

To counter the antagonistic social forces which could be expected to be unleashed by the dominance of the productive corporation might entail the support of a fragmented and specialised environment. The construction of a corporate-dominant order would certainly require the neutralisation of social forces precipitating persistent and effective questioning of the establishing order on such basic and fundamental teleological questions as production of what, for whom and why. To discuss the whole, to seek interconnectedness, or the sociometry of power, was indeed subversive – subversive to the emerging increase in intensity of disparities in wealth and power, discrimination and incessant structural violence which a fragmented and functional corporate world order would unquestionably produce.

The past century has thus seen the industrialisation of the intellectual on a Taylorist scientific management basis, except that without crasis there is no final product. The image of the modern intellectual confined to tinkering at his/her workstation, timed by administration, and (self) disciplined by promotion and material aggrandisement, denied the tools and time to achieve mastery of other areas of knowledge and never united with the final product, is that of an early-twentieth-century production - line worker. Thus it is hardly necessary to note how subjects have been, in this process, shattered and torn from any holistic underpinning. In political economy it was the conversion into economics (Harrod, 1981); in International Relations it was the displacement of international history as the traditional base of the field; in sociology it was the introduction of empiricism; and in philosophy it was the retreat into linguistics. Marxism remained the potential for holistic subversion but the flood to its ranks of those capable only of promoting the binary model – of labour versus capital – prevented perhaps the holistic nature of Marx's work from challenging effectively the conventional specialised wisdom. It was within this context then that all attempts to connect fragmented disciplines had to take place. It is not sufficient simply to make reference to various fields and disciplines – crasis requires a study and understanding of the areas to be connected in the sense of a re-search for a lost completeness.

'Social forces' and the two IRs

The attempt to make International Relations into International Political Economy, and International Political Economy into an area for the contemplation of the condition of humanity would have to begin with, following Dilthey, a 'unifying' characteristic of humankind. If there were any excuse for division in human intellectual endeavour it might be in relation to the arguments and counter-arguments concerning the nature of a unifying characteristic.

A strong candidate for a 'unifying characteristic' is production, which, of course, had already been used in that role by Marx and the earlier materialists. Production is ubiquitous in so far as it exists in all places and at all times. Production is, in that sense, life, for the dispensation of energy (work) which results in life (product). 'Social forces' was the identifiable social energy precipitated by production, the expenditure of which affected directly or indirectly the existing order. For Cox the crucial universal was 'the organisation of production, more particularly with regard to social forces engendered by the production process' (1981: 138). Significantly these social forces need not be classes and would be relative to the type of social relations surrounding production. What was of importance with this concept was that 'social forces' did not necessarily mean a 'working class' as in the two-class Marxist model of capitalism or blue-collar workers in tripartite structures. Accordingly, Cox extends the concept beyond its traditional class confines when he notes that 'the scientific humanistic elite' can be seen as a distinct cultural force (1987: 206). Further, I tried to show the importance in social change of social forces arising from, for example, production centred on self-employment, casual work and household services production (Harrod, 1987a).

Nevertheless, if world orders start with production, which produces social forces, then globally dominant social forces would come from globally dominant production patterns. Thus the study of social forces required the study of those fragmented areas which addressed the details of production relations. For some areas this was found in peasant studies, women's studies, sociology of work, urban sociology, urban studies and so on. But for dominant production forms, which yielded globally important social forces, what was needed was, first, a field of studies in which social, economic and thus political power was made central to the field and not, as was often the case, contained within constricting methods and approaches, such as the voting behaviour trend in political science. Secondly, it would be a field in which the focus was work and its relationship to production.

Such an existing field of study in the first three-quarters of this century was Industrial Relations – hence the attempt at the joining of information generated on social forces in Industrial Relations (Cox, 1971; Cox, Harrod et al, 1972), which is here called IR(1) to the study of the behaviour of states in International Relations, here called IR(2). Here then, 'Industrial Relations' will be used as synonymous with the North

American 'labor relations' although at the international level the latter is the preferred term. IR(1) plus IR(2) could potentially provide a synthesis, a *crasis*, to create an International Political Economy which would be more than just a perception of some economists who had discovered power, or some Marxists automatically extending domestically derived concepts to the global plane.

Industrial Relations as a field had much to offer the student of social forces arising from production. The early Anglo-Saxon Industrial Relations scholars established a tradition of a macro-level, if not holistic approach, partly because one of the foci of their studies was trade unions and bargaining which involved, therefore, situating the subject within 'organised social forces' and considering the latter's power attributes. The questions posed by the early scholars in the field concerned the role and function of trade unions (Commons, 1919; Perlman, 1928) and the solution to workplace conflict. In Europe the macro-level approach grew from both the creative period of social theorists and their concerns with the future based upon town and industry.

Subsequent scholars in the field had, as perhaps have all contemporary scholars of holist intent, the advantage of being involved with the (creative) tension of the Cold War and competing ideologies. Doeringer, in discussing topics for Industrial Relations research, claims that:

In the Anglo-Saxon countries, for example, research is generally categorised by subject area, whereas in those countries with Marxist influences (and for those authors working within a Marxist framework), Industrial Relations issues are only one component of a larger concern with the evolution of society and relationships between classes. Thus any overview of Industrial Relations research organised by topic must necessarily do some violence to Marxist research by arbitrarily dividing the whole into parts. (Doeringer, 1981: 5)

In addition to the study of trade unions, Industrial Relations also encompassed managerial-oriented subjects, thus providing the user bent on synthesis with the ideologies and practical objectives of authority, power and values within industrial production. The battle between the Taylorist and the Human Relations School, essentially that between two schools of thought on how to enhance labour productivity, provided lively debate which was at the core of the notions of labour control, capitalist production, distribution, power and state orientation within international society. It is not surprising that these debates and research objectives during the 1950s in IR(1), again from the standpoint of the user of the material for purposes other than *within* Industrial Relations, helped consolidate its macro-level, power-oriented and humanity-considering potential.

The two books which symbolised and crystallised this trend were

Dunlop (1958) *Industrial Relations Systems* and Kerr et al. (1960) *Industrialism and Industrial Man: the Problems of Labor and Management in Economic Growth*.[4] Dunlop introduced the fashionable notion of systems to Industrial Relations in which the three forces of unions, state and employers interacted on the basis of their different power endowments and, in relating to their different environments, produced rules governing production. The 'industrial relations system' represented a sophisticated exposition of the 'tripartite' model of distributive mechanisms which had been incorporated in the constitution of the International Labour Organisation (ILO) in 1919. But the notion of 'system' allowed a relativity to be introduced in which several distinct systems could be identified as having different social forces interacting with rule-making and distributional results.

With Kerr *et al.* (1960) the full potential of the Industrial Relations field's contribution to an International Political Economy was manifested. Kerr and his co-authors, who included Dunlop, applied the Industrial Relations theories and materials in teleological fashion to produce a support for a 'convergence thesis' of industrial development. Similar in its determinism to modernisation theory, the end result of all industrialising societies was indeed Dunlop's tripartite system, which at that time was extant and flourishing in its almost ideal type in Anglo-Saxon societies.

Intellectually and politically these books were condemned as conservative on two counts. In the first case, although systems could indeed be transformed this was not inherent in the world of Dunlop's Industrial Relations system and it thus appeared that this was a system for all time in which all parties were satisfied and operated to sustain an equilibrium. Secondly, especially in the case of Kerr *et al.*, class as a social force was eliminated as irrelevant. Thirdly, in both cases, a liberal capitalist industrial world order was firmly predicted and because the tripartite system was essentially Anglo-Saxon the prediction was ethnocentric (Harrod, 1994).

From within the current framework of Industrial Relations these authors can now be seen as political conservatives but intellectual progressives as they expanded the purview of the field, considered interconnectedness and attacked the big question. They made it legitimate, for at least part of the academic personnel of Industrial Relations, to be devoted to questions to be answered empirically, analytically or critically concerning the social power of trade unions, motivation (consciousness) of workers, comparative labour productivity, neo-corporatism, enterprise corporatism, employment and distributional systems which have crucial relevance to the emergence of social forces and, therefore, social change.

Furthermore, these questions were framed from a position which was at least cognisant of what occurred at the workplace. For the theorist of social forces knowing about, or observing, the workplace would be like a proponent of the 'great person' theory of history actually observing the activities of the neurones in the dominant leader's brain (mind).

Industrial Relations then up to the early 1970s had the potential for, and was moving in the direction of, connecting workplace to world order. As in so many other disciplines the rapidity with which these broader trends, intentions and efforts were marginalised and eliminated must stand as testimony to the fickleness, and the transitory nature and the lack of defensive vigour of any so-called intellectual movement or school.

In the case of Industrial Relations the macro-level orientation has been followed with extraordinary rapidity since the 1980s. Within the field it has been marked by the coming to power of the proponents of so-called human resource management. This orientation, in fact, represents the triumph of the practitioner over the analyst and a further restriction of the academic as one asked to provide a deeper analysis. Industrial Relations as a field of study had the advantage, or the misfortune, depending upon how it is viewed, of having within it both academics and practitioners in a relationship different from that which, say, International Relations academics might have had with diplomats. Thus labour officers, mediators, trade union industrial relations officers, personnel managers were served in a direct way by the academics in the field.

The personnel management section of Industrial Relations had always been present in the field and indeed then, as now, provided considerable insight into the development of social forces from the workplace. According to Kaufman (1993) the broader-based literature mentioned above had been essentially the work of institutional labour economists (which itself is significant for International Political Economy because these were economists forced to deal with the real world of labour control rather than assumptions of equilibrium theory). The personnel management practitioners had not been in a position of influence within the structure of the IR(1) field until the 1980s but, once on the scene, rapidly eliminated the more eclectic approach. Pockets of resistance remain, particularly in Comparative Industrial Relations, and both old and new writers continue to maintain the earlier traditions (Adams, 1995: Hyman, 1991). Others are intent on revitalising the associated field of labour history and the neo-corporatist issue is still debated. While these may be sites from which change in the field may be generated they do not at the moment significantly challenge the human resource management domination and although this latter area is defined in so many ways that nothing need be excluded (Bratten and Gold, 1994) it has meant essentially that the primary concern of IR(1) has been with productivity enhancing management micro-techniques. In the presidential address at the 1992 International Industrial Relations Congress, Niland noted:

This (the HRM) is no ordinary new wave, for it has the potential to shift dramatically the underlying power bases within the discipline. Among academics there is a concern that responsibility for Industrial Relations is moving to business schools where a different paradigm operates. Among practitioners the concern is that the devolution approach and the techniques of Human Resource Management serve to mainline the industrial relations function with the importance of the line manager growing at the expense of the expert. It is not being overly dramatic to wonder whether the discipline will survive much beyond the year 2000. (Niland, 1992)

It could be argued that IR(1) was responding to the social forces which themselves had precipitated the corporate age. In its most liberal form Human Resource Management is welfare-oriented, anti-Taylorist and therefore expensive. HRM is not really found in smaller enterprises unless it is defined as merely an entrepreneur's use of labour. Thus in the corporate age it could perhaps be expected that the discourse in industrial relations would respond by transforming HRM or some similar paradigm. Such a move in itself would mute the sources of criticism of corporate-dominated use of labor, enhance the possibilities of controlling labor within the corporation while changing (the precarious, marginalised, casual and unprotected workers) even more in favour of those inside. However, what could not have been expected is the rapidity with which the field and those within it abandoned the need or possibility to extend their findings to the greater concerns of international order or the general human condition.

This enforced truncation of a logical sequence from workplace to world yields the malaise of any human being not able to pursue the logic of a finding or opinion to its end in the chain of causality. This is especially the case with academics, some of whom believe that they are supposed to be something more than tinkerers at a fragmented workstation. An eloquent example of such malaise is found in Locke, Kochan and Piore (1995), reporting the preliminary findings on 'the transformation of employment relations in advanced industrial nations'. Within one page of the article, the title words 'employment relations', which are not far from labour relations, become 'employment practices' and then 'employment systems' whereby the relational aspects, that is power and conflict potential, are muted. Despite this initial derogation from the constrained larger intent, the authors cannot help, it seems, but refer to the societal impact of their micro-level findings. Unfortunately when they do so the comments appear to be the most commonplace and lay opinions. Thus in relation to the increased inequalities in income employment opportunities experienced by most of the OECD countries in the past twenty years, they note: 'This threatens not only to polarise these societies into haves and the have nots but also to undermine the solidaristic principles around which labour movements have traditionally organised', and further 'social strains arise from increased wage inequality and the widening gap between those who benefit from those left behind by the new economy and the new employment practices.'

If at this conjuncture then IR(1) has not as much to offer as it did in the past to IR(2) this is not to say that the International Political Economy which exists has been overly receptive to placing social forces at the core of its search for structural explanations of globally peripheral phenomena. In a recent study of texts used at British universities it has been shown that the texts which contain the least cognisance of social forces tend to be most used in International Political Economy courses (O'Brien, 1995). Further, what increasingly is being represented as IPE is in fact international economic relations, which starts at the national frontiers rather than with the social forces, even if defined as markets within them or within humankind.

Yet the collapse of societal analysis in IR(1) and the less than enthusiastic response of IR(2) for the social forces within IR(1), and the weak establishment of an International Political Economy that recognises social forces all come at the time when the original concerns of IR(1) are overtaking the original concerns of IR(2). Madrick reports that the declining rate of productivity growth in the United States since 1973 has meant \$25 trillion loss of production or \$75,000 per person and declares: 'Numbers like these change history' (Madrick 1995:14.) Much productivity growth can be attributed to lack of growth of labour productivity which, in turn, includes the motivational, consciousness and relational aspects of humanity at work. Relative rates of growth and decline of labour productivity unequivocably indicate that new social forces are developing. The first real indicator of the potential implosion of the ex-Soviet Union was chronic labour productivity declines, and the mechanism subsequently and desperately used to restore that productivity was a crucial factor in the historic development of the experiment in state redistribution (Harrod, 1987b). As Madrick considers and I have suggested (Harrod, 1994, 1995) a similar process may now be unfolding in the United States.

Again, the much discussed competitiveness of nations (Porter, 1990; Best, 1990; Hart, 1992; Womak *et al.*, 1990; Thurow, 1992) is a debate about the substantial, if not crucial, component of labour relations and labour productivity. Likewise the debate on forms of capitalism such as

Albert's (1991) formulation of Rhineland and Texas types is based upon views of the social forces within industrial relations systems. International Monetary Fund and World Bank structural adjustment programmes imposed upon indebted Southern countries invariably require social force engineering of the adopting regimes, and a change in labour market and industrial relations structures and policies in order to increase exportable surpluses designed to service sovereign debt (Harrod 1992). The nature and the future of rapidly industrialising countries (as well as countries such as South Africa and entities as Hong Kong) can be more easily considered from the standpoint of the 'real' economy of production and power relations surrounding it than from macro-level financial and national accounts indicators (Frenkel and Harrod, 1995).

Some of these latter examples raise the hope that the future development of International Political Economy (and perhaps even IR(1), IR(2)) will indeed move in a more inclusive direction. But there are also competing paradigms to provide a global perceptual apparatus in world orders.

World orders, world views and academic fields

In contemporary history it is possible to argue that there are successive perceptual, intellectual and disciplinary underpinnings to foreign policy and the attempted creation of world orders. The world view provided by economists was important in the immediate post-war period, followed by that of the new behavioural discipline of International Relations and in particular the realist branch of it. The inability of a successor world view from the humanities in the 1970s, the reasons for which I have tried to illustrate above, left the opportunity open to non-humanities. While the current description of the policies emerging from the social forces in dominant societies is described as neo-liberal, it is at the same time also social Darwinism supported by socio-biology, ecology and environmental science.

The socio-biological world view became bolstered by the scientific view that it is almost certainly impossible for the whole of humanity to achieve levels of consumption enjoyed by the top 20 per cent which substantially produces and entirely devours 85 per cent of world income. The first half of the twentieth century was devoted to creating such a pattern of world income and the last half to maintaining it. The main thrust of the socio-biological world order argument is then as follows – the dominant wealthy 20 per cent of the population, in view of the limits to the growth of their consumption, have restrained their population growth. The rest of the world's peoples/populations are characterised by the condition of population growth which makes it even more impossible to achieve privileged levels of consumption. In short, those not counted as wealthy are breeding themselves out of existence. Further, biological studies have shown that animal and insect behaviour under conditions of over-crowding and resource depletion result in undirected violence, stress and depression.

It follows that first, privileged levels of consumption will come under threat and efforts must be made to sustain and increase the income for the already wealthy; second, any attempt to redistribute world income is futile, inasmuch as the redistribution would be towards those who are already doomed; third, under these circumstances violence and conflict will be the norm rather than the exception in the underresourced and overpopulated world; and fourth, military policy then should be directed at preventing the spill-over of such conflicts into the privileged areas. Such spill-overs can occur only from chemical-biological and nuclear capacity and transnational terrorism and these must be dealt with by nuclear leveraged buy-outs, surgical bombing of chemical and biological capacity and increased surveillance of immigrants, especially from the South.

This is the neo-liberal, socio-biological world order – the extension from ant to atom bomb in the absence of anything approaching a similar extension of workplace to world order. The prospects for transformation to humane world order must start with an analysis of social forces arising from production and their potential role in creating new historical structures. If, in the final analysis, Dilthey's unifying factor of humankind appears to be the violent defence of the material status quo then that factor must be changed, to show that rather it is the potential for change which is the unifying factor.

NOTES

1 This is not to say that such capable scholars in International Relations do not exist nor that some of them may not be found writing in this collection. If this volume is part of the challenge to existing structures then the announced purpose also contains an indication of the direction to proceed, namely to conceptualise 'International Relations' as its stands, out of existence in favour of approaches and groups (departments) devoted to consideration of current and future universal human orders whether or not they are democratic or sustainable.

2 The subtitle I proposed for *Power, Production and the Unprotected Worker* was not allowed, but given that it was in a series 'The Political Economy of International Change', it was to have been on the lines of 'Subordination and Social Change'.

3 Strange (1988) notes the dominance of church and then state in the 'knowledge structure' but does not fully extend this quality to the corporation.
4 Dunlop (1958) was important in formulating and legitimising the first efforts to construct a 'social formation' from several different systems (Cox, 1971; Cox, Harrod *et al.*, 1972).

8   Transnational class formation and state forms

Kees van der Pijl

This chapter explores aspects of the process of transnational class forma-tion of the capitalist class or bourgeoisie in historical perspective. It looks at forms of imagined community (Anderson, 1983) by which this class established a new identity literally outside the pre-existing community and outside the reach of prior social and political structures. Freemasonry, operating within and across a range of state–society com-plexes from the late seventeenth century on, serves as one model for such imagined communities supporting a class identity.

Bourgeois class formation itself was also subject to aspects of socialisa-tion in the sense that separate bodies branched off from the broader class networks to assume a collective intellectual or planning function. The Rhodes/Milner group in the British empire, which was connected to the American ruling class, was the first of such bodies on a transnational level. Ultimately, all these structures serve(d) to reinforce the capacity of the capitalist ruling class to expand its mode of production to global dimensions and eliminate obstacles resisting such expansion; and, within its established sphere of influence, to raise the rate of exploitation of labour and shape social life and politics accordingly. Since this takes place in the context of struggle, there are inherent limits to these designs, and the development of capital itself upsets any particular pattern of exploita-tion by the contradictory advance of commodification and socialisation.

We will first outline our concept of class and some other, corollary notions; and then present a brief overview of some instances of transna-tional class formation in the English-speaking heartland of capital, and in its periphery of contender states.

Class and International Relations

The concept of class, understood as a social agency logically prior to global structures such as the state system and the 'world economy' (Palan, 1992), derives from the notion of exploitation. Across all known history, society's interactions with nature have been mediated by the appropriation of unpaid labour. Since the beneficiaries have unfailingly sought to consolidate their privileged access to society's and nature's wealth by symbolic and material means of power, we may speak of ruling and subordinate classes. Their origin in some structure of exploitation defines the mutual relationship of classes as one of struggle. In this respect, any advance in the level of control of the forces of nature, by creating new opportunities for appropriating unpaid labour, necessarily develops through a restructuring of the existing configuration of classes.

While the term 'social forces', as used by Robert Cox and others, may perhaps serve to capture a broader range of agents in a descriptive analysis, the concept of class takes the central dynamic of social development as its point of departure. This is because it links a structure of exploitation, the stage reached by the control of the forces of nature, and the notion of struggle as a means of explaining social change. The struggles involved in exploitation determine the priorities of a broad range of actors. These struggles propel these actors in their mutual relations and also reduce the possible choices suggested by, for example, Weberian rational action theory. Before social forces can engage in their leisure pursuits, so to speak, the classes of which they are made up face a number of necessary confrontations from which they cannot escape.

Once exploitation is made part of a system of market relations, in which labour power, too, has become a commodity sold in the market, the structure of exploitation is transformed. From a hierarchical order in which wealth is redistributed upwards by tributary mechanisms, society now appears as a collection of, formally speaking, equally entitled members. Formal equality and the explicit freedom to dispose of property at will, on which equal exchange is premised, once codified, cover society with a veil of equivalence, of which the modern state, to which each citizen has equal access, is the ultimate embodiment. We need not here repeat the standard Marxist critique of this market/political equivalence, *viz.*, that it is confined to the market and hides the (occasionally benevolent) despotism of the workplace.

What is important for our argument is that with the coming of market relations and private property, the traditional community dissolves into individuals. And whether as owners of land and mobile wealth or as proletarians without any, all individuals now come to face the economic process (that is, capital in its competitive multiplicity) as a self-propelling system over which no person or group can exercise effective control. Hence, even the contemporary, secularised and property-owning inhabitant of uptown Manhattan remains a fearful, superstitious primitive when confronted with the vacillations of the Dow Jones index. Marx calls this the fetishism of commodities and of capital (*MEW*, 23:85; see also Rupert, 1993: 70).

Compared to the traditional community with its transparent structure of exploitation and stratification, the structure of exploitation of capitalist society therefore is characterised by a prior alienation from community bonds (and from nature, of which they constitute a direct outgrowth; see Marx, 1973: 495). But the individuals cut loose from the immediate relations with nature and with each other by commodification are to some extent reintegrated into units of social cohesion by a parallel process termed socialisation (from the German *Vergesellschaftung*).

Socialisation means that the elementary exchange relations by which a market or any other contractual connection is established, create complex, quasi-organic interrelations in which the initial division of labour implied in exchange becomes objectified in machinery and organisation. Although markets continue to provide the basic framework of society, exchanges to an ever greater degree become internal to an already functioning system of productive and organisational relations, in which all labour and social activity have generally become social, part of a collective social labour process.

Class formation under these conditions can be understood as a process of socialisation and is subject to its further development (functional internal differentiation such as separation of planning and control functions, etc.). It necessarily remains subject to commodification and alienation as well. Social cohesion is persistently fragmented. The very force by which people are collectively employed or enriched and which directs the different structures into which socialised labour breaks down – capital – is not understood as a product of social development and collective effort but as the fetishised 'economy'. The collective bonds people experience and cherish reflect some quest for lost community, which may or may not coincide or overlap with units of socialised labour.

In the class structure, this contradictory unity of objective socialisation and the community reflex works out in two ways. On the one hand, class structures will become ever more complex and ephemeral to the degree commodification and the parallel socialisation of labour advances. While initially, the workers thrown off the land or otherwise separated from their means of production will still directly engage in face-to-face, wage-labour relations with managers of capitalism, ultimately there emerges some universal citizen in paid employment but also owning some shares through a pension fund or otherwise – what Marx and Engels in an optimistic mood called 'world-historical, empirically universal individuals' (*MEW*, 3: 35), for whom exploitation ceases to have a direct social reference. On the other hand, the quest for community as well as the structures of social power and authority carried over from previous social orders in the form of states or otherwise, reproduce patterns of class relations retarding this eventual universalisation.[1] While class therefore assumes a new meaning under capitalist conditions, it remains grafted on ethnic/community, estate and gender bonds which existed prior to the market economy and capital and which continue to imbricate with class relations. The modern state, too, by its national content, continues to rest on an 'imagined' community to sustain its cohesion (Anderson, 1983).

The historical sequence of segments, or fractions, of a nascent bourgeoisie crystallising outside the reach of a given national community and adopting particular quasi-community forms of organisation itself while submitting to certain transnational planning bodies, interacts with a shift in forms of state. As Robert Cox has argued (1986: 205), 'there has been little attempt within the bounds of International Relations theory to consider the state/society complex as the basic entity of international relations. As a consequence, the prospect that there exists a plurality of forms of state, expressing different configurations of state/society complexes, remains very largely unexplored.' In our own work (van der Pijl, 1989–96) we have developed the thesis that the 1688 Glorious Revolution in England created a state/society complex in which the previous, tentacled and mercantilist configuration inaugurated by Cromwell was replaced by a state allowing and guaranteeing the self-regulation of property-owning civil society and separating its public functions from this private sphere. After the author of the *Two Treatises of Government*, this ideal-typical state/society complex may be called 'Lockean'; its predecessor, 'Hobbesian'. The dynamics of interstate rivalry interacting with the varied relationship between state and society from the late seventeenth century on created an evolving pattern which may be described in these terms.

Whereas capital and society could expand from the British Isles to areas overseas, and over several centuries constitute an integrated social basis supporting a bloc of states in and from which capital expanded further (what we term a *Lockean heartland*), its challengers, beginning with France, and for a variety of reasons, remained locked in the Hobbesian configuration of a tentacular state still in the process of demarcating and unifying its social basis. The forms of state as distinguished by Cox (1987) can thus be grouped together under a continuum with two outliers: the Lockean heartland and Hobbesian contender states (Table 1). This is not an exhaustive range of forms of state, because a substantial outer ring of 'proto-states' (1987: 218) which have not yet effectively reached the stage of unification/autonomy remains invisible in this table. However, all state forms distinguished by Cox can be situated in this dichotomy except for the welfare nationalist state – which was straddled across the divide and marked the moment in international history when,

Table 1. *State forms according to Cox on the heartland/contender state divide*

Era	Lockean heartland	Hobbesian contenders
eighteenth and nineteenth centuries	liberal state (Britain) instrumental liberal state (USA)	Bonapartist state (France)
late nineteenth to early twentieth century	welfare nationalist state (Britain)	welfare nationalist state (Prussia/Germany) fascist state (Axis Powers)
mid-twentieth century	corporate liberal state[a] (USA/North Atlantic Bloc)	redistributive party-commanded state (Soviet Bloc) cartel state (South European/American dictatorships) neo-mercantilist developmentalist state (late industrialising Third World states)
late twentieth century	hyperliberal state (Thatcher/Reagan model)	

Note:
[a] Cox uses 'neo-liberal state' which more often is employed to denote what he terms the hyperliberal state.

at the outset of the twentieth century, Germany came alongside Britain as a challenger for world power.

Transnational class formation in the heartland

We will now take up these ideal-types as the reference for our analysis of transnational class formation along the lines indicated above.

The requirement of equivalence for commodity exchange explains why market relations originate historically at the extremities of a community, at the meeting points with members of other communities (*MEW*, 23:102; Polanyi, 1957: 58). Capital develops once the exchange of equivalents is pursued for profit and profit-seeking entrepreneurs start to reorganise their activities with an eye to the exploitation of living labour power. Exploitation in its most extreme forms, such as slavery, historically begins as the enslaving of foreign peoples defeated in war. The mercantile prehistory of capital builds on these foreign expeditions, channelling goods and funds home and establishing far-flung networks of plunder and commerce which eventually also begin to restructure the domestic community.

Now state authority since the Middle Ages (in England even more so than in France) had been built on successive steps demarcating the 'national' against such cosmopolitan forces as the Jews, crusading knightly orders, Venetian merchants and Florentine bankers, and the Roman Catholic Church. The resulting 'imagined community' for which the Stuarts for instance still felt responsible, placed a limit on the exploitation of one's fellow men. Therefore, if the ascendant bourgeoisie was to continue its rise, it would have to develop a new identity and mental distance from its own community in order to develop opportunities for the exploitation of living labour power at home; and also, there would have to be a rehabilitation of the transnational links cut off in the earlier process of state formation to facilitate international exchanges.

Freemasonry served to provide the bourgeoisie with that new identity with which it could look at its community through 'foreign' eyes (Rosenstock-Huessy, 1961: 364), while at the same time allowing the doctrines of free trade and religious tolerance to link up transnationally. Masonry was not only 'catholic' in the sense of universal or ecumenical, but also rehabilitated earlier transnational links by its myths about Templar origins and other references to the crusading orders (Waite, 1994, I: 434). With its agnostic, paganised Christian ritual, it allowed the inclusion of various Christian denominations – as well as Jews and agnostics of all persuasions. The beginning of (non-manual) Freemasonry has been traced to the aftermath of the Glorious Revolution of 1688 which consecrated what we call the Lockean state/society complex. To the extent that a political bond existed among Masons it was the concern to keep the king's authority limited – although in the early eighteenth century an element of conservative entrenchment against further attacks on royal authority also crept in (Knight, 1985: 21–2; Waite, 1994, I: 26).

It can be suggested then, that the class compromise between the old aristocracy and the bourgeoisie in Britain may have been facilitated and in some respects actually achieved within the institutional context of the Masonic lodges, whose membership reached into successive royal families beginning with the Hanoverians (Knight, 1985: 37). On the other hand, the entrepreneurs who became the standard-bearers of the industrial revolution belonged rather to Protestant sects such as the Quakers. The exploitation of living labour power in manufacturing fell to these outsiders and, throughout the nineteenth century, would remain the preserve of 'socially marginal groups such as Quakers, Jews, and immigrants, especially from central Europe' (Overbeek, 1990: 45).

Since bourgeois cosmopolitanism did not sit well with the national and democratic tendencies in Protestantism, Freemasonry seems to have bridged the gap between counter-revolutionary Roman Catholicism and explicit political liberalism. In an age still under the sway of mercantilism, Freemasonry provided the free-thinking, cosmopolitan aristocracy (who paradoxically would be among the leaders of the bourgeois revolutions of the 1770s and 1780s) with a passport of gestures and signs of recognition that allowed otherwise anonymous members of the upper classes to gain access to the good society abroad (Waite, 1994, I: 101; cf. Rich, 1988: 186). The eighteenth century saw the spread of Freemasonry throughout the North Atlantic area and the European continent. Lodges were set up in continental Europe – often, paradoxically, by Jacobite English aristo-crats in exile. The Duke of Wharton set up a lodge in Madrid in 1728; three years later one was launched in the Kingdom of Naples; in 1733, the Earl of Strathmore authorised a lodge in Hamburg (Waite, 1994, II: 50–2). In North America, the New England colonies and Virginia became pivots in its further spread. The first Canadian lodge was set up under Massachusetts jurisdiction in 1749 (Knight, 1985: 34).

More generally, Freemasonry was part of the complex of forces which subtly transformed the universal doctrines of natural law to the more nar-rowly circumscribed citizens' rights doctrines of cosmopolitan law, thus putting in place the class dimension of the 'Rights of Man' (Archibugi, 1995: 441). It was part and parcel of the pervasive spread of the Lockean mind-set, seeping across the borders of states reinforcing their hold of society to confront British commercial supremacy as well as circulating, more freely, in the heartland itself. Among the peace plans of which Kant's 1795 pamphlet of course is the most conspicuous today, circulated others which, as in the case of Carl Hofheim's, actually propagated an international Masonic union (Archibugi, 1995: 451).

The rise of strong contender states in the late nineteenth century, inter-acting with the advance of the organised working class, forced the English-speaking countries to draw together again. This in part could build on the Masonic infrastructure put in place in the previous century. As R. Hyam writes, 'The role of freemasonry in building up the empire, and of its doc-trines of brotherhood in sustaining the world-wide activities of traders and empire-builders, is not easy to document. Its role in spreading British cul-tural influences has thus been seriously underrated' (quoted in Rich, 1988: 187, note 1). Or, in the words of Knight, 'The British . . . remained throughout the nineteenth and twentieth centuries the chief propagan-dists for the movement . . . Undaunted by the loss of the first empire and with it direct control over American Masonry, the British took Masonry with the flag as they created their second empire' (1985: 34).

By 1872, there were about 4 million Freemasons in the British empire compared to half a million trade unionists and 400,000 members of the co-operative movement (Rich, 1988: 176). A parallel, non-religious and non-secret fraternity that was part of a transnational class network, Rotary, was set up in the United States as a businessmen's luncheon club by the lawyer, Paul Harris, in 1905. It was expanded to Rotary International in 1912 (*Chambers' Biographical Dictionary*, 'Harris'). The function of these networks was to knit together the English-speaking bourgeoisie into a quasi-tribal unity. As Gramsci comments, we may understand the lodges and their equivalents as contributing to the achievement of particular political results, 'functioning as international political parties which operate within each nation with the full concentration of the international forces'. 'A religion, freemasonry, Rotary, Jews, etc., can be subsumed into the social category of "intellectuals", whose function, on an international scale, is that of mediating the extremes, of "socialising" the technical discoveries which provide the impetus for all activities of leadership, of devising compromises between, and ways out of, extreme solutions' (Gramsci, 1971: 182 note).

The development of transnational class networks, too, was subject to processes of socialisation, separating certain functions between them which then in turn were connected into chains of (tentative) control and direction. Thus emerged, in response to forces challenging the self-evidence of liberal internationalism and British hegemony, actual policy planning groups. The paradigmatic example of these was the quasi-Masonic secret society set up by Cecil Rhodes, the British financier and South African empire-builder. Rhodes's 'Society of the Elect' marks the divide between allegorical middle-class collusion under royal patronage such as Freemasonry, and attempts at actual planned direction of the conduct of social and world affairs by the transnational English-speaking bourgeoisie.[2] According to Carroll Quigley (1981: 5), the Union of South Africa, the British Commonwealth, as well as the League of Nations, were largely shaped by the planning work of the Rhodes group, operating behind the scenes at crucial junctures and in the places that mattered. Backed by Rhodes's fortune, and subsidised by the Rothschilds, Lazards and other City magnates with world-wide connections, the 'Society of the Elect' shared Rhodes's vision of the British empire as the realisation of a moral idea of freedom. These ideas reflected the transition towards industrial society and the imperialism in their concern for educating the working classes – a concern of which the emergence of the Welfare Nationalist State at this juncture was also an expression. Although a Freemason himself (Rich, 1988: 188, note 6), to Rhodes the model for a secret society were the Jesuits. His society was to be 'a church for the extension of the British empire'.[3] The 'reclaiming' of the United States was a crucial ambition in the Rhodes project (Shoup and Minter, 1977: 12–13). The Rhodes group subsequently developed and extended and came to be called the Milner Group as Alfred Milner took a leading role. By reference to the journal it launched after 1909, it became known to the wider public as the 'Round Table group' and still later, after the Astors' country estate, also as the 'Cliveden Set'.

The power of a body like the Milner group was a function of its being a nodal point in the intellectual, economic and political nervous system of the British empire.[4] It operated through the following key higher education institutes, which were also recruiting grounds: Oxford colleges such as All Souls, Balliol and New College, and the Geneva School and Graduate Institute of International Studies. The latter was set up as part of a larger intellectual network by Alfred Zimmern (Quigley, 1981: 193, 259). Also of key importance were the Rhodes Trust which to this day recruits promising English-speaking students; the Royal Institute of International Affairs (RIIA) and its publications; powerful philanthropies such as the Carnegie foundations in the United States; and publications such as *The Times* of London. By operating through these channels, a body like the Milner Group could bring cohesion to the outlook of the class it was serving, and on an imperial/Atlantic scale at that.

Yet here also we can establish what distinguishes a class analysis from elitism or conspiracy theory. For after reading Quigley's work and running through the lists of members of the Milner Group in Britain, the Commonwealth, the United States and Germany, one realises that *only the function of providing ideological cohesion is a constant*. Otherwise, all the points of disagreement between fractions of the ruling class emerge within the Milner Group itself. On a question like appeasement with Germany or supporting the League of Nations, the dividing lines run straight through the Milner Group; both International Relations 'idealists' like Alfred Zimmern, and their fiercest critic, E. H. Carr, are listed among the membership (Quigley, 1981: appendix). What remains, then, is the notion of class power operating through a shifting structure of processes of capital accumulation and international relations, negotiating challenges in its relations with the exploited and/or intermediary classes, as well as with contender states; but seeking to hold its own through the changes.

After the First World War, there were attempts to actually bring about direct trans-Atlantic planning bodies by building on the activities of Wilson's 'Inquiry' (a body of intellectuals assembled for the Peace Conference also engaging in intelligence work (O'Toole 1991: Ch. 26)), in which Walter Lippmann, a confidant of Wilson's and envoy to the

Milner Group, was the animating spirit. Key figures from the Round Table network such as Lionel Curtis, and powerful Anglo-American bankers such as J. P. Morgan were in the background. The planned, joint Anglo-American Institute of International Affairs did not materialise, however, which resulted in a separate RIIA and the American Council on Foreign Relations (CFR) (Shoup and Minter, 1977: ch. 1). On the eve of the Second World War, the Milner group still had to dispatch Clarence Streit to the US to work for Atlantic unity under the supervision of the leader of the Milner group at the time (and ambassador to Washington), Lord Lothian (van der Pijl, 1984: 110–15).

We cannot here describe the planning bodies which functioned as nodal points of class formation and elite realignment in the subsequent transnational extension of the New Deal/Second World War class compromises with their mass-production blueprint for the economy and a counter-cyclical, welfare model for the state. These included the CFR, the Committee on Economic Development, as well as, in wartime London, the subsequently named European League for Economic Co-operation (ELEC) linked to the International Chamber of Commerce in Paris. These bodies attempted to guide corporate strategies and popular ambitions into a comprehensive framework. The unity of purpose remained tentative and fragile and, in the early 1950s, many of the same people involved in these bodies had to set up a new forum to settle mutual differences between the Atlantic partners – the Bilderberg Conferences.

Significantly, in the 1970s, a new wave of activity and the establishment of actual new forums of transnational consultation emerged in the context of fresh challenges posed by the youth and working-class movements, Third World revolt and détente. But what appeared to become the ultimate triumph of informal policy planning with the creation of the Trilateral Commission in response to Nixon's unilateralism (Gill, 1990) was outflanked by outsider and more right-wing planning groups such as the Mont Pélèrin Society, the Heritage Foundation, the Pinay Circle and the Committee on the Present Danger. Responding to a mood among the ruling class no longer confident in the smooth compromises of the post-war era, these groups embarked on a strategy of confrontation and on which the blue-chip networks such as the Trilateral Commission and Bilderberg only later converged.

This illustrates at the same time the tentative, experimental nature of policy planning from a class perspective, the need to adjust to unforeseen contingencies. The absence of true opposition elements within their ranks reduces the capacity of these groups to anticipate the drift of class and international struggles, compared for instance to political bodies where such elements are not denied public representation.

Passive revolution and class formation in contender states

Let us now turn to the contender state category. The industrial revolution in England turned a major part of the world into a periphery (Senghaas, 1982: 29) and only a limited number of states have been able to challenge this supremacy. Between the heartland of capital, and the contender states congealed in the Hobbesian configuration, a dividing line emerged limiting the relatively unhindered, organic development of social classes. Here state control implied a compulsive shaping of social relations, too. Yet in their attempt to catch up with Britain, and the later expanded heartland, the contender states not only reinforced the position of the state class, but also, by emulating particular aspects of the capitalist order, unwittingly created opportunities for elements both within and outside the state class, to adopt bourgeois perspectives.

This can be analysed with the help of Gramsci's concept of passive revolution (Gramsci, 1971: 114). This concept denotes the impact of an original revolution in a different society resisting it. In our case, the revolutions that put the heartland ahead were the English and American, in conjunction with the first and second industrial revolutions which in the setting of the Lockean heartland served to develop their full leadership potential. A passive revolution (that is, the contender states' reaction), however, combines:

1 a 'revolution from above' without mass participation (Gramsci speaks of 'successive small waves of reform' and 'interventions from above of the enlightened monarchy type'), and:
2 a creeping, 'molecular' social transformation, in which the progressive class (here the aspiring bourgeois elements) finds itself compelled to advance in a more or less surreptitious, 'compromised' fashion.

Let us briefly review the previous patterns of transnational class formation under passive revolution conditions, by reference to the concrete forms of contender state distinguished by Cox (1987).

First, the Bonapartist state. Already at the time of the Glorious Revolution, the Cardinals and Louis XIV had laid the foundations for the tentacular state which was explicitly rejected by Locke (the manuscript of the *Two Treatises* was cover-titled 'On the Gallican Illness' by reference to French despotism (Lasslett in Locke, 1965: 75)). In the eighteenth century, however, cosmopolitanism and Freemasonry still allowed for a relatively unhindered spread of bourgeois ideas. Both enlightened rulers such as Frederick the Great of Prussia and dissident aristocrats such as the Duc d'Orléans, Philippe Égalité, were Freemasons.[5] The American and the French revolutions, in each of which the Masonic element was pronounced (and linked directly – Benjamin Franklin and Helvétius, for example, were members of the seminal Lodge of the Nine Muses in Paris) sharply terminated whatever complacency had existed with respect to the lodges. Continental European Masonry now virtually had to go underground. In 1792, the Austrian lodges closed of their own accord to avoid being subject to persecution, while in Russia, Tsar Paul I outlawed them (Waite, 1994, II:72–3). In France itself, the revolutionary lodges had disintegrated in the disturbances, but, with support from above, they revived under Napoleon and spread with French influence across Europe, now as a network of the powerful, notably in the civil service, the precursors of today's *énarques* (Markov, 1989: 114–15, 106). In the Latin American revolutions inspired by the French revolution, Freemasonry likewise provided the nodal points for transnationally connected bourgeois emancipation and many of its most famous leaders were Masons – Hidalgo, Bolívar, Martí and many others (Nederveen Pieterse, 1990: 135; Waite, 1994, I: xxxv).

In the wave of revolutions that began with 1848, Freemasonry again played a prominent part, but after the Crimean War conservatism, balance of power politics and ascendant nationalism began to disrupt the transnational Masonic connection. In France, with Louis Blanc at its head, Freemasonry claimed the revolution as its own, and following the *coup d'état* of 1851 could not but suffer accordingly (unlike the previous Bonapartes, Napoleon III was not a Freemason (Waite, 1994, II: 26)). The common concern of the European rulers was to contain further democratisation and to prevent their mutual conflicts from flaring into a full-scale war. This concern was shared by the *haute* finance on which they relied for foreign funds. Marx noted for instance that 'the more Austria has opposed the demands of the bourgeoisie for political power, the deeper it must bow before the unlimited despotism of a part of this class – the financiers' (*MEW*, 10: 104). Napoleon III in turn was dependent on English finance, while the tsar relied on the Amsterdam capital market. With transnationalism thus aligned with conservatism, Freemasonry took a national turn, as in the movement for Italian unification – a movement supported by France, but which was mainly against Austria. Garibaldi, who came back a Mason from South America, set up a Grand Orient of his own; eventually, a national convention in 1873 established Masonry in Italy as a political institution (which had 'little communion with England' (Waite, 1994, II: 9; *Chambers' Biographical Dictionary*, 'Garibaldi')).[6]

The centrifugal drift of the era coincided with the emergence of the welfare nationalist state, which was the low point for transnational classes in terms of legitimacy. Between France and the heartland, Masonic links were cut when the Grand Orient declared itself atheist in 1877 (Waite, 1994, II: 297). With Prussia-Germany, the war of 1870–71 destroyed whatever intimate bonds had existed, although towards the First World War, there were attempts by French and British Freemasons to seek conciliation with their German brethren in 1905–9 and 1912, respectively. Only after the war transnational links were restored, however, especially between France and the heartland into which it gradually became integrated. The First World War, as the *Encyclopaedia of Freemasonry* notes, 'welded fresh bonds of union between America, France and Belgium, which in their turn have raised, and in a spirit favourable thereto, the question whether a rapprochement is possible between Freemasonry in Latin countries and that of the English-speaking race at large' (Waite, 1994, II: 4).

At this point, more powerful nodal points for transnational ruling class collusion had formed. Their membership began to look at Germany through different eyes. The forces from Germany, Japan and other contender states willing to align on the anti-Bolshevik orientation sought by the Milner Group in the post-war period, such as Carl Goerdeler in Germany, were weak and divided – as was, in this case, the Milner Group itself (Quigley, 1981: 146–7; van der Pijl, 1984: 128–9). After the Dawes Plan of 1924, a German contingent was admitted into the International Chamber of Commerce – in conjunction with the penetration of new capital into Germany. On the German national committee of the ICC in 1938, Nazis such as Kurt von Schroeder of the Hamburg investment bank sat with liberals such as the Jewish textile magnate, Abraham Frowein (Ridgeway, 1938: 21).

By the time the Second World War broke out, transnational channels of class formation and policy planning had been closed in the most radical attempt to suppress all transnational networks, not only the supposed 'Jewish-Bolshevik' conspiracy which the Nazi imagination had conjured up, but also that of Freemasonry. The small Milner Group membership in Germany (H. J. von Moltke, A. von Trott zu Solz) perished after Goerdeler's failed 1944 coup attempt against Hitler.

Of class formation in the remaining forms of contender state, we can only present some illustrations. Thus in a cartel state like Spain, we may observe the mechanisms of alienation and socialisation into structures providing a new social identity in the phase of the 'opening' of the country's economy in the late 1950s. This was led by technocrats of Opus Dei who had entered the government in 1957. Their aim was to adjust class relations in Spain to the pattern of the newly established EEC but simultaneously, to guarantee continuity with the authoritarian Spanish political order (Holman, 1996: 57). In this classic example of a passive revolution, Opus Dei, a secret Catholic lay organisation committed to modernisation in a rigidly conservative socio-political framework, was part of a transnational network extending to Latin America notably, and including a number of major banks (van Wesel, 1992: 263–7; Holman, 1995: 31–3). Ultimately, this entailed the unforeseen consequence, upon Franco's death, of a transformation of the state form itself to a corporate liberal one coinciding with southern Europe's tentative integration into the heartland (Holman, 1987:8).

The redistributive party-commanded state, Cox's term for the Soviet-type contender state, certainly did not seek integration, and the state hold on society here was much more monolithic. Taking one's distance from the existing social order necessarily involved emigration. Only when state control was relaxed, as in the USSR under Gorbachev, could transnational bodies link up with the aspiring elements of a capitalist class. Thus one of the nodal points of the international and US new right, the Unification Church of Reverend Sun Myung Moon of South Korea, began sending missionaries into the Soviet Union in 1983. In 1990 it had advanced to the point where Gorbachev invited Moon to the Kremlin. Under the free scholarships in the United States offered by the Korean on that occasion, 3,500 Soviet students and teachers went to the United States in the second half of 1990 alone.[7] Once the Soviet sphere of influence in Eastern Europe collapsed, direct transnational links could surface/be established, as in the case of the Czech premier, Vaclav Klaus, who is a prominent member of the neo-liberal Mont Pélèrin Society. But otherwise, the element of émigrés coming back to their country as quasi-strangers is a crucial phenomenon here. This applies to new Czech investment banks such as Harvard Capital and Patria, whose owners have applied their experience in the West to appropriate large chunks of privatised assets; but also, on a much larger scale, to a country like China.[8]

Finally, the element of emigration and return as a form of transnational class formation may be observed also in India, which in Cox's nomenclature is an example of the neo-mercantilist developmental state. Now that capital is establishing itself outside the paternalistic structures of Congress state capitalism, it can be established that what seems to emerge as the real vanguard of a neo-liberal bourgeoisie not only is closely linked with foreign capital, but actually operated from outside India for at least a considerable time in the past. The Reliance group of the Ambani brothers, the Chhabria and Mallya families, the Ispat group and the house of Hinduja all are examples of this trend (Roy, 1994: 23). Whether the unitary state will survive the radical restructuring of class and state/society relations that is involved here (and elsewhere in Asia) remains to be seen.

Conclusion

From these summary notes, very few definite conclusions can be plausibly drawn. Yet, understanding the ways in which an emerging bourgeoisie has historically sought to disentangle itself from its original communities or national quasi-communities in order to exploit them, may be a precondition for understanding the potential and the limits of the moment of resistance to bourgeois class formation, which in the recent period has surfaced again after a period of protracted defeats. Such resistance remains underinvestigated in the transnational historical materialist approach (Drainville, 1994).

Understanding the modalities of how alienation has functioned in bourgeois class formation is a precondition for its being overcome by transparent socialisation and the growth of a planetary, self-conscious community of fate. But the concrete history of our present world, and the development of its ruling classes to global unification under a common, neo-liberal doctrine, teaches that such a community cannot come about in a single act but rather involves the cumulative momentum of a series of particular, largely contingent episodes. Not as the product of a linear and didactic form of univeralism, but from often coincidental, unique historical combinations, the moment of resistance may then emerge to impose limits on capitalist exploitation of people and nature and attempt to reverse its suicidal drive.

NOTES

I owe a debt to Stephen Gill for his thoughtful editing and support and to an anonymous reviewer for pointing to some serious weaknesses in the original manuscript of this chapter.

1 This is even disregarding the inherent and meanwhile manifest limits to capitalist development which mock the very idea of a prosperous planet spinning safely towards a capitalist millennium.

2 Rhodes' 'Society of the Elect' to which an 'Association of Helpers' was to be added, was composed of Rhodes himself; William T. Stead, the journalist; Reginald Balliol Brett, the future Lord Esher, confidant of Queen Victoria; King Edward VII (who was also Grand Master of British Freemasonry in his days); and King George V. Soon after, Alfred Milner was added to this narrow circle. It was after him that the Rhodes network has been named in its further development. Other labels used in this connection are the Round Table groups set up in 1909, or the 'Cliveden Set', after the country estate of the Anglo-American Astors which in the 1920s became a meeting point for the group and its foreign contacts.

3 W. T. Stead claimed afterwards that 'Mr. Rhodes . . . aspired to be the creator of one of those vast semi-religious, quasi-political associations which, like the

Society of Jesus, have played so large a part in the history of the world' (quoted in Quigley, 1981: 34, 36).

4 In his study in the subject, Quigley shows how the Milner group was grafted on the older 'Cecil bloc', named after the family of Lord Salisbury which stood at the centre of a wide-ranging web of intermarried ruling class dynasties but began to lose its effectiveness when Arthur Balfour, a nephew of Salisbury's, became its informal leader. Helped by the Rhodes connection, 'Milner shifted the emphasis from family connection to ideological agreement.' Quigley writes (1981: 29): 'The former had become less useful with the rise of a class society based on economic conflicts and with the extension of democracy.' This as we saw also was the basis of the Welfare Nationalist State.

5 The Duc d'Orléans became Grand Master of the National Grand Lodge of France in 1771; two years later it was transformed into the Grand Orient which still exists today (Waite, 1994, I: 292). See also *Le Monde*, 23 January 1996, 'Jacques Lafouge est élu grand maître du Grand Orient de France.'

6 Today it is known widely through the lodge Propaganda Due which functioned as a shadow government for several decades. Incidentally, the *carbonari*, which as a secret society were of course most notably involved in the quest for Italian unity, were unrelated to Masonry except for the analogy of a political body naming itself after a craft guild. Their function, however, falls into the same category in the sense of the alienation which is part of bourgeois class formation. From the literature on Freemasonry in the heartland that we have studied, it is obvious that it (and parallel networks such as Rotary, Lions, etc.) continues to function to the present day, but with very different roles within the broader class. Of the people listed in the 1982 *Who's Who in the World*, the author's own counting so far has resulted in an estimate of about 10 per cent listed as members of one of these three networks. Since some nationalities such as the British do not identify themselves as such (in contrast to Americans), the real percentage must be higher; but then, the significance of membership cannot be established on the basis of numbers only.

7 See *NRC-Handelsblad*, 4 December 1993; also *Le Monde Diplomatique*, February 1985.

8 See *Newsweek*, 7 July 1995 and *Business Week*, 6 March 1995, respectively.

Part III

Transformation, innovation and emancipation in global political and civil society

The objective of Part II is to develop methods and approaches to explore the meaning of transformation and innovation in terms of potentials for emancipation and democratisation associated with various social forces in global political and civil society. Political and civil society is defined broadly here to include the state, political and civic associations, the institutions of social and economic life, strategic relations and civilisational patterns.

Karl Polanyi's idea of the 'double movement' is a link between Parts II and III of this book and it enables us to see that some social forces that the authors are analysing may be far from benign – as was the case with the right-wing extremism and authoritarianism of the 1930s that produced new forms of state and helped to produce the increasingly violent conditions for the outbreak of the Second World War. Part of the problem of reconstructing world order involves the assessment of the nature, extension and depth of such forces operating locally and globally, and their potentials for democratisation or reaction. Some of the thrust of social movements of both right and left involves the way that they attempt – often in contradictory ways – to challenge the 'common sense' of a dominant set of social and political forces. That is, some subordinate forces or social classes seek emancipation in part through a challenge to not only the ideology but also the knowledge-forms representative of dominant forces. By analogy, each chapter critiques a certain type of theoretical-practical orthodoxy: Mark Rupert that of corporate liberal internationalism; Fantu Cheru, the orthodoxy of the Bretton Woods financial organisations' neo-classical approach to Third World development; Randolph Persaud, of a new racist realism of the right; Spike Peterson, of dominant 'masculinist' forms of representation and the politics and forms of state they embody.

Also, by investigating real forces at work both from 'below' and 'above' in a global hierarchy of social forces, social relations and forms of state, some of these chapters may provide not only substantive analysis but also a method for analysing other cases. For example, the chapters by Rupert and Cheru reflect not only their personal involvement in and knowledge of emancipatory struggles at the grass-roots level, but also they use an ethnographic element in their methodology to identify sites of innovation and transformation.

Indeed, to fully grasp the movement of social forces, a global perspective is needed, and one that looks at the movement of such forces in a dialectical way. Moreover, innovation may or may not imply emancipation. Thus some of the authors demonstrate that 'multilateralism from above' can be innovative in a number of ways, but how, at the same time, it may be far from democratic in nature. For example, Rupert highlights innovations associated with efforts to reinforce the dominance of corporate elites through the discourses, design and implementation of NAFTA in the USA. Cheru deconstructs and criticises neo-classical political economy discourses associated with the World Bank and IMF. These are now being reshaped to stress 'democratisation' in the era of globalisation. Cheru shows the hollowness of the association of the free market and formal democracy in Africa. Indeed he demonstrates its irrelevance to the majority of peasants and the urban poor.

By contrast, both Rupert and Cheru mainly explore political innovations 'from below', such as the populist challenges from right and left to elite perspectives in the NAFTA debate in the USA and the 'silent' revolution of peasants and urban poor in Africa. Rupert's analysis suggests that global restructuring may be creating conditions that might be favourable for reconstructions of 'popular common sense'. In this context, any progressive political movement must define itself not only in terms of opposition to corporate power and neo-liberalism, but also it must distinguish its democratising conceptions from reactionary visions such as the individualism-nationalism of the populist right in the USA.

Cheru's essay documents the development of new, local tools of transformation by ordinary Africans. Written from a perspective sympathetic to the plight of peasants and urban marginals, Cheru offers examples of the innovatory creativity of Africans in resisting the predatory state and externally validated or imposed development paradigms. Moreover, as Cheru points out, in doing so, peasants are offering indigenous knowledge as an alternative form of moral and ethical political economy. Using the phrase of James C. Scott, Cheru suggests that 'every day forms of resistance', independent of traditional political parties, and outside the state, appear related to a critical theory approach to social transformation. Indeed Cheru stresses that it is vital that the agenda for study in International Relations include movements and innovations from subordinate positions in the global social hierarchy in order to fully understand structural change and the future potential for democratic forces.

Randolph Persaud's chapter explores some of the constraints and tensions in the emerging world order. The author suggests that Frantz Fanon's innovative conception of the racial character of colonialism remains pertinent today in a changing context of Third World subordination. Although many of Fanon's ideas were flawed, he was able to point to 'constitutive antagonisms' of global power relations: antagonisms found in the interrelationships between civilisation, exploitation and violence in the reproduction of the colonial world order. For Fanon, exploitation had not only a racial and a class dimension, but it also encompassed civilisational struggles and social relations that had a spatial and dichotomising quality. Applied to contemporary global politics, Fanon's ideas point to ways that race may merge with the contradictions generated by globalisation in a post-colonial era so as to shape the national security conceptions and policies of the West. Persaud concludes, with reference to examples of recent realist political discourse: 'The proximate concerns about too many migrants (and refugees), combined with the larger fears of civilisational erosion, have already given rise to a siege mentality type of politics in the West. If this new attempt at a racio-civilisational dominance is left unchallenged, a Manichaean world order is not that unthinkable.'

Finally, Spike Peterson also shows that emancipation, at least when defined in terms of an approximation of gender equality, is far from being achieved in any known society. Her chapter focuses upon gender and emancipation as a process or form of ideological and political struggle. For Peterson, the power of masculinity is closely connected to the early origins, history and contemporary development of the state. She argues that 'masculinist' representations and understandings have become part of the common sense and *longue durée* of state formation – that is, she offers a feminist interpretation of the history of the state that stresses its essentially patriarchal nature. Her analysis seeks to expose how the dichotomy of masculine-feminine fuels multiple forms of oppression. Today, however, partly as a result of the structural development of the feminist movements, and in the context of global socio-economic and cultural restructuring, she detects a crisis in the social reproduction of masculinity. This can be considered part of a more general global crisis of modernity. It is perhaps a key element in the contemporary ontological shift. Gender is becoming progressively more 'visible' as a dimension of social relations in ways that may open new avenues for democratic change.

The relationship between democratic change and the redefinition of civil society forms the bridge to Part IV. Part IV consists of a number of contrasting reflections on the questions, problems and forces that have shaped, and will help to shape, the emerging world order in the next millennium.

Mark Rupert

Drawing on the theoretical resources of Gramsci and of the historical materialist tradition, Robert Cox has defined a vision of global politics in which social forces, states and world orders are seen as organically related aspects of social reality, historically produced through processes in which material social relations and social self-understandings are together deeply implicated.

Viewing the world through the lenses of Cox's Vichian historical materialism (1981: 132–59, 171), it becomes possible to interpret relations and processes obscured from (and by) more mainstream state-centric visions of International Relations and International Political Economy. Taking the stance of a critical theorist, Cox has challenged us to look for and make explicit the political possibilities latent in the social relations and dynamics of the present.

In the spirit of this challenge, I will suggest that changes are underway in the nexus of relations linking the United States to the global political economy, changes which present possibilities for significant political reconstruction. The extent to which any of these possibilities are realised depends upon struggles in which social self-understandings and ideologies of globalisation will play a crucial role. An important prelude to my more substantive discussion, then, is a brief digression on the importance of popular 'common sense' for an historical materialism of this kind.

Historical materialism: from Marx to Gramsci

To me, the primary significance of historical materialism is that it offers critical resources for the dereification of capitalism and its various forms of appearance (Rupert, 1995a: ch. 2). On this view, commodification of social life, and especially commodification of labour, are not natural, necessary, universal or absolute; nor, therefore, is the separation of the political from the economic which is presupposed by the capitalist wage relation. Paul Thomas argues that the complex of social relations associated with capitalism – including the modern state – entails an 'alien politics' which profoundly limits possibilities for communal self-determination: 'The thoroughgoing denial of democracy in civil society, where the chief activities of daily life most immediately take place, is the ongoing, institutionalised counterpart to the concentration, distillation and fusion of all features of common action and collective concern within the state' (1994: xii; see also Wood, 1995). Critiques such as these imply that the abstraction of politics from the economy and the naturalisation of a civil society of abstract individuals are historical conditions which are open to question and hence potentially to transformation. This transformation would necessarily entail (but not necessarily be limited to) the repoliticisation and democratisation of the economy and of civil society, such that they cease to be pseudo-objective and apparently natural conditions which confront isolated individuals as an ineluctable external 'reality'. Rather, they would become sites for – and objects of – reflective dialogue and contestation, mutable aspects of a broad process of social self-determination, explicitly political.

Marx suggested that such a transformation might emerge out of the confluence of capitalism's endemic crisis tendencies, the polarisation of its class structure and the relative immiseration of the proletariat and, most importantly, the emergence of the latter as a collective agent through the realisation of its socially productive power, heretofore developed in distorted and self-limiting form under the conditions of concentrated capitalist production (Marx, 1977). Accepting in broad outline Marx's analysis of the structure and dynamics of capitalism, Gramsci (1971: 201–2) was unwilling to embrace the more mechanical and economistic interpretations of Marx then circulating in the international socialist movement.

It may be ruled out that immediate economic crises of themselves produce fundamental historical events; they can simply create a terrain more favourable to the dissemination of certain modes of thought, and certain ways of posing and resolving questions involving the entire subsequent development of national [and transnational] life. (Gramsci, 1971: 184)

Progressive social change would not automatically follow in train behind economic developments, but must instead be produced by historically situated social agents whose actions are enabled and constrained by their social self-understandings (1971: 164–5, 326, 375–7, 420). How, indeed whether, such change occurs depends upon struggles to delimit or expand the horizons of these social self-understandings. Thus, for Gramsci, popular 'common sense' becomes a critical terrain of political struggle (1971: 323–34, 419–25). His theorisation of a social politics of ideological struggle – which he called 'war of position' to distinguish it from a Bolshevik strategy of frontal assault on the state (1971: 229–39,

242–3) – contributed to the historical materialist project of de-reifying capitalist social relations (including state-based conceptions of politics) and constructing an alternative – more enabling, participatory, democratic – social order out of the historical conditions of capitalism.

For Gramsci, popular common sense could become a ground of struggle because it is not univocal and coherent, but an amalgam of historically effective ideologies, scientific doctrines and social mythologies. This historical 'sedimentation' of popular common sense 'is not something rigid and immobile, but is continually transforming itself, enriching itself with scientific ideas and with philosophical opinions which have entered ordinary life. [It] is the folklore of philosophy' (1971: 326). As such, it is 'fragmentary, incoherent and inconsequential, in conformity with the social and cultural position of those masses whose philosophy it is' (1971: 419). Gramsci's project thus entailed addressing popular common sense, making explicit the tensions and contradictions within it as well as the socio-political consequences of these, in order to enable critical social analysis and transformative political practice. 'First of all,' Gramsci says of the philosophy of *praxis*, 'it must be a criticism of "common sense" basing itself initially, however, on common sense in order to demonstrate that "everyone" is a philosopher and that it is not a question of introducing from scratch a scientific form of thought into everyone's individual life, but of renovating and making "critical" an already existing activity' (1971: 330–1). At the core of Gramsci's project, then, was a critical pedagogy which took as its starting point the tensions and possibilities latent within popular common sense.

Contested common sense in the United States

With its dual commitments to individual rights and liberties on the one hand – including pre-eminently the right to private property – and, on the other, to popular sovereignty and self-government, liberalism has historically been a key element of popular common sense in the United States (Arblaster, 1984: 75–9, 196–202, 309–32; Augelli and Murphy, 1988: 35–57). In such an historical context, declarations of universal liberty, fundamental equality and democracy are potentially subversive in so far as these aspirations represent unfulfilled promises of liberal capitalism, promises which could not be fulfilled without endangering the class relations which are at the core of capitalism (e.g., by acknowledging that the economy entails intrinsically political relations, and that social self-governance therefore requires democratisation of social relations previously understood in terms of private property). Thus within popular common sense divergent interpretations of the liberal legacy may be brought into explicit conflict, and challenges to the predominant understandings of liberalism – and to the prevailing organisation of society – may be mounted.

Such ideological struggles have played an important role in the construction and reconstruction of American capitalism and the global hegemony based upon it. In the first half of the twentieth century, the social organisation of production was being reconstructed in the manufacturing heart of the US economy: craft-based production was being supplanted by Fordist mass production, and new relations of power were being constructed and contested in the workplace. Fordism entailed increased mechanisation of the labour process and the potential for heightened capitalist control over the pace and intensity of work. Emerging from a decades-long process of political struggle, the institutionalisation of this system of mass production was associated with a socio-political regime which elicited – albeit imperfectly and inconsistently – the consent of industrial workers to the expanding social powers of capital. This process entailed bouts of explicit class conflict during which the socio-political conditions of liberal capitalism were opened to potential challenge: responding to liberal capitalism's valorisation of individual rights, and especially the right of private property, industrial workers counterpoised conceptions of 'industrial democracy' and collective participation in work life in order to legitimate their new and embattled industrial unions. In the post-war context of Cold War fears and access to an unprecedented affluence (rising real wages secured for unionised industrial workers through pattern bargaining, the linking of wages to productivity growth, cost of living adjustments (COLAs), etc.), such challenges were contained within the bounds of a vision of liberal capitalism as the social system best able to secure – on a global basis, and with the active collaboration of 'free trade unions' – individual rights and liberties and a more generalised prosperity. On the basis of their participation in this hegemonic world vision and their acceptance of its implied commitment to the prioritisation of individual rights over collective self-determination, industrial unions were accepted by the state and capital as junior partners in the post-war project of reconstructing a liberal capitalist world order (Rupert, 1995a: chs. 4–7).

In the last decade of the twentieth century this hegemony is transforming itself. The Cold War was officially pronounced to be over as the Soviet Union disintegrated: anti-communism could no longer serve as a crucial ingredient in the ideological cement which bound together the post-war historic bloc. Further, the post-war prosperity which US industrial labour had enjoyed as a result of its participation in the hegemonic bloc is evaporating. Unions – the central institutions of 'industrial democracy' in the United States – have been openly attacked by the state and capital, memberships are in long-term decline, and real wages have been effectively reduced even as productivity growth rebounded during the 1980s (Rupert, 1995a: 179). With the mutation of the post-war historic bloc such that transnational financial and industrial capital are increasingly predominant and industrial labour within the United States is no longer a relatively privileged junior partner, socio-political relations and popular ideologies which once seemed firmly grounded are now increasingly up for grabs. We might expect the latent tension between capitalism and democracy to be addressed all the more effectively in an environment characterised by long-term tendencies towards transnational production, corporate 'restructuring', subcontracting and outsourcing, plant closings and layoffs, concessionary bargaining and union-busting, declining real wages, widening and deepening poverty, intense economic uncertainty and real fear among average Americans, all of which has in recent years been juxtaposed to resurgent corporate profits and happy days on Wall Street (Rupert, 1995a: ch. 8).

Globalisation and contested common sense in the United States

I want to suggest now that the hegemonic liberal narrative of globalisation is increasingly being contested from at least two distinct positions – one which might be described as the cosmopolitan, democratically oriented left (a position I will call 'progressive'), and another – the nationalistic/individualistic far-right – and that these contests over popular common sense have potentially important implications for the nexus of relations linking the United States with the global political economy. In the remainder of this chapter, I will sketch what I take to be the defining features of each of these perspectives, and draw out the different possible worlds towards which each points.

The contested meanings of globalisation in the United States have surfaced most explicitly in the intense public discussions surrounding recent agreements fostering further international liberalisation, especially the North American Free Trade Agreement (NAFTA). I want to suggest that NAFTA is important not just as an agreement to create a continental free trade area, but as an occasion for political argument in which the central tension of liberal capitalism – long submerged beneath the terms of the post-war hegemonic order – was once again represented in public discourse as an open question and a terrain of active socio-political struggle.[1]

A powerful phalanx of social forces has arrayed itself behind the agenda of intensified market-led globalisation: academic economists, major corporations and corporate associations such as the Business Roundtable, and the mainstream press all vigorously supported NAFTA as part of a larger project of continuing global liberalisation (Rupert, 1995b: 664–9). There were two primary themes which consistently emerged from their pro-NAFTA representations. First, it was claimed that NAFTA would encourage greater specialisation according to comparative advantage, that this specialisation along with intensified continental competition and greater economies of scale would result in significant efficiency gains, and that in these ways NAFTA would produce lower prices for consumers and, in the long run, more jobs and higher incomes continent-wide. These economic benefits were expected to be relatively greater for the smaller Mexican economy and more modest for the larger American (see e.g., Dornbusch, 1991; Hufbauer and Schott, 1993–4; Krugman, 1993). Second, influential newspapers such as the *New York Times* (17 November 1993) and the *Washington Post* (16 November 1993) editorialised in favour of the pact on the grounds that failure to enact it would represent not just a lost opportunity but a (potentially catastrophic) US abdication of its historic role as promoter of international liberalisation, peace and prosperity, a giant step backward into the era of isolationism and protectionism. Generally portrayed as promising economic benefits to the American public and serving the national interest by sustaining a more open and liberal world, NAFTA received predominantly favourable press coverage and was editorially endorsed by numerous papers large and small (Rupert, 1995b: 667, 687 n. 11). Sandra Masur, of Eastman Kodak and the Business Roundtable, explained that the US corporate community supported the pact for the immediate business opportunities it would present, but also as part of a larger global agenda: 'The companies of the Roundtable are seeking across-the-board liberalisation of trade in goods, services and investment' (Masur, 1991: 102). This perspective was aggressively promoted to the public and to Congress by major corporate supporters and lobbies such as USA*NAFTA (Rupert, 1995b: 668–9).

Towards transnational democratisation: progressive critiques of the liberal global agenda

The agenda of increasing liberalisation of trade and investment and the global integration of the US economy has not gone unopposed, however. NAFTA in particular prompted vigorous opposition from a constellation of labour unions, consumer groups, environmentalists and citizen activists who represented the trade pact as augmenting the power of multinational capital relative to workers, unions, local communities and citizens more generally. Beginning to frame an alternative vision of global political economy based on democratic self-determination and transnational linkages among working people and citizens – rather than allowing unfettered markets and the criterion of private profit to determine social outcomes – they counterposed the common sense value of 'democracy' to liberalism's traditional valorisation of private property. These progressive NAFTA opponents thus aimed at a central tension in liberal common sense in order to attempt to develop an alternative political agenda to that of corporate capital.

Left-progressive critics found common ground not in a strategy of protectionism and closure, but in a vision of a more participatory global order and a strategy of 'fair trade' – the negotiation of common labour, health and safety, environmental and social standards which would prevent a race towards the lowest common denominator ('downward harmonisation'), enforced by intensified market competition. Unionists believed that NAFTA would enable corporate employers to use enhanced capital mobility and transcontinental competition ('whipsawing') between countries, plants and workers to undermine actual or potential solidarity among workers and communities, and to intensify exploitation throughout the continent (AFL-CIO, 1991; UAW, 1992; Moody and McGinn, 1992). While acknowledging that closer economic ties with Mexico were likely whether NAFTA was approved or not, AFL-CIO officials argued that it was 'neither inevitable nor desirable' that 'economic integration [be] based on an international division of labour in which Mexico supplies cheap labour and lax enforcement of health, safety and environmental standards, the United States supplies the consumer market, multinational corporations derive the profit, and US workers face further wage cuts and loss of their jobs' (Friedman, 1992: 27).

Fears of a continental, hemispheric or global political economy dominated by the institutionalised power of corporate capital brought NAFTA's labour critics together with environmental activists, consumer advocates and others (e.g., Cavanagh *et al.*, 1992; McGaughey, 1992; Nader *et al.*, 1993). Anti-NAFTA coalitions formed which stressed the potential degradation of environmental, health and safety, and consumer protection standards, in addition to the pact's likely effects upon labour. Progressive critics feared that such protections might be directly attacked under the pact as non-tariff barriers to trade. Further, they warned of the indirect effects which the treaty would have upon the ability of communities and political jurisdictions to maintain regulatory standards. In the absence of strong institutionalised protections, the pact could facilitate 'social dumping' in which the exploitation of Mexican workers, communities and their environment would enable MNCs producing in Mexico to undercut producers based in the United States and Canada who are subject to more effective forms of social regulation. In this way, competitive pressure would be brought to bear upon the ability of citizens and communities to regulate producers anywhere within the free trade zone. In full page advertisements which ran in leading newspapers, a group of twenty-five environmental and citizen activist groups denounced NAFTA as a scheme to empower and enrich corporate capital at the expense of workers, citizens and their capacity for democratic self-determination:

Promoted as a boon to all of us, the true purpose of NAFTA is to help large corporations increase their profits. NAFTA does this by undermining laws and standards (in the US, Canada and Mexico) that inhibit uncontrolled corporate freedoms. Freedom to circumvent democratically created environmental, health and safety laws. Freedom to set poor working conditions and keep wages low . . . NAFTA will seriously stifle representative democracy by making local, state or national laws *subject to an unelected NAFTA bureaucracy that citizens cannot control.* (*New York Times*, 15 November 1993)

Some progressives framed the basic issue directly and explicitly in terms of democratisation. In the words of John Cavanagh, 'The key to genuine democracy in this decade will be the struggle by communities and citizens' organisations to control their own destinies, to take control of their own lands and natural resources, to collectively make the decisions that affect their futures. The free trade agreements that are currently on the table appropriate these decisions and toss them to the private sector' (Cavanagh *et al.*, 1992: 6–7). The journalist William Greider argued that to achieve meaningful democracy in the US will require a reorientation of popular thinking in which neither xenophobic nationalism nor a globalism based upon the individualistic ideology of market competition will suffice. Instead, he argued, the future of domestic democracy depends upon an internationalist world view directly addressing relations of global political-economic inequality and domination:

For ordinary Americans, traditionally independent and insular, the challenge requires them to think anew their place in the world. The only plausible way that citizens can defend themselves and their nation against the forces of globalisation is to link their own interests co-operatively with the interests of other peoples in other nations – that is, with foreigners who are competitors for the jobs and production but who are also victimised by the system. Americans will have to create new democratic alliances across national borders with the less prosperous people caught in the same dilemma. Together, they have to impose new political standards on multinational enterprises and on their own governments. (Greider, 1993: 196)

Greider's prescription strikes me as quite remarkable in so far as it crystallises some of the themes more or less explicit in various progressive critiques of economic liberalisation and seems to resonate with the Gramscian historical materialism sketched above: he directly addresses popular common sense and calls for the de-reification of conventional boundaries separating politics/economics, state/society and domestic/international, in order to negotiate a more democratic global economy. And he was not alone in constructing this kind of strategic perspective (Brecher, *et al.* 1993; Browne and Sims, 1993; Cavanagh *et al.*, 1992; McGaughey, 1992; Moody and McGinn, 1992; Nader *et al.*, 1993).

Defending individualism and American exceptionalism: far-right critiques of globalisation

Opposition to NAFTA was not univocal, however. There were sectors of the anti-NAFTA movement which explicitly rejected free trade in favour of protectionism, and which continue to organise against globalisation. These groups, who sometimes identify themselves as 'Patriots', are often dismissively labelled in the mainstream media as 'paranoids' and 'loonies', as if their perspective on politics and globalisation might be explained away by some shared psychological defects. On the contrary, I want to suggest that far-right resistance to globalisation is understandable as a response to changing socio-economic circumstances, a response which draws upon the cognitive resources available in popular common sense to understand a complex and changing world in a way which maintains a stable identity. Far-right anti-globalists tap the most individualistic strains of American common sense in order to construct an image of American exceptionalism, a quasi-religious faith in the superior wisdom of the original US Constitution and of the founding fathers as protectors of God-given individual liberties. This faith has led a segment of the American public to interpret globalisation as an alien tyranny engulfing the United States through a treacherous conspiracy and relentlessly eroding individual rights and liberties. On this view, globalisation is profoundly threatening, and acts of resistance ranging from ideological struggle to mass violence may be justified in these terms. In a context where working people and large segments of what used to be thought of as the 'middle class' are experiencing chronic socio-economic degradation unprecedented in post-war experience, and in which formerly hegemonic ideologies increasingly appear threadbare, reconstructions of popular common sense which seem to explain a reality otherwise seemingly inscrutable, and which point towards urgent political action, potentially pose far more serious socio-political issues than the widespread image of ridiculous dementia suggests.

Viewing the world from within the limits of a rigidly individualistic ontology, the organic intellectuals of the far right suggest that 'there are really only two theories of history. Either things happen by accident, neither planned nor caused by anybody, or they happen because they *are* planned and somebody causes them to happen' (Abraham, 1985: 9). As a consequence of this world view, they are unable to envision, explain or critique the interrelated structures and processes which left-progressives see at work in the nexus between the United States and the global economy; such explanations are dismissively equated with belief in 'mysterious and unexplainable tides of history' (1985: 9). The only apparent alternatives, then, are a view of history as essentially random, accidental, a string of implausible coincidences, or a view which looks for 'cause and effect' in terms of the purposeful – and morally significant – actions of individuals and groups. In this way, conspiracy theory and its Manichean construction of the world elevates itself to the status of scientific analysis of cause and effect (1985: 7–16; also North, 1985: x–xi; Robertson, 1991: 8–9).

Far-right ideology generally takes it as axiomatic that the American system of government is properly understood as a *republic* and not as a democracy: the latter is seen as dangerous insofar as it subjects individual rights and liberties to the will of the community. As one subscriber to a Patriot listserv (an electronic mailing list that serves a certain audience) wrote, 'Democracy is . . . the foundation of communism' (USA-Forever, 16 June 1995; see also Welch, 1986). The republican system of government which the US founding fathers designed to protect individual rights and the economic liberty which flourishes in such a context – i.e., strictly limited government and the 'free enterprise system' – are divinely inspired and the best possible social arrangement (Abraham, 1985: 31, 84; McManus, 1995; 91, 99–100; North, 1985: x–xi, 246–9; Robertson, 1991: 59, 203–5, 239–47). If something is terribly wrong in America it can't be due to flaws intrinsic to the social system, it must be that somebody somewhere is corrupting our political legacy.[2] John F. McManus, president of the John Birch Society – long the most influential source of conspiracy doctrine on the far right (see Mintz, 1985: ch. 7; Durham, 1995) – exemplifies this kind of reasoning and points towards 'treasonous' and 'satanically inspired' forces as the cause of America's ills (1995: 12, 70; see also Robertson, 1991: 9):

most Americans know something is eating away at the foundations of this great nation. Unemployment, national and personal indebtedness, economic slowdown, loss of faith, declining national stature, a vaguely defined 'new world order,' broken families, and much more have stimulated worries from coast to coast . . . Sadly, we witness the presence of powerful forces working to destroy the marvellous foundations given us by farseeing and noble men 200 years ago. (McManus, 1995: ix–x)

The basic conspiracy theory which circulates widely on the far right holds that cliques of evil individuals have been scheming to subjugate and exploit the world at least since 1776, when Adam Weisshaupt, a Bavarian scholar, is alleged to have formed a secret society known as the Illuminati. Plotting to 'overthrow . . . civil governments, the church, and private property' (Robertson, 1991: 67) and to supplant these institutions with their own power and control, the Illuminati infiltrated European Freemasonry in order to insinuate themselves into elite networks of social power. This sect of Illuminated Freemasons, including the fabulously wealthy Rothschild family, are said to have been associated with the French Revolution and the Terror, and subsequently to have provided the model – and the funding – for the Marxist-Bolshevik conspiracy for global domination. 'All Karl Marx really did was to update and codify the very same revolutionary plans and principles set down seventy years earlier by Adam Weisshaupt . . .' (Abraham, 1985: 41, 91; and Robertson, 1991: 67–71, 115, 180–5, 258). Far-right intellectuals are able to assimilate Marxism into a global elite conspiracy because they do not recognise meaningful distinctions between political ideologies of 'left' and 'right'; rather, they see the world in terms of a continuum which stretches from complete and anarchic individual liberty on one end to total government domination on the other. The most desirable point on the spectrum is the 'Constitutional Republic', that is, just enough government to avoid the extremes of anarchy but not enough to destroy individual liberty or to constrain the 'free market'. Monarchy, socialism, fascism and elite-dominated and government-supported cartel capitalism are not seen as significantly different, but as forms of the same anti-individualistic monopoly of power (Abraham, 1985: 32; Perloff, 1988: 44–6; Robertson, 1991: 71, 183).

So it is not inconsistent for far-right intellectuals to claim that international bankers and the super-rich are also part of the conspiracy to undermine individual liberties and their republican-free market sanctum. And indeed the second major tentacle of the conspiracy involves the rise of a clique of international bankers, whose almost unfathomable wealth allows them to grant or deny credit to governments, manipulate economies, extract super-profits and exercise world-historical power. Advancing the conspiratorial design first laid out by the Illuminati, the Rothschilds, Rockefellers, Morgans and their agents are said to have institutionalised their financial powers through the creation of a US central bank in order to control the money supply and directly manipulate the macro-economy, and to facilitate the creation of credit-money and the expansion of private and public debt. They were the driving force behind the establishment of an income tax through which taxpayers' income might be extracted to pay for public debt and fill the coffers of the mega-bankers. And they are alleged to have bankrolled the Bolshevik revolution, providing an 'enemy' against which the governments of the West would have to defend themselves, further deepening public debt, expanding the scope of centralised government activity and laying the basis for comprehensive social control by the financial elite (Abraham, 1985: 43–87; Perloff, 1988: 19–48; Robertson, 1991: 61, 65, 71–3, 117–43).

The third major tentacle of the conspiracy has involved the fostering of an international 'establishment' which would serve as the basis for a 'new world order', the comprehensive political unification and socialisation of the world under the domination of the elite conspirators, 'a one-world government that scorns individuality, personality, nationhood, and even private property' (Robertson, 1991: 156). In 1891, the Rothschilds and Cecil Rhodes allegedly established the Round Table – 'a semi-secret internationalist group headquartered in London' (Perloff, 1988: 36) – as a vehicle for promoting their global agenda. The Round Table then spawned both the Royal Institute of International Affairs in Britain and the Council on Foreign Relations (CFR) in the United States. The CFR was putatively dominated by the American members of the Round Table group and associates of the Rothschilds such as J. P. Morgan – and, later on, by the Rockefellers. This international establishment has had members in influential posts in government, business, law, journalism and academia and has quietly but profoundly influenced the policies of the world's most powerful states. In the aftermath of the Second World War, they promoted the United Nations, the Bretton Woods system, the Marshall Plan, NATO, the entire institutional infrastructure of post-war world order. More recently, the CFR has worked in parallel with the Trilateral Commission and the Bilderberg Group towards the globalist agenda (Abraham, 1985: 89–108; McManus, 1995: 1–24, 61–3, 81–2; Perloff, 1988: 3–38, 71–4, 81–6; Robertson, 1991: 33–58, 65–7, 95–115). McManus makes it clear how some Americans may perceive that individual liberty requires resistance to this global agenda, and thus how far-right ideology fuses individualism with nationalism:

The world government sought by the architects of this new world order would mean an end to the nation we inherited, and the destruction of the greatest experiment in human liberty in the history of mankind. World government would also establish socialism in place of the free market system, a certain route to conversion of this nation into another Third World dead-end . . .The stakes are nothing short of a future marked by national independence and personal liberty. (McManus, 1995: 70, 103)

Preserving an individualistic, capitalist, Christian United States in the face of an insidious transnational threat is the necessary condition for avoiding the destruction of individual liberty, limited government, free enterprise and religious freedom, and their replacement by the unlimited power of global monopoly-socialism and its Godless humanism. Viewed from this kind of perspective, the significance of a free trade agreement such as NAFTA far exceeds its economic costs or benefits, as the following statements demonstrate:

NAFTA creates an economic union among Mexico, Canada and the US, a step paving the way for political union – a favoured route to world government. Predictably, one after another of the Insiders' big guns fired off salvos urging its passage. (McManus, 1995: 85)

Today, it is obvious that NAFTA is part of the overall plan for the 'New World Order' . . . Today, the operating plan is a step-by-step progression to the final goal of ownership and control of all natural resources and every square inch of land and everything on it by a consortium of international supercapitalists: a gigantic holding company, a super-Bilderberg Society of mega-plutocrats. (Carto, 1993: 22)

Variants of this conspiracy narrative circulate within and among the following communities: the John Birch Society (claims 40,000–60,000 members); the Liberty Lobby and readers of its publication, *The Spotlight* (claims a circulation of 120,000); the Patriot/Militia/Gun-Rights/anti-Tax/anti-Environmental/anti-Abortion movements; Neo-Nazi and affiliated white supremacy groups; Pat Robertson's Christian Coalition (claims 1 million members, 1.8 million adherents on its mailing list, and Robertson's publisher claims about 500,000 copies of *New World Order* in print); and the presidential campaign of Pat Buchanan. Chip Berlet (1995) estimates that there may be as many as 5 million persons in the United States who are influenced by far-right movements and their conspiratorial anti-government and anti-globalist ideology. And the worldview of right-wing populism is making inroads into mainstream politics through the growing influence of Pat Robertson's Christian Coalition (Durham, 1995; Lind, 1995), members of the Republican Congressional majority who are sympathetic with far-right ideology (Stern, 1996: 128, 212–14) and Pat Buchanan's right-populist presidential campaign (Bennett, 1995). Buchanan has described NAFTA and globalisation in terms of the narrative of elite perfidy and the destruction of national identity and individual liberty:

Though advertised as 'free trade', [NAFTA] is anti-freedom, 1,200 pages of rules, regulations, laws, fines, commissions . . . setting up no fewer than 49 new bureaucracies . . . it is part of a skeletal structure for world government. (Buchanan, 1993)

Real power in America belongs to the Manhattan Money Power, the one power to which neither party is any longer able to say 'No!' [Treasury Secretary Robert] Rubin said, 'There must be a broad understanding that we really and truly are in a new world where we are dependent on other nations in ways that we never were before.' That is the authentic voice of Goldman Sachs, and regrettably, of our own Republican elites. They are saying, all of them, that America's sovereignty, independence and liberty are things of the past . . . We must all accept our dependency on the New World Order . . . But we never voted our sovereignty away. If it is gone, they sold us out; they traded it away, without our permission. (Buchanan, 1995)

To protect individual liberty and enhance national competitiveness, Buchanan (1993) called for 'free markets at home', protected by a high tariff wall, and a minimal 'Night Watchman State', a golden age recipe he represents as the historic 'foundation of American prosperity'.

Conclusion: popular common sense and alternative possible worlds

I contend that popular common sense in the United States is currently being contested and that these struggles have important potential implications for the relation of the United States to the global economy. The world view of neo-liberal internationalism – in which states and corporations create the rules for global economic integration – is facing challenges which emphasise different aspects of popular common sense in order to envision alternative possible worlds. Drawing on the democratic strains of popular common sense, what I have called the left-progressive position would construct a world in which the global economy is explicitly politicised, corporate power is challenged by transnational coalitions of popular forces, and a framework of democratically developed and enacted common standards provides some social accountability for global economic actors.

The anti-globalist position of the far right, on the other hand, envisions a world in which Americans are uniquely privileged, inheritors of a divinely inspired socio-political order which must at all costs be defended against external intrusions and internal subversion. This latter vision also entails a challenge to corporate power, but it implicitly constructs this challenge from within the bounds of capitalism's structural separation of politics and economics. Unable to understand capitalism in terms of historical structures and the progressive possibilities they may entail, the far right offers instead a reactionary vision which implies a reversal of processes of capital concentration and the transnational socialisation of production which have been central to the historical development of capitalism. In so far as it seeks to preserve capitalism while reversing its central processes, we might anticipate the ongoing frustration of the reactionary vision, and an attendant intensification of scapegoating and hostility towards those seen as outside of, different or dissenting from its vision of national identity.

I have no way of knowing whether either of these ideologies of globalisation will be able to sustain a serious challenge to the orthodoxy of neoliberal internationalism, but I would suggest that the restructuring of the post-war order is creating conditions which are increasingly favourable for reconstructions of popular common sense. In this more fluid context, it will be important for a progressive political movement to define itself not only in terms of its opposition to corporate power and neo-liberal internationalism, but also clearly and explicitly to distinguish its democratising vision from the reactionary individualism-nationalism of the populist right.

NOTES

1 I make no claims to 'objectivity' here. For several months during 1993 – the year that NAFTA was submitted for Congressional approval – I was active with the Fair Trade Coalition of Central New York. I remain sympathetic to the position of progressive NAFTA opponents.
2 While some variants of this conspiracy narrative are explicitly racist or anti-Semitic, others (e.g., Abraham, Robertson, John Birch Society) have attempted to distance themselves from overt anti-Semitism (on Robertson's attempt, see Lind, 1995).

10 The silent revolution and the weapons of the weak: transformation and innovation from below

Fantu Cheru

In the arcane and isolated world of academia, the 'everyday forms of resistance' of ordinary poor people across the globe rarely attract the attention of researchers or funding agencies until these local level struggles break out into spasms of violence that could threaten the *status quo*.[1] The conventional view is that everyday resistance represents trivial coping mechanisms that are non-political and these merit no serious investigation. This view completely misses the point. The consequences of such silent resistance on the policy decisions of governments may not always be visible on the surface and one must carefully search for their long-term effects. Nevertheless, like an army of termites eating away the wooden structure of a house inch by inch, silent resistance by millions of poor peasants can have the same result, eroding the foundations of a political system – perhaps even making for a 'silent revolution'.

Thus this chapter highlights various forms of resistance with reference to a number of African cases. Indeed, I hope to provide an account of both innovation and transformation 'from below' as seen and practised by marginalised groups in rural Africa. Although peasants in Africa have had no formal training in International Relations, they understand from experience how historical forces are constituted and how the prevailing global strategy of the Group of Seven nations and the dominant international financial institutions (e.g., World Bank and IMF) is based on the cold-blooded abandonment of large numbers of humanity. Peasants also understand how such forces might be changed, that is, by relying on 'hidden' forms of everyday resistance. In this context, peasants are raising innovative issues of moral or ethical political economy.

Indeed these forms of resistance, independent of traditional political parties, and outside the state, appear related to a critical theory approach to social transformation. Indeed it is vital that the agenda for study in International Relations focuses on a wider range of dimensions of transformation and innovation, including those that come from 'below', from subordinate positions in the global social hierarchy. This agenda should also involve the development of institutions which can express grass-roots democratic concerns and deal with the kinds of community and global problems that can no longer be ignored.

A peasant perspective on myths of development

It is a well-known fact that the post-independence history of Africa is replete with examples of broken promises and unfulfilled dreams. The policies of both colonial and post-independence governments have had disastrous effects on the silent majority of African peasants and landless labourers (Leys, 1974; Watts, 1983; Palmer and Parsons, 1977; Beckman, 1981). Peasants, by and large, have been treated with less respect than that accorded to cattle. The granting of formal political independence to African countries brought neither participation nor accountability to local structures (Hyden, 1983; Coulson, 1980).

The post-independence development model has, in more ways, been very similar to the colonial development model which stifled peasant autonomy and production (see the chapter by Randolph Persaud on Fanon). Rural development policy has, by and large, been geared towards the production of primary commodities for the export market to pay for prestige development projects. Like their forebears in the colonial era, peasants are expected to provide the bulk of resources required for national development through increased taxes and by engaging themselves in primary resource production (Andrea and Beckman, 1987). Far from being a war against poverty, development has turned out to be a war against the poor and the natural resource base that sustains them.

In some African countries, the forced removal of peasants and pastoralists from fertile areas to marginal lands to make way for export plantations and game parks has been justified by the authorities on the grounds of advancing the 'national interest' (Cheru, 1992; Rosenblum and Williamson, 1987; Timberlake, 1986). In northern Nigeria, for example, the World Bank funded Talak-Mafara irrigation project near the Sokoto River resulted in the displacement of 60,000 peasants in a three-year period. In Ethiopia, the Awash Valley Development Authority irrigation projects, largely funded by donors, resulted in the eviction of thousands of nomadic Afars from their traditional pasture land in the Awash Valley (Zerihun, 1983). These projects also attracted absentee landowners and merchants to engage in extensive mechanisation in the adjacent areas which resulted in excessive land speculation, further compounding the problems of the local people. Similar strategies are still being followed faithfully in many countries at the expense of self-reliance, social justice, political autonomy and ecological harmony.

Independence has largely meant more power and privileges to the urban elites while the rural poor were left to fend for themselves. Elite bureaucrats and party loyalists, far removed from the reality of rural life, continue to dictate what peasants can and cannot produce, to whom they can sell and at what price (Bates, 1981; World Bank, 1989). What the peasants and the urban poor know and what they might need are of no concern to them (Chambers, 1989; Rahmato, 1989). This situation is compounded by insecure tenure systems, inadequate marketing, storage facilities and weak extension services in rural areas. The onset of subsequent droughts has simply compounded their vulnerable condition. Millions perish needlessly in far-away scattered villages through 'silent genocide' of hunger, lack of clean water and basic health services.

The peasants could demand neither better prices for their goods nor a fair distribution of land and other productive resources since they are effectively shut off from the decision-making process. Those who migrated to urban areas in search of scarce jobs live in slums under a constant threat of eviction, and they face daily harassment by the police when they try to sell their fruits and vegetables at street corners. This explains why ordinary people see governments as their number one enemy and try to avoid them altogether.

Does poor people's knowledge matter?

Paradoxically, the present African economic crisis, painful as it may be in the short term, could provide the poor for the first time with a real chance to experiment with alternative strategies of their own. As a person of peasant roots and twenty-five years of work in the field of social justice, I have come to the conclusion that those in a position of power and privilege not only ignore the demands of the poor for fundamental change, but they actually hate the poor. The peasantry, on the other hand, regard elite-initiated development as a threat to their existence. In an environment of mutual suspicion, the poor take matters in their own hands since they know from experience that 'the oppressors never make change; only the oppressed do' (Freire, 1971).

Let us now explore how far and in what ways the delegitimation of the post-colonial state has opened up room for individual and collective defensive action, and more recently, for the elaboration of new civil-society relations as a moment of political innovation. The first example I discuss involves organising around subsistence both at the household and community level (Taylor and Mackenzie, 1992). The second concerns mass political mobilisation to challenge oppressive systems of government.

Individual/household level struggles for subsistence

The peasant sector   Peasants and the urban poor in Africa experience similar problems on a daily basis: poverty, hunger, unemployment, landlessness, intimidation and down-right scorn and disdain from those who govern 'from above'. At the same time, I am humbled by the capacity of the poor to laugh at their own misery and, more importantly, the tenacity that appears to propel even the poorest of the poor to make a living out of thin air, to fight for their dignity.

After many years of being treated like donkeys, the peasants in Africa have realised their powerless situation within the context of orthodox politics, and have drawn conclusions: it is better to avoid the state altogether and withdraw within their local communities on a subsistence basis and to engage in collective action to find solutions to common problems. In some communities, peasants have switched from growing export crops to food production for local consumption. Where quota delivery of grain to marketing boards is mandatory, as was the case in Ethiopia between 1980 and 1989, peasants traded a small portion of their high grade maize or wheat for large sums of low quality grain which they delivered to the marketing board. I have documented a similar experience in Kenya where mandatory delivery of milk by peasant farmers to Kenyan Creamers at state-determined prices had forced farmers to dilute the milk with water, thus making a sizeable profit on the undiluted portion which they withheld to sell privately. Such actions are logical because, for peasants and the urban poor, the future is not necessarily more predictable and thus they prefer security and subsistence to uncertain conceptions of 'progress'.

Indeed, for a peasantry living in acute destitution and imminent danger, survival considerations are always paramount, and every peasant learns the techniques of survival as part of his/her everyday experience. These techniques may be crude or ingenious, depending on the perceptions of the people and the stock of accumulated knowledge having to do with production and survival, the resources of the community, and the social relations and communal values existing at a given time. Everyday forms of resistance are not simply spur of the moment reactions by the marginalised to the problems they confront daily. Rather, the desire to resist is based on a rational calculation of both risks and gains by the participants. Such resistance requires little co-ordination, avoids direct confrontation with authorities and is not subject to elite manipulation (Scott, 1993; Cheru, 1989). I will illustrate this with reference to the Ethiopian case.

Growing up in rural Ethiopia, I had the privilege of being both a participant in and a witness to everyday forms of peasant resistance. Starting with the feudal rule of Emperor Haile Selassie and the military socialist regime that governed the country from 1974 until May 1991, the Ethiopian peasantry had fought hard, first to keep body and soul together and then to liberate themselves from oppressive regimes (Pausewang *et al.*, 1990; Rahmato, 1993). Although the struggle for democracy and sustainable development remains elusive, Ethiopian peasants have demonstrated that undemocratic governments could be brought to their knees. The sudden collapse of the entire military and socialist apparatus of the regime of Colonel Mengistu Haile Mariam in May 1991 was due largely to the prolonged resistance of the peasantry rather than to the military strength of the largely Tigrean-led Ethiopian Peoples Revolutionary Defence Forces (EPRDF) which came into power in 1991.

Throughout the feudal rule of Emperor Haile Selassie, peasant agriculture stagnated partly due to the parasitic nature of the feudal lords and the land tenure system, but more so because of bad economic policies of the regime. The imperial regime continued to starve peasant agriculture of capital investment, technical services and extension support until the early 1970s when an experimental green revolution package called Minimum Package Programme was introduced in easily accessible parts of high potential areas to help improve the performance of peasant production. This minimal programme was initiated after prodding by the donors, not in response to the needs of the peasantry (Aredo, 1990).

The condition of the peasantry deteriorated further by the absence of any channel of communication to air their grievances to the highest authorities. The emperor had made it a policy that no major mass organisation be formed without his approval. The Office of Association in the Ministry of Interior was granted broad authority to judge the registration application to be 'unlawful or immoral' or 'against the national unity or interest' (Clapham, 1969). In practice, the ministry used its authority under the Association's Registration Regulation of 1966 to outlaw all organisations posing a potential threat to the interest of the regime. Similar control measures exist in many parts of Africa in an attempt to suffocate civil society.

In the absence of any democratic opening, peasants had no choice but to resort to innovation, that is, to ingenious forms of resistance. In my own family, such resistance took many forms: underreporting of crop output to the tax collectors, illegal cutting of trees from a state forest designed to supply fuel wood for urban residents, and illegal grazing in government owned land. From the point of view of the peasantry, repeated encroachment on government owned lands was a justifiable act. The land, which used to be communally owned, was the only grazing area available for the entire village before it was forcefully taken away by the government.

When the traditional water sources that sustained my village and the surrounding community were diverted towards a government owned irrigation project that was growing carnation flowers for export, the peasants in the community disrupted production for a prolonged period by cutting down several big pylons that carried electricity to the power transmission station at the project site, while other peasants chipped away sections of the dike in the cover of darkness, allowing water to escape in the direction of the village and the surrounding farms. With operating costs running high, the government had no choice but to accommodate the demands of the community by allowing the peasants in my village to have water for their farms at scheduled hours. Call it tax evasion, bootlegging or stealing, these activities represent a defence of self and community.[2]

Indeed, the adoption of agrarian socialism in the mid-1970s gradually became – as did Mao's periodic slogans for radicalising China – a politically centralising instrument which inflicted suffering on the mass of peasants. In Ethiopia, for example, the land reform of 1975 – the great achievement and pride of the revolution – had been so thoroughly undermined by successive socialist programmes that, by the latter part of the 1980s, it had lost its meaning and came to be employed as a weapon against peasants for whose benefit it was originally designed. Agrarian socialism came to stand for rapid collectivisation on the one hand, and a vigorous offensive against private peasant production on the other (Rahmato, 1985; Pausewang *et al.*, 1990). Collectivisation was promoted under a variety of conditions, including resettlement and villagisation, voluntarily if possible, forcibly if not. In the end, it was these hard-line policies that deeply alienated the peasantry and prepared the ground for the collapse of the government in May 1991.

The destructive policies of agrarian socialism had the following consequences. First, the policies fostered peasant insecurity since land is now considered the property of the state. Long-established traditions regarding land, locality and settlement and customary practices regarding land use and the environment, were declared invalid and irrelevant. While party loyalists justified their actions on the grounds of 'empowering the peasantry', the peasants, on the other hand, viewed themselves as being dispossessed and turned into tenants of the state. State and party agents proceeded to redefine rights of possession, to relocate peasants at will and to threaten the recalcitrant with eviction.

The number of peasants who suffered relocation and marginalisation will never be accurately known, but it is estimated that more than 400,000 households (over 1.8 million people) suffered eviction of one degree or another (Rahmato, 1993). The scale of human displacement occasioned by the resettlement programme affected as many as 750,000 households, of which some 600,000 during 1984/5 alone (Rahmato, 1989). Peasants were forcefully moved from their place of origin and resettled elsewhere, often in areas of low agricultural potential and high health hazard. Out of this total of about 3.5 million people, some 6 to 8 per cent may have perished due to disease, malnutrition and food shortages. The settlement programme was plagued throughout by high rates of desertion (Pankhurst, 1992).

The scale of destabilisation caused by 'villagisation' was equally massive; up to 3 million people may have been involved in the programme, and in some provinces the rural areas were almost totally villagised, often by force and intimidation. Peasant society was shattered as a consequence; families were torn apart, communities were dislocated and property wantonly destroyed. In socio-psychological terms, the shattering experience of destabilisation brought new insights and perceptions to the peasantry, enabling them to penetrate and decode the ideology of military socialism in a way they had not done before.

Finally, the impoverishment of the peasantry was accelerated by excessive taxation to fund the government's ongoing war and its failed socialist experiment. Peasants were burdened with taxes, an unfavourable structure of prices, and by a variety of state exactions (Pausewang, 1990). On the average, peasants gave up to one-third of their annual disposable income in the form of taxes and other contributions. Peasants who engaged in trade or other forms of endeavour to supplement their income were condemned as petty-capitalists and threatened with punishment, and the inter-rural movement of goods and people was highly restricted for a greater part of the 1980s.

Agrarian socialism eventually came to be associated in peasants' minds with the ideology of poverty – a determination on the part of the authorities to level everyone down to destitution.

In response, peasants began to sabotage government projects, fed and protected armed groups bent on overthrowing the socialist government, while some actually joined in liberation movements. Similar actions were consistently applied by the peasantry in other African countries against the colonial powers. When independence was achieved, however, the new rulers turned their backs on the peasantry whose support they actively sought during decolonisation.

The conclusion that can be drawn from the above analysis is that peasants will never be able to undermine the vicious circle of marginalisation and mass exclusion until they organise themselves politically to gain influence on the national level. On the other hand, their precarious economic condition – that is, the daily struggles around subsistence – makes the task of developing a counter-project exceptionally difficult and slow. While peasants, by and large, are aware of their situation at the local level, they have neither the capacity nor the resources required to influence events in the world beyond their villages. The well-publicised 1994 peasant uprising in Mexico by the Zapatista movement seems to be an exception. Africa is yet to experience a well-organised peasant movement ready to challenge autocratic regimes in a credible way.

The urban informal sector   The struggle for dignity by the urban poor must be viewed as being part and parcel of the broader rural struggle. Urban poverty and unemployment are structurally linked to the decay of rural society. Again parallels with the period of enclosures and industrialisation in Britain could easily be made.

In urban areas, the portrait of official joblessness does not reflect the work taking place in the informal sector that keeps thousands of families from starving. Millions are engaged in trades of every description, from back-alley foreign exchange houses, road-side restaurants, curb-side automobile and small appliance maintenance shops, to production and distribution of farm equipment made out of scrap metals, often at much cheaper prices than imported ones. In countries where the supply of medicine is hampered either by the lack of foreign exchange or by official corruption, imaginative individuals who can barely read and write, have stepped in to fill the void and are providing valuable service to the population by opening up their own underground pharmacies, stocked with medicine brought into the country by middle-men who make their living at cross-border trade.

Let me illustrate my point clearly. In a recent trip to western Kenya, I wanted to make an urgent telephone call to the capital. When I inquired at the front desk of my hotel for assistance, the attendant informed me that the line had not been working for many months. All the copper wiring connecting the town to the capital had been stolen by ingenious individuals who supply the Nairobi blacksmith who makes and sells beautiful bracelets to foreign tourists. Although this attitude of 'eat or be eaten' may appear irrational for a Western observer, copper smuggling represents the main source of income for poor citizens who feel forgotten by their own government. The smugglers do not experience a crisis of conscience for taking down government property since they neither have a telephone nor could they expect in the future any type of public employment programme in their region if they behave differently.

Although the driving force for self-help and improvisation is survival, the millions of poor Africans operating outside of the official market are in fact providing vital services where governments have failed to carry out their responsibilities. Instead of castigating the poor and characterising their professions as 'criminal' or 'illegal', we should celebrate them for elevating the human spirit, for fighting to preserve their dignity, and for allowing the rest of us to find our own humanity. The revenge of the poor against oppressive systems could open the way for a far more fundamental transformation of society, for equal justice, liberty and the pursuit of happiness. This is what I call the 'silent revolution' of the poor.

Organised struggles for subsistence

As the state has become increasingly irrelevant in the eyes of ordinary peasants, traditional institutions have assumed greater responsibility in mobilising and facilitating the creative adaptation of the poor. Communities pull their resources together to raise income and family nutrition, to build their own schools, mobilise savings and informal credit to help their members start a business, or push back the desert by planting crops that hold the soil together, and reclaim the self-reliance that was theirs until the advent of the modern nation-state. In the process, peasants and the urban poor in Africa are educating themselves in organisational dynamics and self-government. Several cases are worth mentioning.

The detrimental effects of marketing boards in Africa have been noted. In many parts of Africa, peasants now market their produce and livestock through their own channels, disregarding political boundaries and marketing boards. For example, in the Kaolack region of Senegal, peasants have formed a federation called the Peasant Association of Kaolack (ADAK), which established barter agreements with farmer groups. They exchange millet and salt for palm oil, dried fish and honey, thereby avoiding the market, taxes and government boards (Pradervand, 1989). In eastern Senegal, the Federation of Sarakolle Village has successfully resisted efforts by the state agricultural agency and the United States Agency for International Development (USAID) to promote rice production via large-scale irrigation schemes and centralised control over production and marketing (Adams, 1981). The federation's persistence has forced changes in the state marketing board's approach in other areas where it operates.

Like the colonial system, the post-colonial state has lost its role as an instrument of development and ordinary citizens do not expect anything from the state. Instead, they are determining their own development. In Burkina Faso, for example, thousands of innovative village development groups have been transforming their communities. The most visible institution has been the Naam, the traditional Burkinable village co-operative. These groups grew spontaneously in the early 1970s in response to the rapid and far-reaching environmental and economic crises facing their communities. Using the traditional concept of self-help, the Naam groups organised themselves at the village level and began constructing dams and dikes, reforesting, opening new roads, digging wells and undertaking soil conservation projects. The groups also introduced basic literacy, improved cooking stoves, and constructed cereal banks, grain mills and village pharmacies (Cheru and Bayili, 1991; Pradervand, 1989). Six S, another indigenous organisation, provides the funding for local communities. Six S is organised so that it can respond to local needs without intimidation.

In Kenya, the Green Belt movement, headed by Wangari Maathai, assists Kenyan women in planting trees in their homesteads and in other activities such as job creation for the handicapped and the promotion of sound nutrition. The movement has established more than 1,000 nurseries, producing over 10,000 seedlings per year and involving more than 50,000 households, comprising half a million villagers (Maathai, 1985; Topouzis, 1990). But when the group publicly challenged President Moi's plan to build a 67–storey skyscraper for $250 million at the centre of a popular Nairobi city park, arguing that the money could best be spent to alleviate poverty and ecological degradation in the country, Maathai and the movement were publicly condemned by the parliament and the group lost its limited funding from the government. Still others, such as the Semi-Arid Land Use movement in Kenya, are organised on a co-operative basis to develop land that had been given up as unreclaimable.

In Zimbabwe, the Organisation of Rural Associations for Progress began as a series of women's clubs which rapidly expanded to over 600 affiliated groups of women and men engaged in a variety of village-based development actions. Among its activities are the propagation and use of indigenous seeds, rain water catchment, inter-village food marketing and community grain stores. Its staff take the lead from village-level analysis of problems and offer assistance in negotiation with external contributors, including pressing demands on the government for expanded land redistribution (Nyoni, 1995).

There exist thousands of similar, locally initiated self-help experiments in villages all across Africa. The few examples cited above are indicative of the fact that, as people become more active in their own organisations, they build skills and self-confidence, and thus their capacity to participate in political life more broadly. In the long run, they will be able to undermine the vicious circle of mass exclusion and marginalisation. After all, development is not what the experts claim it to be; it is what people do at the local level to change their situation and to reaffirm their dignity. Locally based co-operative movements are the only ones that can realistically articulate an alternative vision of world order by creating new avenues of social and political mobilisation.

But the success of groups organised around subsistence has so far depended on two factors: the ability to remain 'invisible' to those outside the society (Bratton, 1989), or to generate needed resources from outside the community (including the state) without losing control of their initiatives and institutions. Any attempt by these institutions to openly rearrange the allocation of resources on which the power of the state rests runs the risk of political repression (Bratton, 1990: 95).

This brings us to our final point: the role of the state in national development. While the state in Africa has been part of the problem, it would be a serious error to underestimate its critical role in any effective development strategy. The crucial challenge is how to dismantle the 'disabling state' and replace it with 'a state which is not only protector and supporter, but also enabler and liberator' (Chambers, 1989: 20). If local initiatives are to succeed, then it is clear that new power-sharing relationships must be worked out with powerful state actors. Decentralised processes and choice are central to the reversal of current paradigms. A political space must be opened to allow local communities to establish new relationships between themselves and central governments. This is the Achilles heel of Africa's democratisation and development.

From silent to overt resistance: limits and contradictions

The second form of resistance, growing out of the first, is the challenge to the nation-state and the demand for substantive democratisation, as evidenced in the growth of democracy movements over the past five years. As ordinary citizens have become more and more aware of what they want and how they might attain it, they have entered into political action and organisations to demand an accounting from those who govern. Flag-bearers of this new renaissance are social movements based in the church, informal sector, human rights, environment and development communities that have sprung up all across Africa in the last decade to articulate alternative visions of survival and democratic governance (Cheru, 1996). Popular protests and movements have challenged not only the policies but even the character of the regimes. The concerns of these movements have been economic (unemployment, declining real wages), social (cuts in welfare services), and political (repression, lack of human rights) – all a testimony to the misdirection of resources and accountability.

It would be a great mistake, however, to attribute the growth of democracy movements strictly to the mobilisation efforts of elite-led parties that have sprung up in recent years. Rather, the movement owes its success to the debilitating economic impact of the 'silent revolution' of ordinary peasants on the capacity of African governments to provide even the most basic services to previously protected groups (teachers, civil servants, doctors, etc.). This process dates back to the mid-1970s when peasants began to drop out in large numbers from the formal economy to demonstrate their anger at the perceived hostility of the state towards them.

The demand for fundamental change has been born of a decade of painful economic decline and disenchantment with autocratic rule. The crucial factor which provided the impetus for mass political mobilisation in the decade of the 1980s has been the resistance to externally imposed structural adjustment programmes (SAPs), which have had a disastrous impact on peasants and the urban poor as well as previously protected (or privileged) groups, such as the urban elites and the middle classes. As many people began to draw a direct connection between their economic plight and the paucity of basic liberties, local grievances very quickly escalated into popular challenges to the established systems of governments that are seen domestically as predatory and corrupt and internationally, servile executors of the economic agenda of the ruling classes of the major OECD nations.

Yet, the euphoria over multiparty democracy has been short lived for many reasons. Incumbent regimes were able to use resources at their disposal to splinter civil society either through more repression or co-optation. But, more importantly, opposition parties lacked vision, organisation and leadership. Ethnicity, elitism and corruption further undermined their credibility. The creation of new parties has not directly involved many citizens from outside of extant political elites, and particularly not on the basis of pre-existing grass-roots organisations and interest groups in rural areas. In country after country, the new opposition leaders are often none other than people who served the single party long and faithfully without any great sign of a crisis of conscience.

This did not come as a surprise to the peasantry who are suspicious of elite-led initiatives. As elections in Kenya and Zambia had demonstrated, multiparty systems could lead to new forms of old hierarchies. Although USAID proudly advertises that many countries in Africa had made the transition from military or autocratic rule to democracy in the past ten years, the collapse of one-party states is rarely accompanied by a substantial reorientation of power relations between urban and rural areas. Many citizens, particularly those in the rural areas, have been excluded and broad based programmes of economic and social reforms have rarely been pursued.

Given these facts, peasants have been reluctant to participate in formal political parties or pin their hopes on democracy. Rather, they view the democratisation drive as another ideology of domination, an attempt to turn them into destitutes just the way agrarian socialism did. They particularly find the decisions of newly elected governments to impose austerity measures, requiring them to make more sacrifice, to be harsh and unacceptable. In response, peasants seek to secure greater autonomy from the state through disengagement just as they had done before (Beckman, 1992). In short, democratisation in Africa has little chance of success if it cannot revive economic fortunes.

International Relations in an age of marginalisation: problems and prospects

With the so-called end of the Cold War, the abstractions of free elections and free markets have assumed greater importance in the foreign policies of Western powers and in the programmes of both multilateral and bilateral aid agencies. The shift in the rhetoric and to an extent the practice of official Western policy is in response to the rapid growth of popular movements (environmental, women, indigenous groups and human rights groups) giving voice to the poor and disenfranchised throughout the Third World, challenging not only the character of regimes, but also the basic assumptions of conventional development strategies. Innovation from below, in this sense, involves some marginal political innovation from above so as to transform popular pressures into a co-opted frame of reference – what Gramsci (1971) called *trasformismo*.

When closely scrutinised, therefore, the new foreign policy of 'democracy and free markets' is inconsistent with the views of popular movements in Africa. The USAID Democracy Initiative, for example, states that 'democracy is complementary to and supportive of the transition to market-oriented economies and sustainable, broadly-based economic development'. This same view is expressed by the World Bank, which defines its new mission to be the rapid transformation of developing countries to market-oriented principles (World Bank, 1989). In this context, democracy simply means multiparty elections and implementation of market-oriented economic policies: it is democracy in form but does not contain the substance of participation and popular control over people's everyday lives.

In other words, while multiparty elections and universal suffrage are important formal criteria, they are by no means sufficient to judge the democratic qualities of a society. Northern interpretations of democracy suffer from the same flaw as did their interpretation of development, that is, that democratisation is not a process but a product that the North imposes upon the South. As André Gunder Frank (1992) succinctly put it, 'freedom of the market does not equal democratic freedom', because, in the market, it is one dollar, one vote; so that many dollars mean many votes and no dollar no vote. In a free market system of 'one dollar, one vote', there will not be a place for small farmers and poor people in general unless they increase their leverage to exert influence over decisions. Only then can markets be structured to ensure the allocation of resources to small farmers.

In contrast, most discussions of democratisation in the South stress the need to loosen the links between indigenous governments and national elites with Western governments, and the empowerment of the people so that they can define and steer a democratic development process. While the connections between economics and democratisation are clearly made, the assumptions behind this linkage differ sharply from the common Northern assumption that democratisation and free-market economic policies go hand-in-hand. For example, SAPs that have introduced or reinforced free-market policies across much of the South are widely considered to be anti-democratic. The formulation of these policies does not reflect a democratic, participatory process and the impact of SAPs is not spread evenly across societies. The cost of adjustment has been borne by the poor, particularly women and children in urban areas – a new urbanisation that forms part of what Karl Polanyi (1957) called the 'stark utopia' of the self-regulating market society that the West seems now to be attempting to foster in post-colonial Africa (on ecological aspects of this see the chapter by Mitchell Bernard).

In addition to the above, the notions of accountability, decentralisation, civil society and popular participation mean different things to Northern policy makers and Southern activists. In the North, accountability primarily refers to financial accountability and the need to challenge corruption; in the Southern context, the term is used more broadly to include financial, economic as well as political accountability. Similarly, decentralisation in the North is used in reference to the decentralisation of authority from the level of the state to the local government and on to the people. In the Arusha Charter, decentralisation begins in the North and includes decentralisation from the state to local government to popular levels (UNECA, 1990).

The notion of civil society may or may not be innovatory or emancipatory. Civil society in the North has traditionally referred not necessarily to the grass-roots organisations, but to professional associations such as lawyers, public interest groups, political parties, business associations, churches, the media and universities; usage in the South needs further specification but commonly refers to grass-roots and popular organisations – it is in some ways a more democratic conception (for a contrasting conception see the essay by Yoshikazu Sakamoto). Similarly, popular participation, when used in the North tends to refer to participation at the project or programme level in Third World development; Southern development activists expand the notion of popular participation to include policy formulation at national, regional and international levels (Melin, 1995).

The fashionable notion of 'transnational civil society' also masks many contradictions. While Northern and Southern non-governmental organisations (NGOs) are collaborating together to lobby governments through the United Nations system on issues of human rights, ecology, poverty and other social issues of global dimensions, or in cofinancing of community development projects, their strength and capacity to conduct human-centred transnational foreign policy, independent of states, are exaggerated (Korten, 1990; Ekins, 1992). NGOs are no substitute for governments. Not only are their activities governed by official laws, but their success is partly attributed to the support they receive from host governments in the form of exemptions from tax, import duties, etc. Furthermore, the relationships between Northern and Southern NGOs are characterised by unequal power and influence. It is not uncommon to hear complaints from African partners that Northern NGOs are spreading clientelism, thus undermining collective action. In this sense transnational civil society is antithetical to notions of grass-roots innovation and emancipation.

To a significant degree, the transition to democracy, and equitable and environmentally sustainable development is one that the people of Africa can undertake themselves. However, the current fad of multiparty elections and economic reforms, largely crafted in the North, will only help perpetuate the present economic and political crisis. Indeed, it may be easy for outsiders to teach Africans how to speak the English language; but they cannot teach Africans how to govern themselves. That is a task that Africans themselves must figure out on their own, innovating in their own ways and transforming the circumstances that they face. Although both the World Bank and USAID claim that democracy cannot be exported, they both proceed to define the components of democratic governance for the South.

Conclusion

With few exceptions, International Relations has largely been dominated by pro-establishment scholars, more concerned with the protection of privileges, and less about the creation of a more just, sustainable, non-sexist, and non-racial world order. Some of these commentators have gone even further to proclaim the collapse of communism and the triumph of Western liberalism as 'the end of history' (Fukuyama, 1989). Yet, the end of the Cold War has not translated into the end of domination, exploitation and marginalisation of Third World countries. The growing gap between the North and the South is compounded further by the process of globalisation, which has both integrating and disintegrating tendencies, deepening the existing inequalities in incomes and power at various levels of our society (Mittelman, 1996a). This is the study of International Relations 'from above'. It is incomplete unless it is joined with a perspective on the world 'from below'.

In practical terms, peace and security will not be achieved unless International Relations is extended to deal with the threats that stem from failures in development, environmental degradation, lack of progress towards democracy and the challenges posed by the process of economic globalisation. It is here that critical theory is needed to understand historical structures, which contain contradictions, conflict and coherence, and to propose the necessary changes.

This implies that International Relations as a field must embark on a new research agenda aimed at developing alternative sources of innovative knowledge and understanding which will help identify the forces of opposition to the new global conditions of the 1990s. Seen 'from below', the following research questions are apposite in the African context: how can we create a new balance between the interests of a transnational economy and the real needs of local communities in the face of diminishing state power? How would the poverty-induced migration of millions of destitute people affect relations between states and among those people who see themselves as losing out or as threatened? At the same time, we are witnessing a growing trend in core-periphery social co-operation as exemplified in the global environmental and human rights and other solidarity movements. Are these transnational social movements potential agents of transformation? If so, in what ways? In what ways are they not? Research in these and other areas will foster collective awareness, promote cross-cultural understanding, and eventually come closer to constructing a just and more humane world society in which human innovation and emancipation become the 'order' of the day.

NOTES

1 In the title of this chapter, the phrase, 'silent revolution' is from Cheru (1989); 'the weapons of the weak' is taken from James C. Scott (1985). In some ways, this essay is a personal testimony based on my own experience growing up in a peasant household, and as a professional who has lived and worked in poor communities in many parts of Africa. While my accounts of the deplorable condition of the poor peasants and their everyday struggles for fundamental change may not fit neatly into predetermined categories of social theory, and thus by extension be labelled as unscientific, poor peoples' knowledge and their experienced reality counts, for they alone can change their situation for the better.

2 Editor's note (by Stephen Gill). The responses of peasants in Africa outlined by Fantu Cheru are similar to those noted by E. P. Thompson (1980) in his account of the peasantry and urban poor in the period of intensified enclosure of land and expropriation of the commons and the development of industrialisation in eighteenth and nineteenth-century Britain. Thompson's work showed how poaching (one of the most common 'crimes' of that period) was a relatively spontaneous survival mechanism. However, this crime was widely perceived as legitimate action by the bulk of the population under conditions of expropriation. Access to the commons had been denied and such access was perceived as a threat to both moral economy and the means of existence by the mass of the population. It was thus the subject of intense and protracted political struggle (see also Polanyi, 1957 on this point). Similarly, James C. Scott (1993) discusses how the silent and apparently uncoordinated and unplanned resistance of the Chinese peasantry was in direct response to the disastrous collectivisation of agriculture in Mao's ill-fated Great Leap Forward, a leap which produced mass starvation. The subsequent 'Four Modernisations' policy of Deng is only comprehensible in terms of the limits that such structural resistance – akin to a broad-based class force – posed for the state's agricultural policies. Deng's policies merely recognised and ratified what had already become the reality in the political economy of rural China.

11 Frantz Fanon, race and world order

Randolph B. Persaud

This chapter examines the relevance of Frantz Fanon for the study of global politics. While Fanon did not offer a 'theory' of international – or as I would prefer, global – relations, I intend to demonstrate that he did point to some of the *constitutive antagonisms* of global power relations. Of course, whether Fanon may or may not be considered relevant depends on one of the broader concerns of this book, namely, what is the meaning and purpose of theory, and in particular the degree to which critical theory has an emancipatory dimension.[1]

In International Relations realist theorising has served as a form of power/knowledge, thus 'disciplining' theoretical practices in the field. By privileging certain conceptions of power, states and national interest, in realist ontology the histories and experiences of less powerful states (and their peoples) become marginal or irrelevant. In other words, the civilisational and political content of realist ontology involves not only what is considered reality, but also how it represents the realities that are included and excluded: it is, in effect, a kind of colonisation and dichotomisation of the mind. This is, in my view, a dangerous error, both theoretically and politically.

One way to illustrate this is with reference to the writings of Fanon, and in particular with his understanding of domination, violence and liberation. Fanon saw colonial domination as both an epistemological and ontological system as well as a form of structural violence that was much broader than economic exploitation. It was civilisational, and, most importantly, racial, in content. Its characteristic forms of violence have a peculiar spatial logic, a logic reflected in its characteristic frameworks of thought. For Fanon colonialism was a 'motionless Manicheanistic world'. By implication, we can apply some aspects of Fanon's perspective to analyse aspects of the emerging world order.

The political purpose of this chapter then, is ultimately 'critical' and opposed to the possible intensification of Manichaean world order tendencies. From an ontological and epistemological viewpoint, its purpose is linked to the idea that the development of global social thought must avoid dichotomising the world.

The politics of theory and the dichotomisation of reality

A critical theory of global politics ought to serve the purpose of liberation, be genuinely reflexive, and must carry 'an ethical dimension to analysis, so that the questions of justice, legitimacy and moral credibility are integrated sociologically into the whole and into many of its key concepts' (Gill, 1993b: 24).

Thus the 'meaning' and 'purpose' of theory are dialectically related and cannot be completely separated out as discrete problems. Meaning is contingent upon purpose, and vice versa, and both are ultimately political. In this chapter I will use the two broad categories of international theory, namely, problem-solving and critical or emancipatory theory, to demonstrate my argument (see Cox, 1981, 1992b). In problem-solving approaches the necessary and sufficient condition for a 'theoretical claim' is *explanation* of reality, whereas for critical approaches 'good theory' must contain the capacity for *transforming* the reality explained.

However, there is a prior question to be asked: that is, what is 'the' reality in the first place, or more precisely, what are the realities significant in understanding global politics? Every theoretical inquiry has basic ontological assumptions in so far as there must be some determination of the 'significant entities' to be examined. The assumption of what is important simultaneously marks off what phenomena or institutions are not worth studying.

Thus when realism insists that the meaningful objects of inquiry in International Relations are states, national interests and the state system, they do not simply exclude other entities, but relegate the latter to a peripheral status. As Stephen Gill notes in his chapter, by sustaining the acceptance of a given ontology, those who hold important positions in research and government institutions have influence over research programmes, and thus help to shape the accepted boundaries of a discipline. By virtue of their positional power such individuals confer legitimacy on those 'significant entities' deemed to provide useful and reliable knowledge (about global social and political relations). In this sense, it is also institutional power, or more precisely the struggle over institutional power, that influences adjustments in the field. Let me give one example. In the post-1945 period the rise of the United States to a position of 'global leadership' and the challenge from the Soviet Union coincided with the consolidation of realism as the normal science of International

Relations and with the dominance of American scholars of the field. The key ontological assumptions of realists – concerning states, national interest and power – fitted much like a jig-saw puzzle with the 'national security' concerns of the United States (Buzan, 1991: 299–300). Barry Buzan shows how global strategic management emerged as the focus of American policy. Those specialising in the sub-field of Strategic Studies were considered to have authoritative and relevant knowledge about the field as a whole. Strategic Studies politically manipulated discourses on security, and prevented other significant problems in the study or field of International Relations from gaining greater status. Indeed Buzan describes this network of intellectual, civilisational and political relationships as 'an off-spring of Anglo-American, and . . . Western, defence policy needs . . . Its attachment to security is heavily conditioned by the *status quo* orientations of hegemonic countries safely removed from the pressure of large attached neighbours . . . [it] exists within the confines of the Realist model of the struggle for power' (1991: 10–11).

In this realist model, what are 'theorised' are those *states* with considerable *power*, in the pursuit of their *national interests*, states that are deemed capable of affecting the balance of power in the international system. Small and or weak states, therefore, are not worth studying. In Kenneth Waltz's aphorism, 'Denmark doesn't matter' (Cox, 1992c: 143). Realist ontology is such that generalisations about international relations come from the experience of the great powers – the 'we'. 'Reliable knowledge' in the discipline is drawn from these countries. This has marginalised Third World countries by confining them to 'area studies', that is, to the realm of the *particular* and of 'them', that is, of the other. The civilisational and political content of realist ontology, therefore, constructs, simplifies and dichotomises the 'realities' and understandings that are included and excluded in the relevant and practical knowledge of International Relations.[2] Moreover, whilst realism does not assume a 'fixed reality' as such it does have an ontology of what I call *fixed universals* – of interests, states and power. To these fixed universals is then applied a largely positivist scientific method to make explanatory claims about the world.[3]

In this context, I challenge innovations in recent realist, and certain other types of dichotomising, theory that seek to marginalise the perspectives of most of the world. Such innovations arise in a cultural context of 'Orientalising' *and* 'Occidentalising tendencies' in thinking. Some of these tendencies indicate a more Manichean and racist world order. This would especially be the case if the racist conceptions implicit or explicit in recent realist theorising were to gain wider currency within the practices of the national security complexes of the dominant nations.

To understand the potential contours, content and dangers of such a Manichean world order I draw upon and outline Frantz Fanon's novel conception of the racial character of colonialism. I interpret Fanon to explore and to better understand aspects of the subordination of much of the Third World today. Fanon's ideas serve to provide a contrasting ontology to that of realism. They also point to ways that racial issues appear to overlap with the contradictions generated by globalisation in a post-colonial era so as to shape the national security conceptions and policies of the West.

Fanon and decolonisation

In this discussion of Frantz Fanon, I shall try to indicate that he had a unique understanding of domination, violence and liberation. Whilst there are problems with some of his arguments, an exposition is pertinent to revealing some of the silences of recent theorising in the field of International Relations on questions of race, as well as providing us with some of the elements of a critical ontology of the emerging world order.

My argument is that for Fanon (like Marx) colonial domination was much broader than economic exploitation – it was a form of domination which was civilisational in content and in which race played a key role. Further, Fanon showed that the structure of domination has a formative spatial element, and, on account of this, colonial violence had a peculiar logic. In this calculus race was a central and at times a key principle in economic exploitation. Finally, Fanon, in contrast to Marx, argued that the potential for revolutionary transformation, or what I shall call *strategic counter-hegemony*, comes as much from the margins of the spatial and cultural world of the coloniser as it might do from the proletariat. It has to be noted that on this point, however, there is some confusion in Fanon, since he sometimes speaks of 'socialist' revolution, whilst at other times he speaks of 'national' liberation. In what follows then, I shall demonstrate that, through his analysis, Frantz Fanon offered a distinctive explanation of colonial domination, although one that is not complete or without its ambiguities.

Much of what is now called the Third World were once European colonies. Colonialism as it manifested itself throughout the world was not only a structure of economic exploitation; rather, it was equally a structure of domination based on, and nurtured in, a racist ideology. The historical specificity of colonial racist domination and the 'violence' which it elicited in the process of decolonisation, requires, for its understanding, not only a perspective of the coloniser (for example, certain forms of realism associated with discourses of civilising mission, manifest destiny, etc.) but also those of the colonised. These perspectives need to be understood dialectically.

The historical fact of foreign occupation and its recognition by Fanon as the key generative principle governing social relations in the colonies, informed his perspectives on domination, conflict/violence and liberation. While the act of being occupied was itself traumatic, the fact that the occupier was different *and* armed with a narcissistic notion of civilisational superiority, deepened the cultural debasement of the colonised. Thus Ato Sekyi-Otu notes: 'Beneath the coercive social relations of the colonial world, Fanon uncovers not the tragic history of human practical activity, but a primordial reification of roles, a structure of power relations based upon the bastard principle of race' (Sekyi-Otu, 1975: 145). Seen in this way, racial domination was not simply a matter of the coloniser imposing himself on the colonised through force. Rather, colonial domination was organised through the normalisation of the pathological *via* the continuous intensification of the density of everyday representations of the world couched in Euro-Christian common sense and values. Every act of the coloniser was an act of *othering*, of cultural 'infantilisation', of 'institutionalized dehumanization' (Gordon, 1995: 81) and 'every contact between the occupied and the occupier [was] a falsehood' (Fanon, 1965: 65).

One of Fanon's most innovative arguments was that the organisational logic of colonial domination was spatial in nature. Thus, in his characterisation of the colonial world he constantly referred to a world comprised of 'compartments', one divided into 'separate zones' or 'quarters', a world 'cut in two', and, more dramatically, a 'motionless Manicheanistic world' (Fanon, 1963: 36–41). This spatial organisation made it impossible to speak of 'colonial society'; rather every colonial social formation was constituted not only around two distinct spaces, but around two opposed worlds where 'No conciliation is possible' (1963: 39). Although economic exploitation was inscribed in this Manichean world, the index of domination was to be found in the systematic erasure of all that was indigenous and 'original', through what Lewis Gordon calls the 'mundanity' of racism (Gordon, 1995: 38). Fanon himself put it thus: 'This world divided into compartments, this world cut in two is inhabited by two different species. The originality of the colonial context is that economic reality, inequality, and the immense difference of ways of life never come to mask the human realities' (1963: 39–40).

In the colonial world, these 'human realities' were the creation of what Fanon called 'two different species'. The imbrication of the civilisational and spatial logic of colonial domination led Fanon to the position that 'Marxist analysis should always be slightly stretched every time we have to do with the colonial problem' (1963: 40). For Marx, the logic of exploitation is temporal in so far as surplus-value is nothing other than the 'extortion' of that portion of congealed and objectified labour-time, beyond what is socially necessary for the reproduction of the direct producer. Further, it is upon this logic that Marx constructs his theory of class domination, and ultimately, of agency and liberation. Now, while Fanon accepts the general thrust of Marx's theoretical problematic and his broader political programme leading to socialist revolution, he nonetheless passionately insisted on the peculiarities of colonial domination. Some distinctive features of the latter according to Fanon were: (i) the index of domination was as much spatial as it was temporal; (ii) that race was the key organising principle in the mapping of spatial antagonisms; (iii) that class domination was overdetermined by structural racism and a relatively permanent state of violence; and (iv) on account of these peculiarities, the specificity of the political in colonial situations required innovatory forms of *praxis*, which to some extent transcended the politics of class struggle. These were meaningful adjustments and they warrant further attention.

According to Fanon, the civilisational content of colonialism, and specifically its racist ideology find classical Marxist analysis limited in explaining colonial economic exploitation. The disagreement with Marx is to be found in the following: 'In the colonies the economic substructure is also the superstructure. The cause is the consequence; you are rich because you are white, you are white because you are rich' (Fanon, 1963: 40). The essence of the argument here is that the social structure of accumulation is actually configured around race. The relations of production, in other words, cannot be separated from the racial relations of subordination. Further, the reproduction of the objective conditions necessary for the expansion and consolidation of capitalist modes of social relations, *ipso facto* demanded a deepening of the 'mundanity' of racism. Colonial racism, therefore, should not be seen as a (superstructural) consequence of economic imperialism, but as the organising principle through which specific forms of surplus-value extraction took place. If this adjustment in Marx is 'allowed', some important implications of the theorisation of politics follow.

First, if domination is articulated through attempts to construct hegemony, then a counter-hegemonic project leading to decolonisation cannot be restricted to 'economic' questions. It is not only Fanon who has taken Marx to task on this score. Edward Said, for example, argues that Marx himself held an Orientalist view of British colonialism (in India). Said argues that at the heart of this view was the assumption that, despite the cruelty of colonial practices, modern Western civilisation was beneficial to

Asia because it was tearing down archaic structures and institutions, and concomitantly, setting the conditions for social revolution. Thus, in support of his argument, Said cites Marx's *first* sentence in a short article called 'The Future Results of British Rule in India' (1853): 'England has to fulfil a double mission in India: one destructive, the other regenerating – the annihilation of the Asiatic society, and the laying of the material foundations of Western society in Asia' (quoted in Said, 1979: 155). Said equates this with what he argues is Marx's 'Orientalist' position of the supposed civilising mission of (British) colonialism. Said argues that 'in article after article' Marx 'returned with increasing conviction' to the thesis that colonialism is historically progressive (1979: 153).

However, a closer reading of the full text of 'The Future Results of British Rule in India' indicates that Said fails to appreciate that in fact Marx was making an argument based upon a postulate of the dialectical interplay between, and sedimentation of, different civilisational forces in the historical development of India. Thus Marx argues in the *second* sentence of the article:

Arabs, Turks, Tartars, Moguls, who had successively overrun India, soon became Hinduized, the barbarian conquerors being, by an eternal law of history, conquered themselves by the superior civilisation of their subjects. The British were the first conquerors superior and therefore inaccessible to Hindu civilisation. They destroyed it . . . The work of regeneration [of Hindu culture] hardly transpires through a heap of ruins. Nevertheless it has begun. (Kamenka, 1983: 337)

Marx then argues that the unification of India and the introduction of Western science and industry is part of this dialectic of civilisations, and the likely result will be 'Indian progress and Indian power' after a proletarian revolution that overthrows colonialism, leading to 'the regeneration of that great and interesting country' (Kamenka, 1983: 341). In this sense, Aijaz Ahmad is correct that Marx's writings on British colonialism in India are mainly 'conjectural and speculative' (Ahmad, 1992: 226), although they are linked in this case to a somewhat teleological theory of historical change. Indeed, in his article, 'The Indian Revolt' (Kamenka, 1983: 351–5), Marx shows how a dialectic of violence operates in a situation of colonisation. Marx notes that 'torture is an organic institution of [British] financial policy', and contrasts this with the violent outrages committed against the colonial masters in the revolt of the sepoys in 1857 – the primary servants of the colonisers. This revolt is seen as containing the potential for the onset of the overthrow of colonialism: 'The first blow dealt to the French monarchy proceeded from the nobility, not from the peasants. The Indian revolt does not commence with the ryots, tortured, dishonoured and stripped naked by the British, but with the sepoys, clad, fed and petted, fatted and pampered by them' (1983: 352).

In discussing the situation of British imperialism in China, Marx further notes that 'The violations of women, the spittings of children, the roasting of whole villages, were then wanton sports, not recorded by mandarins, but by British officers themselves.' This is hardly a picture of a 'civilising mission'. It thus seems an overstatement, however, when referring to Marx's writings on China, for Ahmad to suggest that the writings of Marx and Engels 'are indeed contaminated in several places with the usual banalities of nineteenth-century Eurocentrism' (Ahmad, 1992: 229). On this reading then, Marx may be closer to Fanon than either Fanon or others have thought. The key point here, however, is that only a careful reading of Marx can do justice to the complexities of his relationship to colonial and post-colonial discourse, as well as the dialectics of violence and civilisational change in the process of emancipation. Such analysis needs to avoid the dichotomising tendencies of Orientalism (what Said accuses Marx of) and indeed of Occidentalising – seeing the 'West' as a single, homogeneous and undifferentiated civilisational complex, a trap that Fanon does not always avoid.

Second, Fanon's rejection of Marx's ontology of liberation led him to the equally critical question of agency, and particularly to the reproblematisation of the social forces 'historically ready' to articulate a project of strategic counter-hegemony. Fanon saw the working class, to whom Marx had assigned the privileged revolutionary position (even in India), as a class too enamoured with colonial Euro-Christian desire. Simply put, the working classes in colonial social formations were too deeply connected to the 'colonising will' of the imperialists; they were part of the problem in that they had become heavily interpellated in the cultural ambition of the coloniser. To fully grasp this point we need to return to the spatial logic of colonialism.

For Fanon, colonialism was a compartmentalised Manichean world with separate spaces of the coloniser and colonised. But the world of the colonised was itself divided in two. On the one hand, there were the largely urban 'townspeople' where the density of European modernisation was high: 'The latter dresses like a European; he speaks the European's language, works with him, sometimes even lives in the same district, so he is considered by the peasants as a turncoat who has betrayed everything that goes to make up the national heritage' (Fanon, 1963: 112). In a separate zone, set apart from the urban order of things, there is the country-person, the peasant, 'the real native'. In the *making of* the native as the trafficking symbol of backwardness, the coloniser first allows the townspeople into the 'world of Europe'. In other words, the spatio-cultural cleavage between the coloniser and the towns*man* was not as deep as between the former and the country-folk. The African townsman – in contrast to at least some of the Indian sepoys – cherished his closeness to the 'world of whiteness', and in the political strategy of cultural hegemony was circulated as the sign of Europe's civilising mission. It was indeed men from the urban areas who became barristers, medical doctors, civil servants, administrators and even advisers. In more general terms, the urban working class also registered its difference with the country-folk as a means of constructing its own supposed modernity. Clearly, the urban/rural division was not only spatial, but corresponded to the economic and cultural arrangements through which the national colonial 'body', as a whole, was configured. The key point here is that the racio-cultural and socio-economic divide between the coloniser and colonised was itself superimposed on a larger frame of inclusion/exclusion, that is, those within the imagined community of Euro-Christian civilisation, and those outside of it. Fanon's recognition of this doubly constituted inside/outside world led him to theorise the *Lumpenproletariat* and peasants as the 'true' agents of transformative action and to dismiss the working class as beneficiaries of colonial rule (Caute, 1970: 77–8). A critical dimension to this dialectic of *praxis* was the peculiarity of revolutionary counter-violence.

Fanon's treatment of violence as an instrument of decolonisation is extremely controversial. Much of the controversy actually stems from the considerable elasticity with which the concept of violence is used. At times violence is *reduced* to 'force', 'pure force' or 'absolute violence', while on other occasions, there is a much broader political employment, where violence designates – 'action', 'liberation' or 'fight'. In some instances these two faces of violence are combined in phrases like 'murderous and decisive struggle', or 'armed resistance'. Despite this confusion, and bearing in mind the generalised 'atmosphere of violence' created by the coloniser, Gendzier is on firm ground in arguing that, for Fanon, revolutionary violence was a form of 'absolute *praxis*' (Gendzier, 1973: 205). Thus, although Fanon meant different things by violence (Hansen, 1977), it seems that his major concern was the employment of all means necessary in a larger historical struggle against colonial dehumanisation, since dehumanisation is indeed a state of war (Gordon, 1995).

Violence is abhorrent if pondered in the abstract, that is, if those who think about it are far removed from the seemingly permanent and total context of colonial situations regulated by violence, or the threat of violence. As such, it was the recurrent practices of organised, state-sponsored violence by the coloniser which, in the end, elicited wars of national liberation. To the extent that 'violence' was an instrument in wars of national liberation, Fanon not only supported it, but saw it as a mythical principle of mobilisation, a principle which he felt would give coherence to a programme of revolutionary action. He was careful to point out that without 'this coherence . . . there is only a blind will toward freedom, with the terribly reactionary risks which it entails' (Fanon, 1963: 59). The violence that Fanon supported, therefore, was not individual, personal or purely instrumental, but collective, politically informed and historically responsible. In this broader perspective, revolutionary violence cannot be set apart from the total strategy of decolonisation, for to do so would trivialise the 'just wars' fought by millions of men and women in the process of recovering their humanity which colonialism had set out to destroy. As Fanon himself put it: 'The natives' challenge to the colonial world is not a rational confrontation of points of view. It is not a treatise on the universal, but the untidy affirmation of an original idea propounded as an absolute' (1963: 41).

For Fanon then, the political cannot be seen as a set of discrete or 'regional' practices. Rather, it is deeply embedded in the totality of socio-economic and cultural relations which obtained in colonial social formations, and in which race was a central principle of articulation. The precise articulation varies according to time and place, as does the nature of violence, structural or direct.

Global politics and world order

Fanon's theorisation of decolonisation may be incomplete and inconsistent. However, I think it can provide some useful insights for the analysis of the emerging world order – especially with regard to questions of race, violence and civilisation(s).

First, the centrality of space in Fanon's problematisation of antagonism and domination seems all the more relevant in the current conjuncture. Under formal colonialism the regulation of compartmentalised spaces of the coloniser and colonised was 'obedient to the rules of pure Aristotelian logic, they both follow[ed] the principle of reciprocal exclusivity' (Fanon, 1963: 38–9). In the colonial situation, therefore, the spatial logic underpinning domination was horizontal; there was no 'ordinary' hierarchy of upper, middle and lower classes. There were simply two different 'species', that is, self (the coloniser), and other (the colonised). The neo-colonial process of globalisation, however, is currently reinscribing the spatial logic of the global economy in a vertical manner, such that, in contradistinction to reciprocal exclusivity, the dialectic of domination is one of integration/differentiation (see Drainville, 1995). If the new world order currently fashioned by globalisation goes unchecked, we may soon end up with the type of 'garrison existence' which Cox (1995b) talks about, a situation which may very well push the globally dispossessed into renewed 'absolute *praxis*'. Put differently, the globalisation of production and exchange is creating enclavisation (for example, walled communities, export processing zones, offshore financial centres) and thus the need for their defence against the dispossessed and marginalised – with similarities to the spatialisation of class and colonial social relations noted by Fanon.

Second, recent fears about civilisational conflicts, and even war between civilisations, give clear indications that Western supremacist ideas which characterised colonialism have not really ended and these configure dichotomising responses to perceived 'threats' (see Huntington, 1993; Connelly and Kennedy, 1994). In Marx's piece on the Indian revolt we read of their antecedents, for example the editor of the London *Times* in 1857, who argued for a violent response. As Marx notes, summarising the sentiments expressed in the British Press: 'John Bull is to be steeped in cries for revenge up to his very ears, to make him forget his Government is responsible for the mischief hatched and the colossal dimensions it had been allowed to assume' (Kamenka, 1983: 355). Indeed I would suggest that many of the representations of the 'post-Cold War' clashes between civilisations can be understood as part of a backlash by elements in the neo-imperialist nations as they react to challenges to their dominance from other parts of the world.

Further, as Cox argues, the civilisational discourses pointing to impending disaster for the West, are not only a continuation of a world imagined in Cold War terms, but also a deflection of the real causes of global tension, namely, 'the socially polarizing consequences of globalizing market economics' (Cox, 1995b: 11). It is not that the new civilisational discourses are oblivious to these polarising consequences; rather the cause for concern is the particular appropriation and discursive re/production of global displacements. Some, for example Connelly and Kennedy (1994), have used assertions from a racist novel – Jean Raspail's *The Camp of the Saints* – as a means of suggesting that the West is being inundated by starving millions from Third World countries. Thereafter, these authors proceed to integrate these fictitious postulates into what they consider to be a newer and more determined realism. Therefore they write, with the clear intention of influencing Western policy: 'We will have to convince a suspicious public and cynical politicians that a serious package of reform measures is not fuzzy liberal idealism but a truer form of Realism' (1994: 84).

In this 'truer form of Realism', migration of peoples from the Third World is presented as a grave threat to Western way(s) of life, and, as such, a pressing problem of national security. In their analysis, the root of the

problem is not simply overpopulation, but the fact that Western governments have been too misled by 'liberal' ideas such as 'international development' and 'egalitarianism' (Connelly and Kennedy, 1994: 89). These
ideas, they explain, have had the long-term effect of enlarging 'family size'
in the Third World, and, as a consequence, have produced a structural
problem of immigrant/refugee generating countries. The logic of this
analysis is that if Western countries cut back on foreign aid, the natural
environment (that is starvation, in my reading), would quickly limit
population. In their words: 'Individuals responding with low fertility to
signs of limits are the local solution' (1994: 91; emphasis added).

This kind of advice is, of course, consistent with Samuel Huntington's
policy prescriptions of cultivating conflicts between non-Western civilisations, maintaining Western military superiority and supporting groups in
other civilisations 'sympathetic to Western values and interests'
(Huntington, 1993: 49). Huntington has one more bit of advice which,
incidentally, brings to life Fanon's depiction of colonial supremacy as a
form of racio-spatial domination. Huntington suggests the reinscription
of a global order in which there would be a world compartmentalised and
divided in two civilisational zones. On one side, there will be Europe,
North America, Eastern Europe and Latin America (with the possible
inclusion of Russia and Japan). On the other side, will be the rest of
humankind. This new Manichean world order, therefore, will be constituted in two zones with no chance of reconciliation – in Huntington's
mind it will be 'the West versus the rest'. It seems clear to me that while
Huntington uses the broad categories of 'civilisation' and culture to
delineate his boundaries of 'West' and 'the rest', there are more specific
identity constituting principles contained in his system of bifurcation. I
think there is a dimension to this view of civilisational compartmentalisa-
tion, which permits, or even invites, the construction of imagined communities in the context of race.

At a minimum, the signifying chain of civilisational *difference* opens up
the possibility of *empowering* those social forces in 'Western democracies'
already politically legitimised through discourses of ethnic nationalism.
In fact, this kind of nationalism has become increasingly and openly
racist, resulting in widespread beatings and even killings of non-white
people in 'Western democracies' (Doty, 1993: 443–5). Huntington and
others who share his perspective, therefore, seem to be doing two things
at the same time: (i) they are expressing and legitimising the views of
xenophobic social forces in the West, and (ii) acting as the 'organic intellectuals' for the new geopolitical grand strategy of Western states. Since
race is subtly implicated in the constitution of the difference currently
being constructed, these intellectuals are also valorising the racialisation

of identity formation in the West, and simultaneously, the marginalisation of 'the rest'.

Conclusion

Accordingly, race is likely to become an increasingly significant site in the negotiation of identities and thus deserves further attention. R. L. Doty explains how this logic works. She writes:

> To regard race as a *site* where issues of identity and difference, self and other, inclusion and exclusion are resolved highlights the importance of racialisation as a dynamic process through which the identities of social groups can be defined and bound. This, of course, is not to suggest that racialisation is the only such process by which identities are constructed and boundaries drawn. It is, however, to suggest that racialisation is an inherently social and cultural process that interacts and overlaps other social and cultural processes that have been important in constructing identities and drawing boundaries. (Doty, 1993: 455–6)

More broadly, certain processes of neo-colonisation – that is of the mind as well as of territories and civilisations – exist today, for example through the increasing globalisation of production and its 'market civilisation', as well as the growth in racist and a Manichean ideology of Western supremacy. Indeed, current trends may be producing a situation where 'a privileged minority of the world's population . . . [is] living a defensive garrison existence' (Cox, 1995b: 9). This is a situation that resembles colonialism, and, like earlier forms of colonialism, it seems unsustainable. A reason is that in the same way as collective and emancipatory violence was the response to structural oppression in colonial Africa (and elsewhere), today's globally dispossessed may engage in not only an innovatory, although defensive and self-preservatory response (what Fantu Cheru has shown, in this collection, to be the 'weapons of the weak' in Africa) but also in what Fanon called 'absolute *praxis*', that is a revolutionary moment of emancipation.

Seen this way, one way to read recent world order tendencies is in terms of how the 'innocent' category of race is politically and culturally activated in struggles over the nature of world order. Put in more abstract terms, the issue is how race becomes a *constitutive moment* in the complex and overdetermined processes of structuration in the emerging world order. It is precisely in its passage from an abstract category to a generative principle of identity constitution that race becomes racialised. It is important to note that while race as a general category is (ultimately) embedded in the social and material conditions of life, the form and content of racialised referents and of racism, are historically specific. This is so because race *per se* is not a fixed and fully constituted entity, and is rarely deployed as an autonomous and self-contained category of difference. Rather, it is almost always combined with other factors which have 'difference-making properties' – such as, immigration, crime, welfare, language, questions of patriotism, and so on. In this sense (that is, of over-determined complexity) racialisation is discursively constructed through articulatory practices.

The discursive constitution of identity/difference through racialisation, however, does not mean that 'race' is simply invented, or that it is an inert object available for endless 'manipulation'. To accept the latter would actually de-historicise the complex process of racialisation and would assume, *a priori*, that which has to be explained – namely, the making of a racialised imaginary. I want to suggest, therefore, that the extent to which race is used as an articulatory principle of mobilisation/exclusion is very much underpinned by specific configurations of social forces, and, more importantly, by the balance of these social forces.

In the context of my larger discussion, therefore, race is likely to overlap with the marginalisation generated by globalisation, and with the new national security concerns of the West. The proximate concerns about too many migrants (and refugees), combined with the larger fears of civilisational erosion, have already given rise to a siege mentality type of politics in the West. If this new attempt at a racio-civilisational dominance is left unchallenged, a Manichean world order is not that unthinkable. In this regard also, there should be concerns about any unreconstructed philosophy of *praxis* which refuses to acknowledge that while hegemonic common sense, by definition, means a disciplined homogenisation of thinking, counter-hegemonic practices involve 'endogenous', plural and differentiated actions. Emancipatory knowledge, therefore, has an important role to play.[4]

NOTES

My thanks to Stephen Gill, James Mittelman, Martin Hewson and an anonymous reviewer for their helpful comments and constructive suggestions for developing and rewriting this chapter.

1 It is worth mentioning at the outset that the term 'global politics' is used here in a deliberate conceptual sense in order to: (a) outline my disagreement with the ontological assumptions of International Relations as a state-centric and Euro-American practice and (b) to accommodate the analysis of global social forces which were important to Fanon and which have been generally ignored in traditional International Relations theorising.

2 It is in this context that one can make sense of Adlai Stevenson's wish 'for the time when the last blacked-faced comedian has quit preaching about colonialism so that the United Nations could move on to more crucial issues like disarmament' (quoted in Doty, 1993: 446).

3 If ontology is about the conceptual determination of 'significant entities' in the discipline, epistemology is concerned with the way in which those entities become connected to provide explanation about an object. The epistemology of the realist school of International Relations (not thus to be confused with scientific realism as a philosophical approach) is intended to provide a particular form of 'scientific knowledge' instead of 'ideology' or 'opinion', which are understood as distortions of reality.

The most important epistemological claims made by the scientific form of realism, which Robert Cox (1981) has called 'neo-realism', are roughly as follows (these are drawn from Morgenthau, 1946; Waltz, 1979; and Holsti, 1985). Collectively, these claims constitute what I would call a neo-realist ideology of its nature as a science:

(a) Realism is concerned with what is, rather than what ought to be, that is to say, realism is ontologically objective.
(b) Objectivity is possible because the subject is not committed to any normative or ethical position.
(c) Realism is value-free in so far as the 'analyst' abandons his/her values in the process of inquiry.
(d) Realism provides scientific knowledge because the phenomena which it studies are patterns and regularities unaffected by time and place.

4 This may well be the reason why, for example, as professor at York University, Robert Cox began many of his courses in International Political Economy with Frantz Fanon's *Wretched of the Earth* as the very first reading on the syllabus.

12   Whose crisis? Early and post-modern masculinism

V. Spike Peterson

In chapter 1 of this volume, Stephen Gill characterises current transformations as 'a reordering and redefinition of the basic components of
social reality . . . involv[ing] changes in consciousness and processes of
objectification'. Having noted the sense of uncertainty attending these
mutations, he suggests that 'the contemporary configuration of world
order is in structural crisis'.

I endorse Gill's sense of the profundity (depth, extent, scope, significance) of today's transformations and, implicitly, the challenges they pose
to conventional theory/practice. What I would additionally emphasise is
the inseparability of empirical, conceptual and 'socio-psychological'
developments: how changes/events in the world 'out there' produce *and*
are produced by changes in how we conceptualise and who we think we
are; how external objective social change and internal subjective self
change are interactive (Bologh, 1987: 147); how ways of being, ways of
thinking and ways of identifying refer to different yet reciprocally constituted dimensions of social relations.

I stress these points because International Relations scholars so fre-
quently appear to resist and/or deny them. Yet I am persuaded that we
cannot begin to adequately comprehend, much less address, the current
'crisis' until we abandon positivist binaries and take relational thinking
seriously (e.g., Peterson, 1992a). This involves understanding the world
'out there' (practices, institutions, structures of social re/production),
how we think (meaning systems, ideologies, paradigms) and who we are
(subjectivity, agency, self and collective identities) as interacting dimensions of social reality. In particular, in so far as 'structural crisis' refers to
incongruent inconsistencies – even contradictions – among these dimensions, then we cannot comprehend the crisis by focusing on only one or
another of its dimensions.

In this chapter, I consider how the dimensions of today's crisis are
linked by gender.[1] More provocatively, I argue that today's structural
crisis can be analysed as a crisis of masculinity: that it is historically particular social structures, collective meaning systems and subjectivity

185

premised on masculinism (and linked by reference to early state institutions; see below) that are undergoing structural transformation. Stated less provocatively, gender relations are central to, and weave throughout, the changes in what Gill refers to as 'consciousness', 'processes of objectification' and 'key institutional aspects of historical reality'. Hence, by attending to gender and its linkages, feminist accounts offer integrative and interdisciplinary (though not homogenising or totalising) theorisation of today's crisis.

My account here focuses on conveying the pervasiveness and power of gender and necessarily highlights patterns at the expense of specificity and variation. I make these trade-offs in the belief that feminist innovations – and their emancipatory promise – cannot be appreciated or assessed until the systemic and structural effects of gender are acknowledged and until feminist scholarship is engaged with this understanding of its significance. The argument has two parts, framed by two related questions. First, why is gender so invisible in IR accounts if, as feminists keep insisting, it is so central?[2] Second, how does rendering gender visible alter our understanding of today's crisis?

Invisibilisation: 'how we got here'

From a feminist perspective, the innovations of critical and post-modern theorists offer important alternatives to mainstream orthodoxy and its disavowal of gender. Certainly, feminist theories have been enriched by critical and post-modern perspectives, even as they move beyond the androcentrism retained in those accounts. Yet, to date, there is little evidence of reciprocal engagement; feminist scholarship in IR remains a token presence, treated as an 'add on' (if acknowledged at all) in the work of most critical and post-modern theorists (Whitworth, 1989; Sylvester, 1994; Newton, 1988).[3] Even as states are historicised, exploitation criticised, production analysed and security deconstructed, gendered power/politics remain invisible. In short, whatever the innovative contributions of these theorists, however dissident, disruptive or deconstructive their inquiries, it is remarkable how they fail to disturb – much less dismantle – androcentric premises.

From a Braudelian perspective, I suggest that one thing this silence on gender tells us is how 'naturalised' masculinism is, how deeply entrenched in the *longue durée* of human history, and how constitutive of socio-historical structures that, as Gill puts it in chapter 1, it 'take[s] on an almost geological, quasi-permanent character'. But however 'quasi-permanent' in appearance, masculinism – like states, capitalism and racism – is historical, contingent and mutable. That it appears ahistorical has a great deal to do with how we conceptualise history: as the unre-corded past or the recorded and interpreted past that only begins, by definition, with the invention of writing (Lerner, 1986: 4). If history begins with writing and writing is a corollary of early state formation and early state formation institutionalises gender hierarchy, then history begins when men begin to rule – and to naturalise that rule through author(is)ing masculinism as the premise of collective meaning systems.

With that as my starting point, the first part of my argument considers feminist theoretical innovations by exhuming masculinism from the *longue durée* of 'Western civilisation'. This involves a history that exposes masculinist premises 'buried' in early state formation's codification – realised through the technology of writing – of particular structures of group re/production, collective meaning systems and subjectivity. Responding to Gill's introductory questions, a feminist account of early state-making thus illuminates 'how we got here' – to naturalised masculinism pervading social relations – and, significantly, how masculinism is rendered so invisible as to be absent in even critical and post-modern accounts.

With this history as background, I then respond to the second question by considering feminist theoretical innovations in relation to today's transformations, characterised in this chapter as a crisis of masculinity. Building on a feminist account of 'how we got here', the second part of my argument illuminates 'where we are' – by rendering gender visible in today's structural crisis.

Whose state? Naturalising masculinism

Whether characterised as 'the urban revolution' or 'the rise of civilisa-tion', early state formation marks a profound turning point in human relations. By definition, the transition involves a number of simultaneous and interactive transformations: the centralisation of accumulation pro-cesses and political authority, institutionalisation of exploitative divisions of labour, reconfiguration of personal and collective identities, and ideo-logical legitimation of these transformations, enabled by the development of writing for record-keeping and juridico/legal purposes. The following sketch suggests how, in 'Western civilisation', this transition established new forms of group re/production (patriarchal states, family 'house-holds', divisions of labour), meaning systems (philosophy, objectivism/ rationality) and subjectivity (heterosexist, dichotomised gender intra-group identities and adversarial intergroup identities). For the purposes of this chapter, the sketch emphasises how the dichotomy of gender is constituted by these interacting dimensions of early state formation.[4]

Eschewing positivist pursuit of the 'origins' or 'causes' of states and gender hierarchy, it is useful to consider how social groups (beyond the mother–infant relationship) might be constituted and reproduced in historically varying contexts. In Jill Vickers' words, 'male groups cannot reproduce themselves without "their" women being committed to both the physical and social reproduction of the group'. Hence, we can view patriarchal sex/gender arrangements as a contingent (one among a number of possibilities), historically specific response to the 'dilemma of how to construct enduring forms of social organisation, group cohesion and identity' (Vickers, 1990: 481, 483). On this view, early state formation organised group reproduction by institutionalising male control over women's biological reproduction (whose children, under what conditions) and social reproduction (whose 'culture', whose identities), and entailed limiting women's autonomy and undercutting their authority (in so far as women were excluded from defining group interests, regulated in expressions of sexuality and loyalty, and denied the status of 'personhood' attached to group decision-makers). In short, the coherence and continuity of the group was achieved 'by limiting the autonomy, freedom of choice and social adulthood of the group's physical and social reproducers' (1990: 482).

Contemporary theorists argue that opposition to state formation was often widespread and long-lasting (Mann, 1986), as decentralised groups struggled to retain their autonomy and state-makers sought to appropriate the labour and resources of kin-communities and eliminate their rival claims to authority. But however much kin-based groups resisted centralisation and/or women resisted their subordination to group interests, patriarchal states, as a form of group re/production, were the 'victors' and kinship structures the 'losers in the civilisational process' (Reiter, 1977: 9). Claims that states are patriarchal are documented by reference to the gender dimensions of the transition to centralised power/authority, which are my focus here.[5]

Whereas kin societies did not distinguish rigidly among 'political', 'economic' and familial/'reproductive' activities, or segregate them spatially, Western state formation constituted such distinctions in processes that simultaneously constituted gendered dichotomies. In particular, states (structured by property not kinship claims) established relatively independent 'family' households as the basic socio-economic unit; they abstracted and centralised authority/power in a 'public/political sphere' that was then distinguished from (while being dependent upon) a 'private/household' sphere of dismembered and domesticated kinship relations, focused narrowly on social reproduction. In this process, propertied men acquired status, authority and resources as patriarchal heads-of-households and by their identification with the now privileged sphere of politics. Women lost a variety of status, authority and resource claims as centralisation constituted new divisions of power/authority, labour and identities.

Divisions of power/authority

The multifaceted, crosscutting and nuanced social relations typical of larger kin networks afforded women various claims to respect, authority and wealth. In the transition to states, women lost kin claims to property, became transmitters of property and were treated as property themselves. Basing citizenship on property claims (and/or military service) precluded women's participation and constituted 'political' authority as a male prerogative in a 'public' sphere. Relatively isolated in individual households, women became more dependent upon fathers and husbands, losing access to the countervailing support of extended kin networks.

Divisions of labour

'Women, by virtue of their involvement in subsistence work and their ability to create other people' provided both productive and reproductive labour (Gailey, 1987: x). The resources made possible by appropriating this 'dual capacity' of women were crucial to centralised accumulation (slavery appeared later (Lerner, 1986)). This form of appropriation was accomplished both by controlling women within the group and seizing women outside of the group. Whether as wives/daughters, concubines or slaves, women's re/productive labour was appropriated to enhance elite power (which benefited some women more than others). In short, state formation institutionalised exploitative divisions of labour (by gender and 'class'), which permitted the accumulation of resources to support non-productive elites, state projects and the continuity of centralised rule.

Divisions of identity

The political significance of (inheritable) claims to property, membership/citizenship and elite power shaped the state's regulation of sexual relations: through establishing the norm of heterosexuality, controlling women's reproductive activities and, as a singularly important consequence, codifying stratification among women. Simultaneously, instituting 'family' households involved stressing women's sexual/reproductive activities, which were previously only a part of their lives and identities. As an effect of these developments, the binary construction of masculine–feminine constituted new social and sexual identities. For example, in Athens, the emerging construction of 'man' as purposive, political agent and rational actor, contrasted dramatically with 'woman' as inferior in political agency, 'closer to nature', sexual/irrational and naturally responsible for reproductive labour. The point here is that 'gender differentiation' – the (heterosexist) dichotomising of masculine-feminine and 'man–woman' identities – is not 'natural' or biologically given but the effect of historically specific configurations of power (e.g., Butler, 1990, 1993; Foucault, 1978, 1985; Ortner and Whitehead, 1981; Stanton, 1992).

Of course, the transition to states also involved coercion. In contrast to the sporadic raiding and feuding of kin networks, states engaged in organised militarism as a facet of consolidating and sustaining centralised rule. This entailed new social roles for (male) warriors/defenders, which constituted gendered divisions of labour as well as gendered divisions of identity and power/authority. Yet however much coercive power was utilised in establishing centralised authority, cultural and ideological dimensions were crucial for the reproduction of state systems. In early state formation, transformations in collective meaning systems – facilitated by the technologies of writing, under the control of exclusively male elites – elevated masculinist (and elitist) symbol/meaning systems, in particular, the institutionalisation of male deities and, by extension, legitimation/naturalisation of the male right to rule.

What renders early state formation unique is the convergence of centralised power/authority, the exploitation of re/productive labour, and the technology of writing such that, once established, centralised authority was able to turn coercive power to historically novel effect through enhanced systemic control. In the words of Ronald Cohen:

there are multiple roads to statehood . . . that produc[ed] similar effects . . . Once a society begins to evolve more centralised and permanent authority structures, the political realm itself becomes an increasingly powerful determinant of change in the economy, society and culture of the system . . . the hierarchical structure itself becomes a selective determinant that feeds back to all the sociocultural features to make them fit more closely into its overall pattern. (Cohen, 1978: 8)

In so far as writing was invented as a function of state-formation and state-formation was the institutionalisation of (elite) male power/authority, the development of thought manifested in written texts was exclusively from (elite) male experience and perspective. The effects of this power to control what was written (hence rendered authoritative and durable, across both time and space) and from whose perspective (that of elite males) have yet to be systematically reckoned. These effects are central to the politics of subsequent Western language/discourse and the

continuity of androcentric meaning systems. And they are crucial for historicising the *longue durée* of male dominance that was legitimated – and
naturalised – by reference to male-author(is)ed history/texts.

From the Athenian legacy, political scientists are most familiar with the
dichotomy of public and private spheres that continues to frame how we
constitute power, politics and 'real' (read paid/politicised) work, where
rational and collectively significant decision-making occurs, and who
should be doing reproductive (read unpaid/naturalised) labour. Less
familiar but no less significant is the objectivist metaphysics (phallogo-
centrism) of Western philosophy. Constraining (and enabling) how we
conceptualise and make sense of our experience/world, this metaphysics
of identity naturalised a now familiar litany of hierarchical dichotomies:
subject–object, culture–nature, mind–body, public–private, etc., that are
based on the dichotomy *of masculine–feminine* (Derrida, 1976; Hekman,
1990; Peterson, 1992a; 1996b). In particular, this binary metaphysics
enhanced our capacity to analyse and objectify, with normatively varying
but certainly extensive consequences. In this sense, it is key to the *longue
durée* of a (Western) mentality celebrating human (read elite male)
agency, control and certainty – a mentality associated in the modern era
with (masculinist) science, capitalism, and instrumental technologies,
and in the present moment, with a crisis in ways of thinking/knowing.

The point here is that contextualising the 'founding' texts of 'history'
and state-making exposes their masculinism as not coincidental to but
constitutive of new (hierarchical and heterosexist) ways of being, thinking
and identifying. Stated differently, the conceptual categories and objectivist philosophy bequeathed to Western theory/practice were the product
of (gendered) power struggles and are themselves contingent and political (Peterson, 1996b).

In sum, while male-oriented customs preceded and enabled early state
formation, the latter institutionalised systemic gender hierarchy:
masculinist authority relations and exploitative divisions of labour were
here backed by the coercive power of the state and naturalised through
ideological reconfiguration of collective meaning systems that enduringly
structured Western theory/practice. This schematic overview greatly
oversimplifies what are complex and often conflictual processes. In particular, it neglects resistance dynamics and variations among states, families,
gender relations and disciplining practices. It suggests, however, the profundity (depth, extent, scope, significance) of the transition to early states
and how that transformation entailed a struggle against alternative ways of
being/knowing. It also suggests how the 'victory' of masculinism was
'deeply' naturalised, hence depoliticised, through elite male control of collective meaning systems that codified agency, authority and reason as

masculine. What that struggle involved, and the alternatives it displaced, were buried under/by the monuments of state-making. Masculinism was naturalised; and that which is natural has no history and no politics – and no visibility in IR.

Modern states and gender complexities

European state-formation took place in a different context, one that was marked by an emerging culture of individualism and private property, an increasingly secular world view enhanced by the development of reason/science, and expanding relations of production associated with early industrialisation and capitalism. Though set in a different context, in so far as the constitutive features of state-making (centralisation of authority and accumulation based on family/households, ideological consolidation under elite control) remain unchanged, modern state-making replicated, in striking ways, the gender patterns of early states. This is most visible in (but not exclusive to) civil/liberal states that revitalised a public–private dichotomy of power/authority, labour and identities (Elshtain, 1981; Nicholson, 1986; Pateman, 1988; Peterson, 1992c, 1997).

At the same time, the context was different: the development of industrial capitalism and urbanisation (inextricable from demographic transitions, applications of instrumental rationality and developments in technology) and commitments to liberal individualism (inextricable from developments in moral reasoning, capitalist relations and new divisions of labour) reframed gender relations in complicated ways. Two 'threads' have particular significance, and illustrate the complexities.

First, by commodifying labour/production elsewhere, industrial capitalism altered the 'economic' role of households and women's position within them. Enduring masculinist ideologies ensured that re/production *in* the family/household was codified as (natural, unpaid) 'women's work', paid labour outside of the home as 'men's work'. These developments shifted the boundary of public and private, in effect creating a third sphere of market/economics, distinguished from government/politics and family/personal spheres. In these shifts (vastly oversimplified here), men took on the prestige afforded by affiliation with political and economic spheres, while women took on increased responsibility for emotional care-taking and family/social reproduction – whether or not they also worked outside of the home.

Second, the emergence and realisation of liberalism – especially its principle of equality and promotion of personal rights – offered ideological support for resistance by women (and 'others') to systemic social hierarchies. Once citizenship was based on the rights of the abstract individual, women insisted on their own inclusion in the category of 'equal individuals'. Liberal doctrines thus fuelled early (and remain central to contemporary) women's liberation movements. At the same time, however, liberalism is inseparable from the masculinist rationalism that fuelled androcentric – often misogynist – science that discriminated against women both materially (witch persecutions and masculinisation of healing/medicine) and symbolically (the insidious identification of woman/feminine with objectified nature, necessity and irrationality).

What we observe is that dynamic and interacting systems of power – masculinism, objectivism, liberalism, industrial capitalism and state centralisation – produced effects that range from mutually enhancing to structurally inconsistent. Some of the structural inconsistencies have 'deepened' in the intervening centuries and constitute today's crisis. In particular, capitalist development has eroded the material basis of the familial household and liberalism has generated multiple theories/practices of equality. In both cases, and reciprocally, masculine dominance is challenged, and those challenges are integral to the structural transformations we confront today.

Visibilisation: a crisis of masculinity

From a feminist perspective, we can analyse today's transformations as a crisis of masculinity and, by attending to gender and its linkages, more adequately comprehend 'where we are'. That is, we can see how profound changes in gender relations affect, and are affected by, changes in forms of group re/production (crises of the family, sovereign state system and global economic restructuring), in collective meaning systems (crises of Western philosophy and instrumental rationality) and subjectivity (crises of humanist man and of identity, manifested in the politics of sexuality and reconfigurations of political agency). In Braudelian terms, a gender-sensitive lens illuminates mounting tensions and even contradictions between the 'deeper historical structures' of masculinism (bequeathed to us by the success of Western civilisation) and multiple transformations in 'events-time' (the dimensions of today's structural crisis). For example, states depend on women's reproductive labour and the ideology of gender hierarchy that obscures this dependence; today, however, both women's labour and gender ideologies are in transformation, with complex implications for states (as well as for how we understand work, re/production, families, sexuality, etc.). My elaboration of these claims is necessarily brief and oversimplified, focusing on major ways in which expressions of and expectations in regard to masculinity/masculinism are in crisis.

Group re/production

Globalisation exposes more than ever the interaction of 'levels of analysis' and how sovereignty (understood in masculine terms of autonomy, independence and military capacity) is eroded. Even the most powerful states find themselves vulnerable to forces beyond their control in ways that undercut (masculine) ability to command military force (eroded by economic constraints, international agreements, domestic resistance), to control national economies (compromised by interdependence and unregulated global finance) and to protect domestic populations (threatened by border-transgressing pollutants, weapons and diseases). In short, the masculine leaders/warriors of the state are unable to defend the 'motherland' – her frontiers, her well-being or her honour – from 'foreign' men/power. In so far as politics is explicitly about manhood (Brown, W., 1988: 4), which is definitively demonstrated by sovereignty/control (Elshtain, 1992: 143), the masculinity of today's states/men is in crisis: men who cannot defend their woman/nation have jeopardised their 'claim' to that body/land (Peterson, 1995: 180).

Globalisation, ironically, also exposes the centrality of 'the private' (gender identities, family/household activities) to IR concerns. First, new global divisions of labour – which are dramatically gendered – reveal how households, states and global economies are linked both structurally (*vis-à-vis* production and reproduction, distribution of resources and power) and ideologically (*vis-à-vis* socialisation practices, personal and group identifications) (Mies, 1986; Mies et al., 1988; Smith and Wallerstein, 1992; Smith, 1993).[6] Second, as global restructuring alters state power and national economic strategies, it affects delivery of welfare, the rights of workers, the politics of citizenship and the political significance of state-centric identifications. In short, changing global divisions of labour are gendered and are changing divisions of identity and power in gendered ways (Peterson, 1996a).

These linkages are clearest when we look at global divisions of labour and how gendered divisions of identity and labour are constituted within households. We know that states structure the family/household to meet re/productive needs. But today's restructuring exposes how states do so in the context of a global economy that shapes those needs: that is, households, states and the global economy are not separate 'levels' but interact and depend on each other. As the site of social reproduction, the family/household is where we learn most about identities, hierarchies (of race, ethnicity, caste, class, gender, age, sexual orientation, religious affiliation), our positions within them, and how to reproduce, reconfigure and resist them. It is where we first learn how labour is divided, delegated and differentially rewarded. It is where we learn who we (and 'they') are, who is expected to do what, and how different ways of being/thinking are valued. It thus shapes our personal identities and group allegiances, even as it may provide the space, resources and motivation to resist domination practices. As the site of informal sector activities, households both sustain capitalist dynamics (by ensuring non-commodified social reproduction) and resist capitalism's commodifying dynamic (by constituting activities that defy exploitation and by refusing the commodification of personal relations (Nash, 1988: 14)).

In short, households are crucial sites of power – with reciprocal effects on states and global economics – and they are undergoing profound transformations. In spite of their importance, they have been excluded in dichotomising analyses that privilege formal/productive/men's/paid labour. Feminists have criticised that exclusion not simply as a political protest against 'ignoring women' but as a formidable critique of economic analysis (e.g., Ferber and Nelson, 1993; Waring, 1988) and economic policy (Bakker, 1994; Elson, 1991). In particular, the theoretical attention feminists have long paid to 'women's work' and household re/production is crucial to current globalisation studies attempting to theorise the dramatic increase in informal sector activities (Bakker, 1994; Boris and Prugl, 1996; Ward, 1990).

As enterprises everywhere seek a reduction in labour costs and increasingly turn from direct to indirect forms of employment (casualisation, subcontracting), fewer workers can anticipate full-time wages and benefits (Standing, 1989: 1079). Structurally located as cheap, 'docile', reliable and flexible workers (Hagen and Jenson, 1988: 10), women's employment globally has increased, often at the expense of men's employment, and especially in ill-paid, semi-skilled jobs typical of export processing zones (Mitter, 1986).[7] The effects are complex and contradictory: women gain resources and often status through employment, and it certainly affects their self-identity, but women are typically entering employment under worsening structural conditions. Increasingly, people in both 'developed' and 'developing' countries engage in informal (and formal) sector activities that are irregular, part-time, unprotected, non-unionised and without benefits or state regulation. Mies draws our attention to the gender of this phenomenon by calling it 'housewifisation': where male workers who expected otherwise now find themselves in the situation of housewives: atomised, unorganised and economically insecure (Mies, 1986).

Restructuring is most visibly gendered when we look at its effects on welfare provisioning, which is key to the reproduction of social groups. In large part due to feminist interventions, economic policy analysts now recognise that restructuring takes its greatest toll on women, and especially poor women (Commonwealth Secretariat, 1989; Mayatech Corporation, 1992; Afshar and Dennis, 1992; Vickers, 1991). While the effects of restructuring have been most severe in 'developing' countries, there are parallel gender (and class) effects in 'developed' countries where cutbacks in public welfare also have their greatest impact on women and the poor. Briefly, these effects include: (i) feminisation of poverty, especially among female-headed households (estimated at 30 per cent worldwide (United Nations, 1991: 18)); (ii) hardship on women who must 'take up the slack' created by shrinking resources and contraction of social services (e.g., increases in re/productive labour; more time ensuring food availability and health maintenance for the family; greater emotional care-taking; more responsibility for ill/elderly dependants); (iii) erosion of hard-won gender equality gains due to public/state cutbacks (e.g., loss of child care, welfare support, training programs, affirmative action); (iv) loss of employment when public sector jobs are cut.[8] Women (and men) are not passive victims in these developments; their resistance to and negotiations with state and market institutions have effects as well. In sum, global restructuring alters the relationships among political, economic and familial activities, which shape (and are shaped by) changing identities of workers and women.

Collective meaning systems

Today's transformations also challenge enduring forms of consciousness, or ways of thinking/knowing. References to a 'new age of uncertainty' express a discomfort with our inability to control or even comprehend the changes around us, as former world views/paradigmmes prove inadequate or are undermined by new and disorienting critiques. From a feminist perspective, the contemporary crisis of thinking/knowing – variously characterised as post-modernism, the death of humanist man/philosophy, or the crisis of instrumental rationality/science – can be viewed as a fundamental challenge to the androcentric system of thought 'inherited' from early Western state-making and revitalised in the Enlightenment.

However the challenges are characterised, the foundations and certainties of Western philosophy and objectivist science are no longer secure. This insecurity is gendered because the rational subject in these accounts is not gender-neutral (as claims of objectivity and references to 'humanism' purport) but masculine. Moreover, they are masculine in the specific sense (as an extensive feminist literature demonstrates) that the qualities constituting reason and the objective/knowing rational subject are those constituting masculinity/maleness as categorically that which excludes femininity (irrationality, emotion, intuition, feeling) (e.g., Lloyd, 1984). In short, it is specifically male/masculine ways of thinking/knowing – inseparable from their history in state-making and capitalism – that are in crisis. Like impotence in the face of threats to the motherland, and failure to economically provide for the family, philosophical uncertainty and loss of instrumental control disturb our understanding of – and belief in – masculinity.

Subjectivity

These observations return us to questions of subjectivity/identity and how the latter articulates with forms of political allegiance and action. In the past decade, identity has become a crucial concern of IR theorists as new and often conflictual identities proliferate: on and off the battlefield, within, across and 'above' the state. All groups/collectivities – whether bounded by ethnicity/race, religion, territory or shared purpose – are gendered because they are comprised of gendered individuals (whose gender identity affects their participation, contributions, allegiances) and the organisation and reproduction of groups is itself gendered (by divisions of labour, roles, and power).[9] A crisis of masculinity applies here as well, because feminists and other critics of domination contest the male privilege in these groups and because 'given' gender identities are profoundly destabilised by current transformations.

Women's liberation and feminist movements have been key to altering – by politicising – how we think about, reproduce and resist traditional gender (and class, race, ethnic) 'givens'. These changes range from the intimate (e.g., sexual politics, reproductive rights, family configurations) to the international (e.g., women in politics, global conferences, women's human rights). The range of these changes is significant. Whether or not structural power dynamics are dramatically modified, feminisms have altered our consciousness of systemic male dominance: in religion, education, healthcare, media, new social movements, business, governments, nationalisms and revolutions. Women disrupt the tradition of male authority/power as they increasingly participate in the public sphere activities of politics and paid work; their presence politicises and problematises the masculinity of these activities. But masculinity is also disrupted in the private sphere when women demand respect, have independent incomes and access to social services (e.g., women's shelters), and expect men to do the laundry. Because it is so central to self-esteem and the cultural dicta are so relentless, gender identity is difficult to reorder; it is not an identity we can simply take on or off. As a consequence, challenges to it are often deeply disturbing, though, for similar reasons, unlikely to be acknowledged.

The politicisation of gender extends to problematising compulsory heterosexuality and the 'naturalness' of dichotomised gender/sex identities, as evidenced in the new studies of sexuality and lesbian and gay political struggles. These challenges to orthodoxy are linked to the crisis in philosophy because the demise of the unitary, rational subject (undermined by psychoanalytic as well as post-modern claims) exposes its assumption of stable, dichotomised gender identities and their heterosexual norm. Rather, 'the rigid distinctions between heterosexual and homosexual identities, which grounded the system of sexuality and which Freud already blurred, are consistently and concretely subverted in the new work on sexuality' (Stanton, 1992: 7). Similarly, these challenges are inseparable from critiques of reason/science that disrupt all 'given' categories – including sex and nature – and insist on historicising the construction of concepts, practices, institutions and, especially, foundational dichotomies. Historicising sex/gender brings us back to early state formation, where, as I have argued, the production of dichotomised gender (now in crisis) is inseparable from the production of Western phallocentric philosophy (also in crisis), and the institutionalisation of exploitative re/production (now in crisis as a contradiction between simultaneously requiring women as productive workers outside, and reproductive caretakers inside, the household).

In sum, challenges to masculinity weave throughout these disruptions: a state that cannot defend/protect its people is stigmatised as feminine; the globalisation of production appears to feminise labour; philosophy becomes feminine by deconstructing masculine reason; and men themselves are feminised by blurred boundaries between public–private, autonomy–dependence and masculine–feminine. The deeply embedded historical structure of masculinism has ensured that femininity is denigrated (women on pedestals notwithstanding), which renders processes of feminisation uncomfortable, even horrific, for those heavily invested in the dichotomy of masculine–feminine. Of course, this is the key: as we identify new agendas for the study of IR/IPE, we must deeply rethink how the dichotomy of gender structures and constrains our lives.

Conclusion

On the face of it, the implications of the preceding for research and emancipatory theory/practice are straightforward: we must make gender visible and move beyond its oppressive dynamics. This involves taking seriously what women do (especially, reproductive labour in its many guises), how gender structures modes of thought and constructions of agency, and how the hierarchical dichotomy of gender sustains and naturalises the objectification of 'women, nature, other' (Trinh, 1989).

Gender is conventionally invisible because the *longue durée* of masculinism obscures the power required to institutionalise, internalise and reproduce gender hierarchy and its associated oppressions. In this sense, gender is hard to see because it is so taken for granted. But gender also resists visibility and critique due to its pervasiveness and our personal investments: it is not only 'out there' structuring activities and institutions, and 'in our heads' structuring discourse and ideologies; it is also 'in here' – in our hearts and bodies – structuring our intimate desires, our sexuality, our self-esteem and our dreams. As a consequence, our investments in gendered selves fuel heroic and self-sacrificing as well as despotic and self-serving actions. In this sense, gender is hard to see and critique because it orders 'everything' and disrupting that order feels threatening – not only at the 'level' of institutions and global relations but also in relation to the most intimate and deeply etched beliefs/experiences of personal (but relentlessly gendered) identity. Yet, however much we are uncomfortable with challenges to gender ordering, we are in the midst of them. Failure to acknowledge and address these challenges both impairs our understanding of the world(s) we live in and sustains relations of domination.

To argue for the power and pervasiveness of gender is not to identify masculinism as the 'primary' or 'always most important' oppression, to subordinate other systemic critiques of domination, or to promote 'femininity' as an alternative. It is to identify gender – understood as always and reciprocally shaped by class, race and cultural hierarchies – as a structural feature of social relations, to insist that the subordination of women is not reducible to other forms of oppression, and to expose how the dichotomy of gender underpins even as it depoliticises multiple domination dynamics; it is to argue that we cannot understand social re/production – continuity and change – or any systemic oppression without addressing gender.

To make gender visible, this chapter recast contemporary structural transformations as a 'crisis of masculinity'. The latter is not necessarily good for women, much less feminism. It is useful for exposing the centrality of gender and linking the multiple dimensions of our current transformations. Feminist scholarship addresses but does not 'resolve' this crisis; it does illuminate 'how we got here' and 'where we are', and it analyses social relations as the mutual interaction of 'what we do', 'how we think' and 'who we are'. It thus offers integrative, interdisciplinary and critical analyses. Most importantly, it exposes how the dichotomy of masculine–feminine fuels multiple forms of oppression – with obvious implications for emancipatory theory/practice.

NOTES

1 Gender refers to the social construction of power inequalities constituted by the hierarchical dichotomy of masculine over/against feminine. Gender hierarchy describes systems of structural power over women associated with (hegemonic) masculinity. Hence, gender is not only about women but *necessarily about men and masculinity*. Neither is it simply about the domination of women but about the domination of all – women, nature, non-dominant males – whose objectification and exploitation is legitimated by casting them as feminine. Patriarchy is used narrowly to describe the absolute power of male heads of households over dependent family members; its broader meaning, as male dominance over women extended to society in general, is similar to gender hierarchy. Masculinism may refer to the system (masculine privileging) and/or to the ideology (naturalisation) of gender hierarchy. I understand feminism *not* as the 'opposite' of masculinism but as theoretical/practical efforts to transform *all* social hierarchies (classism, racism, heterosexism) intertwined and naturalised by the dichotomy of gender.

2 Feminists argue that gender is a structural, pervasive feature of our discourses, practices, institutions and identities. An extensive corpus of such International Relations literature exists. A selected historical bibliography on 'gender and IR' compiled in 1994 totalled 145 pages (Boutin, 1994). Jacqui True provides an excellent, current review of feminist innovations and literature (1996). See also Enloe, 1990, 1993; Grant and Newland, 1991; Pettman, 1996; Tickner, 1992; Peterson, 1992b; Peterson and Runyan, 1993; Sylvester, 1994; Whitworth, 1994; Stienstra, 1994; Beckman and D'Amico, 1994; Tetreault, 1995; Zalewski and Parpart, forthcoming. Feminist IPE citations appear in the text.

3 Feminists are not denying, much less disparaging, the small but steady increase in 'taking notice' of feminism. This is not an insignificant or easily won gain. Rather, we are seeking engagement with feminist scholarship. This involves more than a token feminist chapter while 'most of the work that appears throughout the rest of those anthologies seems unfamiliar with, and unaffected by, feminist scholarship' (Whitworth, 1994, x). It is important to add, as Whitworth does, that 'resistance to feminist work . . . is far surpassed by the continuing resistance to analyses by anti-racist scholars or work by sexual minorities . . . Feminist struggles are only one among many' (xiv).

4 In order to highlight the gender patterns in early state formation, this brief history necessarily oversimplifies and overgeneralises what were contested, complex and uneven transformations. It draws on a synthesis of extensive research in archaeology, anthropology, classical studies, Western philosophy, political economy, state theories and feminist scholarship. For elaboration and citations see Peterson, 1988, 1992c, 1996b.

5 Contemporary terms (family, public, private) are technically inappropriate in so far as they exaggerate the formalisation of distinctive 'spheres' in primarily agrarian economies. I use them for brevity and to highlight the contrast

between kinship networks (without rigid divisions) and states (with their structural divisions and new 'household' base).

6 The international political economy of sex (e.g., Barry, 1995; Enloe, 1990; Pettman, 1996; Truong, 1990) starkly illustrates how the personal (sexed, classed, raced, and ethno-nationally culturalised bodies; individual 'experiences' of sexual exploitation; sex work earnings in support of families/households) is linked to the political (hierarchies of age, gender, class, race/ethnicity and nation-states that structure sexual exploitation and economics; health care politics of sexually transmitted diseases) and the international (foreign currency accumulation from sex tourism and the international traffic in women as prostitutes, mail-order-brides and domestic servants; roles of colonisation and military bases in these dynamics).

7 Standing (1989: 1080) writes: 'Indeed, no country has successfully industrialised or pursued . . . [an export-led] development strategy without relying on a huge expansion of female labour. And in export processing zones of many industrialising countries it is not uncommon for three-quarters of all workers to be women.'

8 On the gendered welfare state and 'public patriarchy' see, for example, Gordon (1990); Hernes (1987); Sainsbury (1994); Sassoon (1987); Watson (1990).

9 Because it is crucial, not peripheral, to the continuity of all groups, reproduction – typically cast as private and natural – is pre-eminently political and as such should be at the centre of socio-political inquiry (Clark, 1976; Clark and Lange, 1979). Moreover, a focus on social reproduction also illuminates the politics of group identification and solidarity, especially relevant for contemporary analyses of nationalism (Vickers, 1990; Anthias and Yuval-Davis, 1989; on gendered nationalism in a foreign policy context, see Peterson, 1995).

Reflections on global order in the twenty-first century

Part IV discusses the overall condition of and potential for global order(s) on the eve of the twenty-first century. The authors offer quite varied perspectives. At this stage in the present transformation, no single viewpoint on the emerging world order could be sufficiently prescient. We appear to be at a cross-roads but cannot rely on the old, taken-for-granted pathways. What seems important for the development of theory is to explore the many paths available in an open, pioneering spirit of theoretical innovation.

The first chapter by Yoshikazu Sakamoto links Parts III and IV. It considers potentials for the globalisation of democracy through agencies associated with new concepts of civil society. In addition, the chapter situates the 'transformative dynamics of the modern world' since the eighteenth century, as involving a set of fundamental contradictions: (i) capitalism vs. socialism; (ii) democracy vs. authoritarianism; and (iii) nationalism vs. internationalism. Sakamoto notes that socialism and authoritarianism have receded in importance, whereas capitalism, democracy and nationalism have gained currency. In this context, James Rosenau examines mentalities associated with the multiple forms of the 'ordering' of the world, understood as overlapping and intersecting in patterns of integration and fragmentation: or 'fragmegration'. Susan Strange argues that large-scale global interstate war and the conflict between capitalism and socialism are of the past. Thus we need to pose new problems (Ps) and questions (Qs) to understand world order. Each of these three authors, albeit quite differently, situates his/her contribution in the context of the 'end' of the Cold War; particularly important are the implications of the dissolution of the USSR as a force in global politics. Strange's points about capitalism vs. socialism and inter-state war, and Sakamoto's views concerning global capitalism and democracy would have had a quite different resonance prior to 1989–91. Finally, returning to the theme of innovation, James Mittelman discusses knowledge production in future world order. He calls for a return to classical social theory to provide a perspective on today and tomorrow.

Tracing the history of the notion of global civil society, Sakamoto argues for an expanded understanding of democracy that applies to the state system, international institutions and the global market. He then assesses the prospects for democratisation associated with 'new' civil society. This concept of civil society is a non-economistic one, unlike, for example, that of Hegel or the Scottish Enlightenment thinkers. It draws on the inspiration of Solidarity and the East European popular-democratic movements in the 1970s and 1980s that sought some form of political autonomy from the state. He concludes, 'the extraordinary resilience of democracy has been demonstrated by the history of the past. It will be further endorsed by the history of the future as contemplated in the context of the development of the last couple of centuries.' By contrast, there will have to be significant modifications in capitalism because ecological constraints are growing, and 'because of the mounting democratic demands for equality and equity'. On the other hand, the forms that democracy will take will be globalised – to meet the requirements of 'internationalism' (regional and global politics). By implication, the extension of a new civil society would engage in a radical re-examination and challenge to the hegemony of the dominant capitalist concept of economy. This concept stands against a civil society conceived in terms of human solidarity, equity and democratic accountability.

Rosenau sketches a terrain for understanding the common sense of the future: 'the ontology that underlies the intersubjectively shared experience of the next generations'. Among and between state and non-state actors, contradictions and ambiguities of world order involve both co-operative orientations, involving unilateralism or subgroupism. The emergent world order partly comprises these perspectives and patterns in a process that involves both systemic integration and sub-system fragmentation. Such patterns overlap in a sphere of emergent activity called 'fragmegration' (See Figure 1, p. 223). Tensions resulting from such opposing dynamics, because of global communications grids and educational development, are now 'widely and intersubjectively understood'. They help to construct popular understandings that are part of a new, post-Cold War ontology. For example, the 'fragmegrative' aspect of ontology contains at least two sets of broadly shared understandings of, and orientations to, world affairs. These are (i) 'that globalisation is the prime source for change in the emergent order even as it produces contrary trends towards localising processes, implosions of societies and the mushrooming of exclusionary nationalisms'; and (ii) the widespread experiences of breakdown of community and state failures.

Susan Strange challenges International Relations to look beyond the key problems and questions of our era. She thinks that questions of global war or peace and capitalism or socialism are 'twentieth-century problems' that have been or are being superseded. Current and future violent conflicts are not likely to be mainly inter-state but principally 'civil' in character. Strange highlights the cumulative and accelerating internationalisation or transnationalisation of production, the 'womb in which the big issues of the next century are already coming to term'. Unlike other authors (see chapters by Cheru, Mittelman and Persaud), who attest that globalisation is marginalising entire zones and enclaves of the developing world, she speculates that internationalisation of production may be closing the North–South gap through the uneven diffusion of industrialisation. Nevertheless, the same processes exact significant adjustment costs for 'workers, and often for whole communities and regions, in the developed countries'. Her '*P*s' and '*Q*s' suggest that the 'conventional rationale for the separate study of interstate politics and domestic politics disappears. Exit 'International Relations' (as heretofore defined). Indeed for Strange the big issues of the twenty-first century concern the peculiar alchemy of economic globalisation, scientific and technological innovation and the environment (noting that questions of race and gender will also be important). The ecological problem stems from the rate of technological change (e.g. the discovery of nuclear power). The financial problem arises from the 'discovery of the magical power of money'. However there is a Panglossian air about the responses of scientists and bankers to warning signals of impending financial collapse and ecological disaster. She concludes: 'How to control and restrain both the scientists and the bankers – much more than the managers of capitalist enterprises – may be the central problematic of International Political Economy in the future.'

Mittelman rounds off the collection by reflecting on some of the limits to and conditions for theoretical innovation and knowledge production. He probes limits, subtle variations in five 'common traps and confusions': determinism, dualism, Western centrism, reification and scientism. Singly, or in varied combinations, 'these misconceptions have restrained innovations in knowledge about world order'. Mittelman criticises recent work on 'scientific revolutions' (it underestimates the ways that paradigms may be modified), 'epistemic communities' (it is scientistic), and 'knowledge structures' (it involves reification). He argues, by contrast, that 'meanings are hammered out in the crucible of social relations', and they relate to the complexity of interests and ideas, an issue that lies at the heart of classical social theory. The chapter calls for a reconstruction of International Relations theory based upon a trialectic between two classical theorists (Karl Marx and Max Weber), and a modern innovator (Robert Cox). This would 'establish systematic ways to explain or achieve future world order'. Moreover, Mittelman revisits the Marx–Weber debate to explore knowledge production and innovation. He sees this avenue as offering a path towards a 'new syncretism'. Finally, drawing on Kuhn, the author observes that successful innovations have a self-destructive aspect – they become normalised when institutionalised as a dominant paradigm. He speculates whether this might happen to the Coxes' work – an unlikely destination that they would no doubt find to be the precisely wrong one for their endeavours.

Taken together, the contributions in Part IV help to frame an agenda for study in contemporary International or Global Studies, the final question posed in the Preface to this book. For the sake of a brevity imposed by the editors, the presentations here – as elsewhere in the collection – are necessarily selective. Nevertheless, they issue challenges to others to innovate in the field. Especially important in this regard are the implications of innovation and transformation for pedagogy. Innovation in education involves transformation and emancipation in knowledge formation. So there is still much to do in developing an understanding of structural change and the potential for democratic agency in the context of past, present and future.

13 Civil society and democratic world order

Yoshikazu Sakamoto

The resilience of democracy

It is surprising that, while Nazism and fascism had perished by the end of the Second World War, communism had collapsed by the end of the Cold War, and post-colonial militarism and developmental authoritarianism had mostly crumbled by the 1990s, democracy has not only survived but also prevailed over all these other forms of political regime. Thus, the extraordinary resilience of democracy has been demonstrated by the history of the past. It will be further endorsed by the history of the future as contemplated in the context of the development of the last couple of centuries.

The unprecedented transformative dynamics of the modern world since the emergence of industrial capitalism in eighteenth-century Europe seem to consist of the following fundamental contradictions which account for major conflicts and changes in modern times: (i) capitalism vs. socialism; (ii) democracy vs. authoritarianism; and (iii) nationalism vs. internationalism (Sakamoto, 1994). Of these forces of change, socialism and authoritarianism have receded and capitalism, democracy and nationalism have gained universal currency in today's world. What will be the world of a century from now?

Capitalism, in the form of competitive free markets oriented to profit maximisation, will have to undergo a significant modification, or even a radical re-examination, because of the ecological constraints that are bound to grow, and because of the mounting democratic demands for equality and equity which run counter to the disparity and inequity resulting from the dynamics of competitive capitalism. These ecological and democratic antitheses will generate counter-trends that will increasingly erode the moral viability of the modern 'spirit of capitalism' (cf. Giddens, 1994).

Nationalism, in the form of the policy and movement for establishing a sovereign state which corresponds with distinct ethnocultural communities, is – after undergoing a number of regressive tragedies – likely to be outdated in a world of rapidly increasing interpenetration and/or interdependence. Although emphasis on cultural autonomy and diversity will continue, it will be separated from the imperative of nation-state building. In contrast, it is quite likely that democracy will persist. It will have to overcome the confines of 'national democracy' to meet the requirements of 'internationalism' on the regional and global levels; but transnational and global democratisation is an extension and universalisation of democracy, not an emergence of its antithesis.

What are the sources of this resilience? There are at least two – legitimacy and reflexivity. First, in the course of history since ancient times, the sources of legitimacy of political power have broadened and deepened – through complex non-linear processes – from a supreme one, whether divine or secular, to a few, many, and finally to all. This change reflects the growing consciousness of the universal equality of human beings, which is rooted in the formation of civil society that laid the groundwork for democracy. Once the claim of democratic values for *essential* universality is established, any anti- or counter-democratic ideology is bound to be particularistic in space and, ultimately, in time. In the 1930s Nazism and Japanese militarism resorted to racist nationalism. Today, Lee Kuan Yew of Singapore and Mahathir bin Mohamed of Malaysia stress the '*Asian* brand of democracy'. This rhetoric is not to defend the diversity of the concrete forms of democracy grounded on the essential universality of values, as illustrated by the obvious difference between American individualist democracy and Scandinavian social democracies. It is for the defence of 'Asia', a concept which is, however, unclear to the Asians themselves. It is intended to reject the further democratisation of their respective regimes, by equating the claim for the universality of democracy and human rights with the 'West'. It may be noted that, unlike in South Korea, the Philippines, and Taiwan, the political regimes in Singapore and Malaysia have not gone through a democratic revolution based on popular movements from below. The particularistic, localised and transient nature of this ideology will be disclosed with the passage of time.

Secondly, of course, this does not mean that democracy is uniform and immutable. On the contrary, democracy is and remains an 'unfinished project' (cf. Wolin, 1989). It constitutes the perpetual process in which the people themselves define and redefine what democracy is in the light of the problems and challenges confronting them. This means that there will be mistakes made. Nevertheless, it is people's reliance on themselves, never on elitist forces, that makes democracy a democratising process. Thus its resilience consists in the reflexivity of civil society, which generates an open-ended, self-transformative process of democratisation. This reflexivity was illustrated by the fact that the socialist revolution which resorted to 'democratic centrism' in the near-absence of civil society led to authoritarian state socialism. Conversely the recent popular struggles in Eastern Europe to build a real civil society have led to the fatal erosion of the authoritarian state.

There seems to be a general consensus that the (re-)emergence of civil society played a critical role in bringing the authoritarian regimes and the Cold War to an end. Views diverge, however, as to what is meant by 'civil society'. Since 'civil society' refers to key agencies of contemporary global democratisation, a conceptual clarification is in order for the purpose of scientific analysis and political *praxis*.

Civil society revisited

To clarify the meaning of 'civil society', a distinction should be made between the term (or phrase) and the concept. The traditional term *societas civilis*, which goes back to the time of Cicero, is coterminous with the state. By the middle of the century from 1750 to 1850, this old concept underwent complex and uneven changes and subdivision (Keane, 1988). If we simplify so as to highlight conceptual shifts, we may point to how the interrelations between the three key terms – nature, society and the state – help to define the meaning of civil society.

In one school of thought, such as that of Hobbes and Rousseau, nature (or the 'state of nature'), on the one hand, and society and the state (including civil society, *état civil*, the concept of civilisation), on the other, stand in antithetical relation. In another school, the state of nature is a state of society, which is distinct from the state. The Physiocrats used the concept *société naturelle*, which refers to the sphere of economic relations based on agriculture. In their conceptualisation it stands in contrast to *société politique*. There is yet a third perspective in the period reviewed by Keane. A focus on the progress of commerce and manufacturing was used by the Scottish Enlightenment school to define a civil (or civilised) society. In this formulation civil society is treated as closely linked to the state but no longer coterminous with it.

Thus it may be noted that nature and civil society, though different in *terminology* corresponding to different schools of thought, bear similarities. They represent a *concept* of a pre-state phase *vis-à-vis* the state in a dualistic or even antithetical manner. This pre-state civil society then increasingly assumed the character of a concept indicating *history* (e.g., Ferguson's civilising 'natural history') rather than nature. In the wake of a political revolution where historical discontinuity requires a rationale in terms of 'nature', this is a reflection of the historical development and consolidation of modern civil society. It reflects a complex self-awareness of the moral implications of the advance of commerce and industry (Becker, 1994).

Beyond these developments lay Hegel's conception of civil society (*bürgerliche Gesellschaft*). It means pre-political society with special reference to the intermediate sphere between the family and the state. Hegel mentions 'the principle of civil society and the feeling of individual independence and self-respect in its individual members' (Hegel, 1942). Nevertheless, the Hegelian conceptualisation of civil society primarily encompasses the system of economic needs, the formation of classes, and also the judicial and administrative mechanism and corporative organisations. In other words, civil society consists of the capitalist market and its external regulations. It is, therefore, no small wonder that Marx equated civil society to the economic relations of bourgeois society which constitute the structural base of the bourgeois state.

By the latter part of the nineteenth century, however, the term 'civil society' went into oblivion as far as the mainstream discourse of political and social theory was concerned. There would appear to have been two contradictory reasons for this eclipse. On the one hand, as a result of the Marxist critique, civil society was identified with class society, particularly the political class domination of the bourgeoisie with all its problematic implications. On the other hand, as a result of the enhanced predominance of the bourgeois class, the bourgeoisie identified themselves with the 'nation-state', promoting the ideology and policy of nationalism. Although these two reasons reflect conflicting perspectives, they have one thing in common – namely, in both cases the conceptualisation of civil society loses distinctive autonomy from the state. In addition, the dominated classes, though finding themselves alienated and separate from the state, generally identified themselves, particularly after the turn of the century, as the 'masses'. That is, they saw themselves acting as the agent of mass movements in a mass society. This is far removed from the bourgeois notion of civil society characterised by liberal, rational individualism (Mannheim, 1940).

There are, of course, exceptions to this schematic outline. In the nineteenth-century literature, the concept, if not the term, of civil society constitutes a major theme of de Tocqueville's perceptive observations on democracy in America, with its emphasis on the importance of civic 'associations' (de Tocqueville, 1954).

The more notable exception in the early twentieth century concerning the conceptualisation of state and civil society is Gramsci. It is true that his concept of civil society is original and of great analytical importance (Bobbio, 1988; Cox, 1993d). Within the context of the dialectical reciprocal determination between the base and superstructure, civil society refers to a 'superstructural level' which corresponds to the function of 'hegemony' as distinct from the state which corresponds to that of 'direct domination' (Gramsci, 1971: 12). It is also true, however, that the concept was developed in the context of the *praxis* of Marxist movements for social revolution in Western Europe, which failed to materialise (Cohen and Arato, 1994), we might add, partly for the reasons outlined by Gramsci.

It is an irony of history that the concept of civil society unexpectedly re-emerged in the 1970s in the democratic struggle against authoritarian state socialism. This concept of civil society (at least when compared with its precursors) is the most relevant to the contemporary world. Thus 'civil society', as it was actually formulated in *praxis*, that is, in the interactions of democratic intellectual opposition forces and the workers' Solidarity in Poland, for instance, had four organisational principles: spontaneous solidarity, pluralism, free communication and democratic participation (Arato, 1981, 1981–2). This theoretical and practical concept of civil society is significant and innovative in three respects.

First, unlike bourgeois civil society which represents the private sphere (Habermas, 1989), it refers to the struggle to create an alternative *public* space which is autonomous *vis-à-vis* the authoritarian state. It is not confined to the sphere of individual freedom; it seeks to construct a public space based on the social solidarity of citizens.

Second, it suggests a political project of 'double democratisation' (Held, 1987: 283), which means the democratisation of *society* as the base of the democratisation of the state. It goes beyond political democracy, seeking to democratise civil society itself. For this reason, the concept of civil society formulated in Eastern and Central Europe is considered pertinent to the activation and deepening of democracy in the West, particularly in the workplace, family, school, hospital and so forth. This is the area where non-democratic power structures are likely to persist irrespective of whether they are under socialism or capitalism.

Third, despite their opposition to state socialism, the forces for civil society did *not* necessarily subscribe to the capitalist market economy. In this respect, their concept of civil society differs from that of either Hegel or Marx (and Gramsci as applied to capitalist hegemony). Their concept of civil society is fundamentally a project for *political* democratisation. Moreover, unlike the long-standing bourgeois version, the East European notion of civil society is, for the first time since the mid-eighteenth century, conceptually separated from the market economy. That civil society and capitalist society no longer remain conceptually undifferentiated has an important bearing on the understanding of the contemporary global transformation as we will argue below.

It is worth re-emphasising then that the relevance of this concept of civil society is that it is applicable not only to the former East, but also to the South in democratic transition, as well as to the deepening of democracy in the West. It is not merely an empirical concept but a *critical* concept which refers to a democratic transformative public space based on the reciprocal recognition of the dignity and equal rights of human beings. Contrary to the traditional equation of civil society with the 'private sector', which includes the capitalist market (Commission on Global Governance, 1995), civil society in this sense is quite distinct from and antithetical to the capitalist market. The latter is, of course, characterised by the commodification of social relations.

Civil society and changing world order

In an era of radical structural change, many human beings fail to conceptualise transformations in world order, relying on an outdated paradigm. This is particularly the case for many people who have political, economic, and/or psychological vested interests in the *status quo*. Persistent or even regressive dependence on obsolete conceptions tend to obstruct the adaptation to the necessities of change and, in so doing, to generate unnecessary conflict. Such contradictions characterise the condition of the sovereign state system today.

During the Cold War period, no state – especially neither of the two superpowers with their capability of mutual annihilation – was willing to accept the erosion of sovereignty, with its military *ultima ratio*. In the post-Cold War phase, despite, or perhaps because of the accelerating erosion of their *economic* sovereignty, states revert to the old concept of *political* sovereignty in a perceived 'multipolar world'. This conception, in fact, is more apparent than real. For example, some have suggested that a relative decline of hegemonic power means the restoration of the time-honoured multipolar state system. In reality, today's world is characterised *both* by the erosion of effective hegemony *and* the erosion of the sovereign state system. *Realpolitik* persists, but, as far as relations among the core states in the North are concerned, it is no longer predicated on the Clausewitzian maxim that war is an extension of politics (and political economy) by other means. The world is much more complex than the picture that these outdated conceptions present. For an adequate appreciation of the present world order, which is in flux, we need analysis in terms of at least four interconnected dimensions: civil society, the market, the state and international organisation.

The collapse of the Soviet Union and of state socialism, a development that is both the consequence and a cause of the globalisation of democracy, exemplifies the need to examine the relations between civil society and the continued global transformation we witness today. The state, international organisation and the market in the contemporary world order must be grounded in civil society, for civil society is (i) the engine of reflexive democratisation, and (ii) the source of democratic legitimation. It is the most resilient constitutive force of world order and the agencies for creating a democratic public space. Thus, examination of how these three dimensions of global social life are grounded in civil society is in order.

Civil society and the state

The interactions between civil society and the state tend to involve the democratisation of the state. Indeed, the conditions of democratic transition from authoritarian regimes as well as the deepening of democracy within democratic states have been the subject of the reflections of a number of democratic theorists. What is new today is the development of transborder or transnational civil society which gives rise to the issue of the transnational democratic accountability of the state. The following examples will help to substantiate my point.

The first is the gradual establishment of the idea that a state bears responsibility for 'illegal' war damages inflicted on an individual victim of the enemy state. According to conventional international law, claims of the individual to compensation for war damage are *prima facie* covered by state-to-state reparations and no direct payment to the individual is required (Oppenheim, 1955). A new precedent was set by the former West Germany in a series of post-war legislation which stipulated payment of compensation to those individual citizens of sixteen states who had been victimised by the Nazis, regardless of whether in warfare or in other forms of genocidal persecution.

In contrast, Japan has been and still is confronted with the protest of Asian people because of its equivocation over responsibility for its wartime criminal acts in the Second World War. The Japanese government paid reparations to several Asian states. They were not only modest in quantity, amounting to one tenth of the German counterpart; they were also, for all practical purposes, a sort of tied aid which served to ensure and expand Japan's post-war export market.

Underlying the claim to direct compensation to individual victims is the principle that a state bears direct responsibility for the protection of human rights not only of its own citizens but also of the citizens of other states – an idea that presupposes the existence of a transborder civil society consisting of citizens who share equal human rights. In other words, a new norm of transnational accountability is gradually becoming established: a state is accountable for its human rights violations regardless of the nationality (or ethnicity) of victimised individuals. Indeed the decisions of the United States and the Canadian governments to make compensation to Japanese–Americans and Japanese–Canadians for their wartime internment are based on a similar idea.

This new philosophy has even more universal implications. In the above case, it is Germany and Japan that were the perpetrators of crimes, infringing on the human rights of the people of other races. But there are other cases of no less importance. If a state is a perpetrator of a crime against humanity in violation of the human rights of its *own* citizens and ceases to be accountable to the civil society within its borders, are other states and other civil societies accountable to the victimised citizens of a 'foreign' country?

Thus the second related example involves the issue of 'humanitarian intervention'. It has been treated by the international community as a debatable subject (Harriss, 1995). It has, however, been put into practice, with varying degrees of success or failure, in Iraq (the Kurds), former Yugoslavia, Somalia, Haiti and Rwanda, in accordance with the resolutions of the UN Security Council. As for the legitimacy of 'humanitarian intervention', a consensus has yet to be formed at the intergovernmental level, even though there is growing agreement that this is an issue that will become increasingly difficult to evade. A broad consensus has already emerged, however, at the level of non-governmental organisations, such as Médecins sans Frontières, that civil society has the right and duty to intervene transnationally. This further illustrates the emergence of a transnational civil society that has laid the groundwork for the claim of the transnational democratic accountability of the state. Thus one of the significant global developments underway is that a state committed to democracy will be bound to contradict itself if it fails to defend and protect universal human rights universally.

Civil society and international organisation

The end of the Cold War contributed to enhancing the trend towards the globalisation of democracy and the reactivating of the United Nations (particularly the Security Council). The legitimacy of the reactivated United Nations must, by implication therefore, be grounded on globalising democracy much more than ever before. The new rhetorical emphasis put by UN officials, diplomats and experts on the opening phrase of the UN Charter, 'We the peoples of the United Nations' is virtually redefining the United Nations as an organisation not of governments but, in the final analysis, of 'peoples'. This is an indication of the growing awareness of where the source of legitimacy of the United Nations in an age of global democratisation should be located.

It is natural, therefore, that the reactivating of the United Nations should be accompanied by public debate on the 'democratisation' of the United Nations. In the course of discussion at the intergovernmental level, however, the democratisation of the United Nations has been reduced to the reform of the Security Council, particularly the numerical increase of its permanent and rotating members. This would be a reform of secondary importance. The essential deficiency of the United Nations in terms of democracy concerns the facts that (i) more than half of the member states are far from democratic, if not in their professed goals, then in the practices of their governments; and (ii) even in democracies, the forces of civil society have no direct representation in the United Nations.

There is no doubt that the reform proposals for the expansion of the Security Council's membership do not serve to consolidate the legitimacy of the United Nations in the context of global democratisation. It must also be noted that what is at issue is not only its legitimacy but also its efficacy. Although it is true that the United Nations is not independent of sovereign member states, it is also true that the world organisation is a 'system' that is more than the mere sum total of sovereign member states (Cox and Jacobson, 1973). The expectation that the United Nations act as a system with relative autonomy has been enhanced in the last few decades. This is a result of the growing public awareness of problems that can not be adequately dealt with by individual states – world organisation is required. In the light of pressing global problems confronting the United Nations, the reform of the Security Council seems almost irrelevant. Will the inclusion of Germany and Japan, for instance, in the club of permanent members serve to eliminate the root causes of regional or ethnic conflicts? Will the expansion of the Security Council narrow the gap between the rich and poor, not only in the South but also in the industrialised societies of the North? Will the enlargement of the Security Council halt and reverse the degradation of the environment?

It has been widely recognised that the major problems of global concern that the United Nations is expected to tackle cannot be resolved without the active participation of the people and the representation of civil society. Let us take up the five global problems confronting the United Nations.

First, the alleviation and ultimate elimination of poverty and inequitable development cannot be attained either by a command economy imposed by the state from above or by the neo-liberal market economy run by competitive corporate forces. Equitable development cannot be achieved without the democratic initiatives of the people in civil society. This has been demonstrated by the innumerable grass-roots projects and movements in the South, such as the Grameen Bank in Bangladesh and other micro-credit projects in developing countries, endogenously initiated to actually create real alternative development.

Second, the most effective way to cope with the 'population explosion' is not to exercise state power from above in order to enforce family planning. Rather, as recognised at the UN Conference on Population and Development in 1994, it requires the establishment of the reproductive rights of the people, particularly of women. This also means the creation of social and economic conditions conducive to the implementation of those rights. A democratic solution to the population question thus requires the active participation of civil society.

Third, to prevent environmental decay and restore ecological balance, it is essential to rely not on the authoritarian discipline and surveillance of an 'eco-fascist police state'. This simply cannot work. A solution requires the voluntary participation of every member of civil society in a change of life-style geared to equitable and sustainable development in opposition to the model of a dehumanised consumer culture.

Fourth, one of the tasks of critical importance to be performed by the United Nations is the universal establishment of human rights. By its very nature this cannot be done by the state from above, as its power is essentially antithetical to the rights of the people. The establishment of human rights is a consequence of the struggle of the people to ensure the autonomy of civil society *vis-à-vis* the state with its monopoly on the means of coercion and violence.

Finally, the primary goal of the United Nations is to maintain peace and security. The fact that the eruption of 'regional conflict' and 'ethno-national conflict' in the post-Cold War phase took place in the predominantly under- or mal-developed regions of the world shows that the sources of conflict and insecurity are generally social and economic. They are rooted in poverty, inequitable development and the scramble for resources under a condition of perceived zero-sum competition. To eradicate ethno-national conflict may not be an easy task. Tensions may stay. But what is urgently needed is to prevent such conflicts from turning into *armed* hostilities. To prevent violent conflict in these regions, the United Nations must fulfil the first task mentioned above – namely, the alleviation of poverty and inequitable development on the basis of the democratic participation of the marginalised local people.

In sum, attainment of all these five objectives calls for the participation of the people and the representation of civil society all over the world.

These tasks cannot be undertaken by the state alone. Non-democratic states in particular lack the efficacy and the competence to adequately cope with these problems of global concern. Thus, the United Nations is bound to face a *legitimacy crisis* and an *efficacy crisis* unless it is grounded in transnational civil society in a more direct way. The post-Cold War euphoria concerning the legitimacy and efficacy of the United Nations quickly receded, mainly because of the UN's failure to pay due attention to the representation and participation of civil society. It is only through the strengthening of this link with civil society that the 'democratisation of the United Nations' will come into being. Contrary to UN rhetoric, no 'democracy' is conceivable on the interstate level.

Civil society and the market

The question of the democratic accountability of the state to civil society has a relatively long history. The democratic accountability of international organisation is a question that came to the fore recently. Although the question of the democratic accountability of the market to civil society carries increasingly greater weight than before, it is still nebulous. There are two grounds for making this point. First, the market, which provides a structural context for individual corporations, is generally diffuse, impersonal and anonymous. A central locus of power and accountability is hard to identify. Second, the predominance of the globalised neo-liberal capitalist market has eroded the authority of the democratic state. In the past the democratic state served as a political vehicle for national civil society to exercise a degree of regulatory power for the public interest.

Here, however, a difficulty arises also from the very concept of civil society. In modern history, the concept of a civil society autonomous from the state emerged as the capitalist economy began to gain autonomy from the mercantilist state. Thus, civil society and the capitalist market economy have long been treated as interrelated, and with each serving to define the other. However, as noted above, it is in the context of the democratisation of the former East that a new political concept of civil society has come to the surface.

And it is in this new, and democratic sense, that potential for the further development of civil society is evaluated in this chapter. Thus, the 'state–civil society' antithesis should not be confused with the 'state–society' dichotomy. 'Society' in the latter context normally includes the market, capital and corporations. Further, 'society' may include fundamentalist, populist grass-roots movements which essentially conform with, or are conducive to, the authoritarian state; these are antithetical to civil society (see the discussion of such forces in the United States in the chapter by Mark Rupert). Still further, the family, school, hospital and non-governmental organisations will *not* constitute elements of the civil society I have in mind in so far as they are subordinated to and incorporated into the market as well as the state. Put conversely, the questions addressed in this chapter centre on, first, how a democratic form of civil society establishes its autonomy and second, how such a civil society is dialectically mediated into the state, international organisation and the market (see the chapter by Fantu Cheru for a case that shows how autonomy is created by peasants and urban marginals in Africa relative to the predatory state and the capitalist market).

This conceptualisation of civil society as an essentially political project has two consequences. On the one hand, it leads to a clear distinction between democracy and capitalism, or democratisation and marketisation. It thus can contribute to the emphasis on the political role to be played by civil society in transforming the structure of world political economy. On the other hand, it faces the problem of having no specific idea of an alternative non-capitalist economic system. An exception is the ill-defined 'self-management' advanced by the workers in the Solidarity movement (Weslowski, 1995). Indeed, with a few exceptions, perhaps such as Vaclav Havel (but not his prime minister, Vaclav Klaus), protagonists of this new form of civil society in the East generally were not prepared to counteract the massive invasion of world capitalism and its collateral consumer culture.

What the forces of the new civil society in fact seek is probably not so much to draw a blueprint for another economic system as to critically redefine the concept of economy itself in terms of democratic accountability. In other words, it is imperative to recognise that the 'capitalist market is a political as well as an economic sphere, a terrain not simply of freedom and choice but of domination and coercion' (Wood, 1995: 290). The question, however, seems to require a deeper analysis – a critical cultural re-examination of the concept of 'economy' premised on competition and scarcity. Here we should turn to Gramsci. What is at issue is a radical re-examination of the 'hegemony' of the capitalist concept of economy that stands against a conception of civil society that is based on human solidarity and equity (Bowles and Gintis, 1987: 144).

Obviously, this conceptual transformation is not an easy task. It calls for a radical critique of the culture of modernity. And one question we should bear in mind concerns who is to do this task of reconceptualisation. It is suggestive to recall, in this connection, that the concept of civil society which was defined in various ways by great thinkers and then went into oblivion has unexpectedly re-emerged through the dialogue and interactions among a number of citizens engaged in the struggle for democratisation. The concept has been defined and redefined by these people and its meanings are bound to be diverse. Only broad generalisations have been made in this chapter, but what is of crucial importance is the fact that civil society is redefined and reconceptualised by civil society *itself*. The same will hold true of the reconceptualisation of 'economy' from the perspective of civil society. These are all part and parcel of the process of democratisation which is an open-ended, unfinished and reflexive political project.

14 Imposing global orders: a synthesised ontology for a turbulent era

James N. Rosenau

> Even a realist like former Secretary of State Henry A. Kissinger is at a
> loss to describe the world in a comprehensive way. He told a conference
> in Washington recently: 'It's probably not possible to have some over-
> arching concept.'[1]

Challenging as may be the task of accounting for the failure of students of
International Relations to anticipate the end of the Cold War (Gaddis
1992/3; Rosenau, 1995b), that of comprehending the basic contours of
global politics that have evolved since the Berlin Wall came down and the
Soviet Union collapsed is both more difficult and important. If it is the
case, as has been cogently argued, that the Cold War 'left so light an
impact on the living memory of states and societies, that it is already *en
route* to oblivion' (Gambles, 1995: 35), then the need to pause and explicitly conceptualise the basic outlines of the global structures now emergent
is all the more urgent. Not to do so is to run the serious risk of assuming
that 'the business of international politics is being conducted as if there
were continuity between the years before and the years after [the Cold
War], as if history was being *resumed*' (1995: 27) – an assumption that is
clearly too simple and ignores the social, economic, political and
technological transformations that have unfolded in the last fifty years
(and that, indeed, significantly contributed to the end of the Cold War).

While the risk of treating history as undergoing resumption is often
underestimated, there does seem to be a widespread recognition of the
need to reconceptualise the foundations of the emergent global order.
The debate over whether a clash of civilisations is the dominant feature of
our time is illustrative of this recognition (Huntington, 1993; Kurth,
1994), as is the burgeoning literature that posits the possible emergence
of a global civil society (e.g. Lipschutz, 1992). Such innovative formulations suggest that many observers, spurred by uncertainty and a mixture
of hope and despair, are today preoccupied with grasping and assessing
those arrangements in world affairs – the emergent order – through which
conflicts are avoided, fostered, waged, resolved or perpetuated. Some
analysts address the problem of global order confident they have uncov-

ered its main outlines, but most are cautious as to the nature of the forces
driving a world that appears to have reached some kind of turning point
with the end of superpower rivalry. For most observers, in other words,
the transition out of the Cold War has been jarring, a reason to pause, to
go back to the drawing board and determine whether the philosophical
ontology from which they derive their empirical paradigms is still intact.[2]

The return to the drawing board has also been jarring. Looked at with
the advantage of hindsight, the Cold War seems more a collage of perceptions than a confrontation of powers, more a vast exaggeration by both
sides than a huge triumph by one of them, more a shadow play than a
stark drama. To discover that the weapons build-ups and arms races were
perpetuated more by unwarranted perceptions and distorted intelligence
reports (Pincus, 1995) than by actual plans for military offensives, thus
serving to prolong rather than end the superpower conflict (Lebow and
Stein, 1994: 366–76; Lebow and Risse-Kappen, 1995), is to realise how
fully the course of events are fictions of convergent imaginations, of intersubjectivities rather than objective conditions. As one analyst puts it,
'After the event, the Cold War looks too much like pretense' (Gambles,
1995: 35).

In effect, the global order sustained by the Cold War was derived from
an ontology imposed by those who observed and participated in it – by
high-level policy-makers, International Relations analysts and, subsequently, publics – all of which indicates that any order which is judged
as now emerging is also an imposed order. Put more specifically, there are
as many post-Cold War orders as there are practitioners and observers
who either perceive different structures as emergent or attach different
degrees of significance to the same perceived structures. As time passes
and time allows for one set of perceptions to emerge as so incisive as to
persuade others of its soundness, the various post-Cold War orders will
shake down to a few widely shared understandings of how the world is
organised and what dynamics sustain it. In all likelihood, too, intense
competition will follow over which of the surviving understandings is
closer to the truth and deserves to be regarded as a paradigm worthy of
serving as a basis for framing policy alternatives and making choices
among them. Then, not long after this new intersubjectivity becomes
commonplace, it will be given a label that evokes widespread usage and
the Cold War era will recede even further into history.[3]

The processes of imposing order derive from the fact that observers can
never grasp reality in its entirety and are thus forced to select some features of the on-going scene as important and dismiss the rest as trivial. As
Stephen Gill points out in an earlier chapter, the way in which the important features are arranged in relation to each other springs from the

ontologies and paradigms through which the course of events is interpreted and order imposed upon them. And the result is intersubjective –
not objective – understandings. As Cox (1995a: 35) puts it, 'Reality is
made by the collective responses of people to the conditions of their existence. Intersubjectively shared experience reproduces reality in the form
of continuing institutions and practices.' In short, 'Ontologies tell us what
is significant in the particular world we delve into – what are the basic
entities and key relationships. Ontologies are not arbitrary constructions;
they are the specification of the common sense of an epoch' (1995a: 34).

This is not to imply that either our ontologies or our paradigms are necessarily complex and pervaded with multiple layers. On the contrary, normally only a few features – such as the systemic attributes of the key actors
and their orientations towards conflict and co-operation – are selected
out as crucial global structures that serve to explain how and why the
course of events moves in one direction rather than another. It follows
that paradigms are so encompassing in their empirical scope, so capable
of accounting for all the developments that are perceived to be relevant to
the maintenance or alteration of the existing order, that we ordinarily do
not shift back and forth between paradigms with the rationale that 'it all
depends on the issue'. For paradigms are cast at that analytic level where
the sources of behaviour in world affairs are presumed to derive from
roots more fundamental than those associated with issue differences.

Reliance on the deep-seated premises that comprise paradigms is all
the greater in this last decade of the twentieth century because of the
unfamiliar nature of some of the patterns that have evolved since the end
of the Cold War. Confronted with surprises and uncertainties, practitioners and International Relations observers alike are all the more inclined to
impose order on events rather than suspend judgement until such time
that emergent patterns have a chance to settle into place. Similarly, they
are likely to converge intersubjectively around what are regarded as the
key questions posed by the main trends they perceive to have marked the
post-Cold War period. Put differently, the need for paradigmatic sensitivity is perhaps especially acute at this time. With the period since the Cold
War marked by ambiguity and contradiction, with a new millennium at
hand, and with tensions at all levels of organisation – local, national,
regional and global – pervading the course of events, the inclination to
reexamine basic premises and search for an underlying order is widespread.

Despite the ambiguities and difficulties that attach to interpretations of
the current period, however, intersubjective consensus does seem to have
evolved around the key questions that our paradigms need to address.
Will the emergent global order resemble the past and be dominated by

the international world of nation-states? Or will its challenges transcend the nation-state and foster their acquiescence to new ways of collectively managing the world's problems? Will states continue to be more conflictual than co-operative in pursuing their national interests? If there is slippage in their capacity to cope with challenges to their authority at home and their sovereignty abroad, what institutions and organisations, if any, are likely to take up the slack? What roles lie ahead for international governmental organisations (IGOs), for non-governmental organisations (NGOs), for regional organisations, for sub-national groups? Are their norms, orientations and activities likely to enlarge the opportunities for the effective management of world affairs? Or are there good reasons to concur in the expectation that 'we are entering a period of world disorder ... The Western world is in bigger trouble than people realise, and as long as people are not aware of it, it only makes the problem bigger'? (Soros, 1995b: D4).

The purpose of this chapter is not to provide answers to these questions, but rather to identify alternative ways of responding to them and then to indicate which of these alternatives is most likely to become the 'common sense' of our emerging epoch and, thus, serve as the ontology that underlies the intersubjectively shared experience of the next generations. The analysis derives five alternative paradigms and highlights one of them as especially conducive to accounting for how and why the habits and practices of the Cold War are being replaced by new orientations towards the basic entities, relationships and processes deemed to be the driving forces of world affairs. My essential argument is that the pervasive contradictions and ambiguities presently at work in the world can be explained by viewing high degrees of both co-operation and conflict among and between both governmental and non-governmental actors as deeply embedded structures of the emergent global order, with the result that the order is conceived to be tending simultaneously towards both systemic integration and subsystemic fragmentation. It is further argued that increasingly the tensions resulting from these opposing dynamics are, through the channels provided by the micro-electronic revolution, so widely and intersubjectively understood as to be the kind of shared experiences that will form the basis of a new, post-Cold War ontology.

To be sure, human history tells a long story of how tensions have arisen as people moved in both integrative and fragmenting directions. What is different about the present epoch, however, is the simultaneity, the immediate interaction, of these contrary movements. Today what is close at hand is also far away, and vice versa – giving rise to what might be called the pervasiveness of distant proximities (Rosenau, 1995b). The dynamism of present-day communications technologies in a newly decentralised era enables people everywhere to observe the interaction of the tensions and to take for granted experientially that such seemingly contradictory dynamics are not contradictory at all, that they are inherent in the course of events and operate increasingly as the normal way in which life unfolds. Such, in bare outline (and as yet unnamed), is the ontology that is emerging to replace that of the Cold War.

To appreciate the logic of a world sustained by interactive and simultaneous co-operative and conflictual tendencies is not, however, to anticipate when one or another tendency will be operative or dominant. Ontologies are not so specific as to anticipate how the course of events might unfold at any moment in time. They involve, rather, broad and general premises – those conceptions people have of where action originates and of what its essential qualities consist. Specification of the conditions under which co-operative structures will predominate and those that are likely to evoke conflictual patterns are subsumed by paradigms and theories, formulations that are hardly comprised of substantive detail, to be sure, but that are not so all-encompassing and abstract in their substance as are ontologies. As indicated, the ensuing discussion is cast in the very general terms of paradigmatic distinctions. It seeks to outline how paradigms that differentiate among key actors and between co-operation and conflict can be subsumed under the even more all-encompassing understanding that is emerging to replace the Cold War ontology. The tasks of assessing the conditions that foster co-operation or conflict are not undertaken here. These are important steps that need to be taken if our understanding of how the underlying arrangements of world affairs are likely to evolve in the future is to be enlarged, but it seems preferable to postpone them until after an attempt is made to achieve ontological clarity.

Some initial presumptions

It might be wondered how it is possible to impose order on a world pervaded by ambiguity, contradiction and change. Irrespective of the order we impose on the world, it can reasonably be argued, the uncertainties, incongruities and transformations are likely to persist. It would be a mistake, however, to treat these attributes of world affairs as obstacles to comprehension. On the contrary, and to repeat, they need to be viewed as constituent parts of the emergent order. Both within and among societies the dynamics of change are deeply rooted and foster orientations and institutions that are contradictory and ambiguous, suggesting that the prime central tendency at work in the world consists of divergent paths, as if everything regresses to a mean that is bi-modal and better grasped as two separate means, one that encompasses efforts to promote co-operation and another that reflects tendencies towards continuing conflict. To be sure, neither mean can readily be calculated in as much as events and trends since the end of the Cold War are still in flux and have yet to exhibit pronounced patterns. Yet, a lack of clarity in this respect does not negate the presumption of an underlying order that needs to be explicated. Officials and citizens alike need to systematise so as to grasp long-term trends, as the epigraph quoting Henry Kissinger implies, even as they acknowledge that the incongruities and transformations necessitate accepting the presence of both integrative and disintegrative dynamics that are feeding off each other (as the epigraph also intimates).

Furthermore, we do not have the luxury of waiting for such contradictions to unravel. Pervasive uncertainty does not relieve officials and publics of the need to impose order on the course of events, and reach conclusions about where world affairs are headed. Ontologies and paradigms cannot be set aside. Pervasive as the uncertainties that mark the current world scene are, it is erroneous to assume they negate ontological or paradigmatic interpretation. However vague and elusive the empirical trend lines may be, an overall perspective is inherent in the process of selecting some aspects of world affairs as important and dismissing others as trivial. Observers will be ensconced in permanent paralysis if they defer reaching conclusions until such time that the underlying dynamics become so manifest as to make clear where the future is heading. For the underlying dynamics only take shape through the perceptions of observers; and one will wait in vain if the task of interpretation is postponed on the grounds that the prevailing uncertainties will somehow get resolved on their own.

In teasing a collective ontology out of the welter of contradictions and ambiguities it is also crucial to presume a widespread appreciation that these opposing forces originate in the dynamics of globalisation that are operative everywhere in the world. The common sense of the emergent era is that market and other forces spreading people, goods, services, ideas and money around the world are not only shrinking social and economic distances and transforming political institutions, but that they are also impelling the contraction of people, goods and ideas within narrowed or heightened territorial boundaries. It is a widely shared experience, in other words, that globalisation is the prime source for change in the emergent order even as it produces contrary trends towards localising processes, implosions of societies and the mushrooming of exclusionary nationalisms.

Without downgrading the importance of localising dynamics, in other words, these are not the main forces driving the course of events. However the contradictory pressures towards expansion and contraction may be linked, it is the processes of globalisation that are setting the terms and shaping the structures of the emergent global order. For better or worse – and there is much that will surely be worse by most normative standards – the peoples, economies and polities of the world conceive of themselves as caught up in long-term processes of overlap and convergence.

Five imposed orders

There are, of course, numerous dimensions – such as cultural predisposition and market forces – that can and do constitute the orders which analysts and practitioners impose on world affairs. In terms of the political dimension of ontologies, however, it is sufficient to organise understanding around two dichotomised dimensions that are pervasive wherever world politics occur. One involves the identity of the actors central to the course of events and the other focuses on their orientations. In the former a distinction is drawn between circumstances under which states and governments predominate and those situations where they are seen as sharing power with diverse non-governmental actors. In the latter dimension the dichotomy is between situations in which conflictual behaviour is viewed as predominant and those in which co-operation is treated as the primary wellspring of action. By juxtaposing these two dimensions, it becomes possible to identify the primary forms of order that most people impose on world affairs. There are five such forms and the logic of their derivation and juxtaposition can be seen in Figure 1.

Four of these forms are familiar, although the labels attached to them may differ from those used here. Perhaps the most familiar is the unilateral order (often called realism) in which central aspects of world affairs are conceived to be driven by states and their governments. All other actors are seen as essentially peripheral and subject to the will of states. There is no higher authority to which states must respond and through which international order and justice is maintained. States have to preserve their independence and well-being through self-help and the maximisation of their power relevant to other states. They may co-operate with other states through alliances and inter-governmental organisations (IGOs) if it is in their interest to do so, but they are seen as being ready at all times to break any commitments they have made to more encompassing international systems if unilateral and conflictual actions are seen as better enabling them to realise their sub-systemic goals in a distrustful and hostile world. To impose a unilateral order on events, in short, is to perceive the world as an anarchic system that fosters conflict in the absence of enduring authorities with which states must comply.[4]

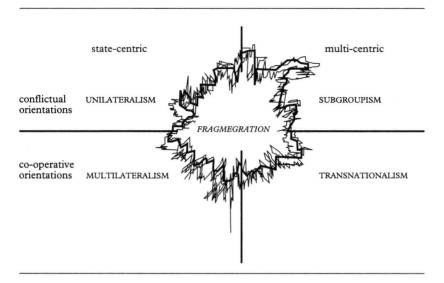

Figure 1 Five imposed orders juxtaposed by units and orientations

A second form of imposed order assumes that, in this era of ever-expanding complexity, the predominance of states is unchallenged but that their interdependence renders them sensitive to shared normative restraints and mindful of long-term goals which can incline them to engage in multilateral co-operation *despite* their immediate interests. Thus states are seen as willing to accord a measure of autonomy and authority to the institutions and regimes of the global system with respect to certain issues even as they may unilaterally pursue their concerns on other questions. In this perceived multilateral order (often referred to as a liberal order) the world is not so much anarchic as it is a system of balanced constraints that allow for co-operation and inhibit states from clinging to narrow self-interests.[5]

Still others, impressed by the erosion of the authority of states, the dominance of markets and the clamour of long-standing ethnic minorities for recognition, have come to perceive the basic structures of world politics as having undergone a bifurcation in which the state-centric world must now interact with a multicentric world composed of subnational, national and transnational collectivities that have extended the key structures well beyond the interstate system. Both as sources and consequences of the bifurcation, the forces of fragmentation are seen as proliferating, the centres of authority as fraying, and the world stage as so dense with actors that all of them have little choice but to enhance their own narrow self-interests. Like states, in other words, numerous actors in many segments of the multicentric world are presumed to distrust co-operative arrangements and to be inclined towards narrow, self-serving courses of action. In effect, they place their subsystemic interests well ahead of larger systemic needs and aspirations. In so doing they seek out like-minded others in their close-at-hand environment for support and psychic comfort, a process that is perhaps best designated as 'subgroup-ism'. This term is conceived to be more generic than that of 'nationalism' since there are many other groups besides nations that have cohered more fully around common identities and sought thereby to advance shared goals (Rosenau, 1990: 132–5). It is not mere coincidence, for example, that in addition to secessionist movements in Europe and Russia (Heraclides, 1994), such diverse collectivities as the Mafia, youth gangs, the Palestinians, the Zapatistas, and the residents of Staten Island have simultaneously experienced rampant subgroupism. Nor does the reloca-tion of authority inherent in this powerful tendency toward subsystems and away from whole systems necessarily reach an end point. It is the nature of the process that subgroupism begets subgroupism (as Quebec presses for autonomy from Canada, for example, so do the Mohawks press for autonomy within Quebec), with the result that presumptions of conflict tend to sustain the dynamics of subgroupism.[6] Accordingly, taken together with states, the bifurcated global system is regarded as closely resembling the decentralised structures of the medieval era. When people impose this neo-medieval form of pluralist order (Bull, 1977: 254–5) – or what I prefer to call a subgroupist order – the world is seen as highly decentralised, conflictual, and disorderly.[7]

A fourth group of observers share the premise that greater inter-dependence has eroded the authority of states, intensified the relevance and salience of other types of actors and thus brought into being bifur-cated structures; but they also perceive these tendencies as having height-ened the necessity of co-operation and as rendering less salient those that foster conflict. This imposed order posits the world stage less as popu-lated with subnational collectivities and more as crowded with non-governmental organisations (NGOs), transnational corporations, social movements, professional societies, epistemic communities and other private entities concerned with environmental, humanitarian and developmental goals that incline them towards participation in interna-tional regimes and organisations in search of co-operative solutions. When this transnational form of order is imposed, the global system is conceived to be increasingly founded on a multiplicity of institutionalised and *ad hoc* arrangements through which governmental and non-govern-mental collectivities accommodate to each other and, in so doing, come to share responsibility for the course of events in a crazy-quilt and yet systemic fashion.[8]

The fifth form of imposed order is the one that seems most likely to emerge as the successor ontology to the Cold War. As indicated by the space in the middle of Figure 1, it springs from the presumption that the underlying order encompasses the pervasive contradictions in world affairs, that powerful tendencies towards co-operation and conflict are both likely to endure, and that thus all four of the other imposed orders reflect some part of the true state of affairs. In effect, the bifurcation of the global system is conceived to allow for the simultaneous operation of uni-lateralism, multilateralism, subgroupism and transnationalism in global life, with each sometimes reinforcing the others and sometimes negating them but at all times at work in one part of the world or another. As a result, the imposed order is viewed as sustaining deep-seated processes that foster both conflict and co-operation.

The terminology available to characterise and analyse this complex order is insufficient.[9] The present offers no dominant relationship such as the superpower competition that underlay the labelling of the Cold War. Nor is the present distribution of power so self-evident as to warrant recourse to hegemonic or balance of power labels. Some have suggested that it be designated a polyarchical order because of the absence of an unmistakable and simple hierarchy among states (Brown, S., 1995: 140–76), but this seems unsuitable in that it implies the new global order rests on a static set of structural arrangements and fails to indicate the tensions between the fragmenting consequences of conflict and the inte-grative effects of co-operation. Perhaps even less suitable is a terminology which characterises the present period as 'the post-Cold War order'. Such a label is 'tentative, vague; it lacks authority' (Atlas, 1995:1); and it is also insufficient because even as it concedes the presence of patterns yet to form, it may also mislead us into overlooking or downplaying the emer-gence of processes that systematically link globalising and localising dynamics.

What is needed, in short, is a terminology that suggests neither a rela-tionship nor a pecking order; rather, terms are needed that call attention to the basic processes on which the imposed order is founded and that enable interested citizens as well as those charged with the tasks of governance to remain sensitive to the underlying dynamics driving the order. Accordingly, a lexicon of three different labels has been developed (Rosenau, 1997) to convey the essential underpinnings of the synthesised form of imposed order represented by the middle area of Figure 1. The distinctions among them are simple. One encompasses first order causal dynamics and is referred to as the turbulence model. Founded on a

conception of three basic parameters of world politics as having undergone transformation in recent decades, the turbulence model posits the
transformations as fostering tendencies towards both subsystemic fragmentation and systemic integration. When the focus turns to the outcomes of these tendencies, to the main characteristics of the prevailing
order, reference is made to the post-international model. And when these
tendencies are viewed as second order causal dynamics, as sources of
further tendencies toward fragmentation and integration, the label
fragmegration is used. The latter term may seem irritating and awkward
at first, but it captures well the simultaneity and interactive bases of the
globalising and localising forces that are propelling some collectivities
toward integration and spurring others towards fragmentation.[10]

Indeed, it is anticipated that eventually this conception of simultaneous
globalising and localising dynamics, though perhaps not the label itself,
will emerge as the basis for the prime descriptor of the collective ontology
that replaces the Cold War. It is a perspective that, given the contradictions and complexity of a turbulent/fragmegrative order, regards the
world as short on clear-cut distinctions between domestic and foreign
affairs, with the result that local problems can become transnational in
scope even as global challenges can have repercussions for small communities. Accordingly, in a fragmegrated order the central units of analysis
are not actors but spheres of authority, diverse arenas in which capacity to
act authoritatively is distributed widely among different types of actors.
The notion that 'the U.S. can destroy a country by levelling with bombs;
Moody's can destroy a country by downgrading its bonds' (Friedman,
1995: A19) is illustrative of an ontological perspective in which the world
is viewed as spheres of authority rather than as a crowded stage on which
actors pursue goals. In effect, fragmegration so disaggregates the global
system that it lacks overall patterns and, instead, is marked by various
structures of systemic co-operation and subsystemic conflict in different
spheres of authority, regions, countries and issue areas.[11] As indicated by
the ragged edges of the space in the centre of Figure 1, this variability is
extensive enough to justify relabelling the second level of causal dynamics
as one of uneven fragmegration, a term that further captures the diversity
of the underlying order.

It is important to note that this stress on diversity is not to imply that
the fragmegrative form of order is a residual category, a catch-all for any
situations, processes or developments that the four other forms of order
do not encompass. On the contrary, while its boundary may be ragged, it
is a separate form of order, one that can overlap with the other forms but
does so in such a way as to sustain interactive processes that are apart
from and independent of the others. In addition, a fragmegrative per-

spective facilitates the analysis of how, say, transnational processes have an impact on unilateral policies or how multilateral endeavours may shape subgroup formation. Indeed, the links between any of the four forms of order can be explored through a fragmegrative approach without collapsing the analysis into a single paradigm.

No less important is the fact that, like the other four paradigms, fragmegration cannot be reduced to any of the other forms of order. It has characteristics that are unique and are not operative in any of the other forms. Perhaps most notable, uneven fragmegration differs from the others in that it involves a non-linear notion of time. This temporal dimension is not to be found in any of the other four types of order. The interactions that mark the latter evolve through standard action-reaction sequences, whereas in a fragmegrative order they can simultaneously cascade across and through systems and thus evolve as sequences not readily explicable in standard time sequences. In a fragmegrative order there are no end points, no final destinations at which events culminate with a resolution of whatever problems sustained them. To the charge that 'you are not telling us where we are going!' the student of fragmegration replies, 'Exactly right, we can't tell you where the course of events will end up because fragmegrative sequences can unfold in so many diverse directions.'

Approximate reality or evasive interpretation?

Since the imposition of the turbulence model on world affairs allows for the operation of unilateral, multilateral, transnational and subgroup dynamics in one or another part of the world, the question arises as to whether or not the fragmegration is likely to frame the collective response that specifies the common sense of the emerging epoch. Earlier it was presumed that such a response would evolve, whatever labels may be attached. Still, it is useful to explore whether such a perspective begins to approximate an emergent, widely shared response or whether it merely evades the reaching of overall interpretations. Conceivably it will not form the basis for a broad intersubjective experience because it seems so profoundly wishy-washy that it cannot be negated by any situation that may arise anywhere. If uneven fragmegration accounts for both central tendencies and any deviation from them, many may conclude, the ontology must be fatally flawed.

My response to this line of reason is that the all-encompassing nature of an ontology is precisely designed to unravel, and thereby account for, seemingly contradictory phenomena. That is what the Cold War ontology did for several generations of publics that may have sensed the superpower rivalry was not as evenly balanced as it seemed, just as the inter-war generation saw the world in balance-of-power terms that allowed for the imbalance that was emerging in Europe – and just as today people have no difficulty grasping that Europe has inched toward more integration even as the former Yugoslavia rushed toward fragmentation. Such an understanding has become common sense today. The apparent contradictions are seen not as contradictions but as logical consequences of the diverse forces that sustain the course of events. In effect, fragmegration is a prime characteristic of globalisation, which is to say that just as integrative tendencies spread across conventional boundaries, so do those that promote fragmentation.

Put differently, the fragmegrative ontology would be quickly abandoned if multilateralism and transnationalism were to become so predominant as to reduce unilateralism and subgroupism to marginal phenomena. And it would also falter if unilateral and subgroup dynamics were to diminish greatly the recognisable patterns reflective of pervasive multilateral and transnational processes. However, neither of these falsifying developments appear to be occurring. Even if it is presumed that globalising dynamics are more powerful than the localising reactions they provoke, neither the co-operative nor the conflictual tendencies appear headed for ascendancy. Unilateralism, multilateralism, transnationalism and subgroupism exist side-by-side precisely because that is the complexity of our time. Such contradictory trends need to be viewed for what they are: reflections of the underlying structures of world politics, few (if any) of which are temporary and most (if not all) of which are likely to become ever more deeply embedded in the course of events. A deeply shared sense of community may be breaking down throughout the world and states may continue to stumble in the absence of resolute publics, but such tendencies are widely understood to be essential features of global affairs in the present epoch.

But if both co-operative and conflictual processes are unfolding throughout the world, if disquieting tendencies are at work among domestic publics even as multilateral institutions become stronger, can it be argued that the world is likely to evolve a measure of order in the years ahead? If the deterioration of societal cohesion everywhere suggests the world is headed for more and more fragmentation – and in some instances for the breakdown of civility into outright warfare – even as shared norms about human rights and environmental improvement become increasingly widespread and valued, can one conclude that the future may be more orderly than unruly, founded more on integrative than disintegrative dynamics?

A post-international answer to these questions stresses that global order is more an emergent pattern than a fixed arrangement. It posits the possibility that order is slowly developing out of the ruins of the Cold War, but that it is not doing so with linearity or with clear-cut dimensions. It is an order that expands as much by small increments at the margins as by wholesale changes at the centre, by widely dispersed reactions to (and often against) different forms of globalisation rather than by hegemonic leadership or great power dominance. It is an order that sustains both fragmentation and integration and that proceeds from the diverse ways in which globalising dynamics are the dominant catalyst of world affairs and localising forces are reactions thereto. The globalising and the localising processes are not necessarily conflictual, but they unfold simultaneously and when they clash, they do so in different ways at different times in different parts of the world, with the result that fragmegration is profoundly non-linear, uneven in its evolution, uneven in its intensity, uneven in its scope and uneven in its direction.

An illustrative conclusion[12]

That the fragmegrative dynamics are applicable to any and all parts of the world can be illustrated by a concrete example. Consider the Caribbean Basin in the present epoch. The unilateral, multilateral, subgroupist and transnational perspectives all serve as useful tools for understanding variability across time and among the several countries in the region. The unilateralist perspective is useful at those historical moments when the United States is pressing its interests on one or another Caribbean state and thereby sensitising all of them to their vulnerabilities to US power. The multilateral perspective accounts for the responsiveness of states in the region to co-operative initiatives designed to cope with new interdependence types of issues – such as the drug trade, environmental pollution and currency crises – that no state can effectively address on its own. The subgroupist orientation provides a way of grasping how and why restless publics and corrupt officials turn to the drug trade and crime to alleviate their problems, thereby fostering authority crises that continually confront Caribbean governments and undermine the integrity of the borders they are supposed to protect. The transnational paradigm serves well the need to explain the ever-widening involvement of non-governmental groups and organisations in the multicentric world beyond the Caribbean.

None of these perspectives, however, are particularly suited to explaining the multiple challenges to the region and the ways in which they might collectively be met. It is here, in the complex arena where problems are shaped by both domestic and foreign dynamics, that a fragmegrative approach can be especially fruitful. It highlights a number of dynamics that are not otherwise the subject of intense analysis – it clarifies how traditional conceptions of national sovereignty are insufficient to cope with continuous flow of messages, money, drugs, diseases, ideas and people from abroad; it calls attention to the ways in which such global-ising forces are rendering the Caribbean ever more subject to complex external events and trends that, in turn, foster internal economic fluctua-tions, unemployment, restlessness and drug consumption; it enables ana-lysts to focus on the processes through which localising, island-specific loyalties inhibit the capacity of the region to develop effective institutions designed to increase its collective security; it opens up analytic room for tracing the ways in which NGOs and other actors in the multicentric world are acting independently of governments to both preserve domestic preferences and absorb human rights, environmental and other norms that are evolving abroad; and no less important, a fragmegrative per-spective accords meaning to developments at the citizen level where expanded analytic skills are likely to have important consequences for democracy in the region and the ability of governments to conduct sensi-ble foreign policies.

In short, equipped with fragmegrative lenses people are able to compre-hend the interaction effects of contradictions and tensions at work in the region. And their policy recommendations are thus likely to stress how the many imperatives that call for the building of collective, region-wide institutions can only be met if account is also taken of the numerous impulses to serve island-centred needs. From a fragmegrative perspective, in other words, not only will the various states and NGOs of the region have to subordinate their particular interests and build region-wide mech-anisms of co-operation, but they will also have to ameliorate the domestic problems that derive from high unemployment, extensive poverty, drug consumption and the many other reasons why people at all levels are 'highly disposed to consume drugs which relax tensions, suppress worries and problems, manage stress in their lives, and give them a feeling of over-coming their problems and being on top of the world' (Stone, 1990: 40). What one wise analyst observed years ago about the Caribbean can readily be applied to the world as a whole: 'The problems are qualitative as well as quantitative – how communities are to be organised; the nature of national identities that are to be forged; the substantive meanings of varied styles of integrating individuals and groups into national and local and suprana-tional communities; the mix of ideologies that can explain and rationalise and stabilise the processes of change' (Silvert, 1971: 195).

NOTES

I am indebted to Walter Truett Anderson, Mustapha Kamal Pasha and Hongying Wang for their critical reactions to an earlier draft of this chapter.

1 News item, see Sciolino, 1995: 3.

2 The concept of an ontology originates in the field of philosophy. It refers to the broad assumptions that one makes about the nature of reality. Here the concept is adapted to the field of world politics and is conceived to involve the broad assumptions people make about the realities of global affairs. A paradigm, on the other hand, is conceived here as an empirical specification of what follows from the assumptions encompassed by an ontology. Stated differently, ontologies are foundational in that they highlight what basic elements are regarded as comprising the existing order, whereas paradigms are seen as referring to the ways in which the elements are organised and order thus imposed upon them. It follows that while one's ontology identifies *what* actors engage in *what* forms of behavior to sustain *what* the world is like, one's paradigm focuses on *how* and *when* the actors and their actions might or might not undergo change. Viewed from the more encompassing perspective in which people perceive and talk about reality, of course, ontologies and paradigms cannot be clearly delineated from each other. We separate them only for analytical purposes (combined together they constitute what is often referred to as the 'social construction of reality'). For a discussion of the nature of paradigms and twenty-one different ways in which the concept is employed, see Masterman (1970: 61–5).

3 For a lengthy analysis arguing that the label presently in use, the post-Cold War era, will eventually be replaced because it is 'tentative, vague' and lacking in 'authority', see Atlas (1995: 1).

4 For succinct statements of the unilateral form of imposed order, see Jackson and James (1993), James (1986), and Mearsheimer (1994/5).

5 Compelling illustrations of the multilateral form of imposed order can be found in Adler and Crawford (1991), Richardson (1994/5), Rittberger (1993) and Ruggie (1993). For a cogent articulation of the multilateral form of imposed order in which it is argued that the long-term history of international organisations has been more successful in facilitating progress and stability than is appreciated, see Murphy (1994).

6 While conflict is the central tendency in a subgroupist order, some fragmentation is motivated simply by attempts to achieve better services through decentralisation without harm to other groups. Some subgroupism occurred in New York City, for example, when numerous municipal services were privatised and 'are filling in for government' through business improvement districts, otherwise known as BIDs. See Lueck (1994: 1).

7 A disquieting example of subgroupism as an underlying global order is available in Kaplan (1994).

8 For affirmations of the transnational form of order, see Ohmae (1990) and Risse-Kappen (1995).

9 For a lengthy analysis of the insufficiency of the terminology available to describe and analyse the present era, see Atlas (1995).

10 This concept was first developed in Rosenau (1983).

11 For a cogent example of the fragmegrative perspective, see Barber (1992).

12 The ensuing paragraphs are based on Rosenau (1995a).

15 The problem or the solution?
Capitalism and the state system

Susan Strange

Behind the question, which theories best help to an explanation, there is a prior and a much more important question. It is this. What is it that we need to explain? It is the perennial question for every researcher, no matter what the field of study. It is said that Alice Toklas, sitting at the bedside as Gertrude Stein lay dying, sought one last word of wisdom from her idol. 'Tell me, Gertrude', she said, 'what is the answer?' (No doubt she had in mind the purpose of human life, the future of literature or some great puzzle.) 'Ah,' replied Gertrude with her last dying words, 'but what is the question?'

That is about where those of us engaged in International Studies, and especially those of us brought up, as it were, in the study of interstate relations, have got to. It is not so much that we stand at a crossroads, uncertain which road to take. It is that we stand in a forest of ideas and facts, in gathering gloom and with no clear path ahead, only a tangle of bushes and overhanging branches. We do not know which way to go. The path that we have followed since our days as students seems, to me at least, to have died out. 'Where to Next in International Studies?' was appropriately chosen as the theme for the 1996 convention of the International Studies Association in San Diego, reflecting a widespread sense of uncertainty about the nature of the questions confronting us in the future.

Others may not feel the same. They may think there is still a field of social science called 'International Relations' with a discrete problematic of its own, and in which students and teachers know and agree, in Gertrude's words, about 'what is the question?' – even if they continue to argue about what is the right answer.

Since some of the connecting themes of this book, as explained in the Preface and in Stephen Gill's chapter involve, assembling divergent ideas on the agenda of future research and different people's ideas about theory and change, there is no requirement that the contributors should all accept the same basic premises. My contribution, therefore, is to question the premise that there is such a discrete field of study as 'International Relations', and also to challenge the relevance of the problematic with

236

which it has been concerned for half a century or so in the United States (and for rather longer in Europe). One, moreover, should confront the notion that international relations can be satisfactorily studied in isolation from the problematics defining other related branches of social science. On the contrary, this chapter will argue that, of the chief problematics of society as they appeared a hundred years ago, some have found solutions while others have shrunk in importance or otherwise gone away and ceased to trouble us. It will further argue that the problematics for human society in the future actually result from the 'solutions' of the past; and that these future problems arise from the internationalisation of capitalist production on the one hand and the incompetence of the state system on the other.[1]

*P*s and *Q*s of the past century

First, the premise of my argument must be explained. It is that at least some of the political and economic problems and questions – the *P*s and *Q*s – that appeared most pressing and important to scholars and policymakers a hundred years ago have by now gone away or been resolved.

For simplicity and brevity, let us consider the two really big questions that have dominated political and academic debate for most of the past century. One is 'socialism or capitalism'? The other is 'peace or war'? Both had already emerged as major issues by the 1890s. Both had faded away, been resolved in one way or another (at least in the form in which the questions were posed) by the 1990s. Let us take first the socialism or capitalism question, together with the secondary issues that followed, assuming that capitalist mode of production prevailed, or until it was replaced.

By the 1890s, the efficiency of the capitalist mode of production in producing wealth undreamt of a century before had been amply demonstrated both in America and Europe. It was about to be demonstrated in Japan and other industrialising countries. Also acutely apparent was the inequity in the distribution of that wealth that seemed inseparable from capitalism. Fifty years after Marx's and Engels' *Communist Manifesto*, a transnational socialist movement was well established at least in Europe. It was dedicated to the destruction of capitalism and its replacement with a system in which wealth was to be distributed according to need rather that the ability to pay. For most of the next century, the burning question was to be socialism or capitalism. And until it was finally resolved towards the end of the twentieth century, it was a question that dominated theoretical and political discourse in practically every society in the world.

What Francis Fukuyama with conscious hyperbole called the 'end of history' arrived with the fall of the Berlin Wall in 1989 and the subsequent disintegration of the flagship of socialism, the Soviet Union and its client socialist states (Fukuyama, 1992). Historians will no doubt continue to argue over the causes of that collapse. But what coincided with it was perhaps equally if not more important. For most of the latter half of the twentieth century, halfway between the United States and the Soviet Union, the opposed champions of capitalism and socialism respectively, there had grown up a non-aligned movement of governments that sided with neither alliance. The counterparts in international politics of social democrats in domestic politics, some of the leaders of these non-aligned countries were united in the common belief that it was possible (and desirable) to follow a middle way between capitalism and socialism both in foreign policy and in national management of their economies. By the early 1990s, this belief had, effectively, been abandoned. Decoupling from the world economy was out. Competition for shares of the world market economy – and therefore much more eager participation in the capitalist world economy and all that went with it – was an almost universal trend. Only Cuba, Myanmar and North Korea held out for a while and by the mid-1990s all three were beginning to weaken.[2]

The premise carries with it some significant riders, just as propositions in physics or mathematics carry with them riders that follow logically from the basic premise. These riders concern the agendas for future research in comparative and transnational (or global) sociology, comparative and transnational politics and comparative and transnational economics. One is that with the disappearance of certain forms of production, the role of labour unions and organised labour will become marginal. Their bargaining power, and their membership, will decline. With that decline goes the rationale of neo-corporatist relations between organised labour, government and management. Another rider is that the social balance of power so tilts against the unemployed, the sick, the old and disadvantaged so that capitalists and their apologists will be persuaded that they no longer need to strive to keep the welfare state alive. The shift is already palpable in the United States, and it is likely to spread to Europe and elsewhere.

The second big question dominating political and academic discourse for the past hundred years has been peace and war. It is both more controversial to assert that it has been 'solved' or gone away; and at the same time, it is closer to the interests and concern of many scholars in International Relations.

Although it was far from new as an issue in human society, it was only towards the end of the nineteenth century that it began to engage popular attention so that governments started to take action and to discuss means of eliminating war or of modifying its impact on society. The year 1899 saw the first real multilateral court of international arbitration set up, weak though it may have been. The Russian tsar made a disarmament proposal – albeit in vain. The Red Cross initiative, taken after the battle of Solferino, led to interstate agreements aimed at limiting the pain inflicted by war on prisoners and civilians. For the rest of the century, under the League of Nations and then the United Nations, the question whether, and if so, war could be avoided or restricted had top priority in the study and, quite often, the practice of International Relations. A vast literature, of which readers will be well aware, resulted.

Is that literature now so much junk? Is it as obsolete, apart from its historical interest, in today's world as instructions on how to use an adding machine, sermons of eighteenth-century divines or theological debates of medieval prelates? If it is not already obsolete, there are reasons for thinking it will soon become so. Why? Because, as many thinkers in the field of security studies are beginning to argue, the end of the Cold War marked a secular decline in the probability, or risk, of major war between states; in a sense, it has 'gone out of fashion' (Mueller, 1991). Only two circumstances remain in which states are still likely to go to war with each other. Rival groups in a collapsing empire, federation or a disintegrating state who want to succeed to the spoils, resources and authority over some or all of its territory may call themselves states (they may even gain some recognition from others and may engage in violent conflict which resembles interstate war). Or, second, existing states may still be tempted to fight for territory in order to gain control over certain natural resources – notably oil or water – which either give access to easily earned foreign exchange, or which significantly increase the victor's invulnerability to foreign pressure. For the rest, the prevailing competition between states nowadays is for world market shares as a means to wealth, and in this game additional territory is largely irrelevant. Meanwhile, both the need for and the possibility of achieving real national autonomy are so far diminished that the state has significantly less need to raise revenues in order to provide for national defence. Of course, vested interests in the military and in defence-related industry and services will strongly resist cuts in defence budgets. They will appeal to atavistic fears and will use, as a last resort, the argument that military force – and especially nuclear capabilities – does still serve to enhance a government's bargaining power over a range of issues unrelated to the defence of territory.

This does not mean the end of violent conflict in human affairs. But the conflicts to come, and already being experienced (in Yugoslavia, in Rwanda, in Chechnya, in Sri Lanka or Chiapas), are not interstate but 'civil'. It does not make them any less bloody. The American Civil War probably still tops the list in ratios of casualties to combatants.

Post-revolutionary Russia and China were not far behind. In both cases, and in post-colonial Africa, the collapse of an old regime was followed by violent conflict over who was to control the succession state or states. But as the current debates about humanitarian intervention in Africa, Yugoslavia or the former Soviet Union clearly show, the issues are not the same as those arising in war between states. To the extent that the latter was the core problematic in the field of *Inter*-national Relations, peace studies and war studies need to be redefined – as indeed is happening in many research institutes and university departments.

Before going on to consider the problematics of the next century, two other problematics that came to the fore in the discourse of the last hundred years deserve mention: race and gender. Both the rejection of white superiority – the premise of concepts of 'civilisation' as defined by Europeans and the white man's burden – and the rejection of male superiority and therefore of special rights and privileges over the other sex (and indeed sexes, if homosexuals count as the third and fourth gender), really emerged as powerful new ideas about the turn of the last century. Bernard Shaw, as on other issues, was ahead of his academic and political contemporaries, as playwrights often are. And unlike the peace or war or the capitalism vs. socialism debates, the race and gender ones are by no means over – as is reflected in several of the contributions to this collection. The problematics of epistemology and ontology and the practical applications of both in society will stay on the agenda for future research and these are explored in more detail in other parts of this book.

*P*s and *Q*s of the next century

Picking the problems and questions that will dominate the political and intellectual discourses of the future is no random process. Unavoidably, perceptions of the relative importance and exigency of issues reflect subjective value judgements. It is very easy – temptingly easy – to say that Issue X will be important in years to come because I think Issue X *ought* to be important. A millennialist, for example, might say that the most important issue today and tomorrow is how best to prepare for the end of the world. But most people would disagree. It does not follow that society will share the value judgements of any one individual.

Even when that individual observer attempts a measure of objectivity in picking *P*s and *Q*s for the future, his or her choice is going to reflect the subjective analytical perceptions of the chooser. These too are never wholly objective. It is therefore incumbent upon anyone who lays out an agenda for future research, a menu for political debate, to explain the analytical process by which he or she has arrived at such an agenda or

menu. The process hinges on perceptions – in part subjective – of important change as opposed to trivial change. Any claim to a measure of
objectivity must show supporting evidence and should be reinforced by
the corroborative opinions of others.

My subjective perception is that the biggest change foreshadowing the
*P*s and *Q*s of the future has been the internationalisation of production
that has been gathering speed in the world economy for the past two
decades. That, in my opinion, is the womb in which the big issues of the
next century are already coming to term. Internationalisation of production means that the processes by which goods and services are produced
have come to be determined according to the demands of a world market
instead of local national markets and in accordance with the supply of
factors of production within the world economy, not according to local
conditions of supply. How you measure the process is debateable and the
debate is inconclusive. The UN's *World Investment Reports* do their best,
but the increased number of multinational enterprises, the rise in the
numbers they employ, in their share of interstate trade, in the percentage
of goods and services they supply and sell in each national market are all
only pieces of circumstantial evidence. Even the definition of a multinational enterprise is contestable since control over production no longer
correlates closely with ownership; a franchisor or a firm licensing its technology to another may keep control without the need to own any part of
the enterprise. Statistics on foreign direct investment, therefore, are only
the roughest of guides to the pace at which the internationalisation of production has taken place in the last quarter of the twentieth century.

What was perceived twenty or thirty years ago by analysts on both the left
and the right as an American phenomenon is now acknowledged as a transnational one. Although US-based companies still account for the biggest
share of the stock of foreign direct investment, it is Asian firms –
Taiwanese, Korean, Singaporean as well as Japanese, whose production of
goods and services outside their home country is now growing fastest.
There were a number of reasons – political, financial, managerial – why the
acceleration of international production was led by US-based firms in the
1950s and 1960s. But forces behind the process were not, it is now clear,
exclusive to American capitalism. Both the radical critics who saw the
multinationals as the agents of American imperialism, and the conservative
business-school writers who saw them as proof of American superiority in
industrial organisation, have been proven mistaken. Reorganising firms to
serve a world market instead of a local one has been driven by forces inherent in capitalism, not in American capitalism. The success of Japanese
multinationals in winning market shares the world over is supporting evidence for that. Nestlé, Asea-Brown Boveri and Nokia (Swiss, Swiss-

Swedish and Finnish respectively) are three non-American, non-Asian firms acknowledged as being 'world class', although all three are based in small, politically insignificant countries.

At this point, two objections, or questions implying dissent, may be heard. The first is that while the internationalisation of production may be significant for the study of corporate management, even perhaps of international trade and investment, it is not clear what it has to do with the relations between states. How is this going to change the problematics of International Relations?

The answer seems pretty obvious. It is to be found in the literature of 'interdependence', beginning back in the 1960s with Richard Cooper's seminal plea for more interallied co-operation on common financial and commercial problems (Cooper, 1968). International production greatly increases the need for co-operation between states to manage a globalised economy; national regulation of financial markets, of interfirm competition, of production and distribution standards for social protection is no longer sufficient or effective. Quickly picked up by Nye and Keohane, Cooper's argument generated a vast literature analysing international regimes (Keohane and Nye, 1977; Keohane 1984; Krasner, 1983). A theory, a methodology, what might be termed the Keohane school of neo-liberal institutionalism, came to dominate the study of International Political Economy in much of North America. Seldom challenged, it nevertheless had a basic weakness. It assumed that regimes were desirable, international co-operation always beneficent, so that all right-minded policy-makers in other countries ought to accept the kind of regime favoured by these American theorists. Yet because the underlying theory excluded economic structure as a powerful determinant of state policy, it continued to remain as obstinately state-centred as the rest of conventional International Relations. Its weakness, however, will become increasingly apparent as the internationalisation of production drives a wedge between the interests of national society and transnational business.

This wedge, raising the old national-interest question – specifically, for Americans, Robert Reich's (1991) question, 'who is US?' – strikes at the heart of conventional International Relations. If some states, and some groups of states, exercise asymmetric structural power to shape the world market economy, and if international production produces great schisms of interest within states – as it is already doing – then the political battle within the structurally influential states becomes a battle with global consequences. The conventional rationale for the separate study of interstate politics and domestic politics disappears. Exit International Relations.

The logical base for this argument is not at all new. The close relation of political power and the ways market economies function is the essence of

Polanyi's claim – and of Schumpeter's – to be fathers of modern International Political Economy. It is central to Cox's major work. It is found in the writings of economists as different as Schumacher, de Cecco or Prebisch. It was central to Wallerstein's contribution to understanding the significance in changes in sixteenth-century agricultural production for the industrial revolution – more enduring a contribution than his better-known observations on hegemonic cycles. All that is happening now is that the acceleration in the internationalisation of production is beginning to have a broader impact on the development of social science. Geographers and the sociologists are starting to take over from the political scientists who chose to specialise in International Politics and International Political Economy.

One reason for the growing influence of human geography and historical sociology is that neither of these disciplines is accustomed – as International Relations people are – to look for causes of change in the relations between states. Such misdirected vision has led some writers on international affairs to expect a future dominated by conflict between trade blocs, even the clash of civilisations (Thurow, 1992; Huntington, 1993). Neither is in the cards. Why they are not, requires some attention to the causes of change in production tailored to a world market instead of to a local market in order to see why this has such a direct bearing on the nature of future problematics in social science.

The explanation has been made elsewhere and is not especially difficult to understand. First of all, it calls for a focus on technological change – although technology is a factor seldom included in basic political or economic theory. Second, it calls for attention to be paid to change in the processes of credit creation in a market economy – another factor too often neglected in political and economic theory.

The accelerating pace of technological change, especially since the mid-century, is not in dispute. Its implications, no matter how great, are usually overlooked, however. Briefly, accelerating technological change in the production of goods and of services means that there is less time for a firm to amortise the cost of the last technological innovation (that is to repay, or write off, the capital invested). New technologies, moreover, are apt to cost more than those they replace. They may save labour costs but they increase capital costs. The firm, therefore, that used to amortise its invested capital from profits made on the local market can do so no longer. There simply isn't time. It is therefore forced to seek profits from other markets, first by exporting and then, in order to counter the risk of raised trade barriers against it, to produce all or part of the product locally, inside its new markets (Stopford and Strange, 1991).

This explanation makes most of the theory of the firm otiose. This theory, based on the nineteenth-century Ricardian concept of rent, built on the work of mid-century economists such as Coase and Williamson. It explains the very existence of firms by the savings of transaction costs consequent upon the internalisation of adding components or processes to production of the finished product. According to this theory, the firm is pulled into international production by the advantages of having control over the whole production. The alternative explanation does not deny that there may be savings in transaction costs, and certainly concedes that enterprises dislike sharing control over their business. But, it insists, firms are pushed, not pulled. They are driven inexorably by technological change which obliges them to seek new sources of profit in order to keep up with their rivals.

The second key factor, without which multinational enterprises could not have managed so easily to keep up with technological change, is the availability and mobility of capital to finance both the research and development and the installation costs of these innovations.[3] This is where – in my opinion – much Marxist and neo-Marxist theory in political economy is based on a serious fallacy. Too many Marxists and non-Marxist writers have tended to assume that capital is created by accumulation, made possible by the exploitation of labour. If that were true the industrial revolution would have taken a thousand years and the internationalisation of production would have been a dream of the distant future. Innovation, and especially competitive innovation, requires a progressive creation of credit. This has been made possible by the mechanisms of banking, a process that has a lineage stretching back to the Fuggers and the Medicis in the European Renaissance. It, too, has accelerated since the 1960s, so that firms have accumulated an ever-increasing load of debt in one form or another – shares, bonds, loans, securitised IOUs. Bankers, too, were responsible for introducing capital mobility across national borders. That too goes back a long way. And capital mobility also increased exponentially with the introduction of Eurocurrency loans and the progressive opening of financial markets to buyers and sellers from all over the world.

These two factors combined to make international production a game that all must play, and, given some willing creditor, are also able to play. Entrepreneurs like Donald Trump, Richard Branson, Robert Maxwell or Rupert Murdoch neither inherited nor 'accumulated' wealth for their enterprises; they borrowed it.

Conclusions

This brief explanation of how the embryos of future problems have grown out of solutions in the womb of the recent past leads to some informed guesses about the future. It would be presumptuous and imprudent to call them predictions. Scholars in International Relations, aping the economists, have sometimes deluded themselves in the belief that prediction was possible.

On the bright side is the potential solution of the problem posed in the Brandt reports – the uneven development of North and South that dominated much debate from the 1960s on. The internationalisation of production is busily closing the much-debated North–South gap by transferring industry from the developed to the developing countries – or at least to a steadily rising number of them.[4]

The downside of this solution is the problem of meeting the adjustment costs for workers, and often for whole communities and regions, in the developed countries. Jobs lost to robots and to transplant factories set up to sell in Asian or Latin American markets will not return. New opportunities for factory jobs in the newly industrialising countries are matched by new risks for factory jobs – and many managers – in Europe, America and Japan (Rifkin, 1995). But there are at least two other important problems foreshadowed by recent political-economic change that are the counterpart or product of apparent solutions. One is ecological. The other is financial.

The ecological one arises from the accelerating rate of technological change. The new technology is already being introduced so fast that its potential for damage to climate, soil and to plants and animals as well as humans only becomes apparent when it is already too late. Distrust of scientific advance – distrust that was first articulated in the 1940s by some of the scientists involved in the Manhattan Project to develop atomic explosives – has already produced a booming market for organically grown food. It could soon stop some research in biogenetics. The next century, in short, could see the end of an era that began with Da Vinci and Galileo, flowered in the Enlightenment and fostered a general belief in reason and in scientific method. For three centuries, society has put its faith in scientists to solve the problems of shortage and poverty. As that faith dies, social scientists too will lose influence and respect.

The financial problem that arises from the discovery of the magical power of money (and still more of created credit) may be just as serious. As with the scientists, it is those who are personally involved in finance who are the Cassandras, predicting sooner or later a 'meltdown' of the global financial system, a disaster that not even they know how to prevent. It is significant that those who are most familiar with the system are the most pessimistic, the readiest to admit that no easy answers can be found. Going back to national regulation of markets and financial operators is all they can suggest, but in the same breath they admit that is not possible (for example, George Soros, the financial speculator who wants to create an 'open society', see Soros 1995a).

But in both cases, the warning voices are drowned out by the great majority of scientists and of financial operators who insist that all is well – so far. How to control and restrain both the scientists and the bankers – much more than the managers of capitalist enterprises – may be the central problematic of International Political Economy in the future. In this regard, the poverty of monetarist economic theory applied piecemeal to national economies regardless of the mushrooming of mobile international capital, is matched only by the poverty of International Relations theory. Once again, the state which was the solution in the early stages of capitalist development now becomes the problem in its later stages. Democracy which was the solution to absolutist tyranny now becomes the problem. A democratically governed hegemon is even less likely than an hierarchical one to make the enlightened choices necessary for the preservation of the global market economy. As Robert Cox once intuitively perceived, the international political system based on states' mutual recognition of each other's formal sovereignty is an obstacle, not a means to co-operation sufficient to preserve social cohesion and stability (Cox, 1982). An alternative task is indeed to discern the coalition of forces that might combine across state frontiers to restore some sanity in the management of human affairs.

NOTES

1 Parenthetically, this interrelationship of the capitalist, or market-oriented, economic system for the production of goods and services, and the international political system composed of territorial states as the prime possessors of political authority, is something on which Robert Cox, for example, has always insisted. That International Relations, and especially the analysis of international organisation, gave him a home or base from which to operate does not alter the fact that his work should more properly be seen as belonging to International Political Economy than to International Relations as conventionally presented. Such tolerance and openness deserves acknowledgement; as much could not be expected from, say, most practitioners and university departments of political science or of neo-classical economics. There are a number of us, like Cox, who have been mercifully free to pursue our interest in International Political Economy under the convenient disguise of 'Professor of International Relations'. Many of us have shared with him a critical concern with the inequities associated with the market economy, at least as great as the concern with the disorders of the international polity that has dominated the study of International Relations.

2 Why socialism lost the contest, and capitalism won, is much debated and will continue to be so. Some will say that it was the inability of centrally planned

economies to satisfy both civilian demands for material comfort and military demands for weapons to match those of the United States and its allies – in short, the pressures of the Cold War. Others, taking a longer view, will say that the failure of workers to show socialist solidarity by refusing to fight for capitalist governments in the First World War foreshadowed the ultimate collapse of international socialism; and that the rest followed that early defeat. Though interesting, the debate about causes does not change the basic end-of-history contention: that the socialism vs. capitalism question belongs to the twentieth century not the twenty-first.

3 There is a further necessary condition for international production which, for reasons of space, I have not mentioned. It is, of course, the mobility of technological information, without which Japanese cars or motorbikes or Korean ships could never have been built.

4 The Brandt solution assumed, unwarrantably, that the social-democratic notion of welfare and income redistribution could be applied internationally, by increasing official aid and giving preferential trade terms. The message, predictably, went unheard in America.

16 Rethinking innovation in International Studies: global transformation at the turn of the millennium

James H. Mittelman

In the preface to this book the editors posed four questions concerning the meaning and purpose of theory, its relationship to historical transformation, the ways that the writings of major theorists can be regarded as 'innovatory' both in their times and as regards world order today, and the agenda for study in the present and the future. Given that the contributing authors are not wedded to any single tradition, it is not surprising that their different backgrounds in terms of discipline, methodological inclination, generation, race, nationality and gender have produced different emphases. To respond to our core questions, the authors have tried to push a range of research genres – normative theory, Marxism, feminism, post-modernism, post-structuralism, post-colonialism and so on.

Whereas this chapter does not presume to present an overview of the contributors' work, it is nonetheless worth noting the broad commonalities that have emerged. There is a shared interest in developing a critical and theoretical perspective on problems of structural change. To do so, several authors choose to focus their research on a series of accelerations and decelerations in history – a set of changes culminating in the current phase of globalisation. Most of the authors take issue with mainstream International Relations, at least with realism, which is the reigning approach. Moreover, some of them seek to theorise resistance movements – that is, opposition to globalising tendencies. Virtually all of the chapters say that while retaining what is valuable, let us leave behind where we were in theory. Although there is no clear point of crystallisation, it is time to innovate, and much is to be learned from the correlation of historical transformation and previous innovations.

Building on the foundations laid in previous chapters, this essay is an attempt to show how theoretical innovation can lead to shifts in research orientations on future world orders. Although in this venue I will not rehearse my reflections on concrete forms of future world order (Mittelman, 1994a; and with emphasis on globalisation as a harbinger of historical transformation, Mittelman, 1996a), this chapter is rather an effort to orient theory productively towards substantive research. I contend that keys to reasoning about future world order are buried in the intellectual past – classical social theory – and may be skilfully and creatively revived in order to bring to light global transformation at the turn of the millennium.

It never occurred to the classical social theorists that International Relations was a separate field of study. Rather, innovators such as Karl Marx and Max Weber regarded International Relations as a specific application of their theories. As with contemporary approaches, their theories generated sets of questions and answers, explained relationships among social phenomena, and provided concepts that practitioners could use as a means of production of collective action.

The great social thinkers of the nineteenth and early twentieth centuries theorised beyond the territorial state. They generated concepts of world order not only as it was, but also as it might be adapted to different value systems, whether emancipatory visions or 'ideal' types. Then as now, connecting the diachronic and synchronic aspects of social change, as well as casting them into alternative futures, necessitated theorising transformation.[1]

In developing my arguments, I will first clear the way by identifying common traps and confusions in thinking about future world order. Next, attention turns to the foremost attempts to comprehend knowledge changes, with emphasis on breakthroughs rather than adaptive innovations. In the third section, I will consider the classical authors, especially Marx and Weber, who spurned what might pass as prophecy and, instead, sought to establish systematic ways to explain or achieve future world order. The conclusion indicates in what directions fruitful approaches might lie – an agenda for study in light of changing global structures.

Analytical traps and confusions

Put basically, theoretical innovation means creative imagination in the production of new knowledge. This activity entails prescriptions and remedies that do not follow established procedures, norms and codes of behaviour. As such, theoretical innovation is just one aspect of the multidimensional process of political, economic and cultural transformation.[2] Depending on the conditions under which they emerge, each innovation may entail rewards and risks – in terms of remuneration, status, career and physical well being – for the agents who challenge the prevailing paradigm.

To determine their intellectual and political sustainability, innovations must be considered in respect to particular sets of structures or institutions. In fact, successful innovations may be regarded as self-destructive to the extent that they are institutionalised or normalised as part of an ascendant paradigm.

Whilst these elemental propositions are broad and must be contextualised, they do suggest five major errors in thinking about future world order.[3] First, there is the pitfall of privileging one aspect or dimension of social change at the expense of others. Sometimes known as determinism, this unvarnished way of thinking about future world order comes in many hues, according to the values and interests of its purveyors. Although economic determinism (often though not exclusively associated with vulgar Marxism) may be the best-known variety, forms of political, technological and cultural determinism also seem to appear, disappear and reappear.[4] For example, in the mid-1990s, long after anthropologists maintained that Confucian values blocked economic advancement in the Orient, there emerged an image of future world order as one of the coming 'Pacific century', with Asian values resurrected as its centrepiece. Joining this debate over hegemony in a globalising, post-Cold War world, Lee Kuan Yew, Singapore's former prime minister, holds that in view of cultural differences between Western and East Asian societies, Western-style democracy will not work in East Asia (Zakaria, 1994). While Lee presents a thinly veiled rationalisation for authoritarian rule in Singapore, some scholars (Baum, 1982; Berger and Hsiao, 1990; Hamilton and Kao, 1987) have also suggested that the rise of the East Asian Newly Industrialising Countries may be largely attributed to their exceptional cultural resources. Confucian values of temperance, collective purpose and sacrifice are identified as distinctive features underpinning East Asian development. Unlike their counterparts elsewhere in the South, the 'four tigers' (Hong Kong, Singapore, South Korea and Taiwan) are said to embody Weberian correlates of capitalist achievement.

The problem with this thesis about Confucian capitalism is that it is rooted in a primordial notion of culture, and denies the historical and changing role of cultural forces. Culture is neither immutable nor homogeneous. In fact, East Asian cultures are medleys of Confucianism, Buddhism, Taoism, Christianity and other traditions. In contrast to culturalist formulations, the more plausible use of culture as one component of an explanation of world order is the appreciation of subjective and selective orientations in contingent terms.[5]

Second, a closely related error in thinking about theoretical innovation in conjunction with global transformation is to impose Western dichotomies on the Third World and seek to universalise them. (On the pitfalls of dualism, see also the chapters by Pasha, Peterson and Persaud.) Of course, Western discussions of International Relations theory are couched in a language that embraces Western concepts and Western experience. That one draws on one's own intellectual heritage is not surprising. When it comes to contemplating world order, Western observers are prone to employ such categories as theory or practice, scientific or unscientific, state or market, public or private, *Gesellschaft* or *Gemeinschaft*, moral or material, legal or illegal, anthropocentric or ecocentric, etc. (Lohmann, 1995: 114).

Application to Southern countries of these Western mental frameworks and presuppositions about the knowledge they are supposed to transmit has an enormous impact on, and may provoke resistance by, those whom research is meant to serve (Lohmann, 1995: 115). This point was brought home to me when I was working in Bukoba, a district in north-western Tanzania. There, *matoke* bananas (the staple food) and coffee are interplanted because land is in short supply; the majority of producers, poor peasants, do not have access to sufficient acreage to grow the two crops in separate areas. The government's agricultural extension officers, however, have advised the small farmer to cultivate pure-stand coffee, since inter-planted bananas draw nitrogen and water from the soil and shade the coffee crop. This advice is based on experiments performed under laboratory conditions. It benefits only the minority of well-to-do farmers with enough land to segregate bananas and coffee. The large landholder cultivates under conditions that resemble those of the research station. In addition, he (not she) is likely to mingle with the government experts in a social milieu that facilitates communication and hence adoption of the proposed innovations.

The poor peasants resist the innovations suggested by the research team because its recommendations are useless or harmful to them. They have been known to fry cotton seeds before putting them in the ground or to plant cassava cuttings upside down. This example of resistance is not a random case. It typifies the way a particular armoury of knowledge is regarded.[6]

There is a widespread Western presupposition that intellectual innovation and social change constitute a two-fold process divided into what has to be done, and how to do it? Historically, the separation of conceptualisation and execution reflects a broader social division between intellectual and subaltern labour, or management and workers, originating in factories in the West (Braverman, 1975). To many non-Westerners, this way of thinking embraces hierarchic and academic, top-down concepts. It ignores the fact that much knowledge and action is generated by different cultures in a fluid blend of theory and practice, and embedded in the everyday activities of ordinary people, sometimes portrayed as the 'weak' or the 'powerless'. Moreover, as the Tanzania illustration suggests, there are no neutral arenas – whether 'science,' laboratories, local pubs or hotels – that do not favour the interests of one group over another or that are free of the contestability of ideas. Indeed, academic science tends to delegitimise local and often unwritten knowledge (Lohmann, 1995: 117–18).

Third, West-centrism is evident in another manner. The problem Westerners often face in gaining access to local and unwritten knowledge lies in the unstated premises of the questions they pose. For example, they present inappropriate hypothetical choices to people who respond either quizzically or more directly by wanting to challenge the presuppositions of the query. I made this error myself when I had an opportunity to carry out research in an *ujamaa* (communal) village along Tanzania's Rufiji River. Following a period of becoming acquainted and establishing rapport, an elder recounted the origins of the community, whose inhabitants had been moved away from their ancestral homeland and resettled by the state. Asked whether she preferred to live in this communal setting or her former domicile, this wizened old lady merely shrugged. My question was too iffy for her taste. Perhaps this subsistence farmer thought that such hypothetical matters may interest Westerners, but what was the point?[7] This epistemological gulf between knowledge sets suggests that the Western framework itself and its variants, purportedly deployed to study other cultures, histories and world order, must be transformed into a subject of inquiry and for criticism.

Fourth, even if one is aware of the dangers of West-centrism, and if one seeks to decentre thinking about theoretical innovation and global transformation, there is still the risk of reification. One of the foundational theoretical works on what makes order possible, an innovative study that influenced subsequent generations of thinkers, is Emile Durkheim's *Division of Labour in Society*. In Durkheim's theory, modern societies are far more complex than are primitive ones, owing to a high division of labour. Although there is a transformation of the prevalent solidarity from a mechanical to an organic form, order as such is preserved – except in cases where anomie and a considerable incidence of suicide mark a pathological state of affairs. With modernity, the more individuals depend on society, the more labour is divided, activities become more specialised, and people are bound together not by a strong collective conscience but by their increasingly differentiated roles. Durkheim thus maintained, contra Marx, that the modern organic division of labour did not necessarily bring deleterious consequences but could create cohesion among otherwise autonomous individuals.

In developing this thesis, however, Durkheim and his many followers have reified overall social structure; very little attention is given to the interactions between structures and agents, to how to join processes and actors. The distinction between mechanical and organic solidarity is a valuable analytical insight, but when hardened to the extent that it is regarded as a reality in its own right, it becomes counterproductive. What happens is that the concept distracts researchers from the real historical processes in which social relations are created and transformed. Whatever Durkheim's intentions, the theory's atemporal aspects have not only been given a life of their own, but also have constituted and imposed an *a priori*, dichotomised order on fluid and varied social realities so that the whole scheme fits neatly together.

Finally, it is important to signal a warning about scientism – the pretence of using hard-edged ontological categories drawn from the predictive ability of the natural sciences as the measure of theory (Sayer, 1992; see also the chapter by Strange). Premised in positivism, this tradition in reasoning about the human future, especially that genre known as futurology, involves linear projections: empirical data are the basis of forecasting trends or extrapolating about the future (e.g., one of the best evaluative studies of this tradition is Hughes, 1985; and in a popular idiom, Naisbitt, 1995). Modellers present particular outcomes as empirical tendency statements drawn from statistical knowledge. The difficulty with this mode of inquiry is that the future is seen as more of the same. Changing bases of power in society and social relations do not enter into the models of the future. There is little understanding of the structures and processes of history (Cox, 1976). History is not seen as a dysrhythmic and spasmodic process in which basic ruptures can tear the social fabric and turn the course of human affairs. Singly, or in varied combinations, these misconceptions have restrained innovations in knowledge about world order.

Thinking about knowledge changes: world order

Eluding these analytical snares, some of the foremost thinking about theoretical innovation may be found in the work on 'scientific revolutions' (Kuhn, 1970), 'epistemic communities' (Haas, 1992) and 'the knowledge structure' (Strange, 1988). It would be remiss not to note both the contributions and limitations of these perspectives, for these constructs can serve as staging posts for more theoretically innovative scholarship on global transformation. (Whereas Gramsci finds his place among major theorists on the role of ideas in historical transformation, his approach does not appear here only because it is assayed in the chapter by Augelli and Murphy, and is a theme in Gill's and Sakamoto's chapters.)

Based on his study of the history of the natural sciences, Kuhn shows that scientific knowledge grows through revolutionary transformation rather than via a linear accumulation of facts or hypotheses. He holds that a scientific discipline begins with forming a paradigm – a common framework, a shared world view that helps to define problems, a set of tools and methods, and modes of resolving the research questions deemed askable. Normal science is a means of confirming the type of knowledge already delimited and legitimised by the paradigm in which it arises. In fact, normal science often suppresses innovations because they are subversive of a discipline's fundamental commitments (Kuhn, 1970: 5).

No part of the aim of normal science is to call forth new sorts of phenomena; indeed those that will not fit the box are often not seen at all. Nor do scientists normally aim to invent new theories, and they are often intolerant of those invented by others. Instead, normal-scientific research is directed to the articulation of those phenomena and theories that the paradigm already supplies. (Kuhn, 1970: 24)

Given the ways that scientific practice normalises knowledge, how do paradigms change? Most often it is either the very young or newcomers to a field who refuse to accept the evasion of anomalies (observations at odds with expectations derived from prior theoretical understanding) – what Gouldner (1980: 299) calls 'the bland form contradiction takes within institutionalised intellectual life'.

A new paradigm emerges when the burden of anomalous phenomena grows too great, when discrepancies can no longer be assimilated into existing paradigms, when there is incommensurability between competing paradigms to the extent that proponents of alternative frameworks cannot accept a common ground of assumptions. Instances known as 'scientific revolutions' that shatter the traditions of normal science are extraordinary occurrences precisely because the stakes are so high: a redefinition of problems, novel methods, new textbooks, different standards, pedagogical shifts, etc. What type of transformation follows? In the aftermath of a scientific revolution, how is a new tradition of normal science formed?

For Kuhn, the transition to a new paradigm is all or nothing: 'Like the gestalt switch, it must occur all at once (though not necessarily in an instant) or not at all' (Kuhn, 1970: 150). In his insistence on the structural power of paradigms to orient intersubjective meaning and mould the culture of scientific inquiry, Kuhn has contributed importantly to understanding theoretical innovation. In explaining transformations, however, Kuhn falls short insofar as he underestimates the tenacity of the early paradigm. In the field of global development, a pertinent example is the modernisation school, which has withstood attacks from the dependency, world-systems and Marxist traditions, and is now ascendant under the mantle of neo-liberalism, revived as part of the reigning orthodoxy. Just as modernisation theorists have adapted to changed conditions, so too is it necessary to abandon Kuhn's notion that normal science is rigid. Surely a paradigm can modify itself, and the dynamic interplay between paradigms must be explored more deeply than merely observing that friction exists.

Moving beyond his initial formulation, in a 1970 postscript Kuhn notes that advocates of a paradigm belong to a shared knowledge community. Subsequently, this concept was reincarnated in the form of epistemic community: 'a network of professionals with recognised expertise and competence in a particular domain and an authoritative claim to policy-relevant knowledge within that domain or issue-area' (Haas, 1992: 3). From this perspective, knowledge formation is a process of specialised inquiry. Equipped with expertise, mutual expectations, and a superior mapping of reality, epistemic communities render information and advice to decision makers who seek to solve problems in a climate of uncertainty.

The important point about the structure of epistemic communities is that the consensus forged by experts over the identification of problems shapes the way that the interests of states are defined. Another matter fleshed out in this research is that technical advice reflects prior social and intellectual conditioning. In fact, the concept of epistemic community seems to draw on the insights of post-structuralist epistemology, which emphasises the importance of the conditions under which knowledge emerges and the relative nature of rationality.

Like Kuhn, Haas stresses that the perpetrators of knowledge can institutionalise their influence and, he holds, infuse their views into international politics. Yet, the epistemic community approach maintains that there is 'a dynamic for persistent co-operation independent of the distribution of international power' (Haas, 1992: 4). Although Haas identifies the role of an important transnational actor, his argument imbues agents with too much autonomy. In many respects, scientific communities are not detached from but constitute an integral component of power structures. What must be decoded is the precise nature of the knowledge-power link. Most often, intellectual innovations are shaped to meet the needs of the powerful, to the detriment of the powerless, thereby constraining political and economic transformations. Moreover, the epistemic community approach is scientistic, stressing as it does that the authority of experts rests on the elucidation of cause-and-effect relationships, hypothesis testing and evidential proofs. This way of thinking about intellectual innovation and global transformation is a validation of positivist methods, and the emphasis on consensus over shared knowledge within epistemic communities and scientistic thinking serves the architects of state power.

In fact, the sometimes understated, very subtle and unmistakably critical thrust of Kuhn's analysis exposes the epistemic, and basically functionalist, approach to portraying intellectual innovation as a way to fulfil a political system's need to reduce complexity and uncertainty.[8]

A different appreciation of the patterns of intellectual innovation may be found in Strange's notion of a knowledge structure, which includes 'what is believed . . . what is known and perceived as understood; and the channels by which beliefs, ideas, and knowledge are communicated – including some people and excluding others' (Strange, 1988: 115). Although Strange's view seems to bear the imprint of Antonio Gramsci's concept of hegemony, which could easily accommodate knowledge structures consisting of beliefs and understandings, she does not discuss this link, or identify the differences. Like Haas, she stresses that new knowledge relies on consent, but for her, knowledge is also a product – i.e., a public good – and its connection to power is crucial to understanding the sutures of leadership. In an era when large philanthropies are a multibillion dollar business dominated by US foundations, mostly the fortunes of large clans such as the Mellons, the Carnegies and the Rockefellers, dynasties that dwarf private donors in Europe, and when only a handful of developing countries have the wherewithal to enter the competition to build knowledge structures in the form of industrial and technological parks – crucial nodes of innovation – who can doubt that Strange has focused on a key ingredient of changing hierarchies in world order?

Yet, by blurring the distinction between knowledge and 'information', she verges towards treating the former as a thing – reifying it. Moreover, she rightly notes that 'knowledge can be stored' (1988: 118), but does not probe the processes and varied conditions under which 'meanings' are socially constructed out of information. Knowledge is, of course, not deposited in a databank and simply transmitted through technological networks. The latter are not neutral carriers. Meanings are hammered out in the crucible of social relations, which do not comprise a unified structure, yet are linked to interests in complex and varied ways.[9] The controversy over the nature of this relationship – the affinity between ideas and interests – goes to the heart of classical social theory. The question of new knowledge begs examination of the links to the structures of social life that underpin it.

Pointing the way forward: going back to the classics[10]

The major classical site of the ideas–interest problem is the Marx–Weber debate. It is well to remember that both of these path-breaking theorists devised methods to understand the world as well as to reason about alternative forms of action for the future. Inasmuch as the conversation between Marx and Weber speaks to potentiality, there is much to be gained by going back to the classical tradition in order to go forward from it. Then one can adapt the old concepts to new problems, albeit ones for which they were not intended.

The role of ideas in history is treated somewhat differently by the two authors. Marx posits a closer correspondence between ideas and material conditions than does Weber in his notion of an 'eclectic' remove from the more directly economic formulations of the dialectical paradigm. Attention to the centrality – not primacy – of economic conditions is evident in Weber's initial publications, but he regarded the 'economic interpretation' of history as a one-sided perspective (Löwith, 1993: 19). Methodologically, he constructed theory by accentuating one or more ideas, producing what Weber himself (1949: 90) called a 'utopia', a mental construct that cannot be found in reality, arrived at by isolating certain aspects of reality.

But what traits are exaggerated and unified into an analytical construct? Weber's formula for selection is flexible, or put differently, subjective. Rejecting the assumption of any objective meaning, Weber sought to restrict the explanations of meaning to the subjective intentions of the actor (Gerth and Mills, 'Introduction', Weber, 1946: 58). Insofar as ideal types are abstracted from certain characteristic social phenomena and constitute a model, they are pure mental constructs removed from reality. In this sense, ideal types differ from the Marxist method of double motion – moving from the abstract to the concrete and from the concrete to the abstract in a series of successive approximations. For Marx, the most general level of abstraction, particularly the concept of mode of production, is a heuristic tool, supplanted by intermediate levels of abstraction, such as the concept of commodity, to study concrete social formations. Marx then employed a historical and dialectical method to identify the contradictions that move history.

In contrast to historical dialectics, Weber's methodological reflections are linked to his ultimate unit of analysis – the individual person. 'Only through ideal-typical concept-construction do the viewpoints with which we are concerned in individual cases become explicit' (Weber, 1949: 110). For Weber, collectivities are a provisional focus, but the whole can be reduced to its parts: the reality is individuals interacting with one another. He thus developed a critique of the 'undifferentiating use of collective concepts' such as the family and the state as units of analysis. Since people who comprise collectivities have diverse interests, concepts and procedures must examine these dissimilarities.

Many of the concepts Weber constructed centred on aspects of personality: 'the scientific man', 'the political man', 'charisma', etc. Weber's methodological individualism is also evident in his belief that the activity of social science is intuitive and inspired by 'flashes of the imagination' – it is a calling. He recognised that the judgement of the scientist depends on his/her mental constructs, not a 'reality' itself. Weber thus argued for a more self-reflexive perspective of intellectual work. In a 1920 letter to Robert Liefmann, Weber encapsulated his methodological and ontological commitments: 'if I have become a sociologist . . . it is mainly in order to exorcise the spectre of collective conceptions which still lingers among us. In other words, sociology itself can proceed from the actions of one or more separate individuals and must therefore adopt strictly individualistic methods' (Weber, 1971: 25).

This emphasis on the individual stands in marked contrast to Marx's focus on big structures and large processes rooted in production. For Marx, the meta-structure – modern capital – is irrational. The irrationality of capitalist economy stems from a contradiction between the rational advances of productive forces and the fetters of private property, the rule of profit and a 'free' market. For Weber, on the other hand, modern capitalism is the epitome of rationality. One of its engines is the large corporation, a type of bureaucracy that promotes rational efficiency. But Weber, unlike Marx, was not interested in exploring the unfolding of capitalism, which the former regarded as the highest form of rational operations.

Reflexive on the problems of their times, Weber, writing in an ascendant, at times hyper-nationalist Germany, and Marx, in exile in England during its industrial revolution and expansionist period, differed in their reasoning about the future order. A liberal individualist and an ardent nationalist, Weber was committed to the statist project. He envisaged a general drift towards secular rationalisation. For him, the cage of history is the bureaucratic division of labour. He maintained that there could be no possibility for the transformation of bureaucratic specialisation through revolution. For Weber, the only hope of escaping the iron cage of bureaucratic rationality is through the agency of charismatic leadership. Rejecting individualistic solutions, Marx was more optimistic, and offered an emancipatory project. He anticipated not only the ultimate resolution of class conflict in favour of subaltern groups, but also the easing of the grip of bureaucratic administration and the loathful release of political control by the capitalist state.

The tensions between these different methodologies, ontologies and political orientations offer a sound basis for thinking about alternative futures. But when pushed to extreme formulations, the two positions run the risks of reductionism (purporting to understand the whole in terms of its parts) and structuralism (not allowing human agents to write their own history). Trying to navigate between these shoals, critical scholars have moved along the currents of Marx and Weber, though not to the exclusion of others, and have attempted to theorise global transformation at the turn of the millennium.

The new syncretism: according to whose paradigm?

In perhaps the most innovative effort to reconcile Marx and Weber, as well as to establish a critical and decentred epistemology in International Relations theory, Robert W. Cox, whose work is an exemplar of innovation, has challenged the canon of normal science. 'Critical' here may be taken to mean erasing the imaginings of society so as to eradicate their deleterious effects and injecting new understandings, which is theory's emancipatory goal (Sayer, 1992: 17, 130, 251–7). Towards this end, Cox adopts the term 'historical structure' 'in the sense of the essential features of an inclusive socio-political entity' (Cox, 1982: 41). In addition, to classify modes of social relations (Cox, 1987), he proposes 'ideal types, or, in the words of Reinhard Bendix, they are contrast concepts of limited historical applicability' (1982: 41).

Drawing on the long-term historical side of both Marx and Weber, Cox rejects Marx's claim to have discovered a logic in history and prefers Weber's reasoning about a succession of forms. Having discarded Marxist meta-theory and some of the economics derived from eighteenth-century notions (including the labour theory of value), Cox (1993b) holds that it was Marx who 'gave a better heuristical tool in pointing to the struggle of social forces as the motor of historical change'. 'Social forces' is of course a more inclusive term than Weber's or Marx's own categories of class.

To rethink world order, Cox makes an important distinction between synchronic and diachronic dimensions of change. One moment of historical change may be analysed in synchronic terms, and may be represented as an ideal type. In this usage, the ideal type is not a teleological construct – i.e., a desirable, achievable, or predetermined outcome. Rather, it is a coherent pattern of interaction of social forces, mental structures and institutions. For Cox, this construct has its own internal contradictions – an inherent dialectic. The resolution of these contradictions explains the diachronic moment. Making allowance for agency, there is nothing inevitable or predetermined about outcomes, only opportunities defining the limits of the possible. History is open-ended. In Cox's view, it is best explained by post-facto ideal types, part of an attempt to understand change by merging the synchronic and diachronic, the coherent and the conflictual, in a dialectic process. Functional analysis, which focuses on coherence, and dialectical analysis, a concern for contradictions within an apparently coherent structure that can lead to its transformation, are thereby combined (Cox, 1993c: 3; 1993b: 5).

On this reading, Weber may be regarded as a dialectician. In fact, Cox (1993a: 4) considers Weber to be 'an historical materialist insofar as he enquires not about the "truth" of a set of ideas but about why they appeal to people in certain material conditions of existence'.

Although Stephen Gill and I (1996) have raised questions about theoretical commensurability in Coxian historicism, an original attempt to unite select aspects of Marx and Weber, this new syncretism provides important innovations in critical theory. The trialectic of Marx, Weber and Cox furthers explanation of new knowledge. The point of entry is through a theme raised in Gill's chapter and bears revisiting in the conclusion: the concept of rationality. As noted here, Marx and Weber pose alternative notions of rationality leading to different accounts of possibility and potentiality. Marx's thinking about the contradictions of capitalism is grounded in what he regarded as the objective irrationality of it all. For him, capital disciplines productive forces but ultimately hinders its further development, thereby limiting its potential.

Weber posited the rationality of the 'systematic thinker', but theoretical mastery largely concerned religious-ethical orientations as they related to the rise of Occidental capitalism. Weber constructed a notion of economic rationalism, which came to dominate the Occident as part of the rationalisation of secular life. This notion derives from his distinction between formal and substantive rationality. The former delimits money calculation and market competition, the products of conflicts of interest and power relationships, whereas the substantive condition of money accounting implies market freedom – an absence of imposed monopolistic limitations which are economically irrational. In other words, the principles of formal and substantive rationality are in conflict. Notwithstanding these important nuances between Marx's and Weber's notions of rationality, Cox encapsulates both of them in an ethical and critical perspective on world order. He probes knowledge structures, paradigms and specific theories in the context of an historical period, the changing nature of capitalism, social interests and power relations, providing a basis for investigating responses to structural changes in the global political economy of the late twentieth century.

For many observers, existing knowledge and intellectual paradigms have proven incapable of adequately explaining the massive changes. An alternative, Cox's multilevel analysis rejected exclusionary dichotomising at the very time when the superpower divide dissolved, the two-fold cleavage between capitalism and socialism mainly shifted into inter-capitalist rivalries, and the North–South polarity gave way to much greater differentiation among developing countries, with a handful of them reaching the cusp of developed-country status. In short, the pressures for a more diverse world order increased markedly.

In contrast to Fukuyama's prognosis (1989) that the triumph of capitalism over communism constitutes a final state of affairs and that there will be no more history, Huntington's projection (1993) that the major global dynamic will be Western culture versus 'the Rest' (especially Islam), and Kaplan's (1994) prediction that despair in many parts of the Third World portends the 'coming of anarchy', Cox views history as a dialogue between past and present, etching other possibilities for the future. By drawing such alternatives from the lived realities of our times, he is able to show their real constraints and opportunities. Like his US counterparts, Fukuyama, Huntington and Kaplan, Cox offers scenarios, but they spring from a different paradigm.

Writing during the Cold War, Cox (1981) used an historically grounded theory and method to elucidate three alternative world orders (also discussed in the chapter by Falk). One vision is that of a new hegemony resting upon the global structure of social power emanating from the internationalising of production. At an interstate level, this configuration would consist of a coalition of Western countries and Japan, the co-optation of some of the more industrialised countries in the Third World, and growing linkage with the (former) Soviet sphere. A second vision of world order is a non-hegemonic structure of conflicting power centres. This could come about through the fragmentation of the international economy into major constellations adopting protectionist policies and lead to competition among neo-mercantilist blocs. A third and more remote possibility is the emergence of a counter-hegemony, a challenge to core countries based on a Third World ensemble with a coherent view of an alternative order. While schematic, these scenarios still seem to portend very real and divergent tendencies in global dynamics.

More recently, he has turned attention to intercivilisational relations (Cox, 1995b) and globalisation (Cox, 1996a), implicitly asking not only, 'what is future world order all about?' but also, 'according to whom?' Cox has in effect, tried to make the reigning Western framework itself into a subject for scrutiny and criticism, seen in the context of its own and other people's history and culture.

Now, Coxian studies are just beginning to gain stature and occupy a recognised place in the scientific community, more or less influential from one zone to another. But if these counter-values do constitute a disruptive element among existing paradigms, and are perceived as a protest movement, will they be absorbed and rendered innocuous by institutionalisation? In Kuhn's terms, will they be normalised? Just as scientific research can be a means of social control, it can also undermine the prevailing order. Just as intellectual innovations are a response to a crisis in world order, they can be crisis-causing for those who occupy the command posts of scientific research and, in the long run, perhaps political and economic power. Just as the adherents of the established order will resist innovations that subvert what they seek to defend, one might go beyond Kuhn to say that it is the duty of critical theorists to resist normalisation.

Towards this end, scenarists may help to rethink long-term global transformation insofar as their work is anchored in tendencies already present in the structure of society. When rooted in historical dialectics, world-order scenarios may combine powerful analytical insights with such value preferences as greater justice, protection of the environment, non-violence and tolerance for different civilisations. Scenarios not only express moral and political orientations, but also, like the theories from which they spring, are means of action. They underline the possibilities for political intervention, subject to structural constraints.

What follows from this analysis in terms of an agenda for study is to ask, more concretely, how is a specific innovation sustained and undermined? This is to pose the question of the politics of ontology and epistemology. Moving beyond the origins and content of an innovation itself in International Relations theory, how do novel ideas become actualised in historical transformations? How do countervalues convert into an integral part of social movements and become a dynamic factor in global transformation? What is the potential for influencing and shaping historical change? Insofar as a theoretical innovation can be a vital element in transforming world order, resolution of these questions is in good part a matter of whose paradigm is violated.

NOTES

I owe a debt of gratitude to Ashwini Tambe for research assistance, especially her substantive contributions, in the preparation of this chapter. I have also benefited from Linda Yarr's and some of the contributing authors' critical comments on earlier drafts.

1 Important explanations for historical transformation are the work of Karl Polanyi (1957), who analysed a double movement comprised of the atomising effects of the market's downward thrust and demands for collective protection emanating upward from society, as well as, at a world level, that of Sakamoto (1994).

2 With the strengthening of civil society in some countries, analysts are increasingly centring attention on innovative strategies of local governance as well. Especially important to my discussion is the work of Tigno (1994).

3 A masterly attempt to contextualise innovatory theories in the field of economics is Heilbroner (1962), a study of the relationships between ideas and the lives of men (i.e., their biographies) without seeking to generalise about the process of paradigmatic change.

4 Elsewhere (Mittelman and Pasha, 1997), we have tried to debunk the notion of technological determinism.

5 I am borrowing from Pasha and Mittelman (1995: 356–7).

6 This example is derived from Mittelman and Pasha (1997: 39).

7 Again, I am drawing an illustration from Mittelman and Pasha (1997: 217).

8 This evaluation of the epistemic community approach owes much to the advice of Ashwini Tambe.

9 I am indebted to Ashwini Tambe's studies of communication.

10 This section draws on and supplements passages in Gill and Mittelman (1996).

References

Abraham, L. (1985) *Call It Conspiracy*. Wauna, WA: Double A Publications.

Adams, A. (1981) 'The Senegal River Valley,' in J. Heyer *et al.*, *Rural Development in Tropical Africa*. New York: St. Martin's Press.

Adams, R. (1995) *Industrial Relations under Liberal Democracy: North America in Comparative Perspective*. Columbia, SC: University of South Carolina Press.

Adler, E. and B. Crawford (eds.) (1991) *Progress in Postwar International Relations*. New York: Columbia University Press.

AFL-CIO (American Federation of Labor-Congress of Industrial Organizations) (1991) *Exploiting Both Sides*. Washington, DC: AFL-CIO.

Afshar, H. (ed.) (1987) *Women, State, and Ideology: Studies from Africa and Asia*. Albany: State University of New York Press.

Afshar, H. and C. Dennis, (eds.) (1992) *Women and Adjustment Policies in the Third World*. London: Macmillan.

Agarwal, B. (ed.) (1988) *Structures of Patriarchy: State, Community and Household in Modernising Asia*. London: Zed Books.

Agnew, J. (1994) 'The Territorial Trap', *Review of International Political Economy* (1) 53–81.

Ahmad, A. (1992) *In Theory: Classes, Nations, Literatures*. London: Verso.

Al-Azmeh, A. (1982) *Ibn Khaldun: An Essay in Reinterpretation*. London: Frank Cass.

Albert, M. (1991) *Capitalism contre Capitalism*. Paris: Plon.

(1992) *Kapitalisme contra kapitalisme*. Amsterdam: Contact.

Altvater, E. (1994) 'Ecological and Economic Modalities of Time and Space', in M. O'Connor (ed.) *Is Capitalism Sustainable? Political Economy and the Politics of Political Ecology*. New York: Guilford Press, 76–90.

Anderson, B. (1991/1983) *Imagined Communities: Reflections on the Origin and Spread of Nationalism*. London: Verso.

Andrea, G. and B. Beckman (1987) *The Wheat Trap: Bread and Underdevelopment in Nigeria*. London: Zed Books.

Apthorpe, R. (1980) 'Distant Encounters of a Third Kind: Problems of Generalism in the Teaching of Development'. *Bulletin of Institute of Development Studies* (Sussex) (11) 3–15.

Arato, A. (1981) 'Civil Society Against the State: Poland 1981–82'. *Telos* (47) 23–47.

(1981–2) 'Empire vs. Civil Society: Poland 1981–82'. *Telos* (50) 19–48.

Arblaster, A. (1984) *The Rise and Decline of Western Liberalism*. Oxford: Blackwell.

Archibugi, D. (1995) 'Immanuel Kant, Cosmopolitan Law and Peace'. *European Journal of International Relations* (1) 429–56.

Archibugi, D. and D. Held (eds.), (1995) *Cosmopolitan Democracy*. Cambridge: Polity Press.

Aredo, D. (1990) 'The Evolution of Rural Development Policies in Ethiopia', in S. Pausewang, F. Cheru, S. Brune and E. Chole (eds.), *Ethiopia: Rural Development Options*. London: Zed Books, 45–57.

Arrighi, G. (1993) 'The Three Hegemonies of Historical Capitalism', in S. Gill (ed.), *Gramsci, Historical Materialism and International Relations*. Cambridge: Cambridge University Press, 148–165.

(1994) *The Long Twentieth Century*. London. Verso.

Ashley, R. K. and R. B. J. Walker (1990) 'Speaking the Language of Exile: Dissident Thought in International Studies'. *International Studies Quarterly* (34) 259–68.

Atlas, J. (1995) 'Name That Era: Pinpointing a Moment on the Map of History'. *New York Times*, 19 March.

Augelli, E. and C. N. Murphy (1988) *America's Quest for Supremacy and the Third World*. London: Pinter Publishers.

(1995) 'Lessons of Somalia for Future Humanitarian Assistance Operations'. *Global Governance* (1) 339–65.

Bacon, F. (1972 [1625]) Essay XXIV. 'Of Innovations', in *Essays*. London. J. M. Dent. Everyman's Library. 74–5.

Bakker, I. (ed.) (1994) *The Strategic Silence: Gender and Economic Policy*. London: Zed Books.

Banks, M. (1985). 'The Inter-Paradigm Debate', in M. Light and A. J. R. Groom (eds.) *International Relations: a Handbook of Current Theory*. London: Frances Pinter.

Banks, M. and M. Shaw (eds.) (1991) *State and Society in International Relations*. New York: Harvester.

Barber, B. (1992) *Jihad vs. Macworld*. New York: Times Books.

Barry, K. (1995) *The Prostitution of Sexuality*. New York: New York University Press.

Bates, R. H. (1981) *Markets and States in Tropical Africa: The Political Basis of Agricultural Policies*. Berkeley: University of California Press.

Baum, R. (1982) 'Science and Culture in Contemporary China: The Roots of Retarded Modernization.' *Asian Survey*, 1 December, 1166–86.

Becker, M. B. (1994) *The Emergence of Civil Society in the Eighteenth Century: A Privileged Moment in the History of England, Scotland, and France*. Bloomington: Indiana University Press.

Beckman, B. (1981) 'Ghana, 1951–78: The Agrarian Basis of the Post-Colonial State', in J. Heyer *et al.* (eds.) *Rural Development in Tropical Africa*. New York: St. Martin's Press.

(1992) 'Empowerment Or Repression? The World Bank and the Politics of African Adjustment', in P. Gibbon, Y. Bangura and A. Ofstad (eds.), *Authoritarianism, Democracy and Adjustment*. Uppsala: The Scandinavian Institute of African Studies, 83–105.

Beckman, P. R. and F. D'Amico (eds.) (1994) *Women, Gender and World Politics*. Westport, CT: Greenwood.

Bennett, J. (1995) 'Buchanan In Unfamiliar Role'. *New York Times*. 31 December.

Berger, P. and H.-H. M. Hsiao (1990) *In Search of an East Asian Development Model*. New Brunswick, NJ: Transaction Publishers.

Bergson, H. (1955) *An Introduction to Metaphysics*. Indianapolis: The Bobbs-Merrill Company, Inc. Translated by T. E. Hulme (1903).

Berlet, C. (1995) 'Armed Militias, Right Wing Populism, and Scapegoating'. Cambridge, MA: Political Research Associates.

Bernard, M. (1994) 'Post-Fordism, Transnational Production, and the Changing Global Political Economy', in R. Stubbs and R. Underhill (eds.) *Political Economy and the Changing Global Order*. Toronto: McClelland and Stewart, 216–229.

Best, M. (1990) *The New Competition: Institutions of Industrial Restructuring*. Cambridge: Polity Press.

Bienenfeld, M. (1991) 'Karl Polanyi and the Contradictions of the 1980s', in M. Mendell and D. Salée (eds.) *The Legacy of Karl Polanyi: Market, State and Society at the End of the Twentieth Century*. New York: St. Martins Press, 3–28.

Block, F. and M. Somers, (1984) 'Beyond the Economic Fallacy: the Holistic Social Science of Karl Polanyi', in T. Skocpol (ed.) *Vision and Method in Historical Sociology*. New York: Cambridge University Press.

Bobbio, N. (1988) 'Gramsci and the Concept of Civil Society', in J. Keane (ed.) *Civil Society and the State*. London: Verso, 73–99.

Bologh, R. W. (1987) 'Marx, Weber, and Masculine Theorizing', in N. Wiley (ed.) *The Marx–Weber Debate*. Beverly Hills: Sage, 145–168.

Boris, E. and E. Prugl (eds.) (1996) *Homeworkers in Global Perspective*. New York: Routledge.

Boutin, J. D. K. (1994) 'Gender and International Relations: A Selected Historical Bibliography'. Toronto: York Centre for International and Strategic Studies Occasional Paper No. 23.

Bowles, S. and H. Gintis (1987) *Democracy and Capitalism: Property, Community, and the Contradictions of Modern Social Thought*. New York: Basic Books.

Braidotti, R. (1991) *Patterns of Dissonance*. New York: Routledge.

Bratten, J. and J. Gold (1994) *Human Resource Management: Theory and Practice*. London: Macmillan.

Bratton, M. (1989) 'The Politics of Government-NGO Relations in Africa', *World Development* (17, 4) 569–87.

    (1990) 'Non-Governmental Organizations in Africa: Can They Influence Public Policy?' *Development and Change* (21) 87–118.

Braudel, F. (1977) *Afterthoughts on Material Civilisation and Capitalism*. Translated by P. Ranum. Baltimore: Johns Hopkins University Press.

    (1978) *The Mediterranean and the Mediterranean World in the Age of Philip II*. London: Fontana/Collins. Translated by S. Reynolds (1949).

    (1980) 'History and the Social Sciences: the Longue Durée', in *On History*. Translated by S. Matthews, Chicago: University of Chicago (1958).

    (1979a/1985a) *The Structures of Everyday Life: the Limits of the Possible*. Volume I of *Civilisation and Capitalism, 15th-18th Century*. Translated by S. Reynolds. New York: Harper and Row.

    (1979b/1985b) *The Wheels of Commerce*. Volume II of *Civilisation and*

Capitalism, 15th-18th Century. Translation by S. Reynolds. New York: Harper and Row. [1979].

(1984/1985c) *The Perspective of the World*. Volume III of *Civilization and Capitalism 15th-18th Century*. Translation by S. Reynolds. New York: Harper and Row.

Braverman, H. (1975) *Labor and Monopoly Capital: The Degradation of Work in the Twentieth Century*. New York: Monthly Review Press.

Brecher, J., J. Childs and J. Cutler (eds.) (1993) *Global Visions*. Boston: South End Press.

Brown, S. (1995) *New Forces, Old Forces, and the Future of World Politics*. New York: Harper Collins.

Brown, W. (1988) *Manhood and Politics*. Lanham, MD: Rowman and Littlefield.

(1995) *States of Injury: Power and Freedom in Late Modernity*. Princeton, NJ: Princeton University Press.

Browne, H. and B. Sims (1993) *Runaway America*. Albuquerque: Resource Center Press.

Bruland, C. (1990) 'The Transformation of Work in European Industrialization', in P. Mathias and J. A. Davis (eds.) *The First Industrial Revolutions*. Oxford: Oxford University Press, 154–69.

Buchanan, P. (1993) 'America First – NAFTA Never'. *Washington Post National Weekly Edition*, 15–21 November.

(1995) 'Where the Real Power Resides'. *The Washington Times*. 8 February.

Bull, H. (1966a) 'Society and Anarchy in International Relations', in H. Butterfield and M. Wight (eds.) *Diplomatic Investigations: Essays in the Theory of International Politics*. Cambridge, MA: Harvard University Press, 35–50.

(1966b) 'The Grotian Conception of International Society', in H. Butterfield and M. Wight (eds.) *Diplomatic Investigations: Essays in the Theory of International Politics*. Cambridge, MA: Harvard University Press, 51–73.

(1977) *The Anarchic Society: A Study of Order in World Politics*. New York: Columbia University Press.

Burnham, P. (1991) 'Neo-Gramscian Hegemony and the International Order'. *Capital and Class* (45) 73–93.

Butler, J. (1990) *Gender Trouble: Feminism and the Subversion of Identity*. New York: Routledge.

(1993) *Bodies That Matter: On the Discursive Limits of 'Sex'*. New York: Routledge.

Buzan, B. (1992) *People, States and Fear: An Agenda for International Security Studies in the Post-Cold War Era*. Boulder, CO: Lynne Rienner.

Camdessus, M. (1996) 'Africa: Adjustment through Cross-Fertilization'. *IMF Survey*, January 8.

Caplan, P. (ed.) (1987) *The Cultural Construction of Sexuality*. London and New York: Tavistock.

Carr, E. H. (1939/1946) *The Twenty Years' Crisis 1919–1939: An Introduction to the Study of International Relations*. London: Macmillan; 2nd edn 1946, New York: St. Martin's Press.

(1945) *Nationalism and After*. London: Macmillan.

Carto, W. (1993) 'The Global Plantation', *The Spotlight*, 17 May.

Caute, D. (1970) *Frantz Fanon*. New York: The Viking Press.

Cavanagh, J. et al. (1992) *Trading Freedom*. San Francisco: Institute for Food and Development Policy.

Cerny, P. (1995) 'Globalization and the Changing Logic of Collective Action'. *International Organization* (49) 595–625.

Chambers (1984) *Chambers' Biographical Dictionary*. J. O. Thorne and T. C. Collocott (eds.) London: Chambers (rev. edn.).

Chambers, R. (1989) *The State and Rural Development: Ideologies and an Agenda for the 1990s*, IDS Discussion Paper 269, University of Sussex.

Chase-Dunn, C. (1989) *Global Formation: Structures of the World-Economy*. Cambridge, MA: Basil Blackwell.

Chase-Dunn, C. and T. D. Hall (eds.) (1991) *Core/Periphery Relations in Precapitalist Worlds*. Boulder: Westview.

Cheru, F. (1989) *The Silent Revolution in Africa: Debt, Development and Democracy*. Harare and London: Zed/Anvil Press.

—— (1992) 'Structural Adjustment, Primary Resource Trade, and Sustainable Development in Sub-Saharan Africa', *World Development* (20, 4) 497–512.

—— (1996) 'New Social Movements : Democratic Struggles and Human Rights in Africa', in J. Mittelman (ed.), *Globalization: Critical Reflections*. Boulder: Lynne Rienner, 145–64.

Cheru, F. and J. Bayili (1991) *Burkina Faso: Assessment of Micro-Economic Policy and its Impact on Grassroots and Non-Governmental Organizations*, Consultant Report, Washington, DC: African Development Foundation, July.

Clapham, C. (1969) *Haile Selassie's Government*. London: Longman Group Ltd.

Clapp, J. (1994) 'Africa, NGOs and the Toxic Waste Trade'. *Journal of Environment and Development* (3) 17–46.

Clark, L. M. G. (1976) 'The Rights of Women: The Theory and Practice of Male Supremacy', in J. King-Farlow and W. Shea (eds.) *Contemporary Issues in Political Philosophy*. New York: Neal Watson Academic Publications, 49–65.

Clark, L. M. G. and L. Lange (eds.) (1979) *The Sexism of Social and Political Theory: Women and Reproduction From Plato to Nietzsche*. Toronto: University of Toronto Press.

Clarke, S. (1992) 'Privatization and the Development of Capitalism in Russia'. *New Left Review* (196) 3–28.

Cohen, J. L. and A. Arato (1994) *Civil Society and Political Theory*. Cambridge, MA: MIT Press.

Cohen, R. (1978) 'Introduction', in *Origins of the State*, (ed.) R. Cohen and E. Service. Philadelphia, PA: Institute for the Study of Human Issues.

Commission On Global Governance (1995) *Our Global Neighbourhood*. Oxford: Oxford University Press.

Commons, J. (1919) *Industrial Goodwill*. New York, McGraw-Hill.

Commonwealth Secretariat (1989) *Engendering Adjustment for the 1990s: Report of a Commonwealth Expert Group on Women and Structural Adjustment*. London: Marlborough House.

Connell, R. W. (1990) 'The State, Gender and Sexual Politics: Theory and Appraisal'. *Theory and Society* (19) 507–544.

Connelly, M. and P. Kennedy (1994) 'Must It Be the Rest Against the West?' *The Atlantic Monthly*, December.

Cooper, R. (1968) *The Economics of Interdependence: Economic Policy in the Atlantic Community.* New York. Council On Foreign Relations/McGraw Hill.

Corbin, H. (1993) *History of Islamic Philosophy.* Translated by L. Sherrard. London: Kegan Paul. (First edn in French in 1964).

Corbridge, S., R. Martin and N. Thrift (eds.), (1994). *Money, Power and Space.* Oxford: Blackwell.

Coulson, A. (ed.) (1980) *African Socialism in Practice – the Tanzanian Experience,* London: Spokesman Books.

Cox, R. W. (1971) 'Approaches to the Futurology of Industrial Relations'. *International Institute For Labour Studies Bulletin* (8) 139–64.

(1976) 'On Thinking about Future World Order'. *World Politics* (28) 175–96.

(1979) 'Ideologies and the New International Economic Order: Reflections On Some Recent Literature'. *International Organization* (33) 257–302.

(1980) 'Production, Hegemony and the Future'. Paper presented to the 1980 Annual Meeting of the American Political Science Association. Washington, DC August. *Mimeo.*

(1981/1986/1996b) 'Social Forces, States, and World Orders: Beyond International Relations Theory'. *Millennium* (10) 127–155. Reprinted with a 1985 Postscript in R. O. Keohane (ed.) (1986) *Neorealism and its Critics.* New York: Columbia University Press, 204–254; and in R. W. Cox, with T. J. Sinclair, *Approaches to World Order.* Cambridge: Cambridge University Press, 85–123.

(1982) 'Production and Hegemony: Toward a Political Economy of World Order', in H. K. Jacobson and D. Sidjanski (eds.), *The Emerging International Economic Order: Dynamic Processes, Constraints, and Opportunities.* Beverly Hills, CA: Sage, 37–58.

(1983/1993d) 'Gramsci, Hegemony, and International Relations: An Essay in Method'. *Millennium* (12) 162–175. Reprinted in S. Gill (ed.) *Gramsci, Historical Materialism and International Relations,* 49–66.

(1987) *Production, Power, and World Order: Social Forces in the Making of History.* New York: Columbia University Press.

(1989) 'Production, the State, and Change in World Order', in Ernst-Otto Czempiel and J. N. Rosenau (eds.) *Global Challenges and Theoretical Challenges.* Lexington, MA: D. C. Heath.

(1991) 'The Global Political Economy and Social Change', in D. Drache and M. S. Gertler (eds.) *The New Era of Global Competition.* Montreal and Kingston: Mcgill-Queen's University Press.

(1992a) 'Global Perestroika', in R. Miliband and L. Panitch (eds.) *The Socialist Register 1992: New World Order?* London: Merlin Press, 26–43.

(1992b) 'Globalization, Multilateralism and Democracy'. The John W. Holmes Memorial Lecture. The Academic Council on the UN System, *Reports and Papers 1992,* No. 2.

(1992c) 'Towards a Post-Hegemonic Conceptualization of World Order: Reflections on the Relevancy of Ibn Khaldun', in J. N. Rosenau and E.-O. Czempiel (eds.) *Governance without Government: Order and Change in World Politics.* Cambridge: Cambridge University Press, 132–159.

(1993a) 'Production And Security', in D. Dewitt, D. Haglund and J. Kirton (eds.) *Building a New Global Order: Emerging Trends in International Society*. Toronto: Oxford University Press, 141–158.

(1993b) Correspondence with J. Mittelman. 12 April.

(1993c) Correspondence with J. Mittelman. 29 October.

(1994a) 'Future World Order and the UN System'. Paper Prepared for *Conference on the UN and Japan in an Age of Globalization*. Yokohama, Japan. 30 November–3 December.

(1994b) 'Global Restructuring: Making Sense of the Changing International Political Economy', in R. Stubbs and G. R. D. Underhill (eds.) *Political Economy and the Changing Global Order*. Toronto: McLelland and Stewart.

(1995a) 'Critical Political Economy', in B. Hettne (ed.) *International Political Economy: Understanding Global Disorder*. London: Zed Books, 31–45.

(1995b) 'Civilizations: Encounters and Transformations'. *Studies in Political Economy* (47) 7–32.

(1996a) 'A Perspective on Globalization', in J. H. Mittelman (ed.) *Globalization: Critical Reflections*. Boulder, CO: Lynne Rienner, 21–30.

Cox, R. W. and Harrod, J. (1972) *Future Industrial Relations: An Interim Report*. Geneva: International Institute for Labour Studies.

Cox, R. W. and H. K. Jacobson (eds.) (1973) *The Anatomy of Influence: Decision Making in International Organization*. New Haven: Yale University Press.

Cox, R. W. with T. J. Sinclair (1996b) *Approaches to World Order*. Cambridge: Cambridge University Press, 85–123.

Crosby, A. (1986) *Ecological Imperialism*. Cambridge: Cambridge University Press.

Cross, G. (1993) *Time and Money: The Making of Consumer Culture*. London: Routledge.

Curtin, P. (1984) *Cross-Cultural Trade in World History*. Cambridge: Cambridge University Press.

Der Derian, J. (1992) *Antidiplomacy: Spies, Terror, Speed and War*. Cambridge, MA: Blackwell.

Derrida, J. (1976) *Of Grammatology*. Translated by G. C. Spivak. Baltimore: Johns Hopkins.

Dhaouadi, M. (1990) 'Ibn Khaldun: The Founding Father of Eastern Sociology'. *International Sociology* (5) 316–335.

Doeringer, P. (1981) 'Industrial Relations Research in International Perspective', in P. Doeringer (ed.) *Industrial Relations in International Perspective*. London: Macmillan.

Dornbusch, R. (1991) 'North American Free Trade: What it Means'. *Columbia Journal of World Business* (26) 73–6.

Doty, R. L. (1993) 'The Bounds of "Race" in International Relations'. *Millennium* (22) 443–461.

Drainville, A. C. (1994) 'International Political Economy in the Age of Open Marxism'. *Review of International Political Economy* (1, 1) 105–132.

(1995) 'Of Social Spaces, Citizenship, and the Nature of Power in the World Economy'. *Alternatives* (20) 51–79.

Druckman, D. (1994) 'Nationalism, Patriotism, and Group Loyalty: A Social Psychological Perspective'. *Mershon International Studies Review* (1) 43–68.

Dunlop, J. T. (1958) *Industrial Relations Systems*. New York: Holt.

Durham, M. (1995) 'The New Christian Right and the New World Order'. University of Wolverhampton. *Mimeo*.

Eckersley, R. (1993) *Environmentalism and Political Theory: Toward an Ecocentric Approach*. Albany: State University of New York Press.

Ekins, P. (1992) *A New World Order: Grassroots Movements for Global Change*. London: Routledge.

Elshtain, J. B. (1981) *Public Man, Private Woman*. Princeton, NJ: Princeton University Press.

(1992) 'Sovereignty, Identity, Sacrifice', in V. Spike Peterson (ed.) *Gendered States*. Boulder, CO: Lynne Rienner, 141–154.

Elson, D. (ed.) (1991) *Male Bias in the Development Process*. Manchester: Manchester University Press.

Enloe, C. (1990) *Bananas, Beaches and Bases: Making Feminist Sense of International Politics*. Berkeley: University of California Press.

(1993) *The Morning After: Sexual Politics at the End of the Cold War*. Berkeley: University of California Press.

Fakhry, M. (1970) *A History of Islamic Philosophy*. New York: Columbia University Press.

Falk, R. (1995) *On Humane Governance*. University Park, PA: Penn State Press.

Fanon, F. (1963/1968) *The Wretched of the Earth*. New York: Grove Press.

(1965) *A Dying Colonialism*. New York: Grove Weidenfeld.

Ferber, M. A. and J. A. Nelson, (eds.) (1993) *Beyond Economic Man: Feminist Theory and Economics*. Chicago: University of Chicago Press.

Ferguson, T. (1995) *Golden Rule. The Investment Theory of Party Competition and the Logic of Money-Driven Political Systems*. Chicago and London: University of Chicago Press.

Flax, J. (1989) *Thinking Fragments: Psychoanalysis, Feminism, and Postmodernism in the Contemporary West*. Berkeley: University of California Press.

Foucault, M. (1972) *The Archaeology of Knowledge*. Translated by A. M. Sheridan Smith. London: Tavistock.

(1978/1980) *The History of Sexuality*. Volume 1. Translated by R. Hurley. New York: Random House. New York: Vintage.

(1985) *The Use of Pleasure*. Translated by R. Hurley. New York: Random House.

Frank, A. G. (1992) 'No Escape from the Laws of World Economics'. *Review of African Political Economy* (50) 20–31.

Freire, P. (1970) *Pedagogy of the Oppressed*. Translated by M. Herder. New York: Herder and Herder.

Frenkel, S. and J. Harrod (eds.) (1995) *Industrialisation and Labour Management Relations*. Ithaca, NY: ILR Press.

Friedman, M. (1962) *Capitalism and Freedom*. Chicago: University of Chicago Press.

Friedman, S. (1992) 'NAFTA as Social Dumping'. *Challenge* (September-October) 27–32.

Friedman, T. L. (1995) 'Don't Mess with Moody's'. *New York Times*, 22 February.

Fukuyama, F. (1989) 'The End of History?' *National Interest* (16) 3–18.
  (1992) *The End of History and the Last Man*. New York: Avon Books. London: Hamish Hamilton.
Gaddis, J. L. (1992/3) 'International Relations Theory and the End of the Cold War'. *International Security* (17) 3–58.
Gailey, C. W. (1987) 'Evolutionary Perspectives on Gender Hierarchy', in B. Hess and M. M. Ferree (eds.) *Analyzing Gender*. Newbury Park, CA: Sage, 32–67.
Gambles, I. (1995) 'Lost Time – The Forgetting of the Cold War'. *National Interest* (41) 26–35.
Garst, D. (1989) 'Thucydides and Neorealism'. *International Studies Quarterly* (17) 3–27.
Gellner, E. (1981) *Muslim Society*. Cambridge: Cambridge University Press.
Gendzier, I. L. (1973/1974) *Frantz Fanon: A Critical Study*. New York: Pantheon Books. (1974) New York: Vintage Books.
George, J. (1994) *Discourses of Global Politics: A Critical (Re)Introduction to International Relations*. Boulder, CO: Lynne Rienner.
Giddens, A. (1987) *The Nation State and Violence: Volume II of a Contemporary Critique of Historical Materialism*. Berkeley: University of California Press.
  (1990) *The Consequences of Modernity*. Cambridge: Polity Press.
  (1994) *Beyond Left and Right: The Future of Radical Politics*. Cambridge: Polity Press.
Gill, S. (1990) *American Hegemony and the Trilateral Commission*. Cambridge: Cambridge University Press.
  (1993a) (ed.) *Gramsci, Historical Materialism and International Relations*. Cambridge: Cambridge University Press.
  (1993b) 'Epistemology, Ontology and the "Italian School"', in S. Gill (ed.) *Gramsci, Historical Materialism and International Relations*, 21–48.
  (1994) 'Knowledge, Politics and Neo-Liberal Political Economy', in R. Stubbs and G. Underhill (eds.) *Political Economy and the Changing Global Order*. Toronto: McClelland and Stewart, 75–88.
  (1995a) 'Globalization, Market Civilisation, and Disciplinary Neoliberalism'. *Millennium* (24) 399–423.
  (1995b) 'Theorizing the Interregnum: The Double Movement and Global Politics in the 1990s', in B. Hettne (ed.) *International Political Economy: Understanding Global Disorder*. London: Zed Books, 65–99.
  (1996) 'Globalization, Democratization and the Politics of Indifference', in J. H. Mittelman (ed.) *Globalization: Critical Perspectives*. Boulder: Lynne Rienner.
Gill, S. and D. Law (1988) *The Global Political Economy*. Baltimore: Johns Hopkins University Press.
  (1989) 'Global Hegemony and the Structural Power of Capital'. *International Studies Quarterly* (33) 475–99.
Gill, S. and J. H. Mittelman (1996) 'Coxian Historicism as an Alternative Perspective in International Studies'. Unpublished manuscript.
Gilpin, R. (1981) *War and Change in World Politics*. New York: Cambridge University Press.
  (1986) 'The Richness of the Tradition of Political Realism', in R. O. Keohane

(ed.) *Neorealism and its Critics*. New York: Columbia University Press, 301–321.

(1987) *The Political Economy of International Relations*. Princeton: Princeton University Press.

Goodman, D. and M. Redclift (1991) *Refashioning Nature*. London: Routledge.

Gordon, L. (1990) *Women, the State, and Welfare*. Madison: University of Wisconsin.

Gordon, L. R. (1995) *Fanon and the Crisis of European Man*. New York: Routledge.

Gouldner, A. S. (1980) *The Two Marxisms: Contradictions and Anomalies in the Development of Theory*. New York: The Seabury Press.

Gramsci, A. (1971) *Selections from the Prison Notebooks*. Translated and edited by Q. Hoare and G. Nowell Smith. New York: International Publishers.

Grant, R. and K. Newland (eds.) (1991) *Gender and International Relations*. Bloomington and Indianapolis: Indiana University Press.

Greider, W. (1993) 'The Global Marketplace: A Closet Dictator', in Nader et al., *The Case against Free Trade*. San Francisco: Earth Island Press, 195–217.

Griffith, I. L. (1993) *The Quest for Security in the Caribbean: Problems and Promises in Subordinate States*. Armonk, NY: M. E. Sharp.

Haas, P. M. (1992) 'Introduction: Epistemic Communities and International Policy Coordination'. *International Organization* (46) 1–35.

Habermas, J. (1989) *The Structural Transformation of the Public Sphere: An Inquiry into a Category of Bourgeois Society*. Cambridge, MA: MIT Press.

Hagen, E. and J. Jenson (1988) 'Paradoxes and Promises: Work and Politics in the Postwar Years', in J. Jenson, E. Hagen and C. Reddy (eds.) *Feminization of the Labor Force: Paradoxes and Promises*. New York: Oxford University Press, 3–16.

Halliday, F. (1987) 'State and Society in International Relations: A Second Agenda'. *Millennium* (16) 215–230.

Hamilton, G. and C.-S. Kao (1987) 'Max Weber and the Analysis of East Asian Industrialization'. *International Sociology* (2) 289–300.

Hampson, N. (1968) *The Enlightenment*. Harmondsworth: Penguin.

Hansen, E. (1977) *Frantz Fanon: Social and Political Thought*. Athens, OH: Ohio University Press.

Harding, S. (ed.) (1987) *Feminism and Methodology*. Bloomington: Indiana University Press.

Harriss, J. (ed.) (1995) *The Politics of Humanitarian Intervention*. London: Pinter.

Harrod, J. (1981) 'The Evolution of the Subject of International Political Economy 1967–1977', in R. C. Kent and G. Nielson (eds.) *The Study and Teaching of International Relations*. London: Francis Pinter, 78–89.

(1986) 'Development Studies: From Change to Stabilization', in R. Apthorpe and A. Krahl (eds.) *Development Studies: Critiques and Renewal*. Leiden: Brill.

(1987a) *Power, Production, and the Unprotected Worker*. New York: Columbia University Press.

(1987b) 'Social Relations of Production, Systems of Labour Control and Third World Trade Unions', in R. Southall (ed.) *Trade Unions and the New Industrialisation of the Third World*. Ottawa: University of Ottawa Press, 33–55.

(1992) *Labour and Third World Debt*. Brussels: ICEF.

(1994) *Models of Labour and Production: The Origins and Contemporary Limitations of the Anglo-American Model*. The Hague: Institute of Social Studies Working Paper, No. 183.

(1995) 'Global Forms of Extraction and Forms of State: From Profit to Interest and Governance to Agency'. The Hague: Unpublished Paper for State/Society Research Seminar. Institute of Social Studies.

Hart, J. (1992) *Rival Capitalists; International Competitiveness in USA, Japan and Western Europe*. Princeton: Princeton University Press.

Harvey, D. (1989) *The Condition of Postmodernity*. Oxford: Basil Blackwell.

Hayek, F. A. (1976/1985) *The Road to Serfdom*. London: Routledge and Kegan Paul [*De weg naar slavernij*. Amsterdam: Omega (1944)]

Hegel, G. W. F. (1942) *Hegel's Philosophy of Right*. Translated with notes by T. M. Knox. Oxford: Oxford University Press.

Heilbroner, R. L. (1962) *The Worldly Philosophers: The Lives, Times, and Ideas of the Great Economic Thinkers*. New York: Time Incorporated.

Hekman, S. J. (1990) *Gender and Knowledge: Elements of a Postmodern Feminism*. Cambridge: Polity Press.

Held, D. (1987) *Models of Democracy*. Cambridge: Polity Press.

Helleiner, E. (1990) 'Fernand Braudel and International Political Economy'. *International Studies Notes*, (15) 73–8.

(1994) *States and the Reemergence of Global Finance*. Ithaca: Cornell University Press.

(1995) 'Great Transformations: A Polanyian Perspective on the Contemporary Global Financial Order'. *Studies In Political Economy* (48) 149–64.

(1996) 'International Political Economy and the Greens'. *New Political Economy* (1) 59–77.

Henderson, H. (1981) *The Politics of the Solar Age*. Garden City, NY: Anchor Press.

Heraclides, A. (1994) 'Secessionist Conflagration: What is to be Done?' *Security Dialogue* (25) 283–94.

Hernes, H. 1987 *Welfare State and Woman Power: Essays in State Feminism*. Oslo: Norwegian University Press.

Hettne, B. (ed.) (1995) *International Political Economy: Understanding Global Disorder*. London: Zed Books.

Hildyard, N. (1993) 'Foxes in Charge of the Chickens', in W. Sachs (ed.) *Global Ecology: A New Arena of Political Conflict*. London: Zed Books.

Hirsch, F. (1976) *The Social Limits to Growth*. Cambridge, MA: Harvard University Press.

Hirsh, S. K. (1985) *Using the Myers-Briggs Type Indicator in Organizations*. Palo Alto, CA: Consulting Psychological Press, Inc.

Hobsbawm, E. (1994) *The Age of Extremes*. London: Michael Joseph.

Hodgson, M. (1974) Volume I. *The Venture of Islam: Conscience and History in a World Civilization*. Volume II. *The Expansion of Islam in the Middle Periods*. Volume III. *The Gunpowder Empires and Modern Times*. Chicago: University of Chicago Press.

Holm, H.-H. and G. Sørensen (eds.) (1995) *Whose World Order? Uneven Globalization and the End of the Cold War*. Boulder: Westview.

Holman, O. (1987–8) 'Semi-Peripheral Fordism in Southern Europe. The National and International Context of Socialist-led Governments in Spain, Portugal and Greece in Historical Perspective'. *International Journal of Political Economy* (17) 11–55.

(1995) 'A Short History of Spanish Banking', *Amsterdam International Studies Working Papers*, No. 40. Amsterdam: University of Amsterdam.

(1996) *Integrating Southern Europe. EC Expansion and the Transnationalisation of Spain*. London and New York: Routledge.

Holsti, K. J. (1985) *The Dividing Discipline: Hegemony and Diversity in International Theory*. London: Unwin Hyman.

Hufbauer, G. and J. Schott (1993–4) 'Prescription for Growth'. *Foreign Policy* (93) 104–14.

Hughes, B. B. (1985) *World Futures: A Critical Analysis of Alternatives*. Baltimore: Johns Hopkins University Press.

Huntington, S. (1993) 'The Clash of Civilizations?' *Foreign Affairs* (72) 22–49.

Hyden, G. (1983) *No Shortcuts to Progress: African Development Management in Perspective*. London: Heinemann.

Hyman, R. (1991) 'Plus Ça Change? The Theory of Production and the Production of Theory', in A. Pollert (ed.) *Farewell To Flexibility?* London: Blackwell, 259–283.

Ibn Khaldun (1950) *An Arab Philosophy of History*. Selections from the *Prolegomena* of Ibn Khaldun of Tunis (1332–1406). Translated and arranged by Charles Issawi. Princeton: The Darwin Press.

(1958) *The Muqaddimah: An Introduction to History*. Translated by F. Rosenthal. Abridged and edited by J. Dawood. Princeton: Princeton University Press.

International Studies Quarterly. (1989) Special Issue: 'Exchange on the Third Debate' (33, 3) September.

Irigaray, L. (1985a) *Speculum of the Other Woman*. Translated by G. Gill. Ithaca: Cornell University Press.

(1985b) *This Sex Which Is Not One*. Translated by C. Porter. Ithaca: Cornell University Press.

Jackson, R. H. and A. James (eds.) (1993) *States in a Changing World: A Contemporary Analysis*. Oxford: Clarendon Press.

James, A. (1986) *Sovereign Statehood: The Basis of International Society*. London: Allen and Unwin.

Jones, C. (1987) *International Business in the Nineteenth Century: The Rise and Fall of a Cosmopolitan Bourgeoisie*. New York: New York University Press.

Jones, K. and A. Jonasdottier (1988) *The Political Interests of Gender*. London: Sage.

Jung, C. J. (1933) 'A Psychological Theory of Types', in *Modern Man in Search of a Soul*. Translated by W. S. Dell and C. F. Baynes. New York: Harcourt, Brace and World, Inc.

Kamenka, E. (1983) *The Portable Karl Marx*. Translated by Eugene Kamenka. New York: Penguin Books.

Kaplan, R. D. (1994) 'The Coming Anarchy: How Scarcity, Crime, Overpopulation, Tribalism, and Disease are Destroying the Social Fabric of Our Planet'. *The Atlantic Monthly* (February) 44–76.

Kates, R. W. et al. (1990) 'The Great Transformation', in B. L. Turner et al. (eds.)

The Earth as Transformed by Human Action: Global and Regional Changes in the Biosphere over the Past 300 Years. Cambridge: Cambridge University Press, 1–17.

Kaufman, B. (1993) *The Origins and Evolution of the Field of Industrial Relations in the United States.* Ithaca, NY: ILR Press.

Keane, J. (1988) 'Despotism and Democracy', in J. Keane (ed.) *Civil Society and the State.* London: Verso, 35–71.

Kelman, H. C. (1979) 'An Interaction Approach to Conflict Resolution and its Application to Israeli-Palestinian Relations'. *International Interactions* (6) 99–122.

(1992) 'Informal Mediation by a Scholar/Practitioner', in J. Bercovitch and J. Z. Rubin (eds.) *Mediation in International Relations: Multiple Approaches to Conflict Management.* New York: St. Martin's Press.

Kennedy, P. (1987) *The Rise and Decline of the Great Powers: Economic Change and Military Conflict from 1500 to 2000.* London. Unwin Hyman.

Keohane, R. O. (1984) *After Hegemony: Cooperation and Discord in the World Political Economy.* Princeton, NJ: Princeton University Press.

(1986a) 'Neorealism and the Study of World Politics', in R. O. Keohane (ed.) *Neorealism and its Critics*, 1–16.

(1986b) (ed.) *Neorealism and its Critics.* New York: Columbia University Press.

(1988) 'International Institutions: Two Approaches'. *International Studies Quarterly* (32) 379–96.

Keohane, R. O. and J. S. Nye Jr (1977) *Power and Interdependence.* Boston: Little Brown.

Kerr, C. et al. (1960) *Industrialism and Industrial Man: The Problems of Labor and Management in Economic Growth.* Cambridge, MA: Harvard University Press.

Khalidi, T. (1985) *Classical Arab Islam: The Culture and Heritage of the Golden Age.* Princeton, NJ: The Darwin Press.

Knight, S. (1985) *The Brotherhood: The Secret World of the Freemasons.* London: Grafton.

Kolko, G. (1994) *Century of War, Peace, Conflict, and Society Since 1914.* New York: The New Press.

Kolko, J. (1974) *America and the Crisis of World Capitalism.* Boston: Beacon.

Korten, D. (1990) *Getting to the 21st Century.* West Hartford: Kumarian Press.

Krasner, S. (1983) *International Regimes.* Ithaca, NY: Cornell University Press.

Krasner, S. and J. Thomson, 'Global Transactions and the Consolidation of Sovereignty', in J. Rosenau and E. O. Czempiel (eds.) *Global Changes and Theoretical Challenges.* Lexington: Lexington Books, 195–219.

Krugman, P. (1993) 'The Uncomfortable Truth about NAFTA'. *Foreign Affairs*n (72) 13–19.

Kuhn, T. S. (1970) *The Structure of Scientific Revolutions* (2nd ed.). Chicago: University of Chicago Press.

Kurth, J. (1994) 'The Real Clash'. *National Interest* (Fall) 3–15.

Laclau, E. and C. Mouffe (1985) *Hegemony and Socialist Strategy: Towards a Radical Democratic Politics.* London: Verso.

Lacoste, Y. (1984) *Ibn Khaldun: The Birth of History and the Past of the Third World.* London: Verso.

Lana, R. E. (1987) 'Ibn Khaldun and Vico: The Universality of Social History.' *The Journal of Mind and Behavior* (8) (Winter) 153–65.

Lapid, Y. (1989) 'The Third Debate: On the Prospects of International Theory in a Post-Positivist Era'. *International Studies Quarterly* (33) 235–54.

Lapidus, I. M. (1988) *A History of Islamic Societies*. Cambridge: Cambridge University Press.

Lawrence, B. B. (ed.) (1984) *Ibn Khaldun and Islamic Ideology*. Leiden: E. J. Brill.

Leaman, O. (1985) *An Introduction to Medieval Islamic Philosophy*. Cambridge: Cambridge University Press.

Lebow, R. N. and T. Risse-Kappen (1995) *International Relations Theory and the End of the Cold War*. New York: Columbia University Press.

Lebow, R. N. and J. G. Stein (1994) *We All Lost the Cold War*. Princeton: Princeton University Press.

Lefebvre, H. (1977) *De l'état*. Volume III. *Le Mode de Production Étatique*. Paris: 10/18.

Lerner, G. 1986. *The Creation of Patriarchy*. New York: Oxford University Press.

Lewis, B. (1976) 'The Return of Islam'. *Commentary* (January) 39–49.

Leys, C. (1974) *Underdevelopment/In Kenya*. Berkeley and Los Angeles: University of California Press.

Lind, M. (1995) 'Rev. Robertson's Grand International Conspiracy Theory.' *New York Review of Books*. 2 February, 21–5.

Lipschutz, R. (1992) 'Reconstructing World Politics: The Emergence of a Global Civil Society'. *Millennium* (21) 391–420.

Lloyd, G. (1984) *The Man of Reason: 'Male' and 'Female' in Western Philosophy*. Minneapolis: University of Minnesota Press.

Lloyd, G. E. R. (1979) *Magic, Reason and Experience: Studies in the Origins and Development of Greek Science*. Cambridge: Cambridge University Press.

Locke, J. (1965) *Two Treatises of Government* (ed. P. Lasslet). New York: Mentor [1690].

Locke, R., T. Kochan and M. Piore, (1995) 'Reconceptualizing Comparative Industrial Relations: Lessons from International Research'. *International Labour Review* (134) 139–161.

Lohmann, L. (1995) 'Visitors To The Commons: Approaching Thailand's "Environmental" Struggles from a Western Starting Point', in B. R. Taylor (ed.) *Ecological Resistance Movements: The Global Emergence of Radical and Popular Environmentalism*. Albany, NY: State University of New York Press. 109–26.

Löwith, K. (1993) *Max Weber and Karl Marx*. London: Routledge.

Lueck, T. J. (1994) 'Business Districts Grow at Price of Accountability'. *New York Times*. 20 November.

Maathai, W. (1985) 'Kenya: the Green Belt Movement', *IFDA Dossier* (49) 4–12.

Machiavelli, N. (1970) *The Discourses*. Harmondsworth: Penguin.

(1977) *The Prince*. New York: Norton.

Mackinnon, C. E. (1989) *Toward a Feminist Theory of the State*. Cambridge: Harvard University Press.

Madrick, J. (1995) 'The End of Affluence' *New York Review of Books*, 21 September.

Mahdi, M. (1957) *Ibn Khaldun's Philosophy of History: A Study in Philosophical Foundations of the Science of Culture*. London and Chicago: Phoenix Books, University of Chicago Press.

Mann, M. (1986) *The Sources of Social Power*. Volume I. Cambridge: Cambridge University Press.

Mannheim, K. (1940) *Man and Society in an Age of Reconstruction*. London: Routledge and Kegan Paul.

Mardin, S. (1991) 'The Just and the Unjust'. *Daedalus* (120) 113–29.

Markov, W. (1989) *Napoleons Keizerrijk. Geschiedenis En Dagelijks Leven Na De Franse Revolutie*. Zutphen: Walburg Pers [1984].

Marx, K. (1973a) 'General Introduction'. *Grundrisse*. Edited by D. McLellan. London, Paladin, 26–57.

(1973b) *Grundrisse. Foundations of the Critique of Political Economy (Rough Draft)* Translated by M. Nicolaus. Harmondsworth: Penguin. [1857–8]

(1977) 'Results of the Immediate Process of Production', in *Capital*. Volume I. Translated by B. Fowkes. New York: International Publishers. 948–1084.

Marx, K. and F. Engels (various years, 1956–1989) *MEW: Marx-Engels Werke* (Collected Works). Vols. 23–25 are *Capital* Volumes I–III. Berlin: Dietz.

Masterman, M. (1970) 'The Nature of a Paradigm', in I. Lakatos and A. Musgrave (eds.) *Criticism and the Growth of Knowledge*. Cambridge: Cambridge University Press, 51–89.

Masur, S. (1991) 'The North American Free Trade Agreement: Why it's in the Interest of US Business.' *Columbia Journal of World Business* (26) 99–103.

Mayatech Corporation (1992) *Gender and Adjustment*. Washington, DC: Mayatech Corporation.

McGaughey, W. (1992) *A US–Mexico–Canada Free Trade Agreement: Do We Just Say No?* Minneapolis: Thistlerose Publications.

McManus, J. (1995) *The Insiders: Architects of the New World Order*. Appleton, WI: The John Birch Society.

Mearsheimer, J. J. (1994/95) 'The False Promise of International Institutions'. *International Security* (19) 5–49.

Melin, M. (ed.) (1995) *Democracy in Africa: On Whose Terms?* Stockholm: Forum Syd.

Mendell, M. and D. Salee, (eds.) (1991) *The Legacy of Karl Polanyi: Market, State and Society at the End of the Twentieth Century*. New York: St. Martin's Press.

Mies, M. (1986) *Patriarchy and Accumulation on a World Scale: Women and the International Division of Labour*. London: Zed Books.

Mies, M. and V. Shiva (1993) *Ecofeminism*. London: Zed Books.

Mies, M., V. Bennholdt-Thomsen and C. Von Werlhof (1988) *Women: The Last Colony*. London: Zed Books.

Miliband, R. (1968) *The State in Capitalist Society*. London: Quartet Publishing.

Mills, C. W. (1959) *The Sociological Imagination*. New York: Oxford University Press.

Mintz, F. (1985) *The Liberty Lobby and the American Right*. Westport, CT: Greenwood.

Mittelman, J. H. (1994a) 'The End of a Millennium: Changing Structures of World Order and the Post-Cold War Division of Labour', in L. A. Swatuk and T. M. Shaw (eds.), *The South at the End of the 20th Century: Rethinking the Political Economy of Foreign Policy in Africa, Asia, the Caribbean and Latin America*. London: Macmillan, 15–27.

(1994b). 'The Globalization Challenge: Surviving at the Margins'. *Third World Quarterly* (15) 427–43.

(1996a) (ed.) *Globalization: Critical Reflections*. Boulder: Lynne Rienner.

(1996b) 'How Does Globalization Really Work?', in Mittelman (ed.), *Globalization: Critical Reflections*, 229–41.

Mittelman, J. H. and M. K. Pasha (1997) *Out from Underdevelopment Revisited: Changing Global Structures and the Remaking of the Third World*. London: Macmillan; New York: St. Martin's Press.

Mitter, S. (1986). *Common Fate, Common Bond: Women in the Global Economy*. London: Pluto Press.

Moody, K. and M. McGinn (1992) *Unions and Free Trade*. Detroit: Labor Notes Books.

Morera, E. (1990) *Gramsci's Historicism: A Realist Interpretation*. London: Routledge.

Morgan, P. M. (1981) *Theories and Approaches to International Politics*. London: Transaction Books.

Morgenthau, H. (1948/1973) *Politics Among Nations*. New York: Alfred A. Knopf.

Morse, E. L. (1976) 'The Westphalian System And Classical Statecraft', in *Modernization and the Transformation of International Relations*. London: Macmillan, 22–46.

Mueller, J. (1991) *Retreat from Doomsday: The Obsolescence of Major War*. New York: Basic Books.

Murphy, C. N. (1994) *International Organization and Industrial Change: Global Governance Since 1850*. New York: Oxford University Press.

Murphy, C. N. and R. Tooze, (eds.) (1991) *The New International Political Economy*. Boulder, CO: Lynne Rienner.

Nader, R. *et al.* (1993) *The Case against Free Trade*. San Francisco: Earth Island Press.

Naisbitt, J. (1995) *Megatrends Asia: The Eight Asian Megatrends that are Changing the World*. London: Nicholas Brealy Publishing.

Nash, J. (1988) 'Cultural Parameters of Sexism and Racism in the International Division of Labor', in J. Smith et al. (eds.) *Racism, Sexism, and the World-System*. New York: Greenwood, 11–38.

Nederveen Pieterse, J. (1990) *Empire and Emancipation*. London: Pluto.

(1992) (ed.) *Christianity and Hegemony. Religion and Politics on the Frontiers of Social Change*. New York and Oxford: Berg.

Nelson, D. (1991) 'Trade Policy Games', in C. N. Murphy and R. Tooze (eds.) *The New International Political Economy*. London: Macmillan, 129–46.

Neufeld, M. (1995) *The Restructuring of International Relations Theory*. Cambridge: Cambridge University Press.

Newton, J. L. (1988). 'History as Usual? Feminism and the 'New Historicism'. *Cultural Critique* (Spring) 87–122.

Nicholson, L. (1986) *Gender and History: The Limits of Social Theory in the Age of the Family*. New York: Columbia University Press.

Niland, J. (1992) 'Change and the International Exchange of Ideas'. Presidential

Address to the Ninth Congress of the International Industrial Relations Association, Sydney.

Norman, E. H. (1975) *Origins of the Modern Japanese State*. J. Dower (ed.). New York: Pantheon Books.

Norris, C. (1993) *The Truth about Postmodernism*. Oxford: Cambridge, MA: Blackwell.

North, G. (1985) 'Prologue' and 'Epilogue', in L. Abraham, *Call It Conspiracy*. Wauna, WA: Double A Publications.

Nyoni, S. (1995) 'Is Democracy Possible? The Role of Grassroots Movements', in M. Melin (ed.) *Democracy in Africa: On Whose Terms?* Stockholm: Forum Syd, 187–96.

O'Brien, Richard (1992) *Global Financial Integration: The End of Geography*. London: Pinter.

O'Brien, Robert (1995) 'International Political Economy and International Relations: Apprentice or Teacher', in J. Macmillan and A. Linklater (eds.) *Boundaries in Question: New Directions in International Relations*. London: Pinter, 89–105.

O'Connor, J. (1994) 'On the Misadventures of Capitalist Nature', in M. O'Connor (ed.), *Is Capitalism Sustainable? Political Economy and the Politics of Political Ecology*. New York: Guilford Press, 125–51.

O'Connor, M. (1994) 'Is Sustainable Capitalism Possible?', in M. O'Connor (ed.), *Is Capitalism Sustainable?*, 152–75.

O'Toole, G. J. A. (1991) *Honorable Treachery: A History of U.S. Intelligence, Espionage, and Covert Action from the American Revolution to the CIA*. New York: The Atlantic Monthly Press.

Ohmae, K. (1990) *The Borderless World: Power and Strategy in the Interlinked Economy*. New York: Harper Business.

Oppenheim, L. (1955) *International Law*, Seventh Edition. London: Longman.

Ortner, S. and H. Whitehead, (eds.) (1981) *Sexual Meanings: The Cultural Construction of Gender and Sexuality*. Cambridge: Cambridge University Press.

Overbeek, H. (1990) *Global Capitalism and National Decline: The Thatcher Decade In Perspective*. London: Unwin Hyman.

Overbeek, H. and K. van der Pijl (1993) 'Restructuring Capital and Restructuring Hegemony: Neo-Liberalism and the Unmaking of the Post-War Order', in H. Overbeek (ed.) *Restructuring Hegemony in the Global Political Economy: The Rise of Transnational Liberalism in the 1980s*. London and New York: Routledge.

Palan, R. (1992) 'The Second Structuralist Theories of International Relations: A Research Note'. *International Studies Notes* (17) 22–9.

Palmer, R. and N. Parsons (ed.) (1977) *The Roots of Rural Poverty in Central and Southern Africa*. Berkeley: University of California Press.

Panitch, L. (1994) 'Globalisation and the State', in R. Miliband and Panitch (eds.). *The Socialist Register 1994*. London: Merlin Press, 60–94.

Panitch, L. and Miliband, R. (1992) The New World Order and the Socialist Agenda. *Socialist Register, 1992*. London: Merlin Press.

Pankhurst, A. (1992) *Resettlement and Famine in Ethiopia: The Villagers' Experience*. Manchester: Manchester University Press.

Parpart, J. L. and K. A. Staudt, (eds.) (1990). *Women and the State in Africa.* Boulder, CO: Lynne Rienner.

Pasha, M. K. and J. H. Mittelman (1995) 'What Future for the NIC Model? Globalisation and the Remaking of the Third World'. *The European Journal of Development Research* (7) 353–65.

Pasha, M. K. and Samatar, A. I. (1996) 'The Resurgence of Islam', in J. Mittelman (ed.) *Globalization: Critical Reflections*, 187–201.

Pateman, C. (1988) *The Sexual Contract.* Stanford, CA: Stanford University Press.

Pausewang, S. *et al.* (eds.) (1990) *Ethiopia: Options for Rural Development.* London: Zed Books.

Perlman, S. (1928/1949) *The Theory of the Labor Movement.* New York: A.M. Kelly.

Perloff, J. (1988) *The Shadows of Power.* Appleton, WI: Western Islands Publishers.

Peterson, V. S. (1988) 'An Archeology of Domination: Historicizing Gender and Class in Early Western State Formation'. Ph. D. Dissertation. American University.

(1992a) 'Transgressing Boundaries: Theories of Knowledge, Gender, and International Relations'. *Millennium* (21) 183–206.

Peterson, V. S. (ed.) (1992b) *Gendered States: Feminist (Re) Visions of International Relations Theory.* Boulder, CO: Lynne Rienner.

(1992c) 'Security and Sovereign States', in Peterson (ed.) *Gendered States*, 31–64.

(1995) 'The Politics of Identity and Gendered Nationalism', in L. Neack, P. J. Haney, and J. A. K. Hey (eds.) *Foreign Policy Analysis: Continuity and Change in its Second Generation.* Englewood Cliffs, NJ: Prentice Hall, 167–86.

(1996a) 'The Politics of Identification in the Context of Globalization'. *Women's Studies International Forum* (19) 5–16.

(1996b) 'The Gender of Rhetoric, Reason, and Realism', in F. A. Beer and R. Hariman (eds.), *Post-Realism: The Rhetorical Turn in International Relations.* East Lansing: Michigan State University Press.

(1997) 'Seeking World Order Beyond the Gender Order of Global Hierarchies', in R. Cox (ed.) *The New Realism: Perspectives on Multilateralism and World Order.* London: Macmillan.

Peterson, V. S. and A. Sisson Runyan (1993) *Global Gender Issues.* Boulder, CO: Westview Press.

Pettman, J. J. (1996) *Worlding Women: A Feminist International Politics.* Sydney: Allen Unwin.

Pincus, W. (1995) 'CIA Passed Bogus News to Presidents'. *Washington Post*, 31 October.

Polanyi, K. (1957) *The Great Transformation: Political and Economic Origins of Our Time.* Boston: Beacon Press [1944].

(1968) *Primitive, Archaic and Modern Economies.* Boston: Beacon Press.

(1974) 'Our Obsolete Market Mentality'. *The Ecologist* (4, 6) 213–20.

(1977) *The Livelihood of Man.* New York: Academic Press.

Polanyi, K., C. M. Arensberg and H. W. Pearson (eds.) (1957) *Trade and Market in the Early Empires.* Chicago: Gateway.

Porter, M. (1990) *The Competitive Advantage of Nations*. Basingstoke: Macmillan.

Pradervand, P. (1989) *Listening to Africa: Developing Africa from the Grassroots.* New York: Praeger Publishers.

Przeworski, A. (1985) 'Democratic Capitalism at the Crossroads', in *Capitalism and Social Democracy*. Cambridge: Cambridge University Press, 205–22.

Quigley, C. (1981) *The Anglo-American Establishment*. New York: Books in Focus.

Rahmato, D. (1985) *Agrarian Reform in Ethiopia*. Trenton, NJ: Africa World Press.

(1989) 'Rural Resettlement in Post-Revolution Ethiopia', Paper Prepared for the Conference on Population Issues in National Development, ONCCP, Addis Ababa, June.

(1993) 'Agrarian Change and Agrarian Crisis: State and Peasantry in Post-Revolution Ethiopia', *Africa* (63) 1.

Rakovsky, M. (1978) *Towards an East European Marxism*. London: Allison and Busby.

Reich, R. (1991) *The Work of Nations. Preparing Ourselves for Twenty-First Century Capitalism*. New York: Alfred Knopf.

Reiter, R. R. (1977) 'The Search for Origins'. *Critique of Anthropology* (3, 9) (Winter) 5–24.

Rich, P. J. (1988) 'Public-School Freemasonry in the Empire: "Mafia of the Mediocre"?', in J. A. Mangan (ed.) *Benefits Bestowed? Education and British Imperialism*. Manchester: Manchester University Press.

Richardson, J. L. (1994/1995) 'Asia-Pacific: The Case for Geopolitical Optimism'. *The National Interest* (38) 28–39.

Ridgeway, G. L. (1938) *Merchants of Peace: Twenty Years of Business Diplomacy Through the International Chamber of Commerce 1919–1938*. New York: Columbia University Press.

Rifkin, J. (1995) *The End of Work: The Decline of the Global Labor Force and the Dawn of the Post-Market Era*. New York: G. P. Putnam's Sons.

Risse-Kappen, T. (1995) *Bringing Transnational Relations Back In: Non-State Actors, Domestic Structures, and International Institutions*. New York: Cambridge University Press.

Rittberger, V. (ed.) (1993) *Regime Theory and International Relations*. Oxford: Clarendon Press.

Robertson, P. (1991) *The New World Order*. Dallas: Word Publishing.

Robinson, W. (1996) *Promoting Polyarchy*. Cambridge: Cambridge University Press.

Rogers, R. (1994) *Nature and the Crisis of Modernity*. Montreal: Black Rose Press.

Rosenau, J. N. (1983) 'Fragmegrative Challenges to National Security', in T. Heyns (ed.) *Understanding U.S. Strategy: A Reader*. Washington, DC: National Defense University, 65–82.

(1989) 'Global Changes and Theoretical Challenges: Toward a Postinternational Politics for the 1990s', in E. O. Czempiel and J. N. Rosenau (eds.) *Global Changes and Theoretical Challenges* Lexington, MA: D. C. Heath.

(1990) *Turbulence in World Politics: A Theory of Change and Continuity*. Princeton: Princeton University Press.

(1995a) 'Hurricanes Are Not The Only Intruders: The Caribbean in an Era of

Global Turbulence'. Conference on International Security in the Greater Caribbean. Cambridge, MA. October. *Mimeo.*

(1995b) 'Signals, Signposts and Symptoms: Interpreting Change and Anomalies in World Politics'. *European Journal of International Relations* (1) 113–22.

(1997) *Along The Domestic-Foreign Frontier: Exploring Governance in a Turbulent World.* Cambridge: Cambridge University Press.

Rosenblum, M. and D. Williamson (1987) *Squandering Eden: Africa at the Edge.* New York: Harcourt Brace Jovanovich.

Rosenstock-Huessy, E. (1961) *Die Europäischen Revolutionen Und Der Character Der Nationen.* Stuttgart: Kohlhammer. Third Edition. [1931].

Rosenthal, E. (1958) *Political Thought in Medieval Islam: An Introductory Outline.* Cambridge: Cambridge University Press.

Roy, A. (1994) 'New Inter-Relations between Indian Big Bourgeoisie and Imperialism'. *The Marxist Review Occasional Letters* (16) 12–34.

Ruggie, J. G. (1982) 'International Regimes, Transactions and Change: Embedded Liberalism in the Postwar Economic Order'. *International Organization* (36) 379–416.

(1993) 'Territoriality and Beyond'. *International Organization* (47) 139–74.

(1993) (ed.) *Multilateralism Matters: The Theory and Praxis of an Institutional Form.* New York: Columbia University Press.

Rupert, M. (1993) 'Alienation, Capitalism, and the Inter-State System: Toward a Marxian/Gramscian Critique', in S. Gill (ed.) *Gramsci, Historical Materialism, and International Relations,* 67–92.

(1995a) *Producing Hegemony.* Cambridge: Cambridge University Press.

(1995b) '(Re)Politicizing the Global Economy: Liberal Common Sense and Ideological Struggle in the US NAFTA Debate'. *Review of International Political Economy* (2) 658–92.

Russell, B. (1946) *History of Western Philosophy.* London: George Allen and Unwin.

Sachs, W. (1992) *The Development Dictionary.* London: Zed Books.

Said, E. W. (1979) *Orientalism.* New York: Vintage Books.

Sainsbury, D. (ed.) (1994) *Gendering Welfare States.* London: Sage.

Sakamoto, Y. (1994) 'A Perspective on the Changing World Order', in Sakamoto (ed.) *Global Transformation: Challenges to the State System.* Tokyo: United Nations University Press, 15–54.

Sassoon, A. S. (ed.) (1987) *Women and the State.* London: Hutchinson.

Sayer, A. (1992) *Method in Social Science: A Realist Approach.* London: Routledge.

Schmidt, N. (1967) *Ibn Khaldun: Historian, Sociologist and Philosopher.* New York: Ams Press.

Schwartz, H. (1994) *States versus Markets: History, Geography and the Development of the International Political Economy.* New York: St. Martin's Press.

Sciolino, E. (1995) 'Call It Aid or a Bribe, It's the Price of Peace'. *New York Times,* 26 March.

Scott, J. C. (1985) *Weapons of the Weak.* New Haven: Yale University Press.

(1993) *Everyday Forms of Resistance.* International Peace Research Institute, Meigaku. Occasional Paper Series No. 15. Yokahama.

Sekyi-Otu, A. (1975) 'Form and Metaphor in Fanon's Critique of Racial and Colonial Domination', in A. Kontos (ed.) *Domination*. Toronto: University of Toronto Press.

Senghaas, D. (1982) *Von Europa Lernen. Entwicklungsgeschichtliche Betrachtungen*. Frankfurt: Suhrkamp.

Shiva, V. (1993a) *Monocultures of the Mind*. London: Zed Books.

(1993b) 'The Greening of Global Reach', in W. Sachs (ed.), *Global Ecology*. London: Zed Books, 149–56.

Shoup, L. H. and Minter, W. (1977) *Imperial Brain Trust. The Council on Foreign Relations and United States Foreign Policy*. New York and London: Monthly Review Press.

Showstack Sassoon, A. (ed.) (1987) *Women and the State*. London: Hutchinson.

Silverblatt, I. (1988) Women in States. *Annual Review of Anthropology* (17) 427–60.

Silvert, K. H. (1971) 'The Caribbean and North America', in T. Szulc (ed.), *The United States and the Caribbean*. Englewood Cliffs, NJ: Prentice-Hall.

Smith, A. (1967) *The Wealth of Nations* (ed.) A. Skinner. Harmondsworth, Penguin. First published in 1776. 29–97.

Smith, Gaddis. (1994) *The Last Years of the Monroe Doctrine, 1945–1993*. New York: Hill and Wang.

Smith, J. (1993) 'The Creation of the World We Know: The World Economy and the Re-Creation of Gendered Identities', in V. M. Moghadam (ed.) *Identity Politics and Women*. Boulder: Westview Press. 27–41.

Smith, J. and I. Wallerstein (eds.) (1992) *Creating and Transforming Households: The Constraints of the World-Economy*. Cambridge: Cambridge University Press.

Smith, S. (1995) 'The Self-Images of a Discipline: A Genealogy of International Relations Theory', in K. Booth and S. Smith (eds.) *International Relations Theory Today*. Cambridge: Polity Press.

Soja, E. (1989) *Postmodern Geographies*. London: Verso.

Sorel, G. (1961) *Reflections on Violence*. London: Collier Books. Translated by T. E. Hulme and J. Roth. [1906, 1907].

Soros, G. (1995a) 'Toward Open Societies', *Foreign Policy* (98) 65–76.

(1995b) Quoted in N. C. Nash, 'At Forum, Peso Draws Attention'. *New York Times*, 30 January.

Standing, G. (1989) 'Global Feminization through Flexible Labor'. *World Development* (17) 1077–95.

Stanton, D. C., (ed.) (1992) *Discourses of Sexuality: From Aristotle to Aids*. Ann Arbor, MI: University of Michigan Press.

Stern, K. (1996) *A Force upon the Plain*. New York: Simon and Schuster.

Stienstra, D. (1994) *Women's Movements and International Organization*. New York: St. Martin's Press.

Stone, C. (1990) *National Survey on the Use of Drugs in Jamaica, 1990*. Kingston: USAID.

Stopford, J. M. and Strange, S. (1991) *Rival States, Rival Firms: Competition for World Market Shares*. New York: Cambridge University Press.

Stowasser, B. (1983) *Religion and Political Development: Some Comparative Ideas on*

Ibn Khaldun and Machiavelli. Washington, DC: Center for Contemporary Arab Studies.

Strange, S. (1981) 'Reactions to Brandt: Popular Acclaim and Academic Attack'. *International Studies Quarterly* (25) 328–42.

—— (1984) 'Preface', in S. Strange (ed.), *Paths to International Political Economy*. London: Allen and Unwin.

—— (1990) 'The Name of the Game', in N. Rizopolous (ed.), *Sea-Changes*, New York: Council on Foreign Relations, 238–73.

—— (1988/1994) *States and Markets*. London: Pinter.

Strauss, G., S. Jacoby and C. Olson (1993) Review Symposium of Kaufman (1993), in *Industrial and Labor Relations Review* (46) 395–406.

Sylvester, C. (1994) *Feminist Theory and International Relations in a Postmodern Era*. Cambridge: Cambridge University Press.

Tarock, A. (1995) 'Civilisational Conflict? Fighting the Enemy under a New Banner'. *Third World Quarterly* (16) 5–18.

Taylor, D. F. and F. Mackenzie (1992) *Development from Within*. London and New York: Routledge.

Tester, K. (1992) *Civil Society*. London: Routledge.

Tetreault, M. A. (1995) *The Kuwait Petroleum Corporation and the Economics of the New World Order*. Westport, CT: Quorum Books.

Tetreault, M. A. (ed.) (1994) *Women and Revolution in Africa, Asia, and the New World* Columbia, SC: University of South Carolina Press.

Thomas, P. (1994) *Alien Politics*. London: Routledge.

Thompson, E. P. (1980) *The Making of the English Working Class*. Harmondsworth: Penguin. [1968]

Thurow, L. (1992) *Head to Head: The Coming Economic Battle among Japan, Europe and America*. New York: William Morrow.

Tickner, J. A. (1992) *Gender in International Relations: Feminist Perspectives on Achieving Global Security*. New York: Columbia University Press.

Tigno, J. V. (1994) 'A New Orthodoxy: Exploring the Bounds of Governance and the Sipaglakas Innovation in Lipa.' *GO-NGO Watch* (5) 22–6.

Timberlake, L. (1986) *Africa in Crisis*. London: Earthscan Publishers.

Tocqueville, A. de (1954) *Democracy in America*. New York: Vintage Books.

Topouzis, D. (1990) 'Kenya Women Fight Deforestation', *Africa Recovery* (4) October-December, 43–45.

Totman, C. (1993) *Early Modern Japan*. Berkeley: University of California Press.

Trinh, T. M. 1989. *Woman, Native, Other: Writing Postcoloniality and Feminism*. Garden City, NY: Anchor Books.

True, J. (1996). 'Feminism', in S. Burchill, R. Devetak, A. Linklater, M. Paterson, and J. True (eds.), *Theories of International Relations*. London: Macmillan.

Truong, T.-D. (1990) *Sex, Money and Morality*. London: Zed Books.

UAW (United Automobile Workers) (1992) *Fast Track to Decline?* Detroit: UAW.

Uchihashi, K. (1995) *Kyosei no Daichi*. Tokyo: Iwanami Shinsho.

UN (1991) *The World's Women: 1970–1990. Trends And Statistics*. New York: United Nations.

UN Economic Commission For Africa (ECA) (1990) *African Charter for Popular Participation in Development and Transformation*. Addis Ababa: ECA.

UNRSID (UN Research Institute for Social Development) (1995) *States of Disarray: The Social Effects of Globalization*. Geneva. UNRISD.

Useem, M. (1996) *Investor Capitalism: How Money Managers are Changing the Face of Corporate America*. New York: Basic Books.

van der Pijl, K. (1979) 'Class Formation at the International Level: Reflections on the Political Economy of Atlantic Unity'. *Capital and Class* (9) 1–21.

——(1984) *The Making of an Atlantic Ruling Class*. London: Verso.

——(1989) 'Ruling Classes, Hegemony, and the State System'. *International Journal of Political Economy* (19, 3) 7–35.

——(1993a) 'The Sovereignty of Capital Impaired: Social Forces and Codes of Conduct for Multinational Corporations', in H. Overbeek (ed.) *Restructuring Hegemony in the Global Political Economy*, 28–57.

——(1993b) 'Soviet Socialism and Passive Revolution', in S. Gill (ed.) *Gramsci, Historical Materialism and International Relations*, 237–58.

——(1995) 'The Second Glorious Revolution: Globalising Elites and Historical Change', in B. Hettne (ed.) *International Political Economy: Understanding Global Disorder*, 100–28.

——(1996) *Vordenker Der Weltpolitik*. Leverkusen: Leske and Budrich.

Van Harvey, A. (1987) 'Hermeneutics', in M. Eliade (ed.) *The Encyclopedia of Religion*, Vol. VI. New York: Macmillan, 287–97.

Van Wesel, A. (1992) 'Catholics and Politics in Europe', in J. Nederveen Pieterse (ed.) *Christianity and Hegemony: Religion and Politics on the Frontiers of Social Change*. New York and Oxford: Berg.

Vickers, J. (1991) *Women and the World Economic Crisis*. London and New Jersey: Zed Books.

Vickers, J. M. (1990) 'At His Mother's Knee: Sex/Gender and the Construction of National Identities', in G. Hoffmann Nemiroff (ed.) *Women and Men: Interdisciplinary Readings on Gender*. Toronto: Fitzhenry and Whiteside, 478–92.

Vico, G. (1970) *The New Science of Giambattista Vico*. Translated by T. G. Bergin and M. H. Fisch. Ithaca: Cornell University Press. .

Viotti, P. R. and M. V. Kauppi (1987) *International Relations Theory: Realism, Pluralism, Globalism*. New York: Macmillan.

Wackernagel, M. and W. E. Rees (1996) *Our Ecological Footprint: Reducing Human Impact on the Earth*. Philadelphia, PA: New Society Publications.

Waite, A. E. (1994) *A New Encyclopaedia of Freemasonry*. New York and Avenel, NJ: Wings Books. 2 Volumes. [1920, 1970]

Waltz, K. N. (1979) *Theory of International Politics*. Reading, MA: Addison-Wesley.

——(1986) 'Reflections on *Theory of International Politics*: A Response to My Critics', in R. O. Keohane (ed.) *Neorealism and its Critics*, 322–66.

Ward, K. B., (ed.) (1990) *Women Workers and Global Restructuring*. Ithaca, NY: ILR Press.

Waring, M. (1988) *If Women Counted: A New Feminist Economics*. San Francisco: Harper and Row.

Waters, M. (1995) *Globalization*. London: Routledge.

Watson, S. (ed.) (1990) *Playing the State: Australian Feminist Interventions*. London: Verso.

Watts, M. (1983) *Silent Violence: Food, Famine and Peasantry in Northern Nigeria.* Berkeley: University of California Press.

Weber, M. (1946) *From Max Weber: Essays in Sociology.* Translated and edited by H. H. Gerth and C. Wright Mills. New York: Oxford University Press.

(1949) *The Methodology of the Social Sciences.* Translated by E. A. Shils and H. A. Finch. Glencoe, IL: Free Press.

(1971) *The Interpretation of Social Reality.* J. E. T. Eldridge (ed.) New York: Charles Scribner's Sons.

(1980) 'The National State And Economic Policy' (Freiburg Address). Translated and Reprinted in *Economy and Society* (9) 428–49 (1895).

Welch, R. (1986) *Republics and Democracies.* Appleton, WI: John Birch Society.

Weslowski, W. (1995) 'The Nature of Social Ties and the Future of Postcommunist Society: Poland and Solidarity', in J. H. Hall (ed.) *Civil Society: History, Theory, Comparison.* Cambridge: Polity Press.

Whitworth, S. (1989), 'Gender in the Inter-Paradigm Debate'. *Millennium* (18) 265–72.

(1994) *Feminism and International Relations: Towards a Political Economy of Gender in Interstate and Non-Governmental Institutions.* London: Macmillan.

Wight, M. (1966) 'Western Values in International Relations', in H. Butterfield and M. Wight (eds.) *Diplomatic Investigations: Essays in the Theory of International Relations.* New York: Columbia University Press, 89–131.

Wolin, S. (1989) *The Presence of the Past: Essays on the State and the Constitution.* Baltimore: Johns Hopkins University Press.

Womak, J. P., D. Jones and D. Ross (1990) *The Machine that Changed the World.* New York: MIT Press.

Wood, E. M. (1994) 'From Opportunity to Imperative: The History of the Market'. *Monthly Review,* July–August, 14–40.

(1995) *Democracy against Capitalism.* Cambridge: Cambridge University Press.

Woodis, J. (1972) *New Theories of Revolution: A Commentary on the Views of Frantz Fanon, Regis Debray and Herbert Marcuse.* London: Lawrence and Wishart.

World Bank (1989) *Sub-Saharan Africa: From Crisis to Sustainable Growth.* Washington, DC: World Bank.

Worster, D. (1993) *The Wealth of Nature: Environmental History and the Ecological Imagination.* New York: Oxford University Press.

Young, O. (1989) *International Cooperation: Building Regimes for Natural Resources and the Environment.* Ithaca: Cornell University Press.

Yuval-Davis, N. and F. Anthias (eds.) (1989) *Woman–Nation–State.* London: Macmillan Press.

Zakaria, F. (1994) 'Culture is Destiny: A Conversation with Lee Kuan Yew'. *Foreign Affairs* (73) 109–26.

Zalewski, M. and J. Parpart (eds.) (forthcoming) *Feminism, Masculinity and Power in International Relations.* Boulder, CO: Westview.

Zerihun, T. (1983) *Rural Settlement Schemes: A Comparative Study of the Awash Valley Settlement Schemes in Ethiopia and the Gezira Settlement Scheme in the Sudan.* M.Sc. Thesis. Uppsala: Swedish University of Agricultural Sciences.

Index of names

Index of subjects

Africa
  marginalisation of sub-Saharan 100–1
  resistance from below 153–69
agency
  in Braudel 103
  in Fanon 177–8
  in Polanyi 80–2
  and structure 77
anthropology 72, 106

bourgeoisie 10, 14, 97, 210 *see also* class,
  capitalist
  transitional formation of 118, 122–31
Braudel, Fernand 71
  and economic globalisation 90–104
  hierarchies 99–100
  'limits of the possible' 11
  longur durée 11–12, 94, 95
  methodology and ontology 11, 90–1,
    93–4, 96, 99
  social orders 96
  space 11–12, 91, 93
  time 11–12, 93–6
Britain
  colonialism in Asia 175–7
  emergence of industrial capitalism 12
  forms of state 121, 122
  'great transformation' 82
  hegemony 16–17
  historical social struggles 13–14
  transitional class formation 122–7
  working-class formation 13
Bull, Hedley
  and critical realism 40–51

capitalism 138–40, 207
  Braudel's concept of 99–100
  emergence of industrial 12, 79, 80–1
  and gender relations 192
  and socialism 203, 207, 237
  and the state-system 237–47
Carr, E. H.
  and critical realism 40–9, 52, 54

civil society
  and changing world order 212–13
  concept of 204, 209–12
  and international organisation 214–17
  and the market 217–19
  in the North and South 167
  and the state 135, 210–11, 213–14,
    217
  transitional 167, 213, 214, 217
civilisations
  business 98
  clashs of 66, 67, 180–2, 220
  discourses of 180
  encounters of 99
  Islamic 2, 56, 63–7
  market 66
  Western 187
class 13–14, 37, 111, 118–21
  capitalist 16 ,118, *see also* bourgeoisie
  exploitation 118–20, 137, 175
  and race 175
  and social forces 109, 119
  transnational managerial 97
  working 13, 16, 30, 32, 109, 124, 125,
    177, 178
class formation 120
  transnational 118, 122–31
Cold War 46, 220–1
colonialism 173–83
commodification 72, 73, 79, 81, 83–5,
  119–20, 138
core-periphery 101, *see also* North–South
corporatism
  enterprise corporatism 111
  neocorporatism 11, 238
counter-movements 73, 75, 78, 79, 84,
  86
Cox, Robert W.
  critical realism 40–1, 43–6, 52–3
  historical materialism 138
  historical structure 103, 259
  and Ibn Khaldun 51
  and neo-realism 44